P9-BXY-060

SOUTH COUNTY

VOLUME THREE

Yen
Press

CONTENTS

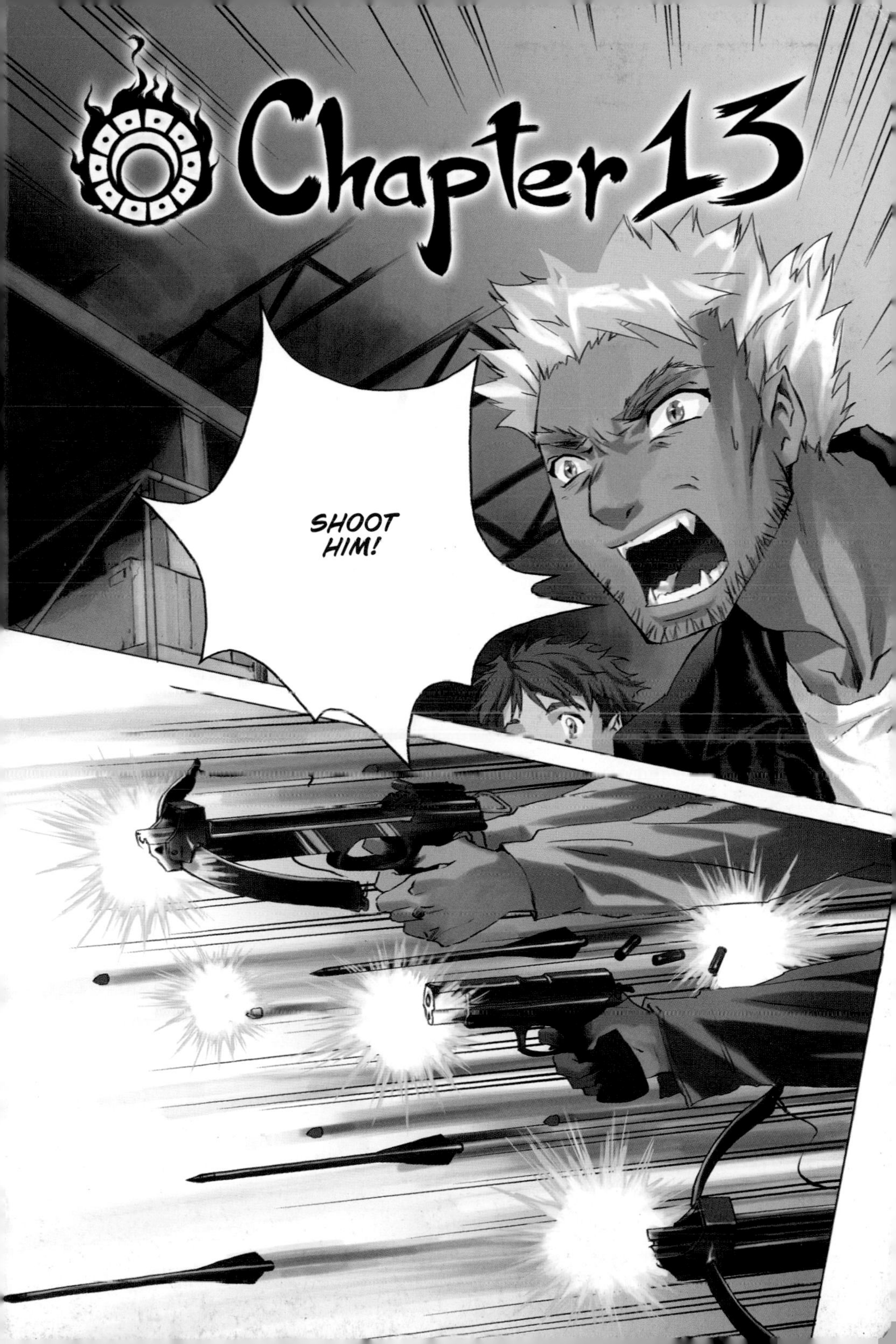
Chapter 13
SHOOT HIM!

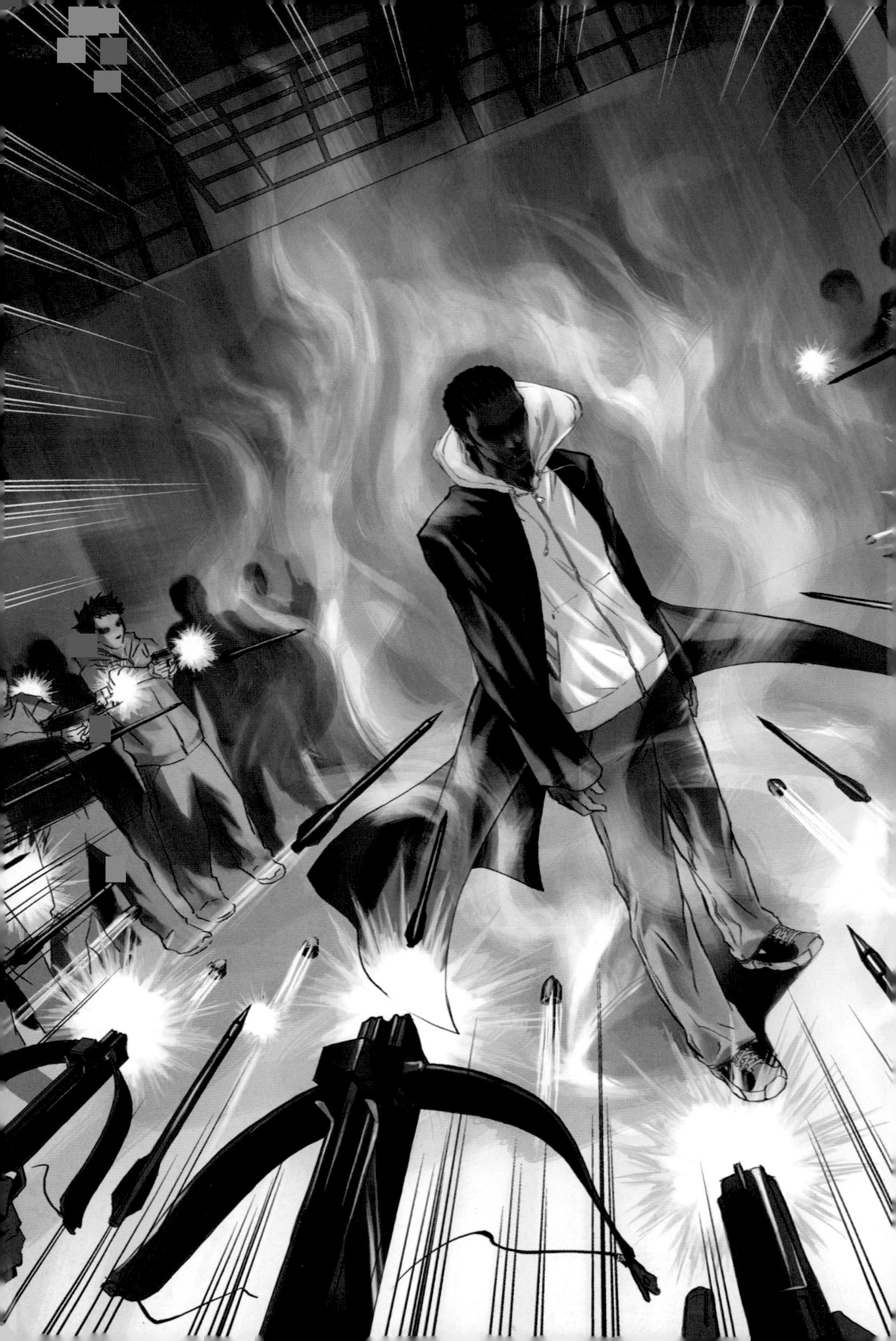

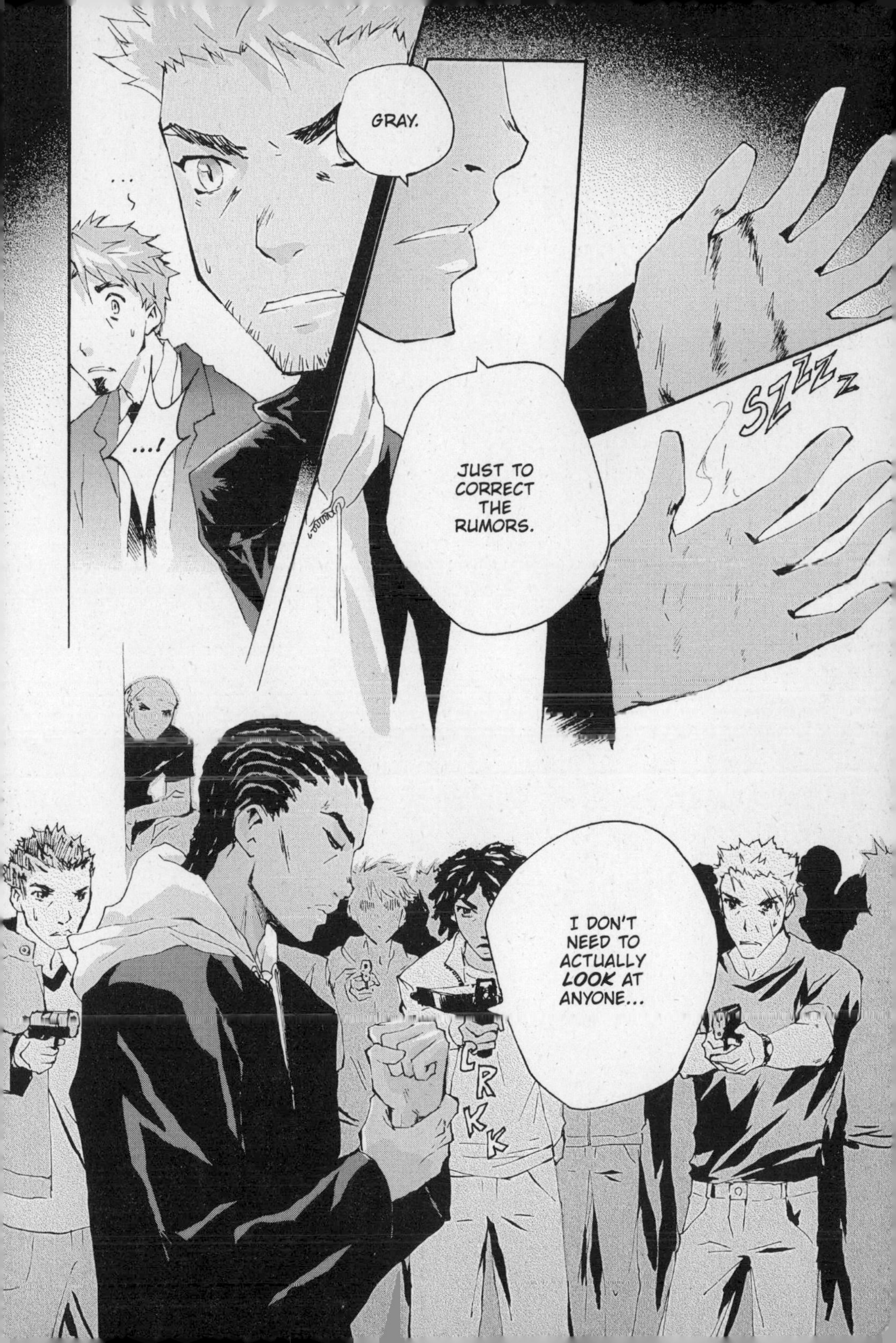
...
GRAY.
...!
JUST TO CORRECT THE RUMORS.
SZZZZ
I DON'T NEED TO ACTUALLY *LOOK* AT ANYONE...
CRKK

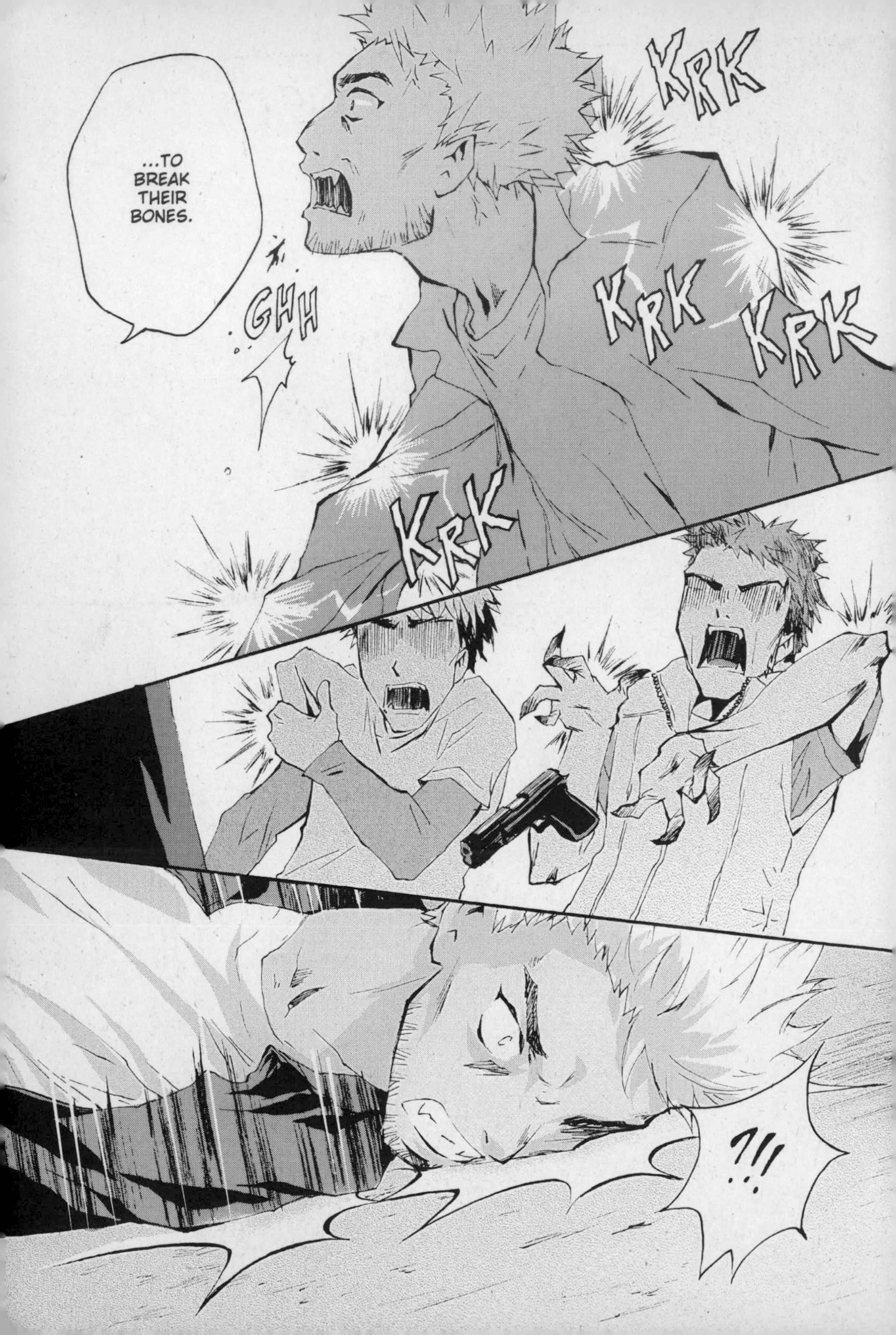
...TO BREAK THEIR BONES.
KRK
GHH
KRK
KRK
KRK
?!!

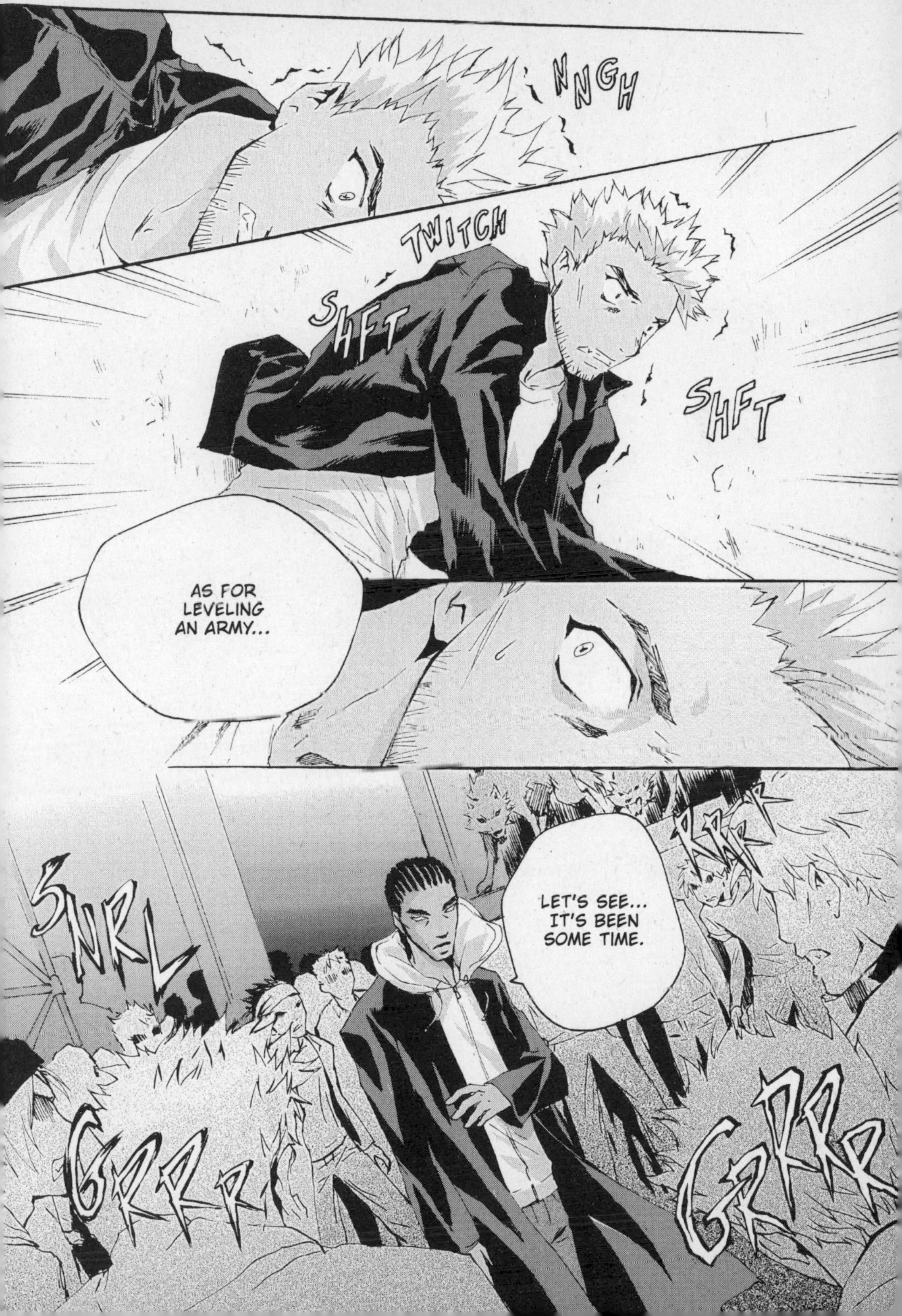
NNGH
TWITCH
SHFT
SHFT
AS FOR LEVELING AN ARMY...
SNRL
LET'S SEE... IT'S BEEN SOME TIME.
RRRR
GRRR
GRRR

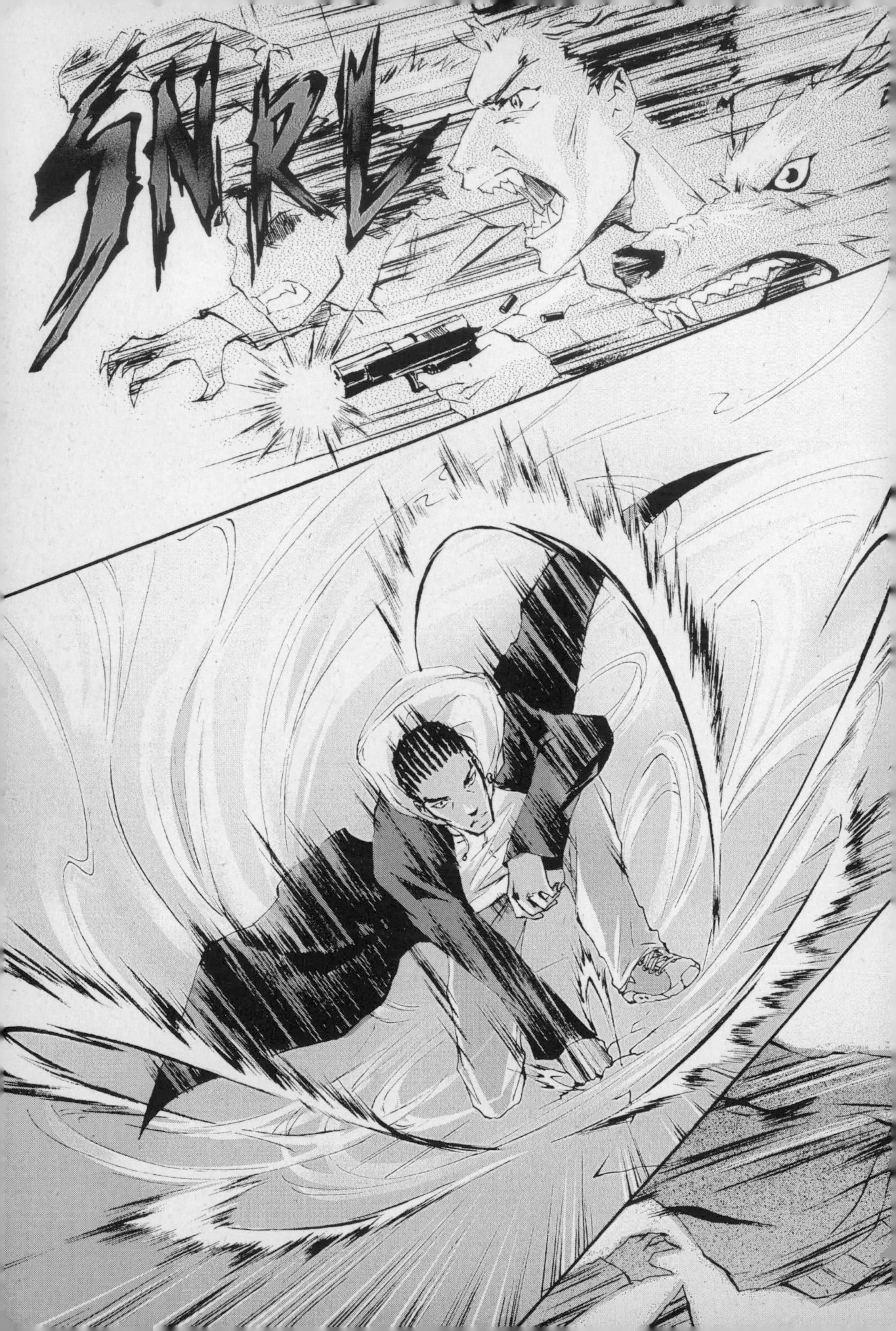
SNRL

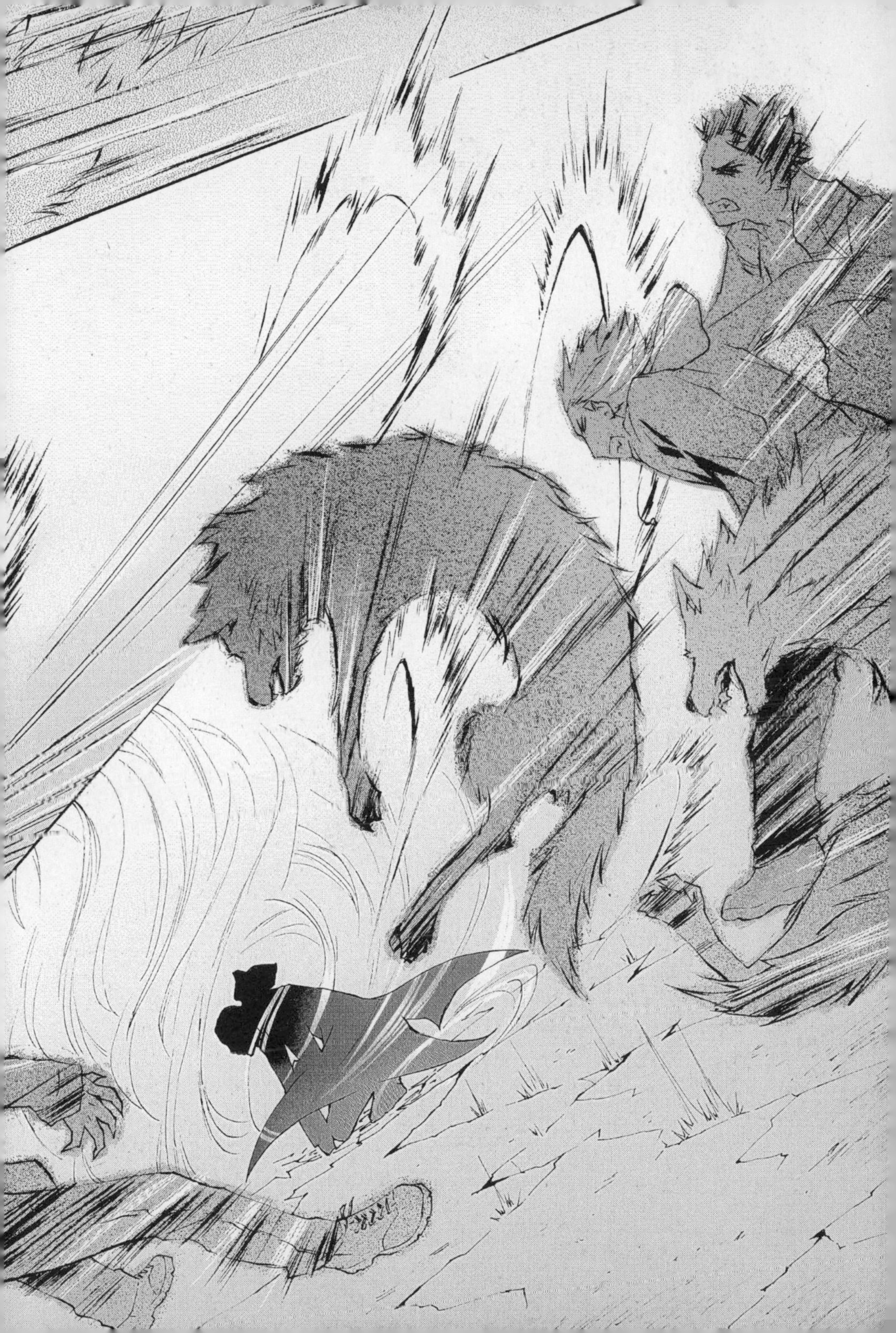

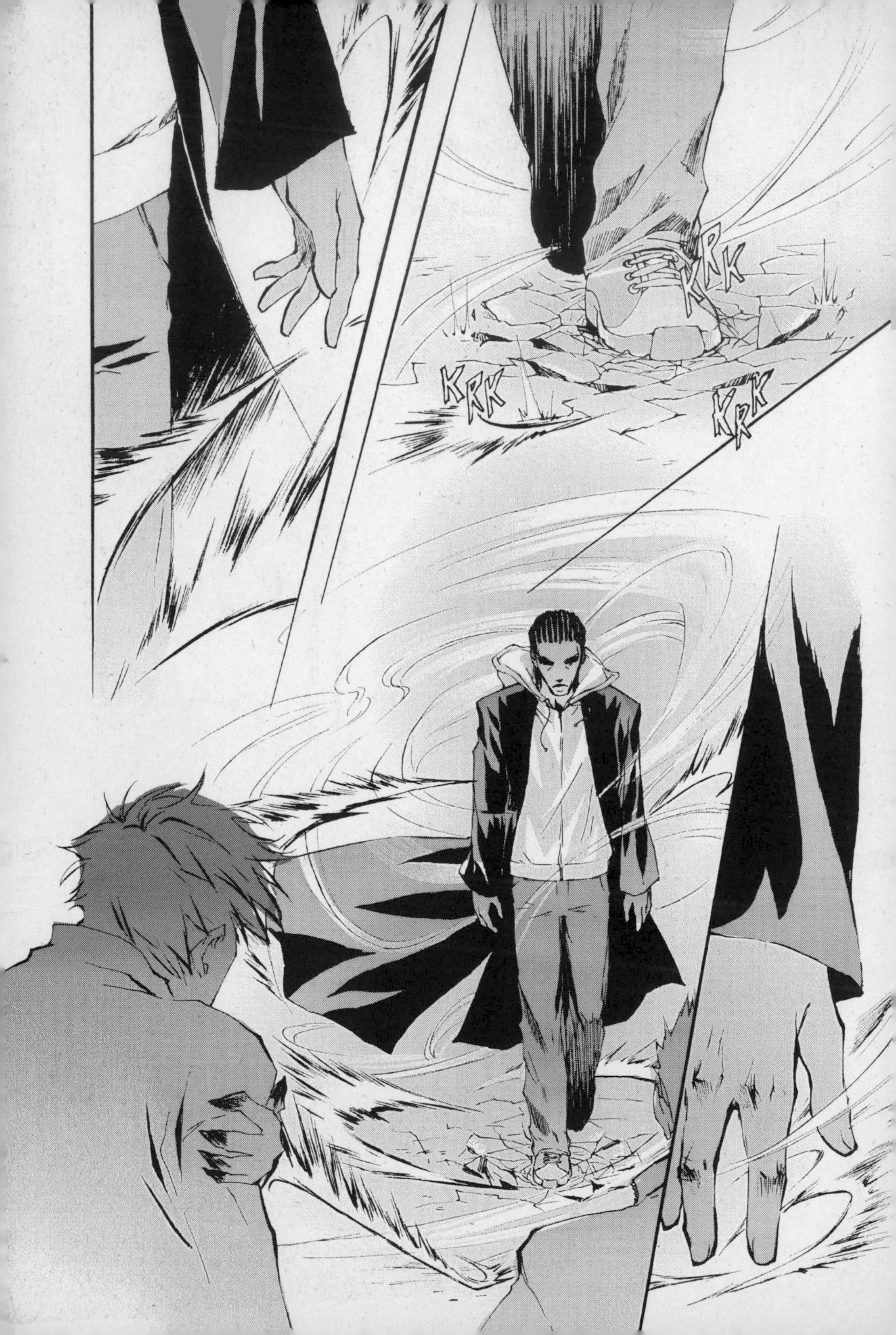

KRK
KRK
KRK
KRK

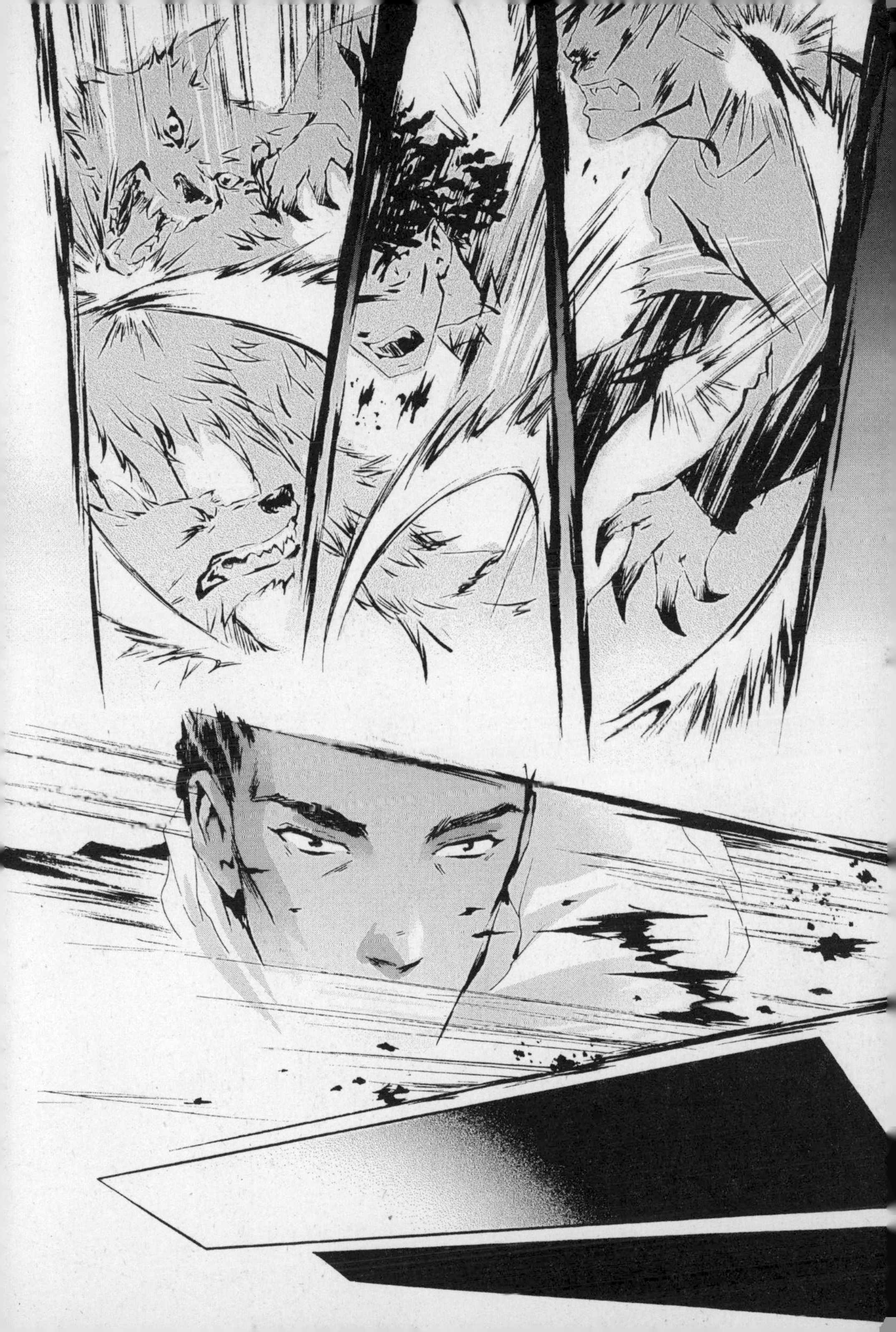

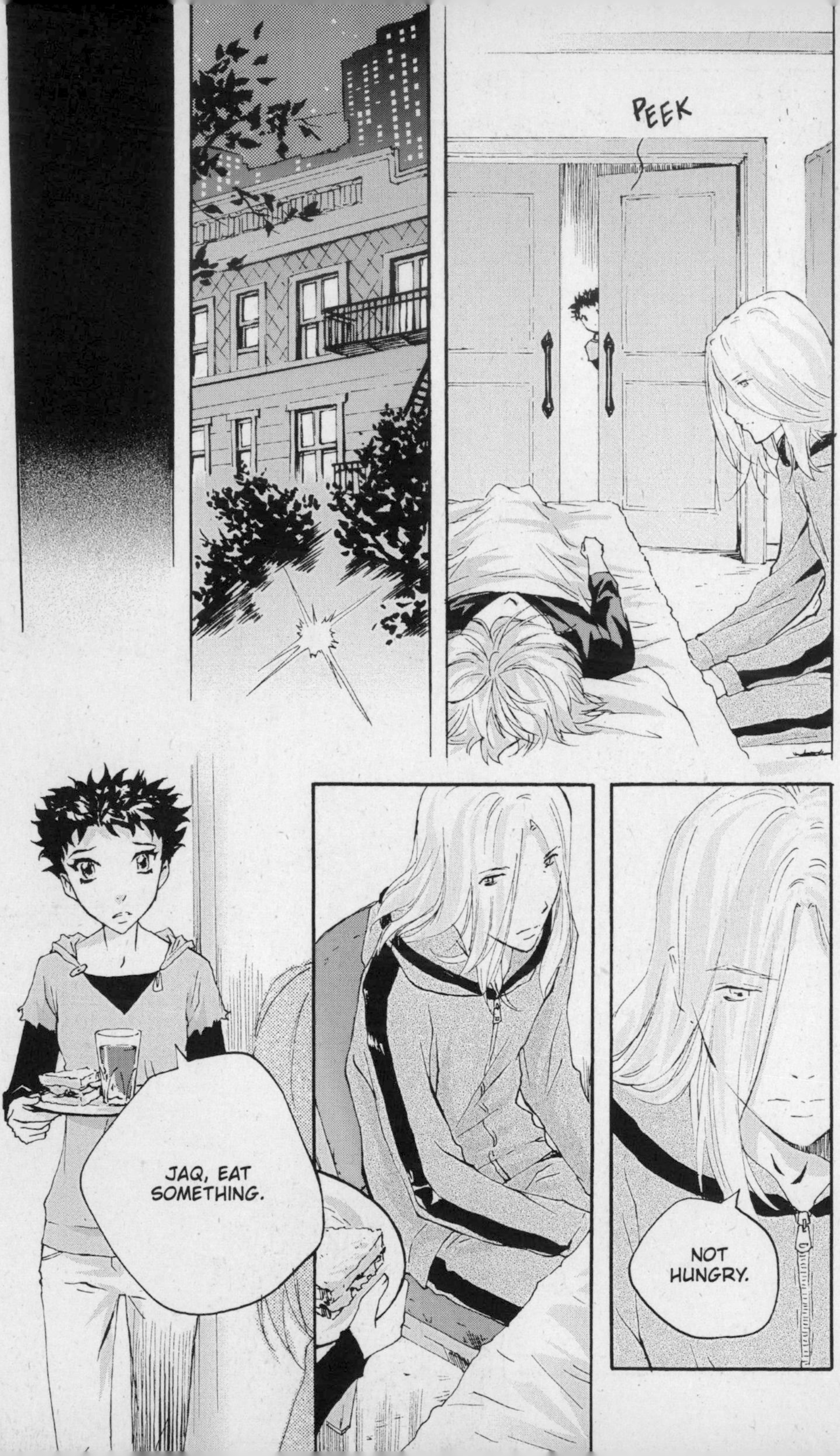
PEEK
JAQ, EAT SOMETHING.
NOT HUNGRY.

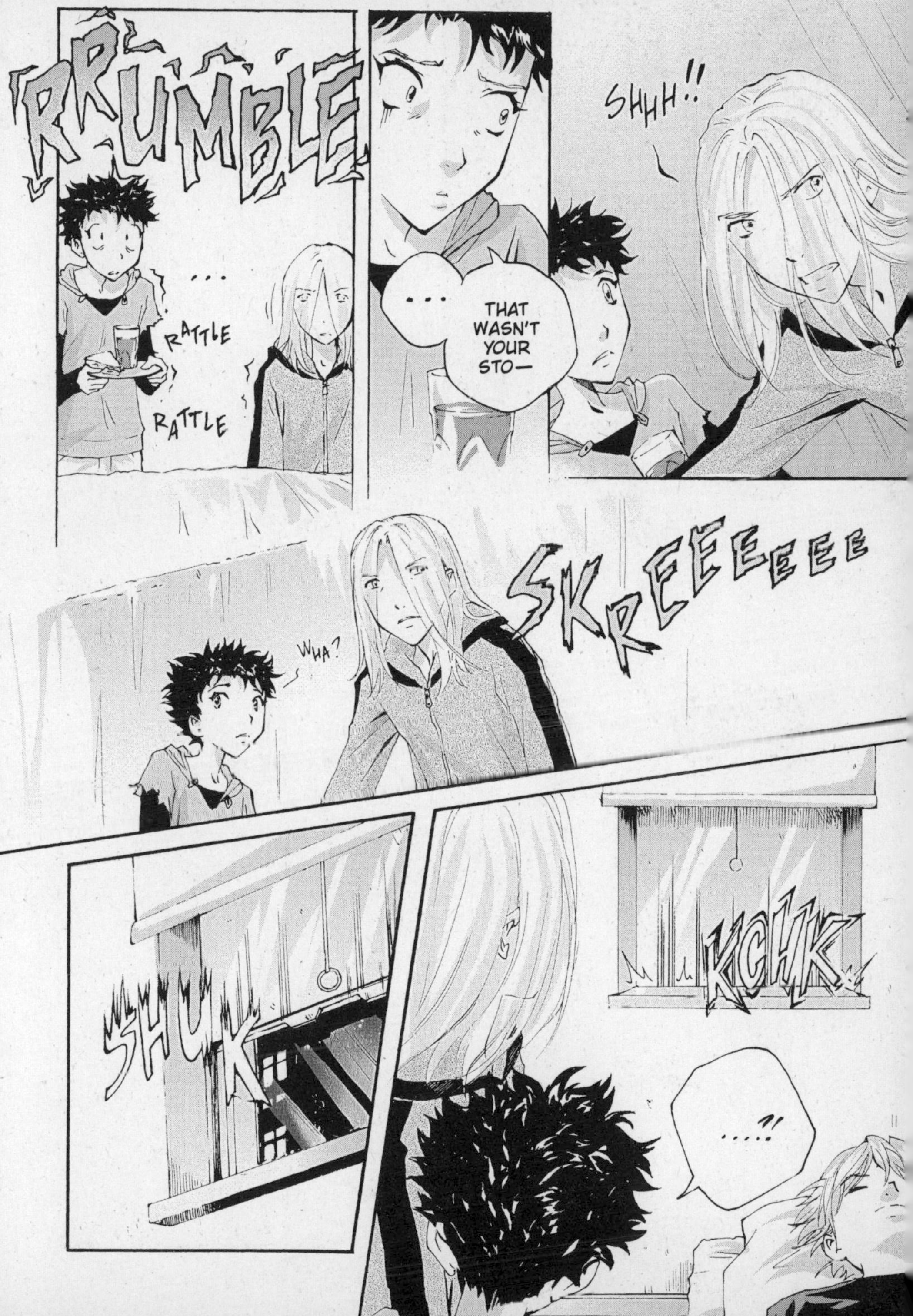
RRUMBLE
...
RATTLE
RATTLE
... THAT WASN'T YOUR STO—
SHHH!!
WHA?
SKREEEEEEE
SHUK
KCHK
.....?!

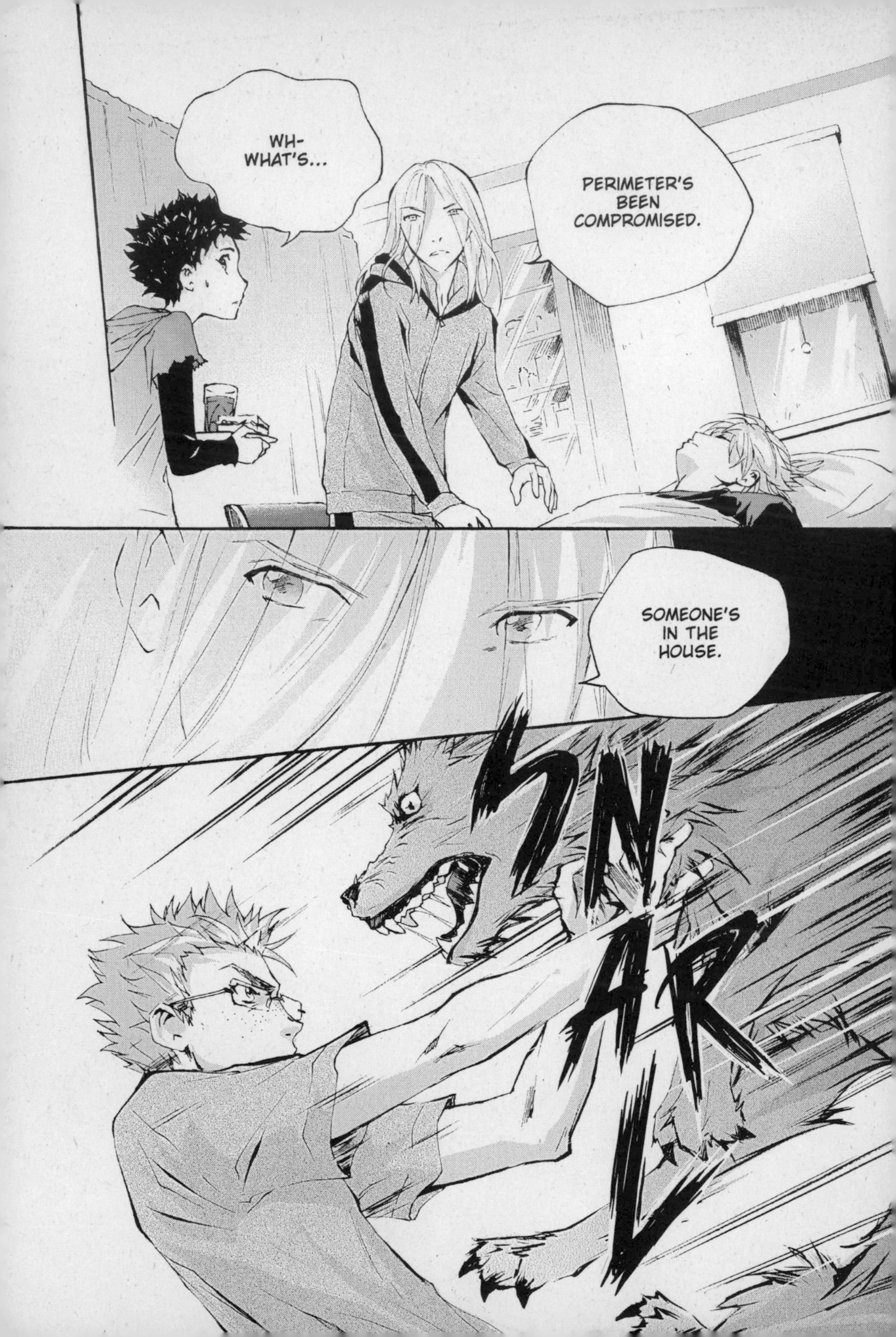
WH-
WHAT'S...
PERIMETER'S BEEN COMPROMISED.
SOMEONE'S IN THE HOUSE.
SNARL

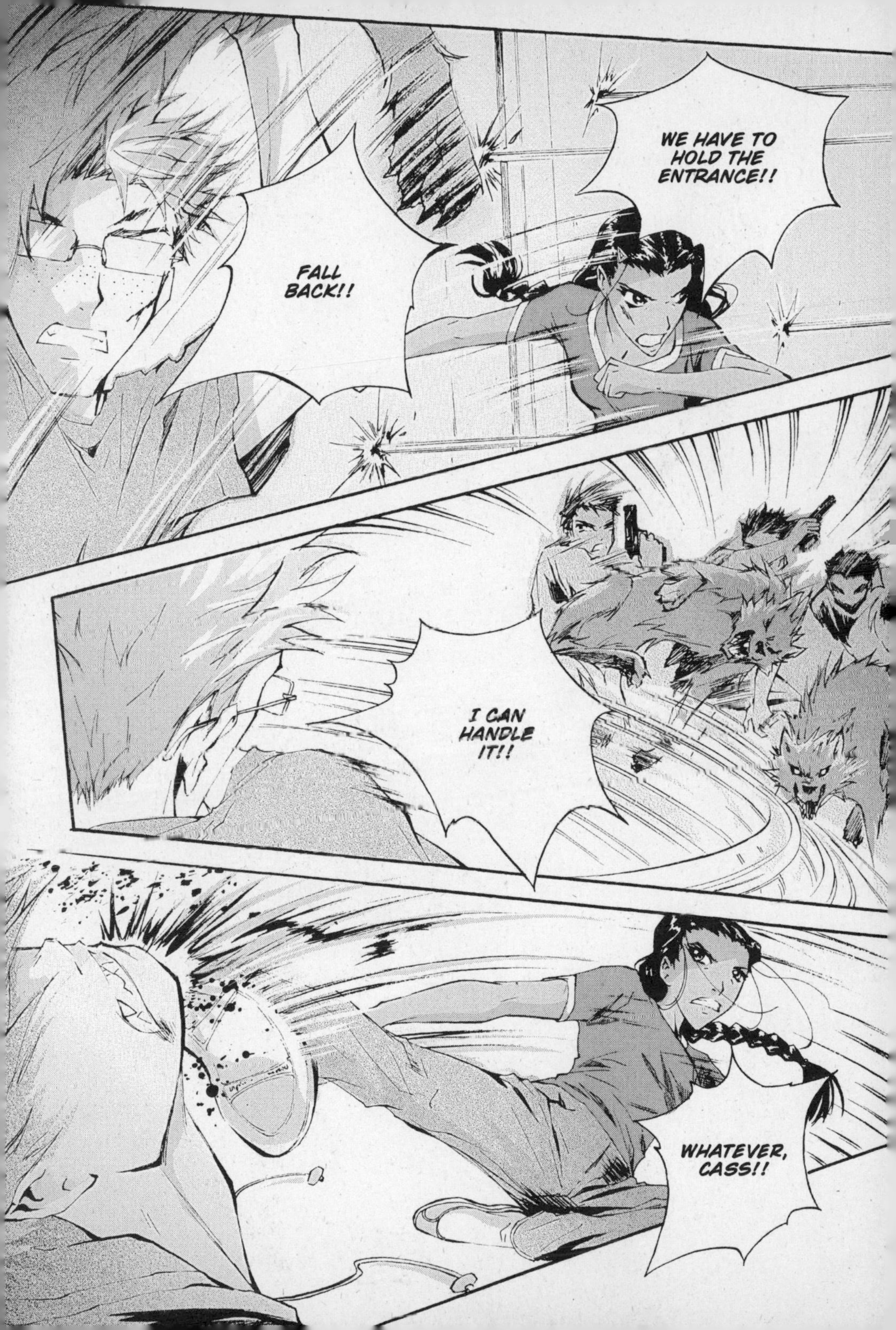
FALL BACK!!
WE HAVE TO HOLD THE ENTRANCE!!
I CAN HANDLE IT!!
WHATEVER, CASS!!

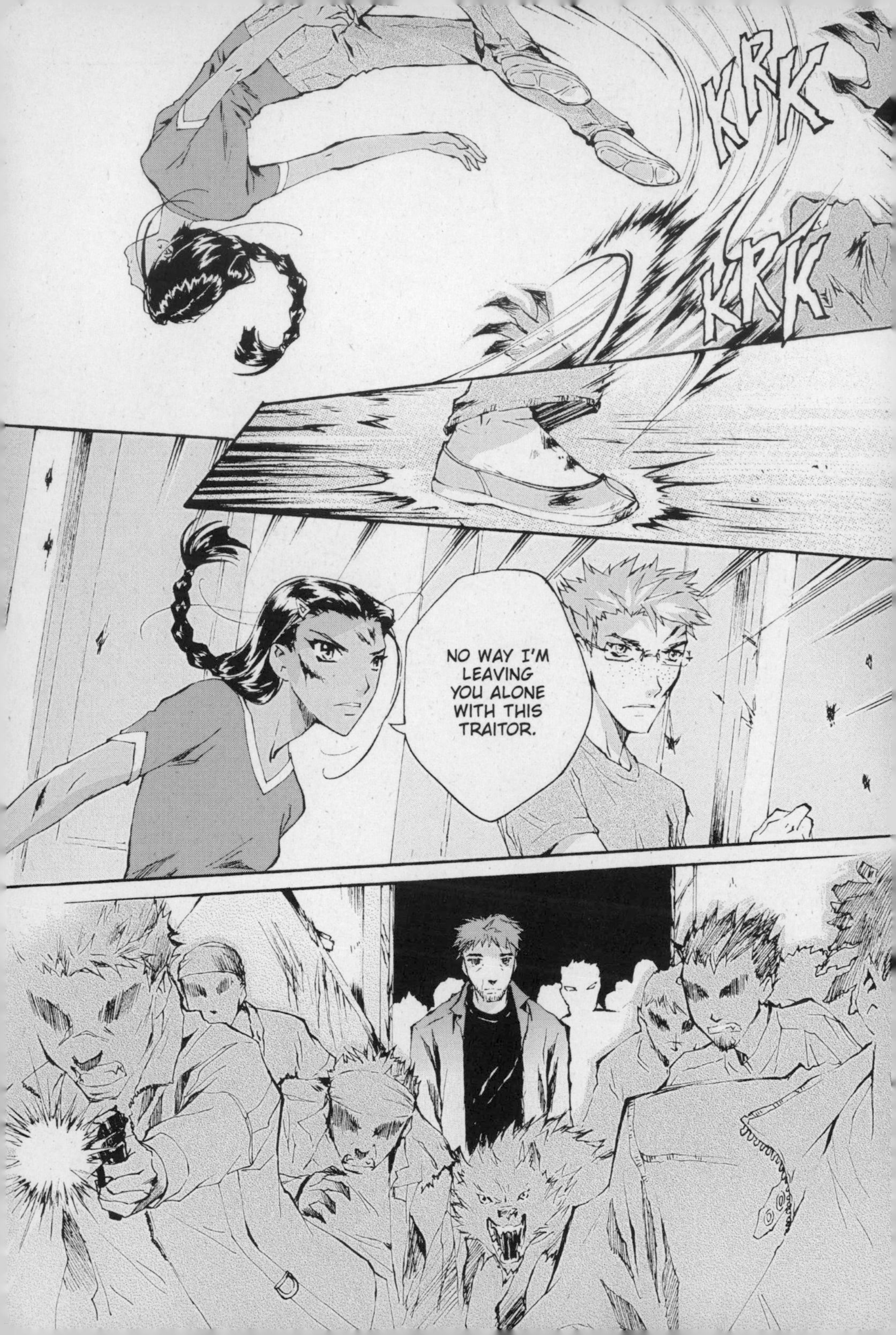
KRK
KRK
NO WAY I'M LEAVING YOU ALONE WITH THIS TRAITOR.

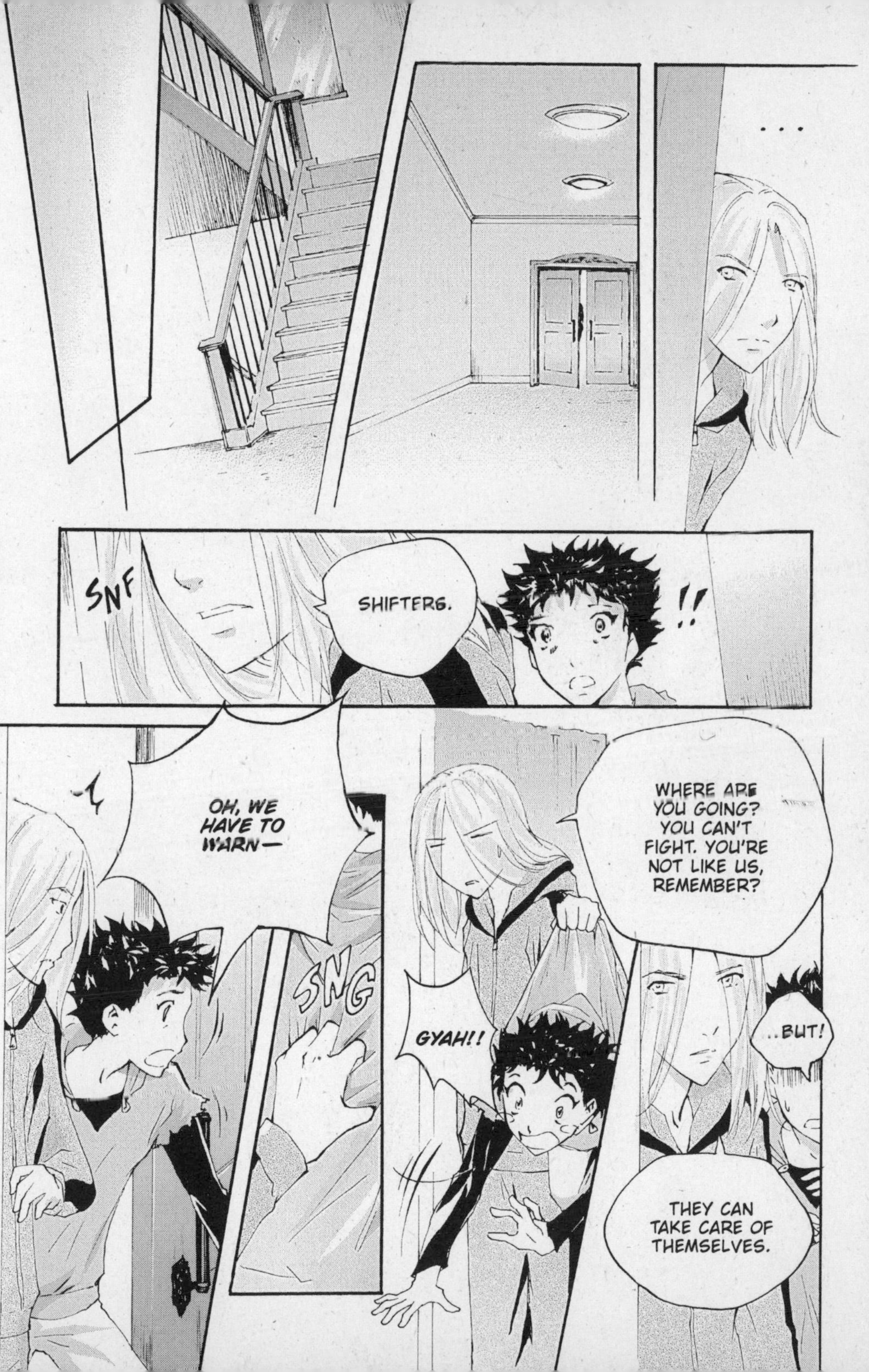
...
SNF
SHIFTERS.
!!
OH, WE HAVE TO WARN—
SNG
WHERE ARE YOU GOING? YOU CAN'T FIGHT. YOU'RE NOT LIKE US, REMEMBER?
GYAH!!
...BUT!
THEY CAN TAKE CARE OF THEMSELVES.

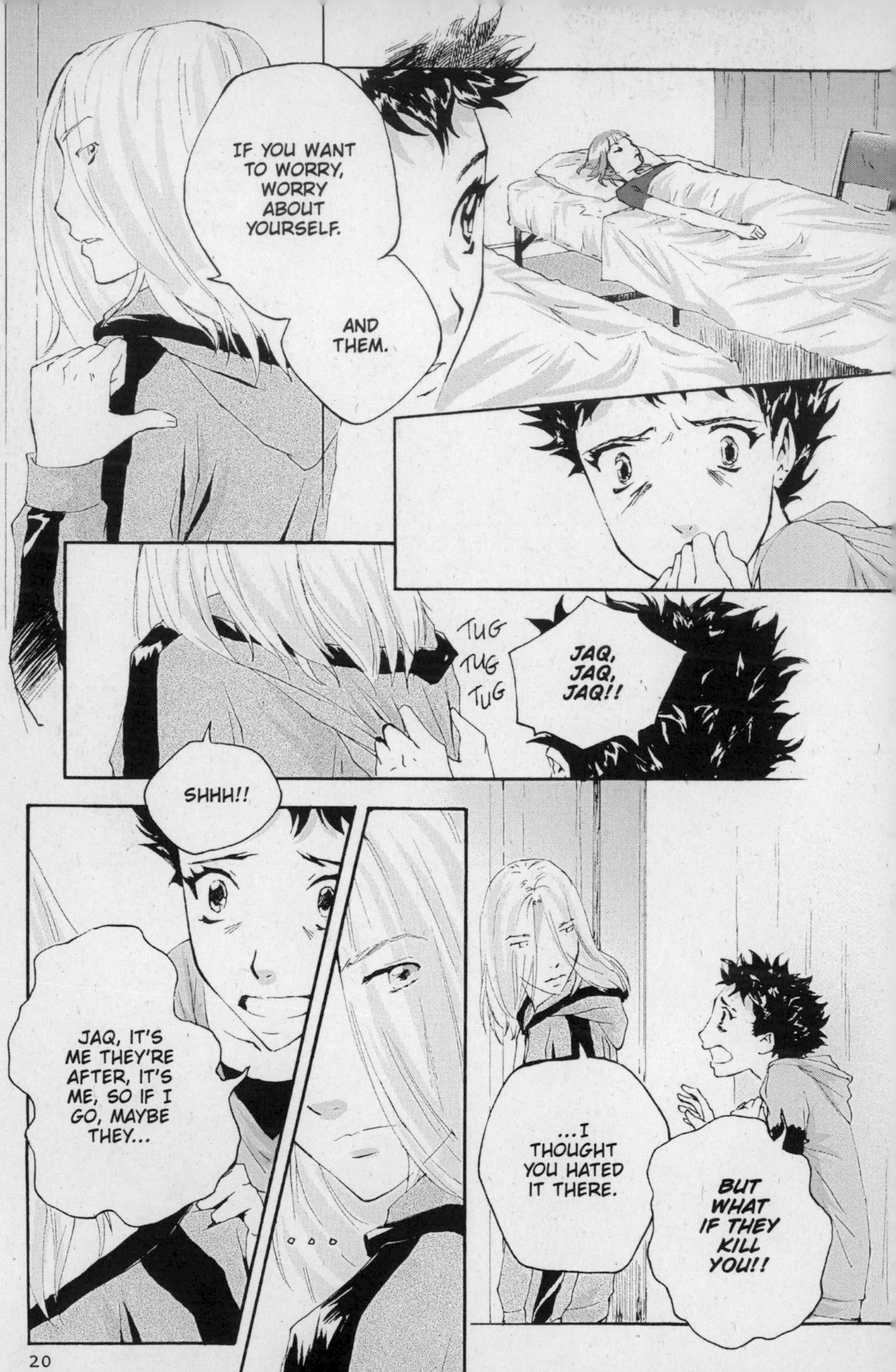
IF YOU WANT TO WORRY, WORRY ABOUT YOURSELF.
AND THEM.
TUG TUG TUG
JAQ, JAQ, JAQ!!
SHHH!!
JAQ, IT'S ME THEY'RE AFTER, IT'S ME, SO IF I GO, MAYBE THEY...
...I THOUGHT YOU HATED IT THERE.
BUT WHAT IF THEY KILL YOU!!

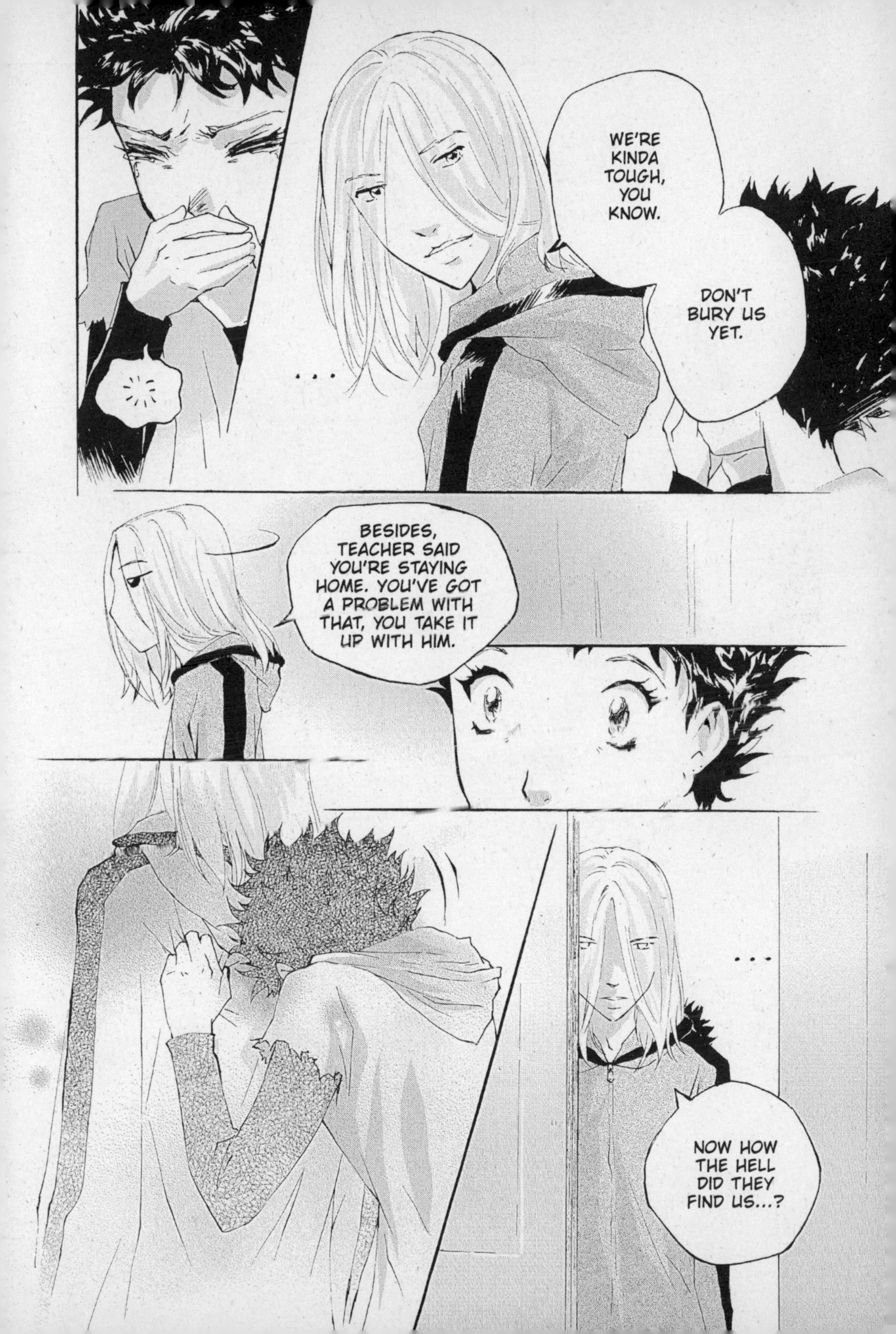

WE'RE KINDA TOUGH, YOU KNOW.
DON'T BURY US YET.
...
BESIDES, TEACHER SAID YOU'RE STAYING HOME. YOU'VE GOT A PROBLEM WITH THAT, YOU TAKE IT UP WITH HIM.
...
NOW HOW THE HELL DID THEY FIND US...?

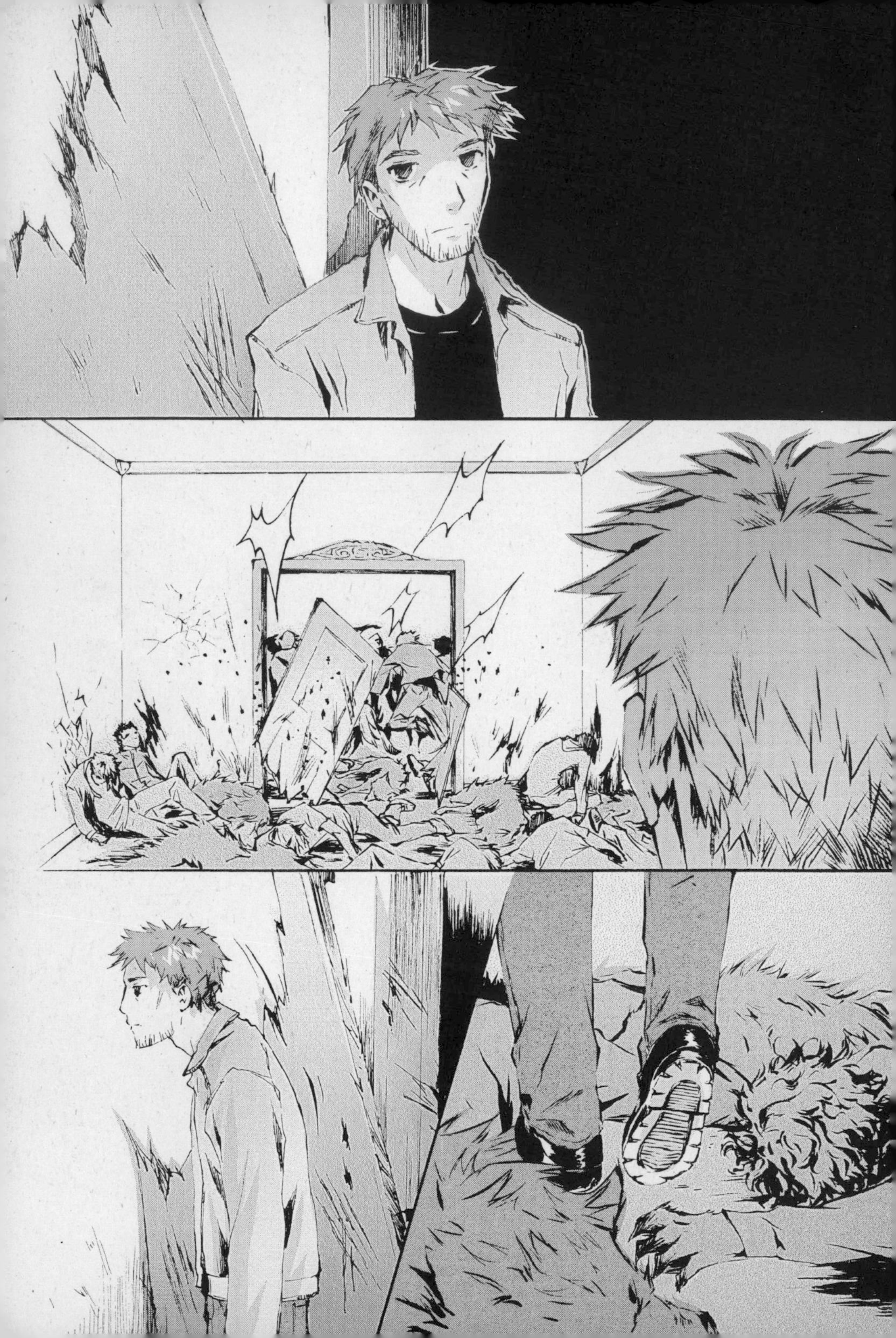

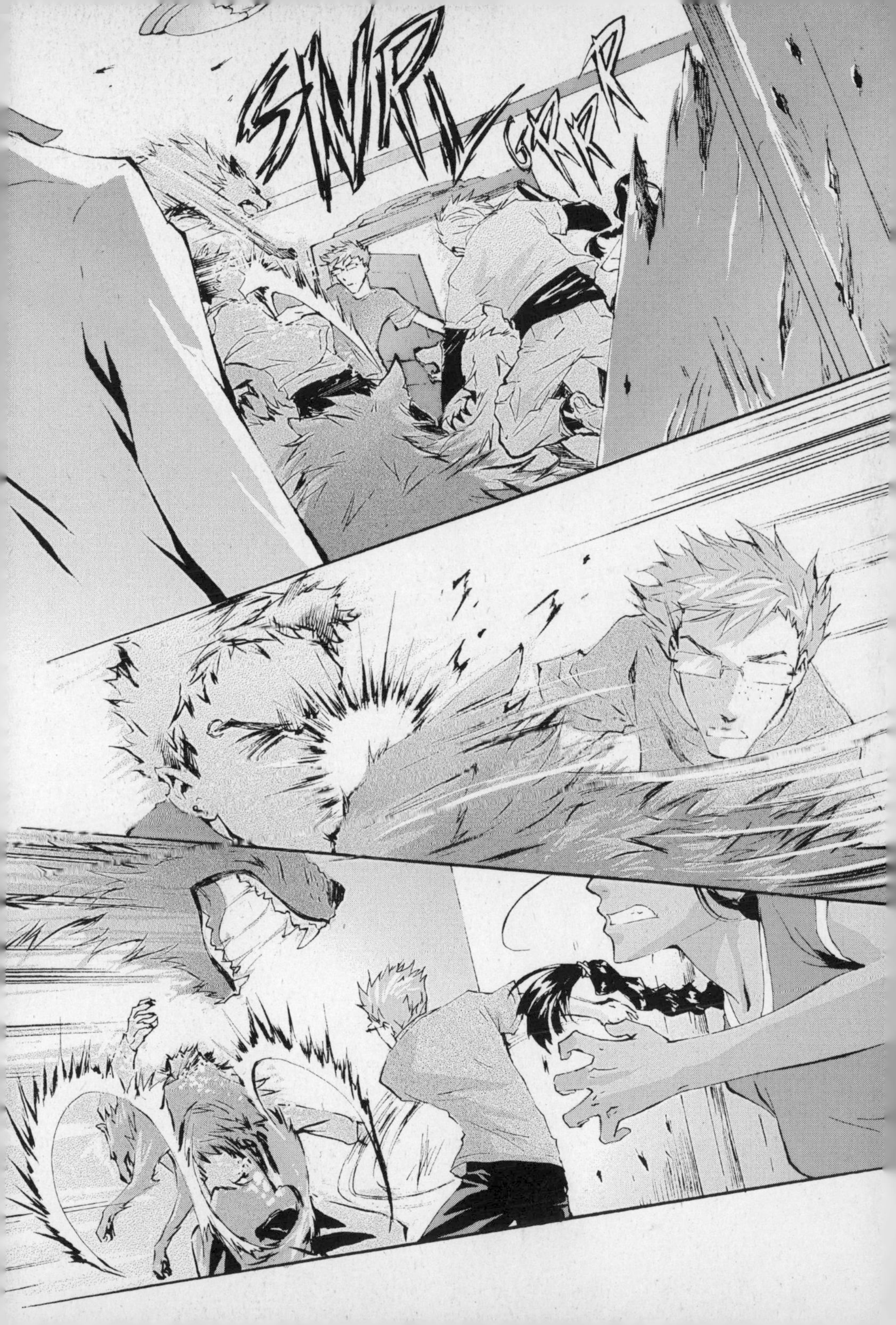
SNRL
GRRR

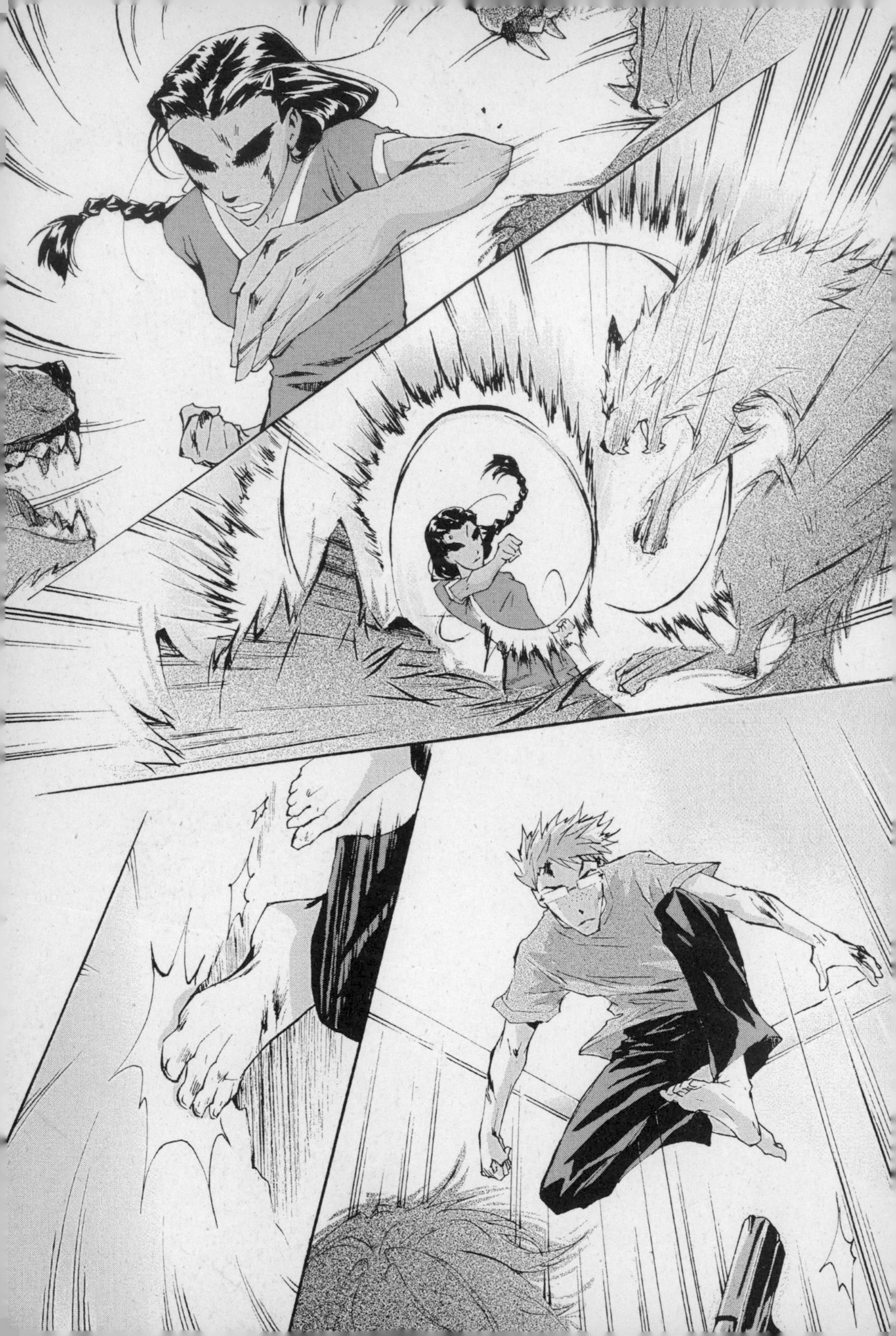

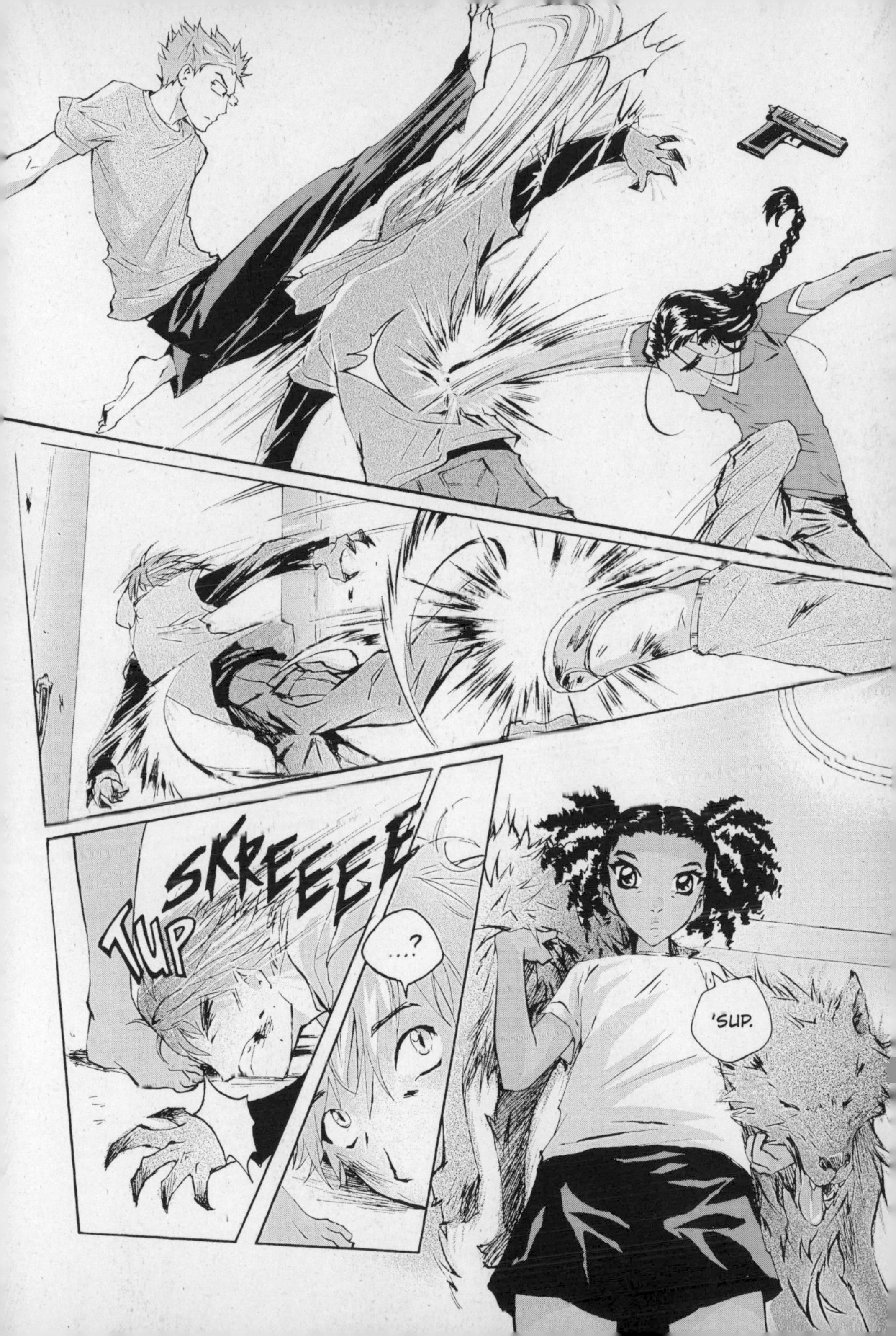
TUP
SKREEEEE
...?
'SUP.

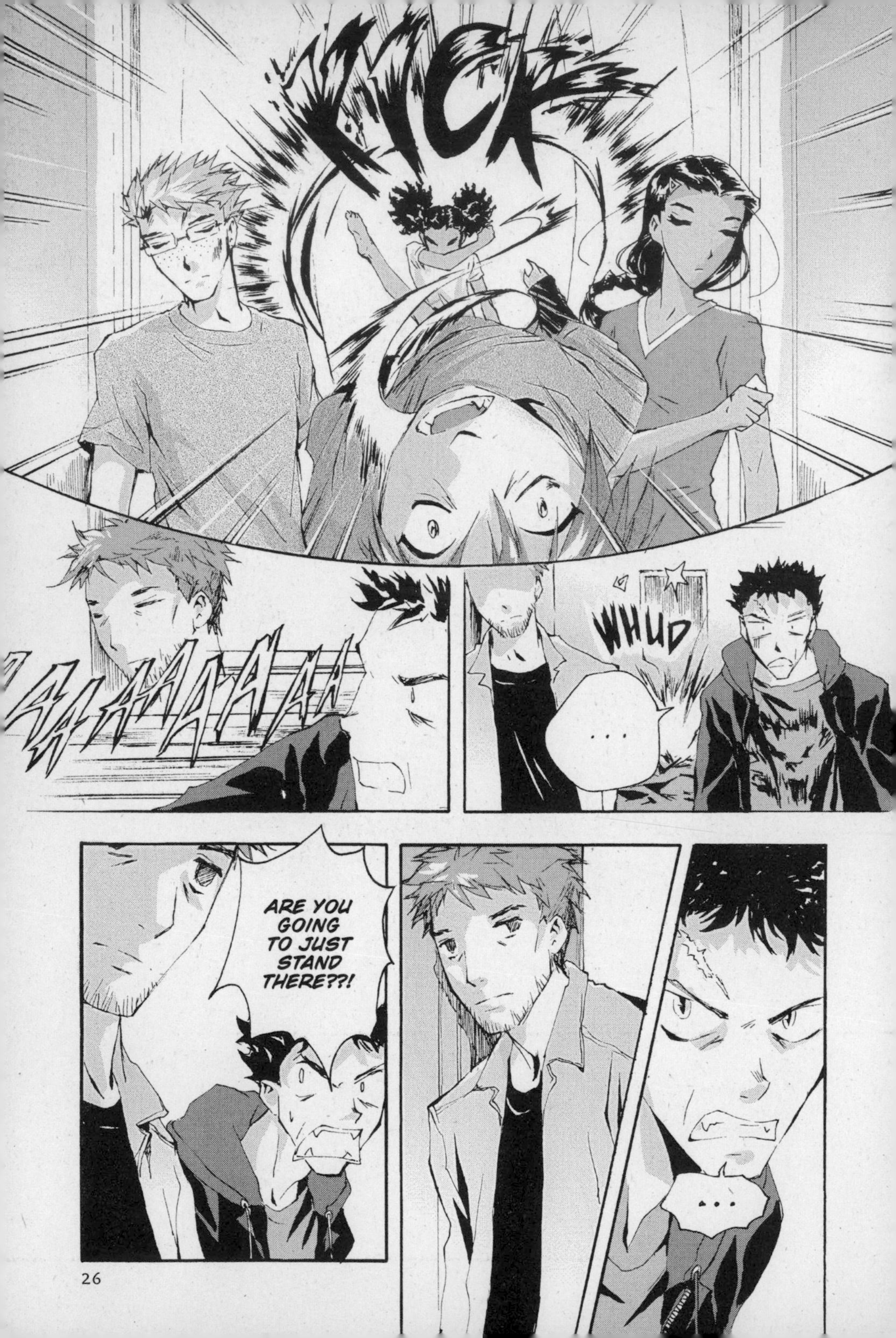
KICK
AAAAAAA
WHUD
...
ARE YOU GOING TO JUST STAND THERE??!
...

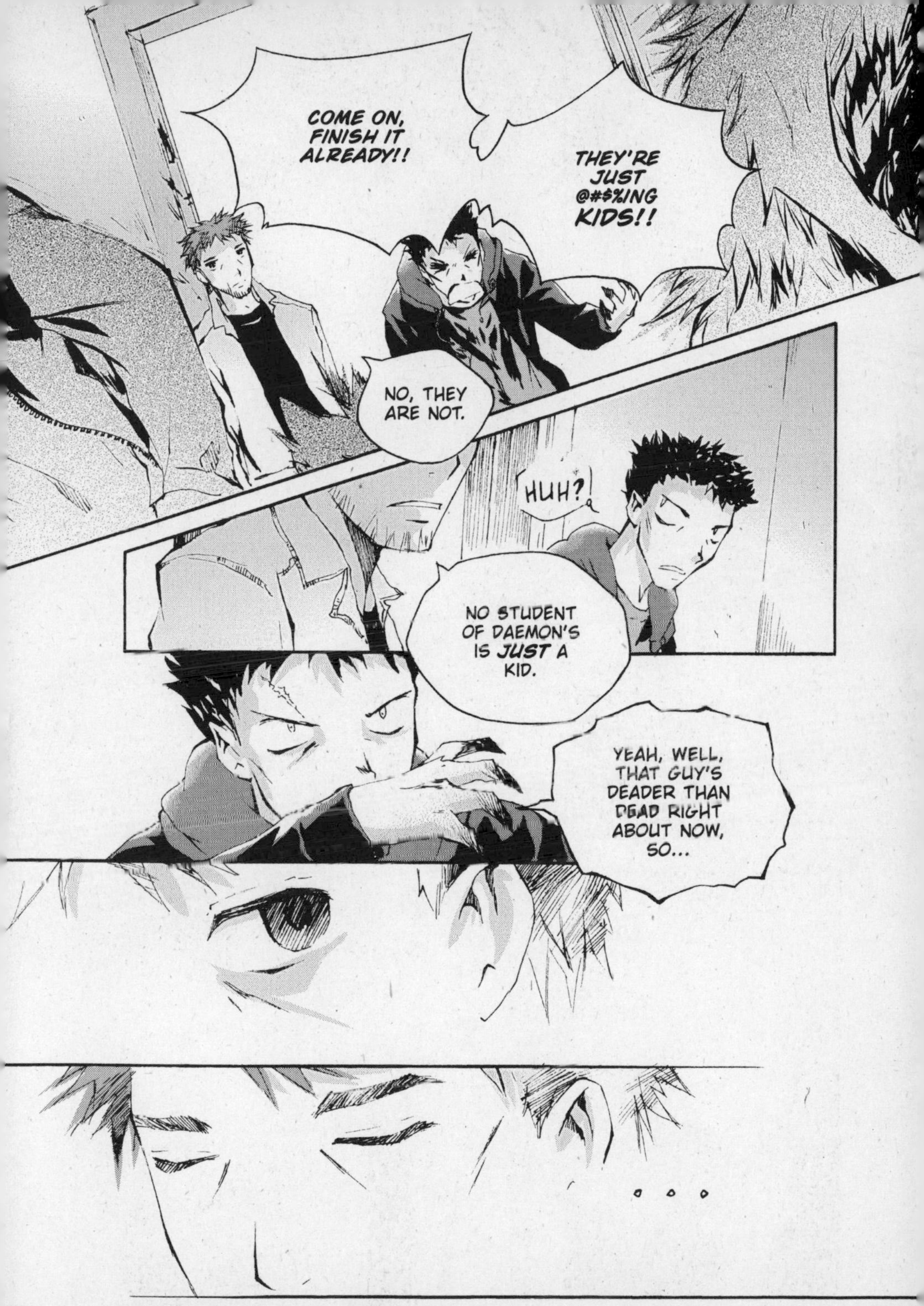
COME ON, FINISH IT ALREADY!!
THEY'RE JUST @#$%ING KIDS!!
NO, THEY ARE NOT.
HUH?
NO STUDENT OF DAEMON'S IS *JUST* A KID.
YEAH, WELL, THAT GUY'S DEADER THAN DEAD RIGHT ABOUT NOW, SO...
...

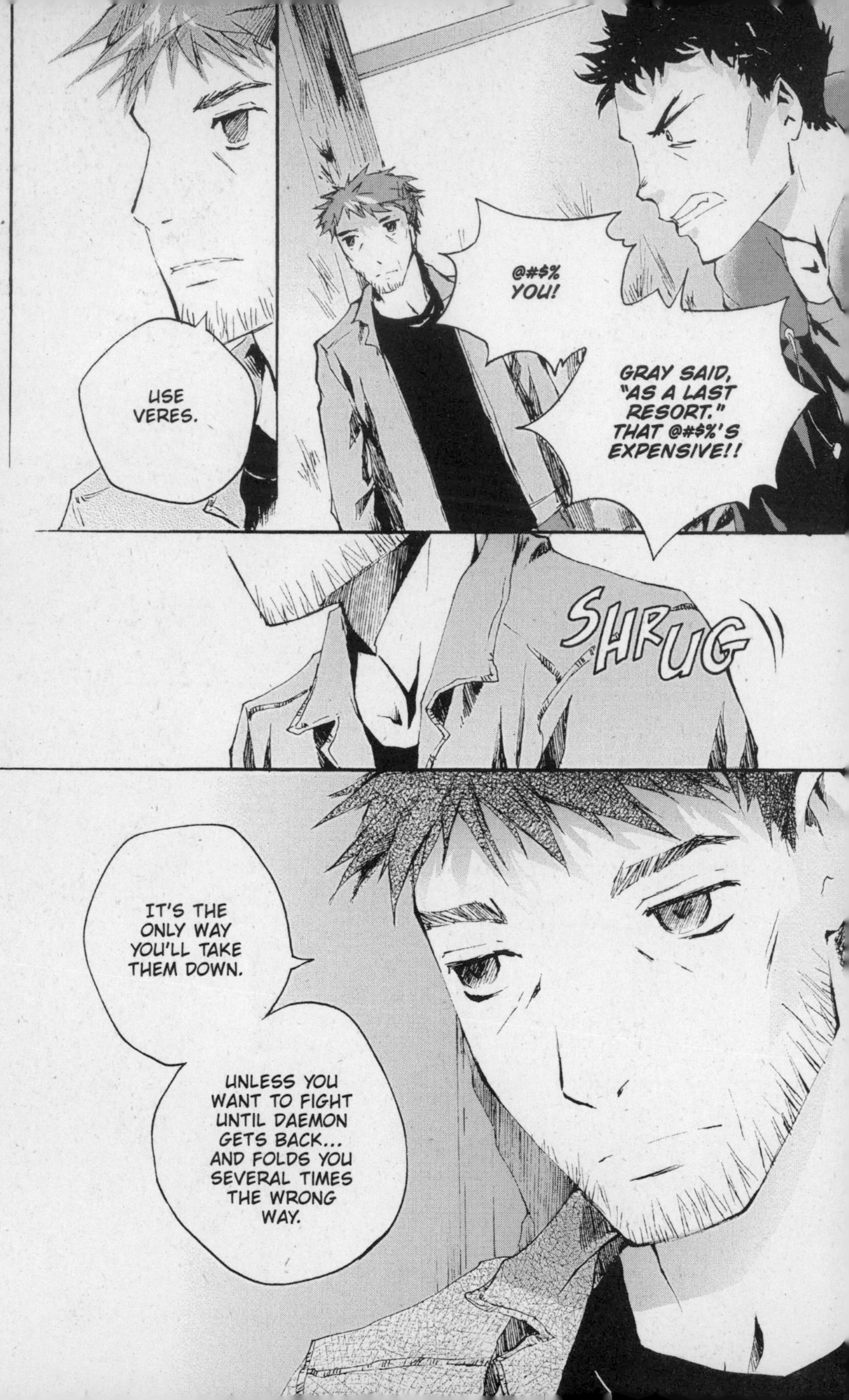
USE VERES.
@#$% YOU!
GRAY SAID, "AS A LAST RESORT." THAT @#$%'S EXPENSIVE!!
SHRUG
IT'S THE ONLY WAY YOU'LL TAKE THEM DOWN.
UNLESS YOU WANT TO FIGHT UNTIL DAEMON GETS BACK... AND FOLDS YOU SEVERAL TIMES THE WRONG WAY.

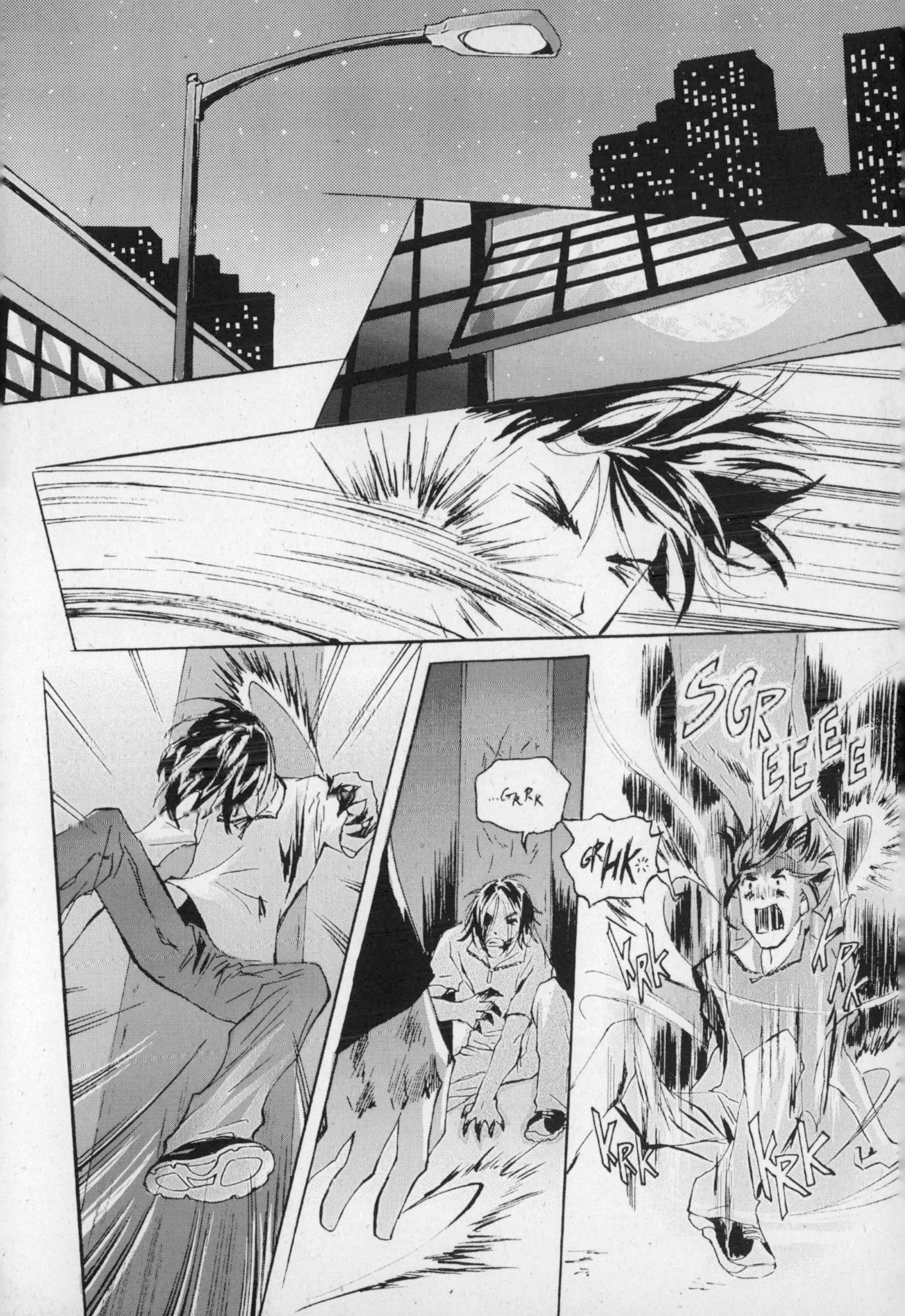
...GRRK
SCREEEE
GRHK
KRK
KRK
KRK
KRK

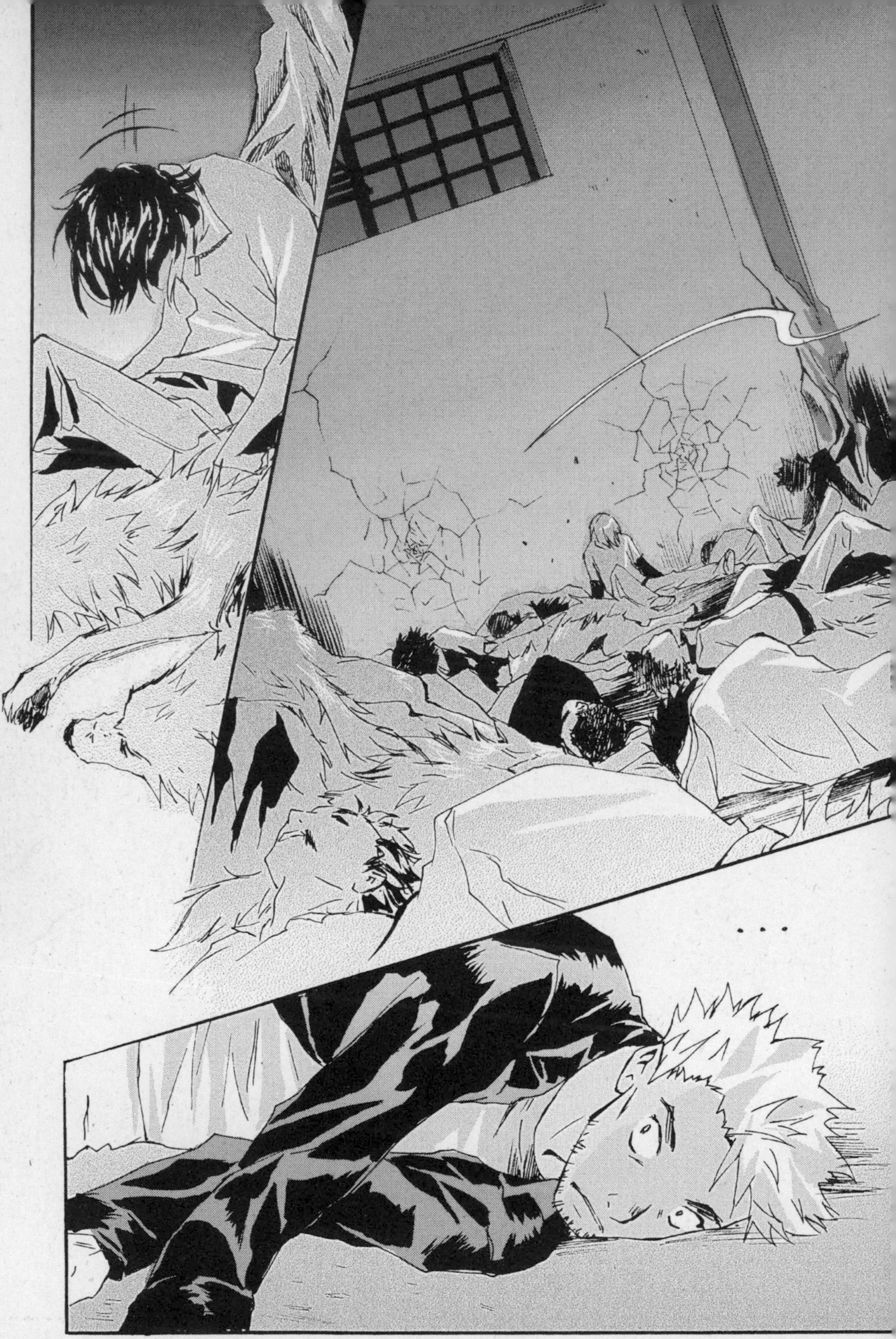
...

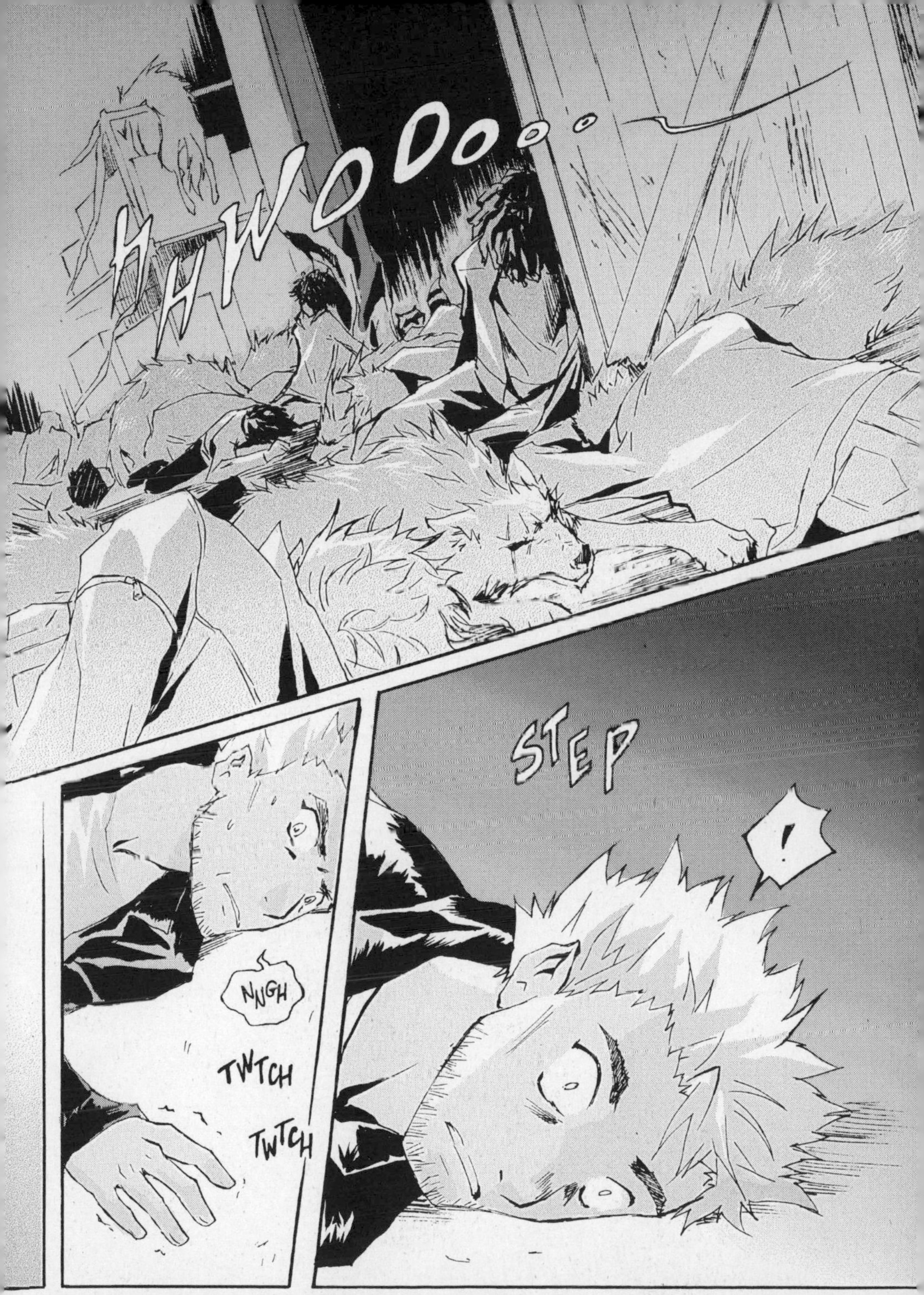
HWOOoo...
STEP
!
NNGH
TWTCH
TWTCH

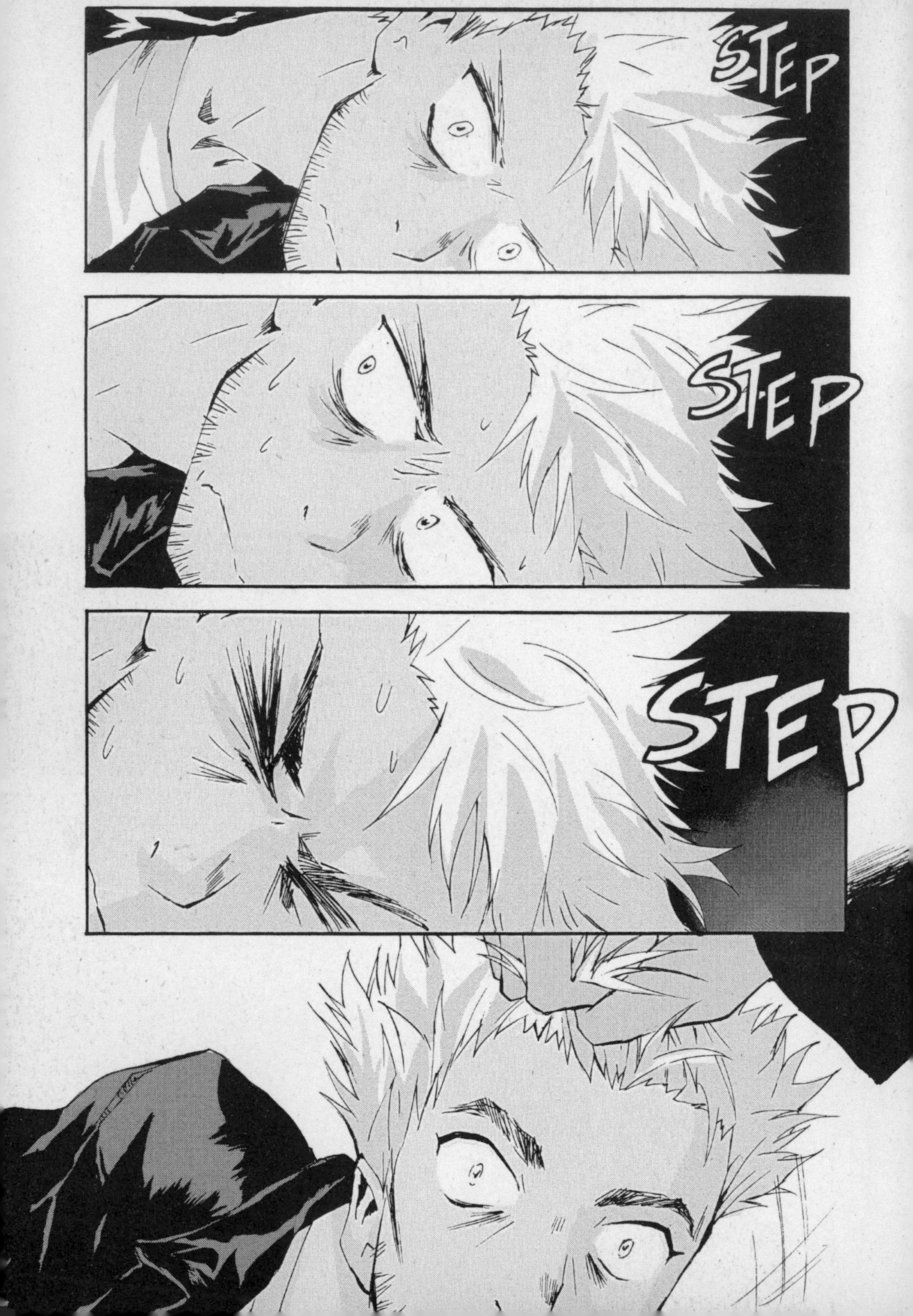
STEP
STEP
STEP

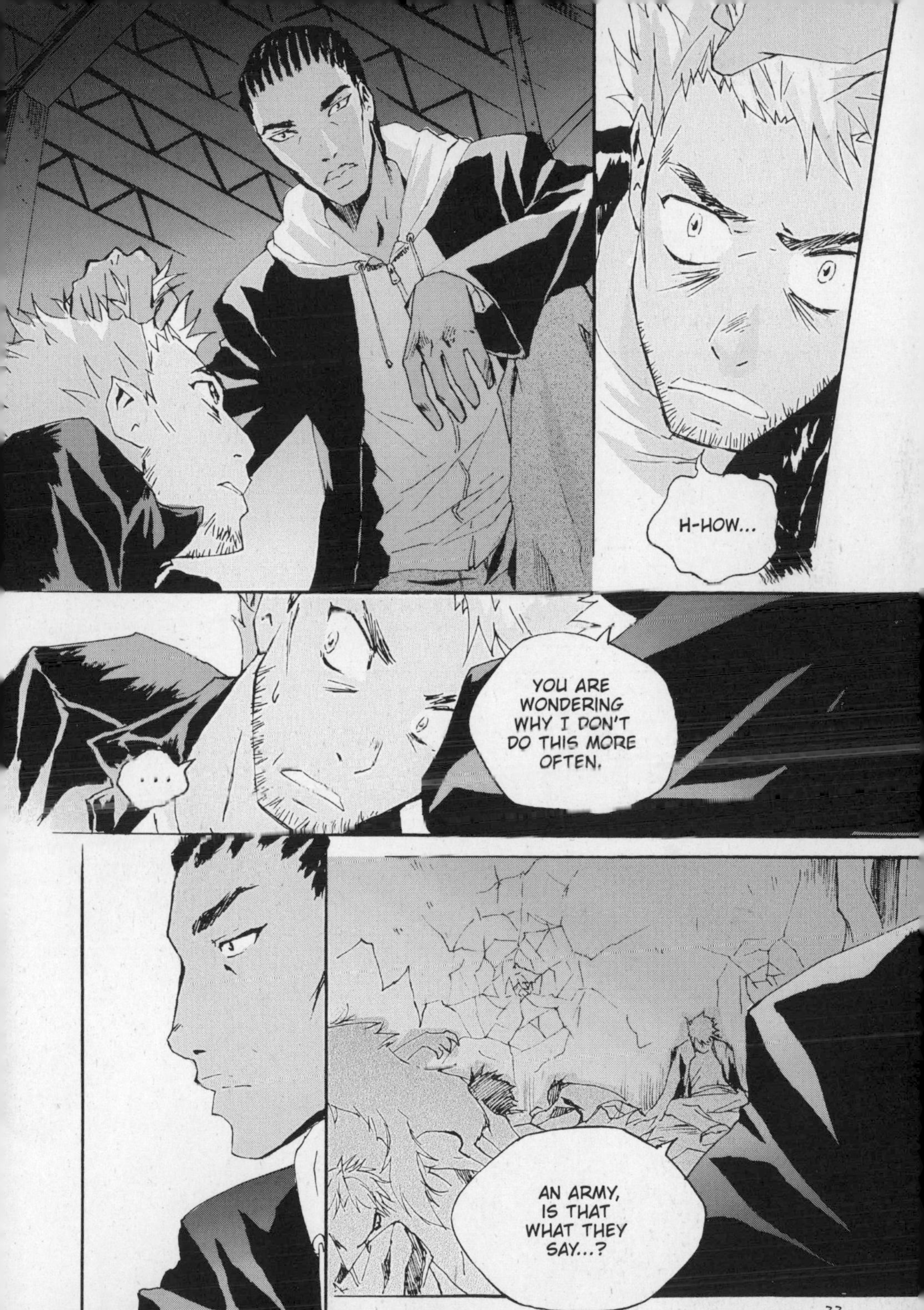
H-HOW...
...
YOU ARE WONDERING WHY I DON'T DO THIS MORE OFTEN.
AN ARMY, IS THAT WHAT THEY SAY...?

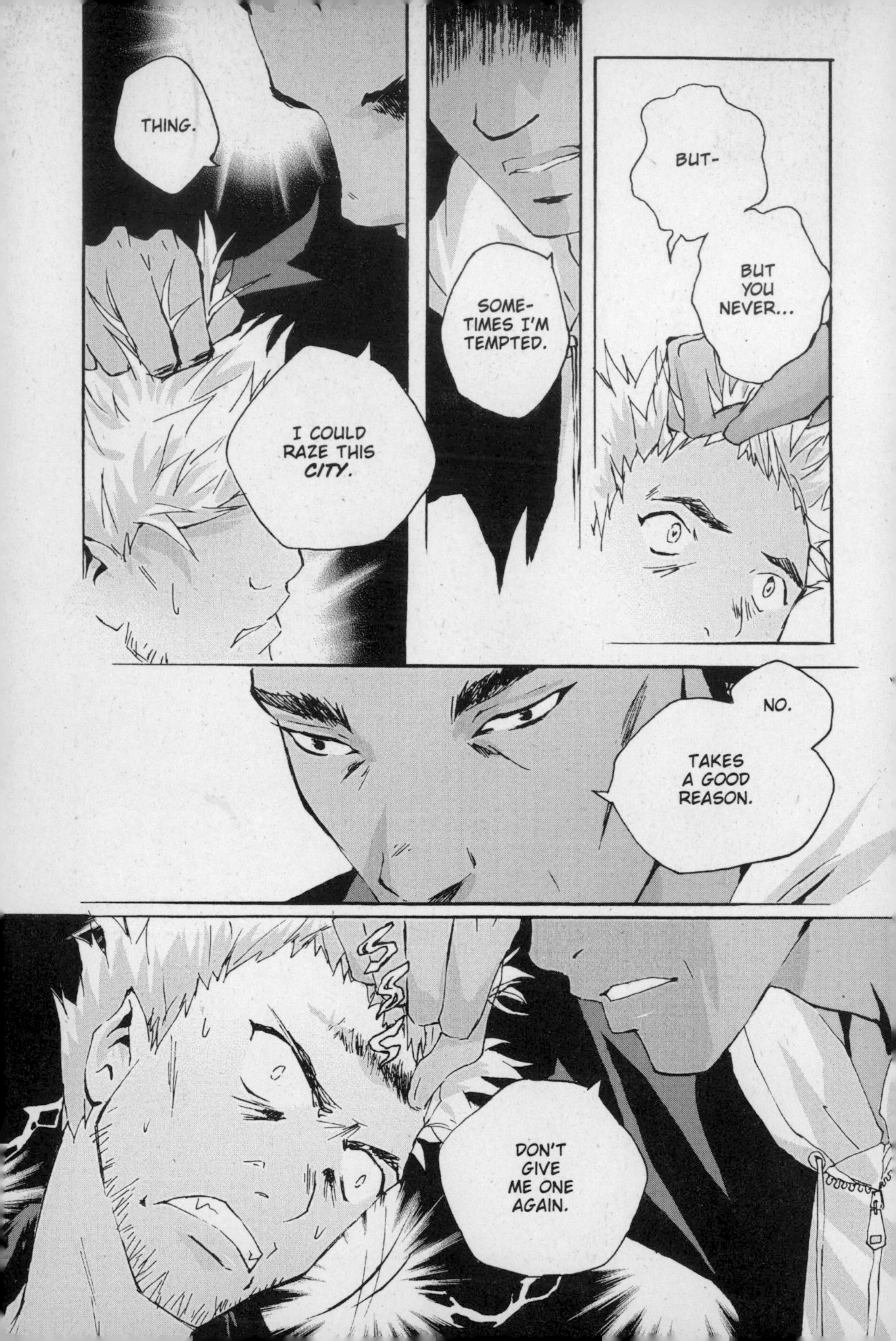
THING.
I COULD RAZE THIS *CITY*.
SOME-TIMES I'M TEMPTED.
BUT-
BUT YOU NEVER...
NO.
TAKES A GOOD REASON.
DON'T GIVE ME ONE AGAIN.

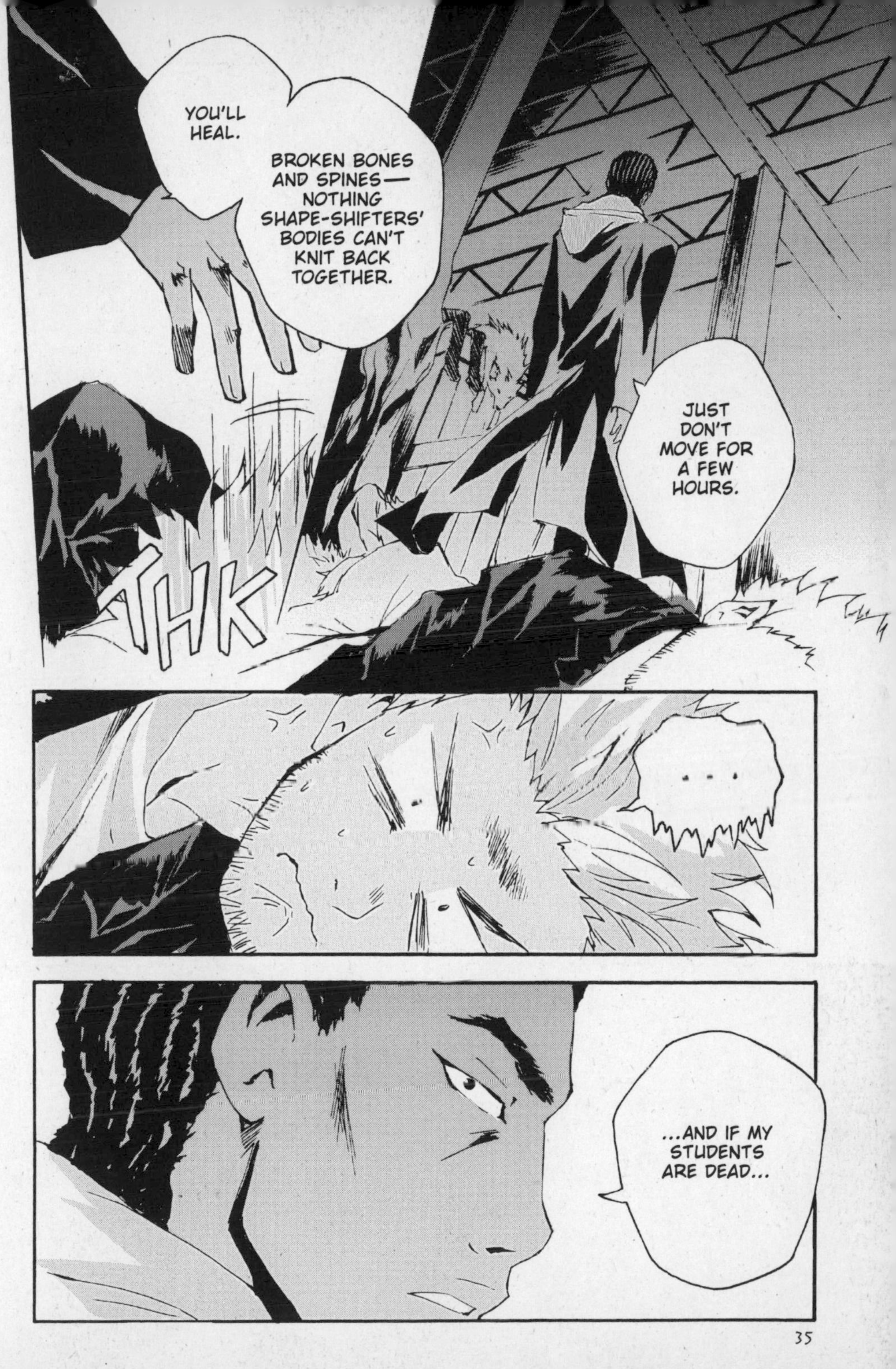
YOU'LL HEAL.
BROKEN BONES AND SPINES— NOTHING SHAPE-SHIFTERS' BODIES CAN'T KNIT BACK TOGETHER.
JUST DON'T MOVE FOR A FEW HOURS.
THK
...
...AND IF MY STUDENTS ARE DEAD...

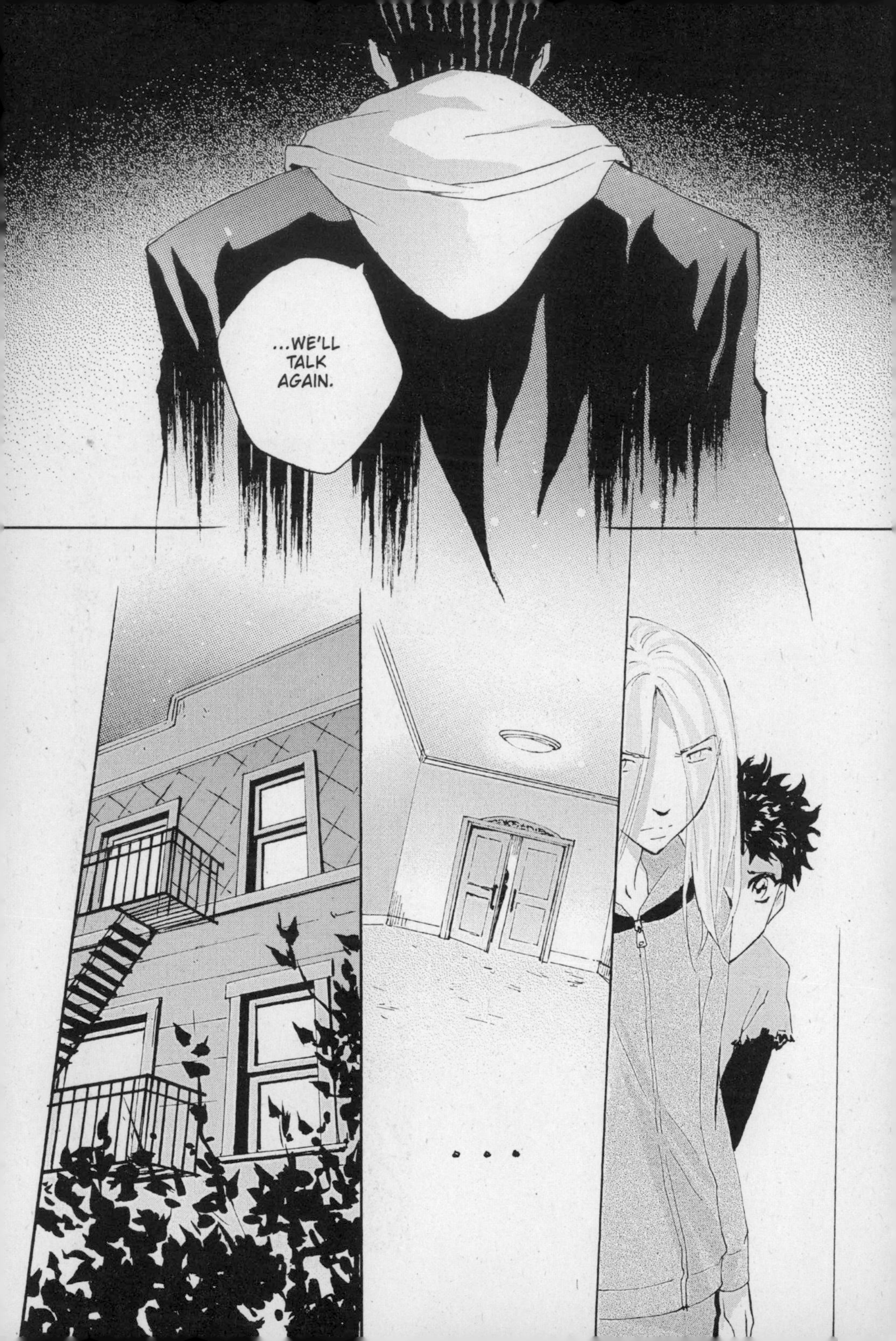
...WE'LL TALK AGAIN.
...

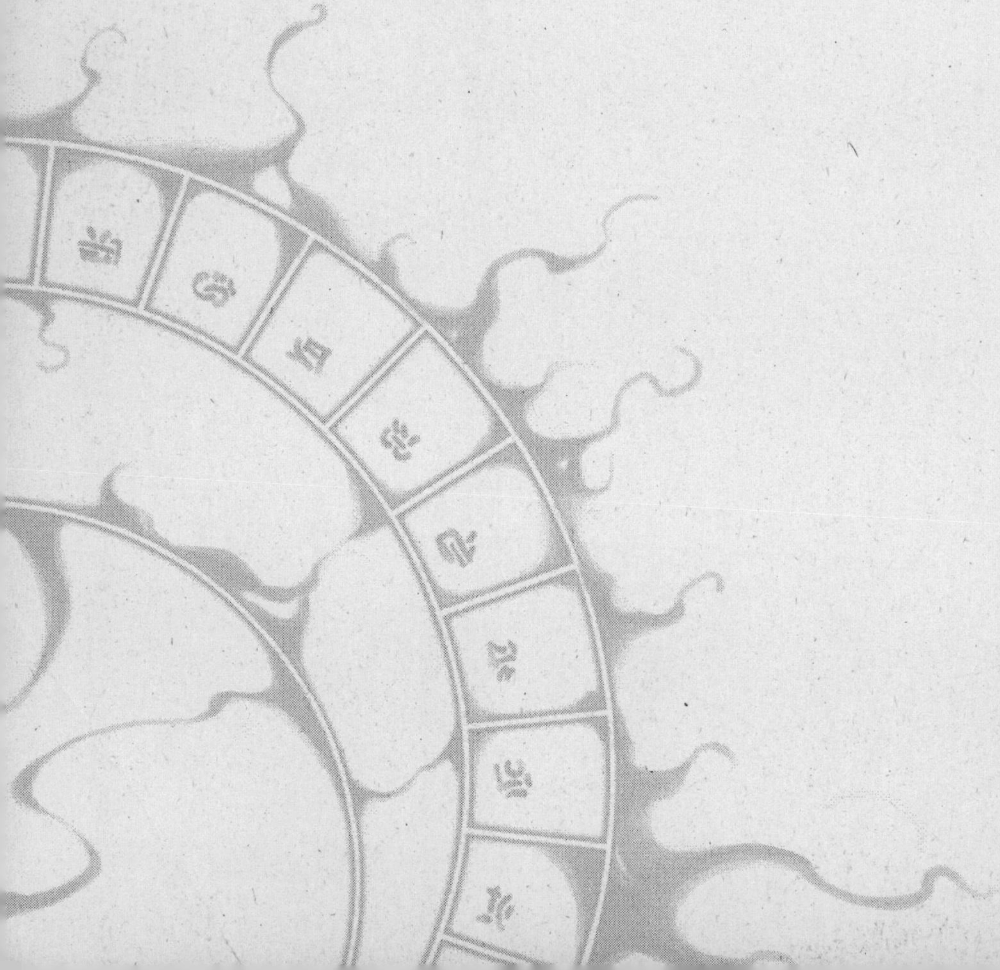

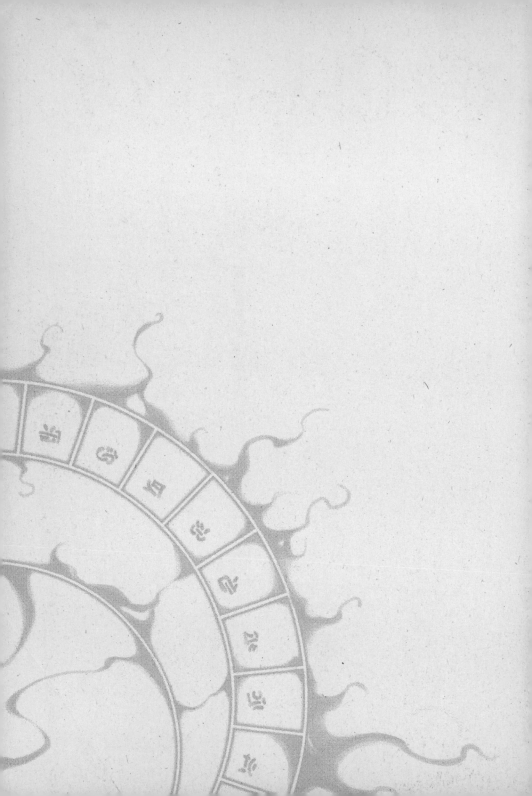

Chapter 14

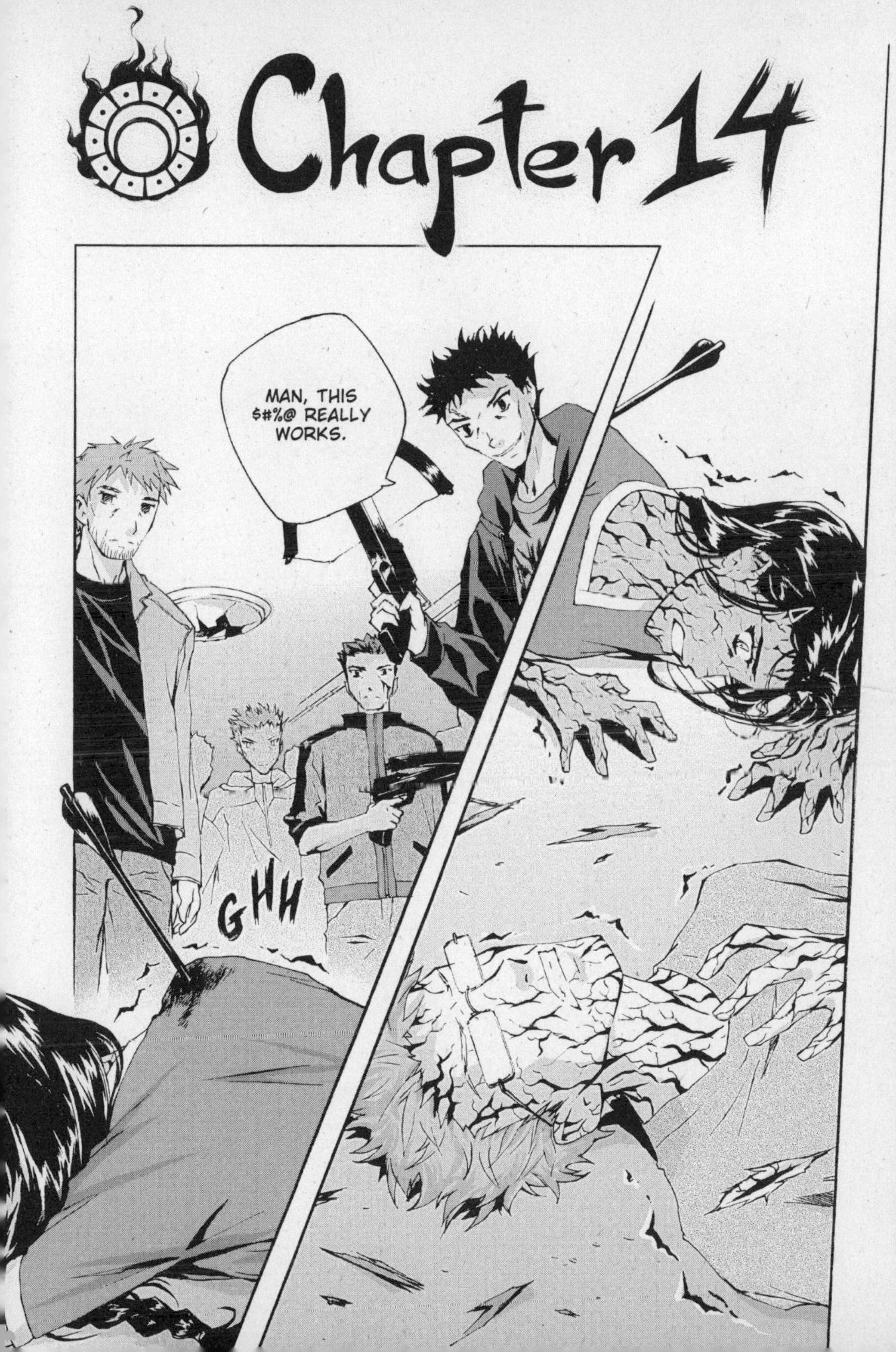
MAN, THIS $#%@ REALLY WORKS.
GHH

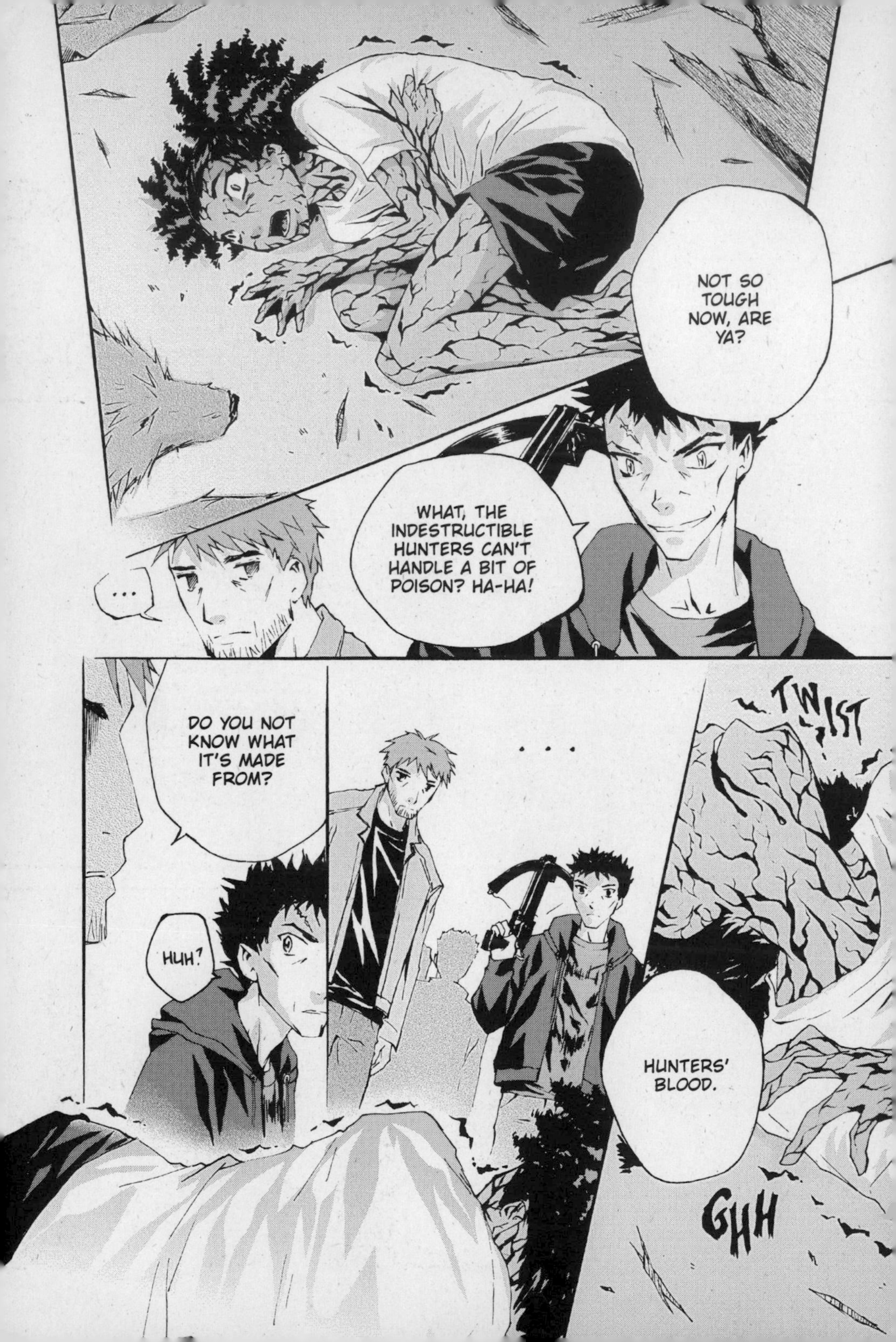
NOT SO TOUGH NOW, ARE YA?
...
WHAT, THE INDESTRUCTIBLE HUNTERS CAN'T HANDLE A BIT OF POISON? HA-HA!
DO YOU NOT KNOW WHAT IT'S MADE FROM?
HUH?
...
TWIST
HUNTERS' BLOOD.
GHH

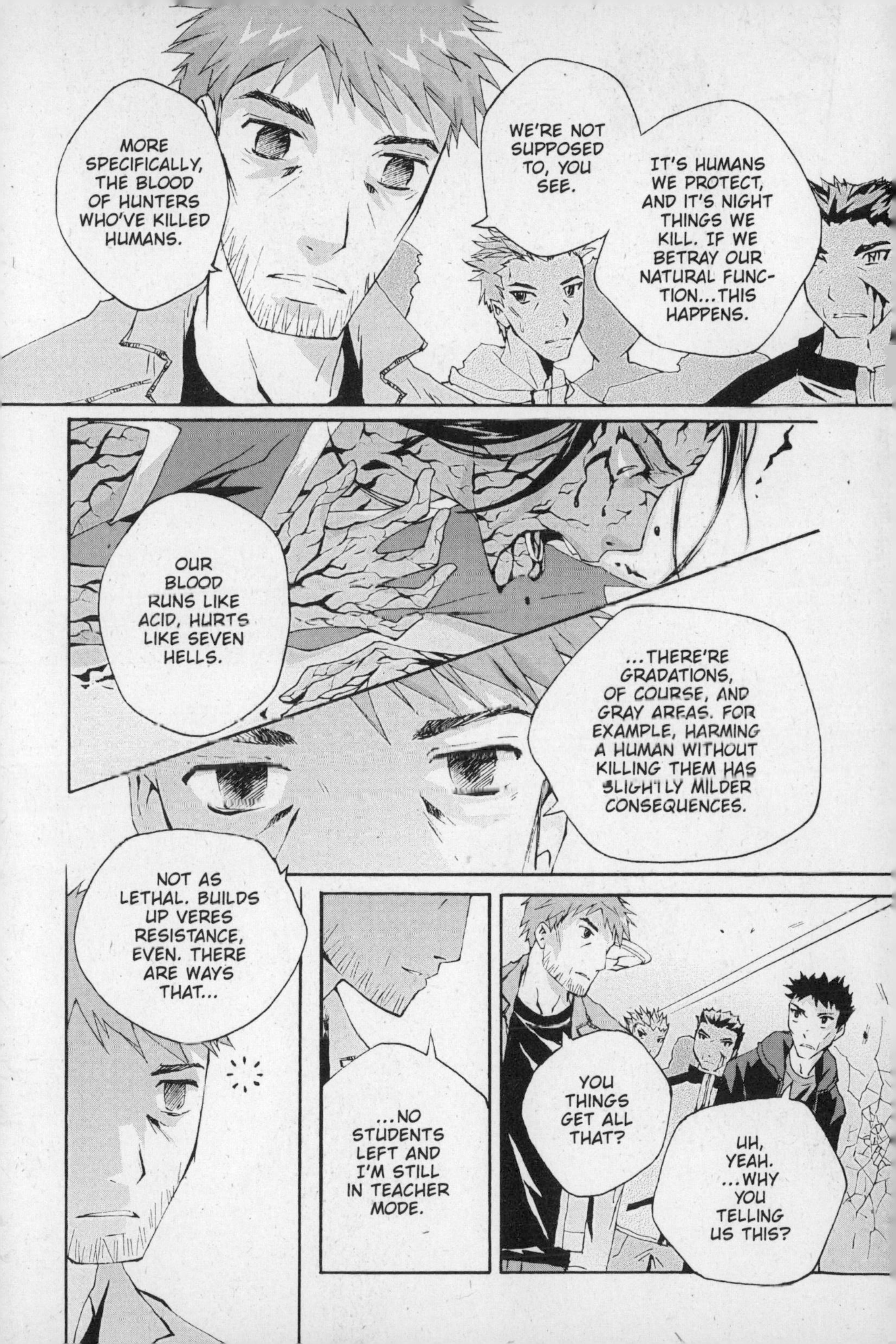
MORE SPECIFICALLY, THE BLOOD OF HUNTERS WHO'VE KILLED HUMANS.
WE'RE NOT SUPPOSED TO, YOU SEE.
IT'S HUMANS WE PROTECT, AND IT'S NIGHT THINGS WE KILL. IF WE BETRAY OUR NATURAL FUNCTION...THIS HAPPENS.
OUR BLOOD RUNS LIKE ACID, HURTS LIKE SEVEN HELLS.
...THERE'RE GRADATIONS, OF COURSE, AND GRAY AREAS. FOR EXAMPLE, HARMING A HUMAN WITHOUT KILLING THEM HAS SLIGHTLY MILDER CONSEQUENCES.
NOT AS LETHAL. BUILDS UP VERES RESISTANCE, EVEN. THERE ARE WAYS THAT...
...NO STUDENTS LEFT AND I'M STILL IN TEACHER MODE.
YOU THINGS GET ALL THAT?
UH, YEAH. ...WHY YOU TELLING US THIS?

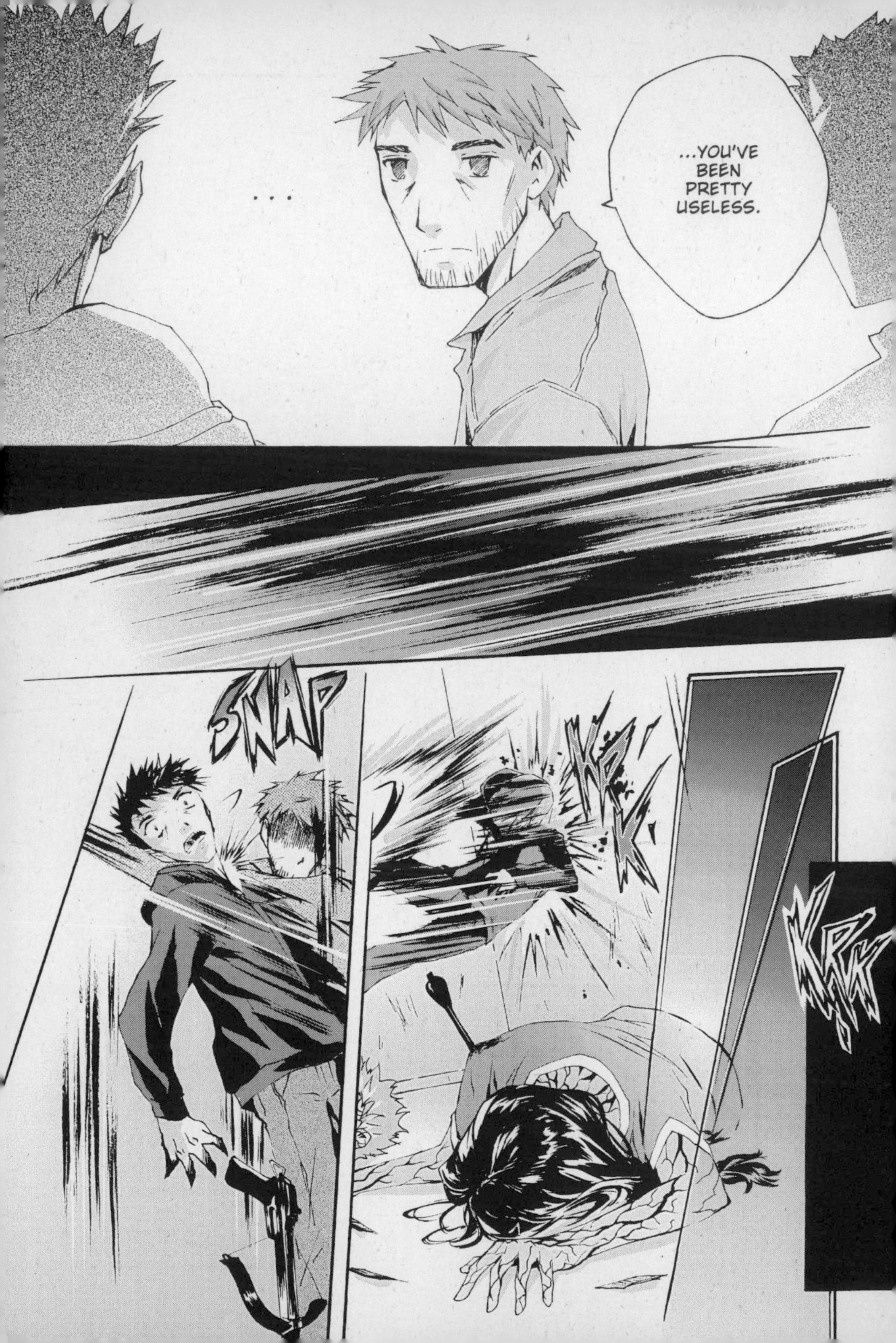
...
...YOU'VE BEEN PRETTY USELESS.
SNAP
KRAK
KRAK

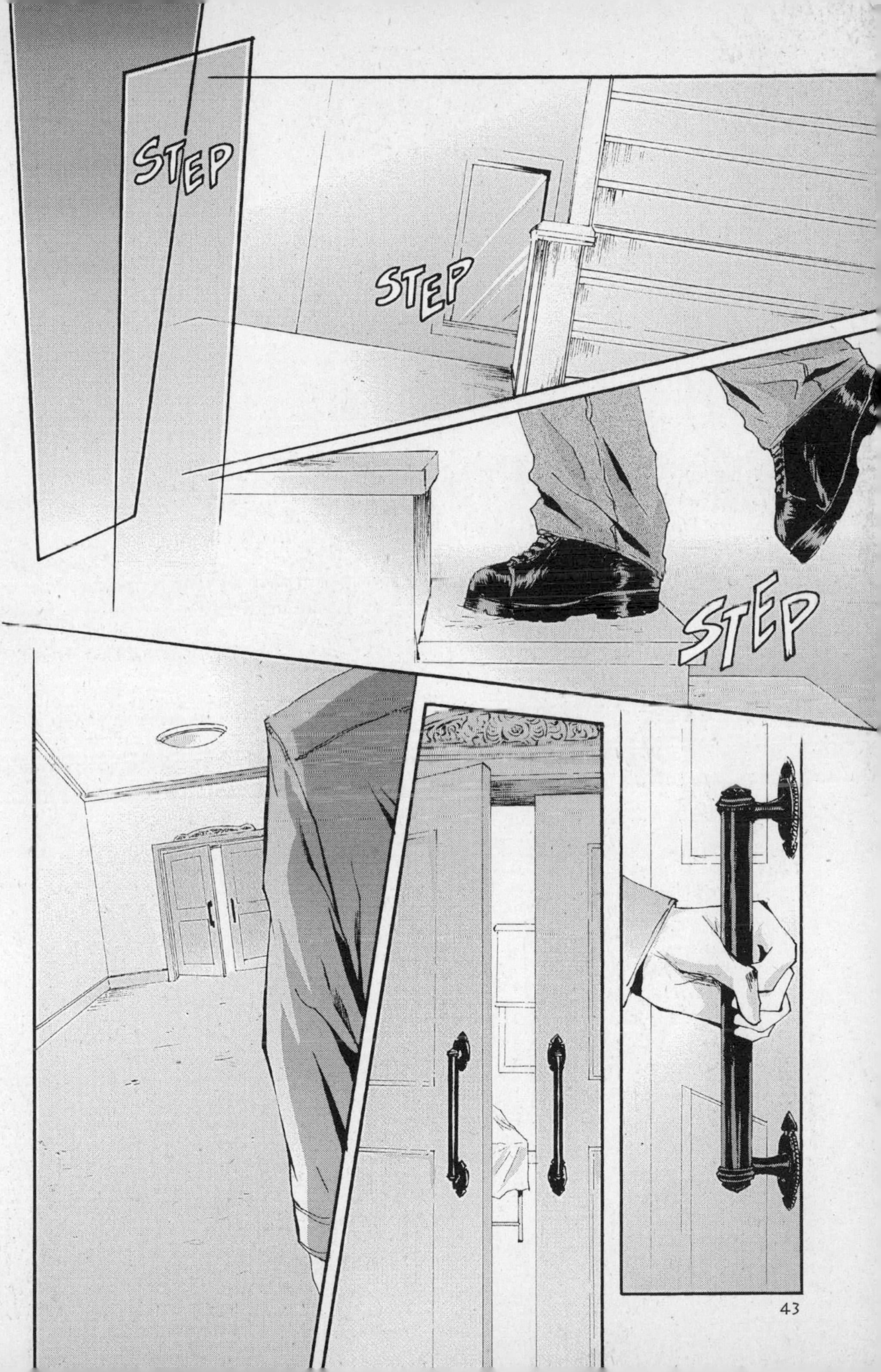
STEP
STEP
STEP

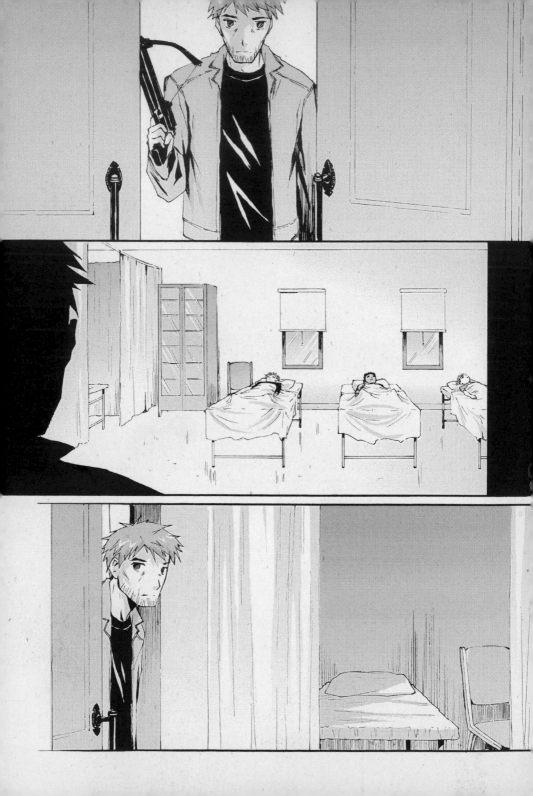

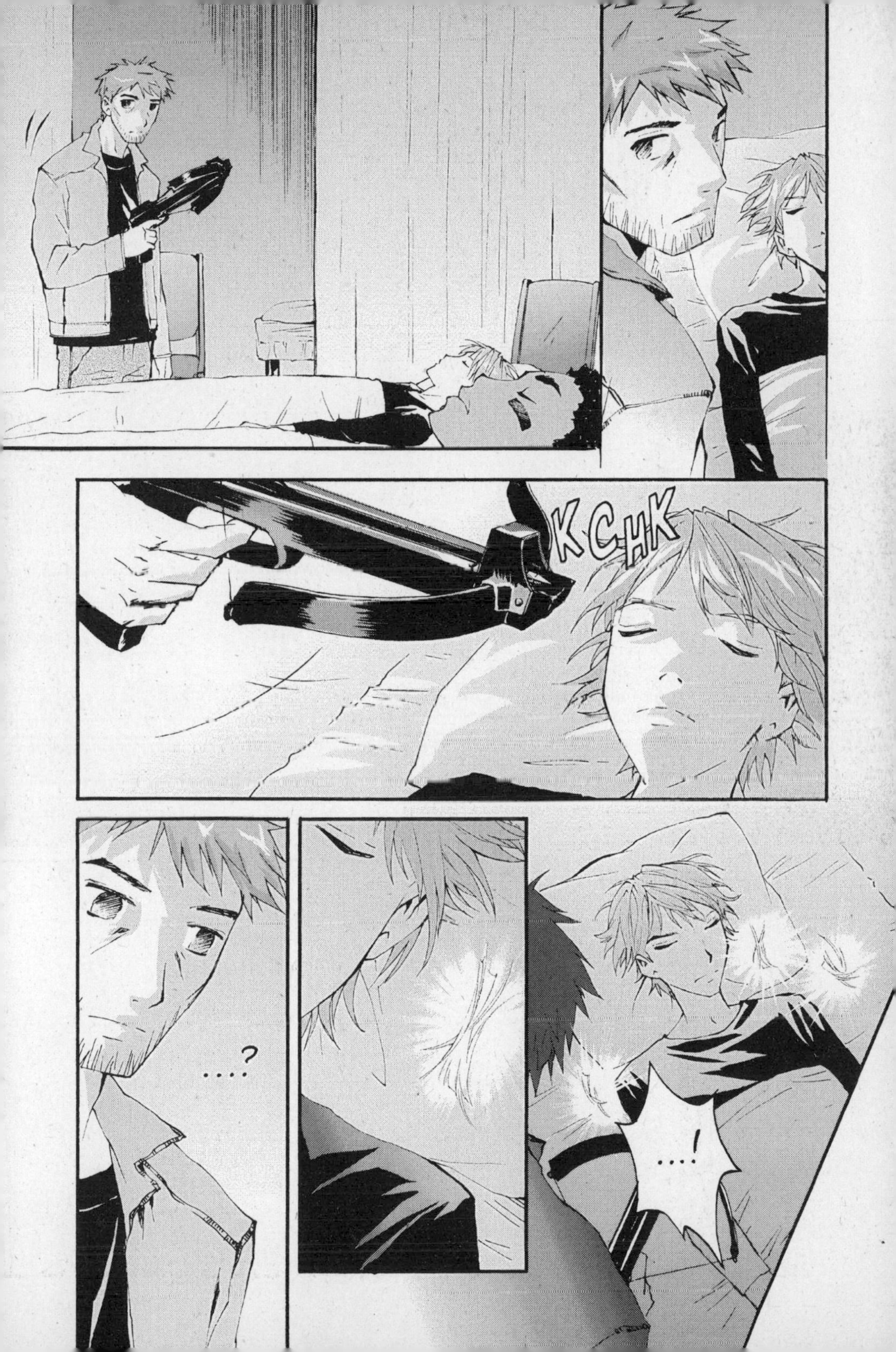
KCHK
...?
...!

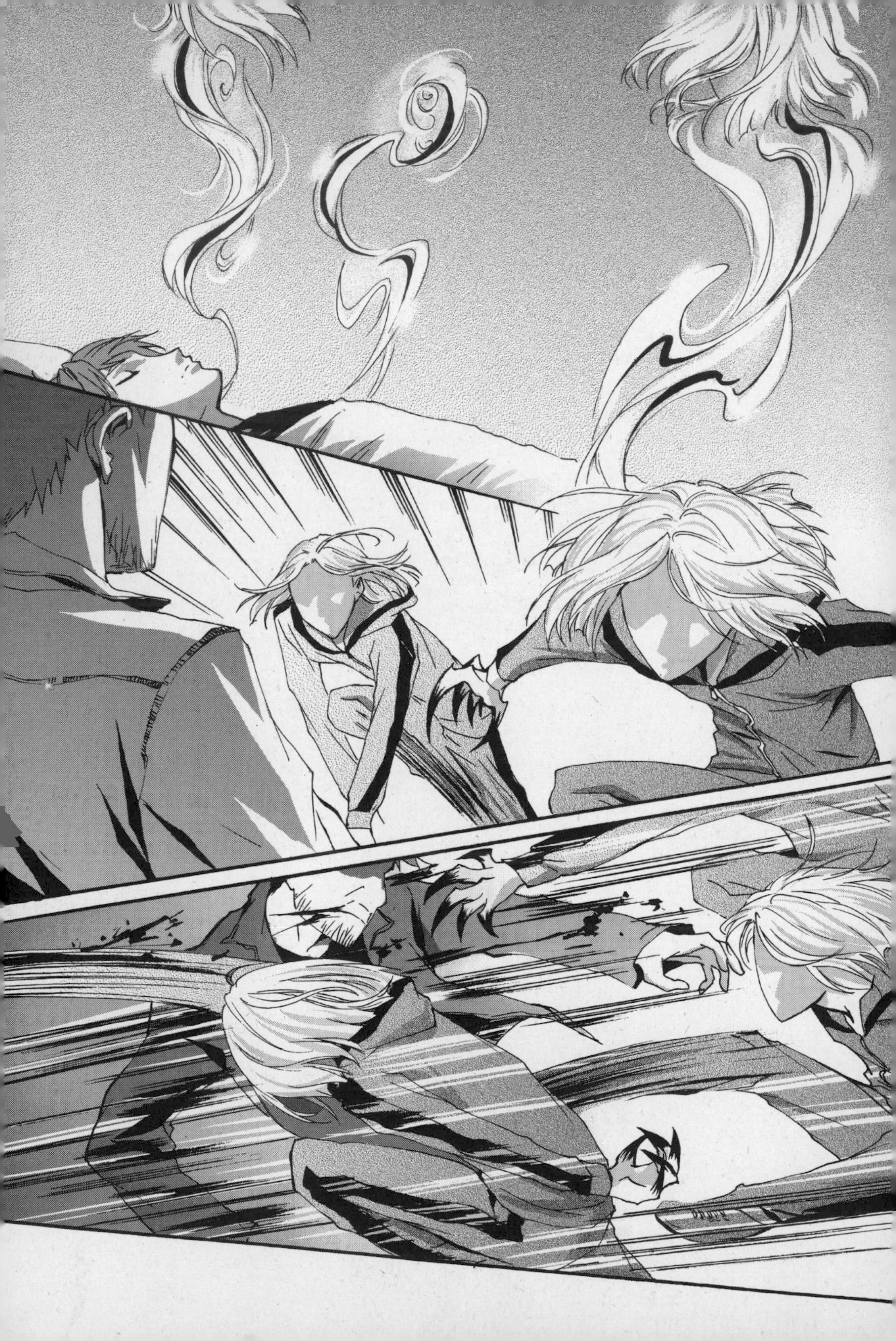

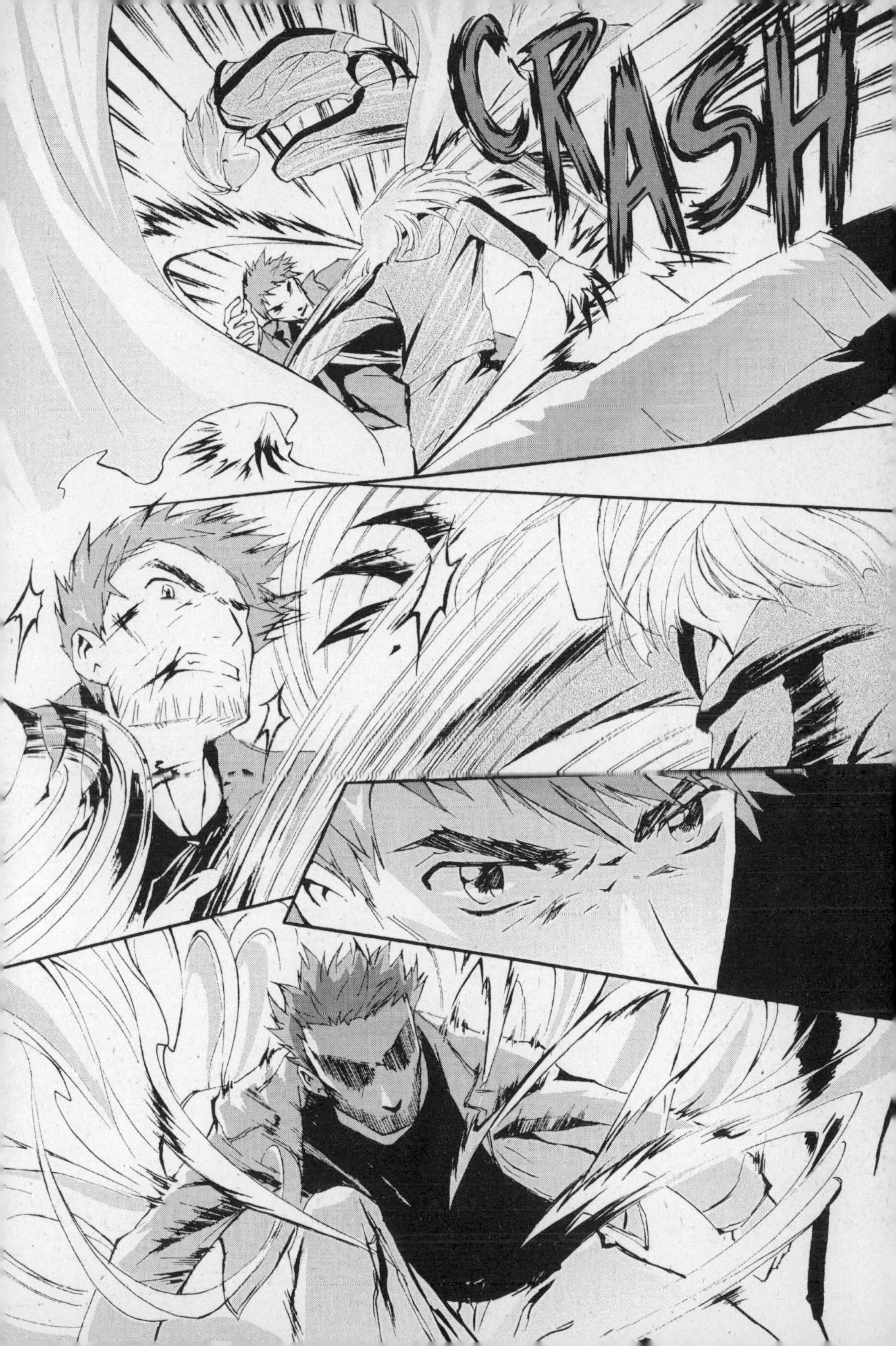
CRASH

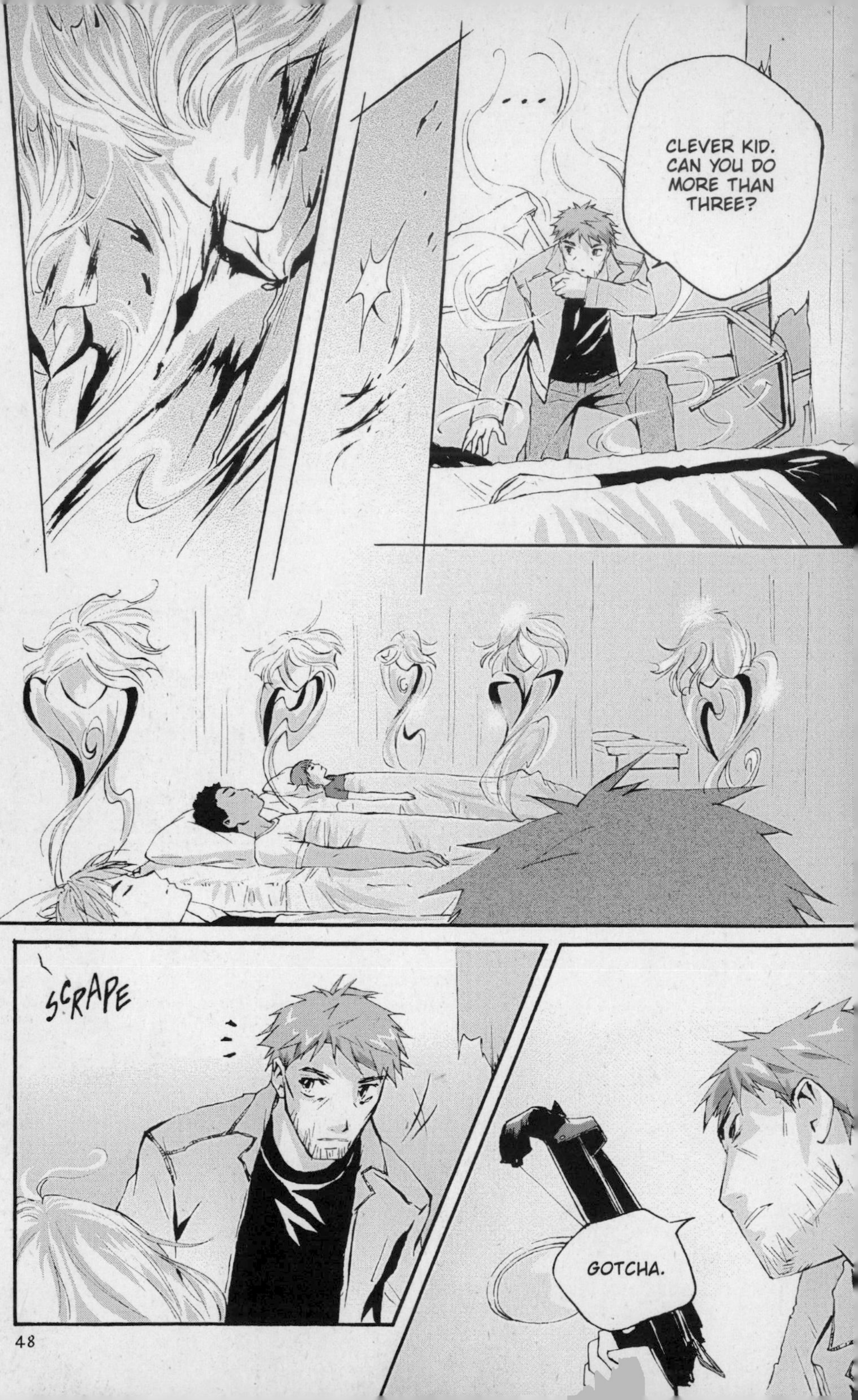
...
CLEVER KID. CAN YOU DO MORE THAN THREE?
SCRAPE
GOTCHA.

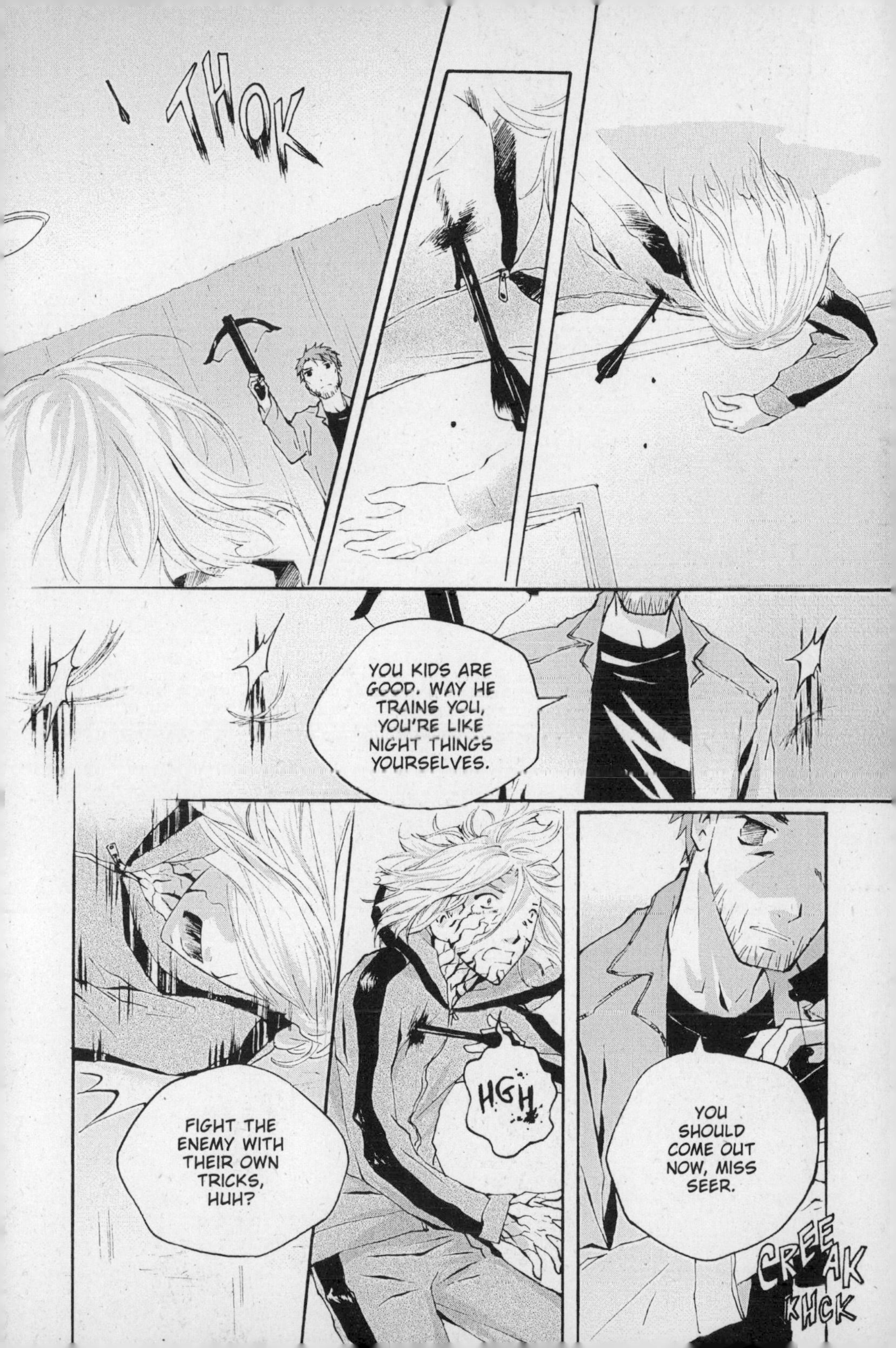
THOK
YOU KIDS ARE GOOD. WAY HE TRAINS YOU, YOU'RE LIKE NIGHT THINGS YOURSELVES.
FIGHT THE ENEMY WITH THEIR OWN TRICKS, HUH?
HGH
YOU SHOULD COME OUT NOW, MISS SEER.
CREEAK
KHCK

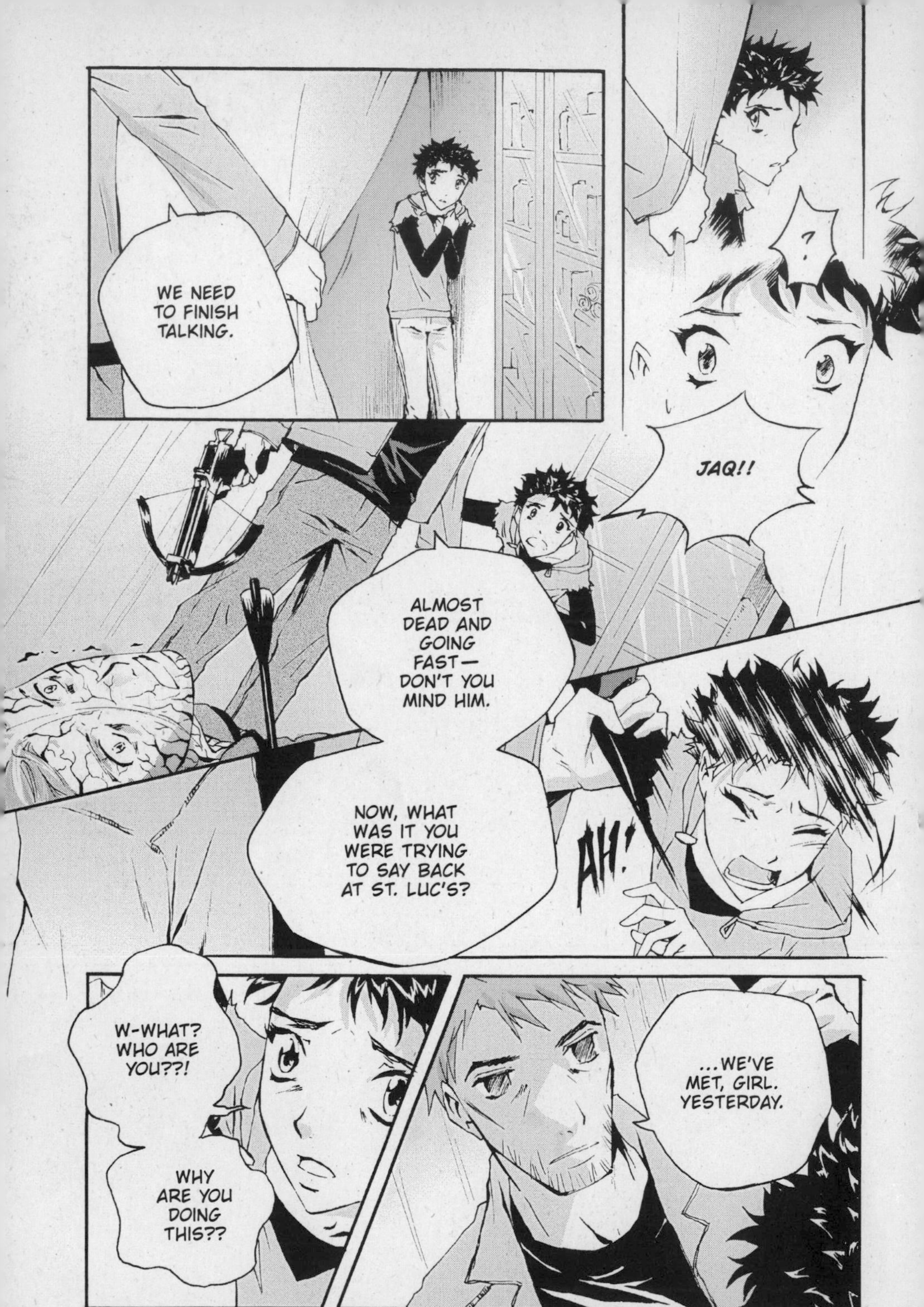
WE NEED TO FINISH TALKING.
?
JAQ!!
ALMOST DEAD AND GOING FAST— DON'T YOU MIND HIM.
NOW, WHAT WAS IT YOU WERE TRYING TO SAY BACK AT ST. LUC'S?
AH!
W-WHAT? WHO ARE YOU??!
WHY ARE YOU DOING THIS??
...WE'VE MET, GIRL. YESTERDAY.

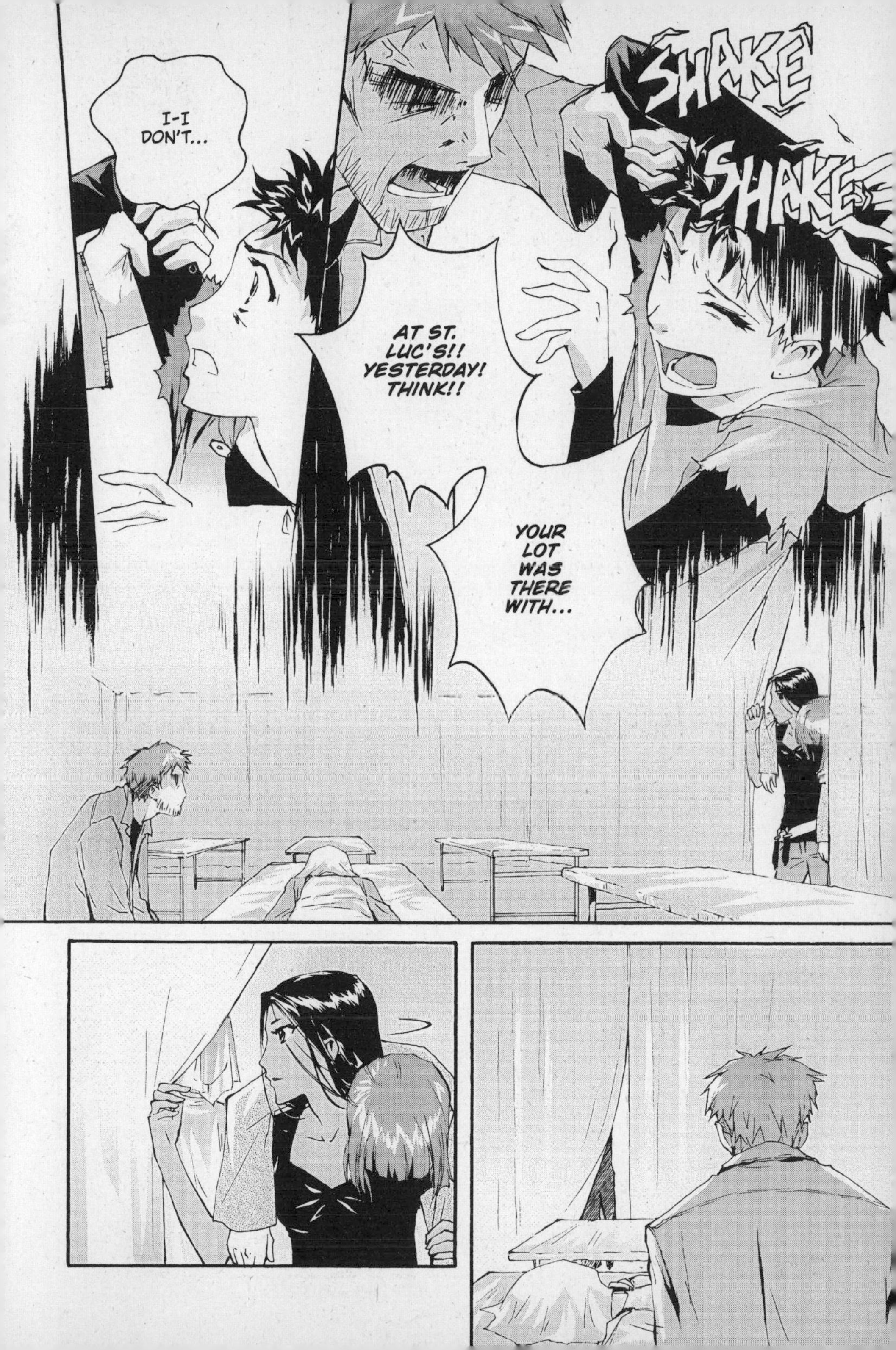
I-I DON'T...
AT ST. LUC'S!! YESTERDAY! THINK!!
SHAKE
SHAKE
YOUR LOT WAS THERE WITH...

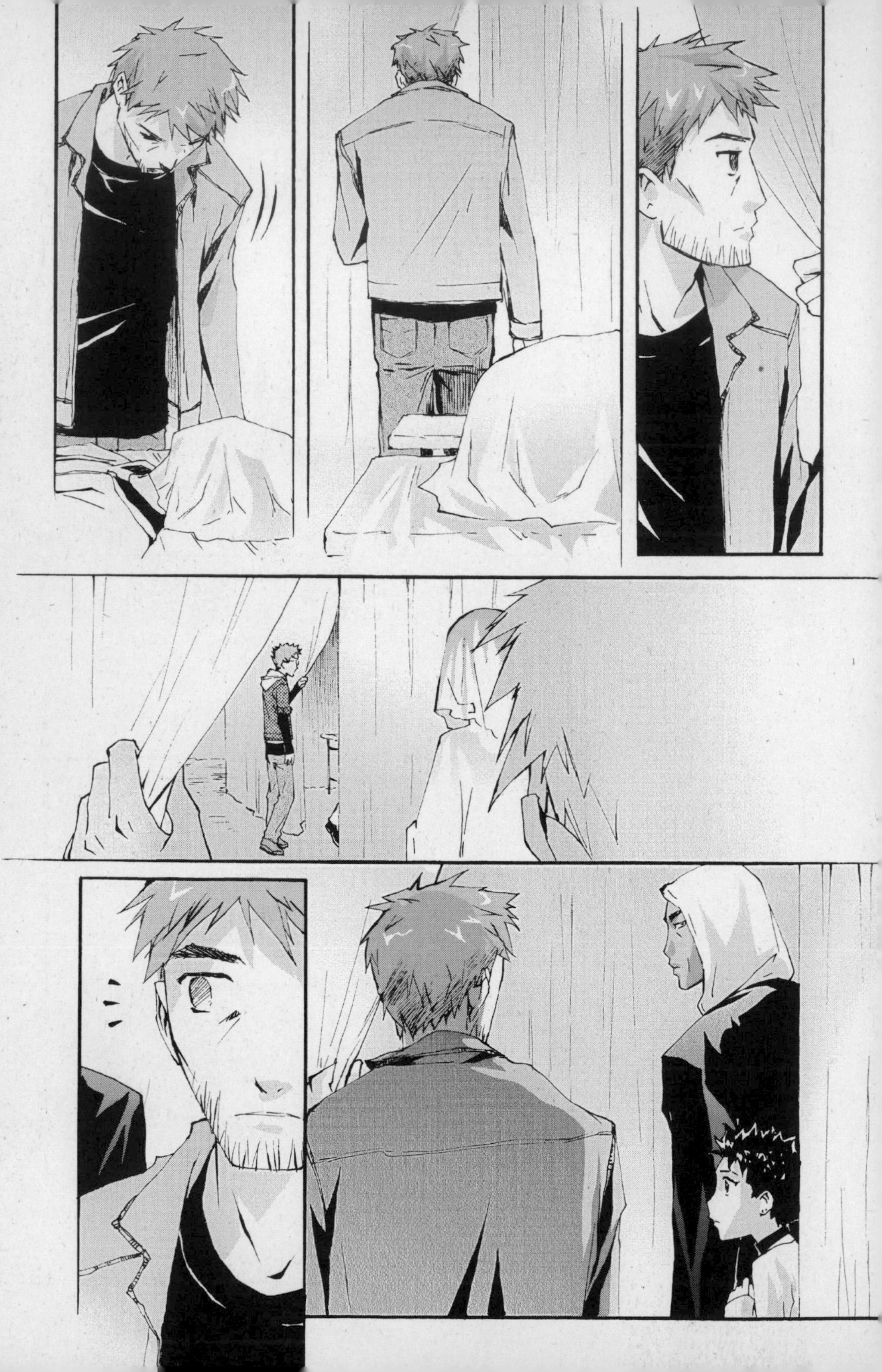

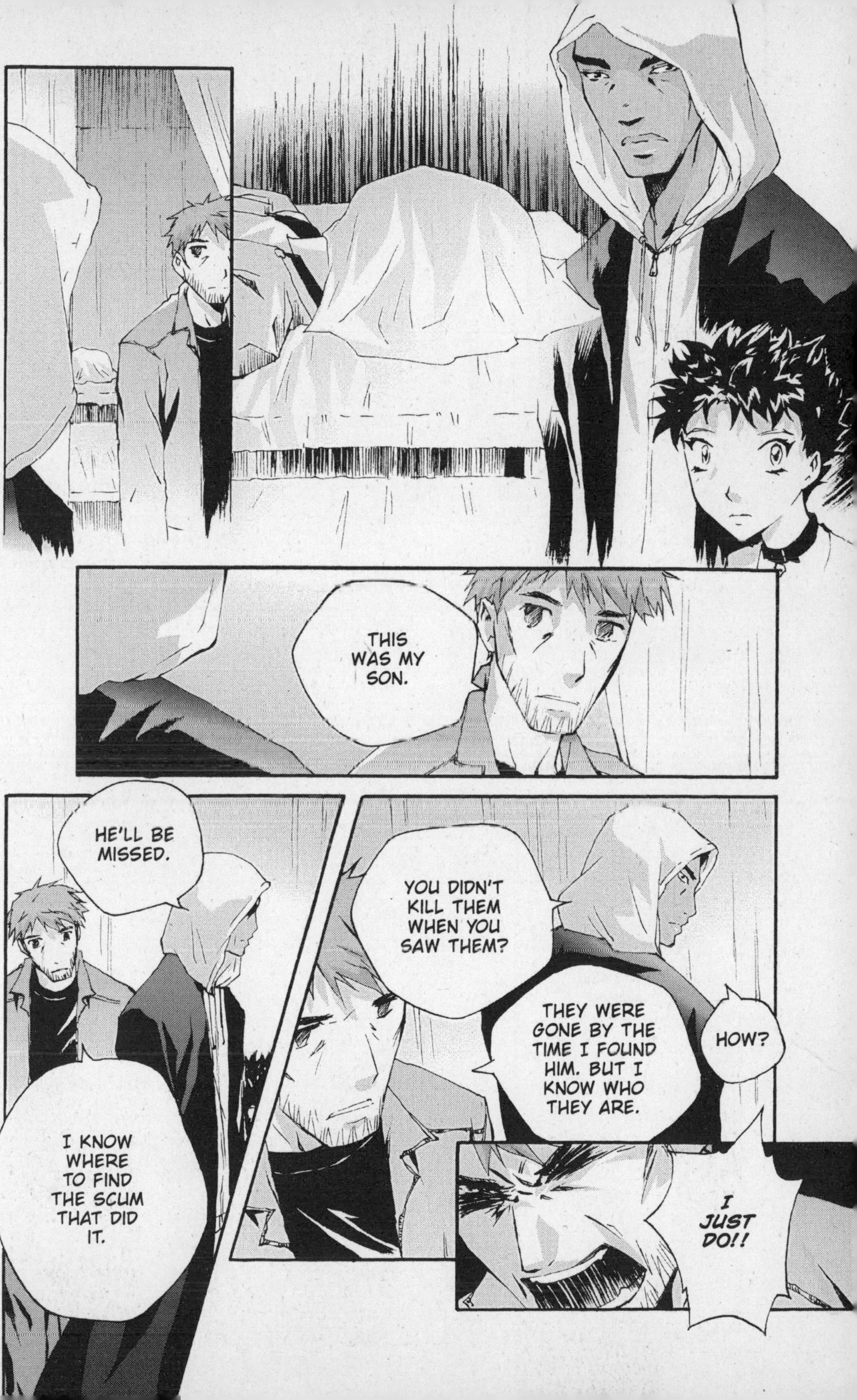
THIS WAS MY SON.
HE'LL BE MISSED.
I KNOW WHERE TO FIND THE SCUM THAT DID IT.
YOU DIDN'T KILL THEM WHEN YOU SAW THEM?
THEY WERE GONE BY THE TIME I FOUND HIM. BUT I KNOW WHO THEY ARE.
HOW?
I JUST DO!!

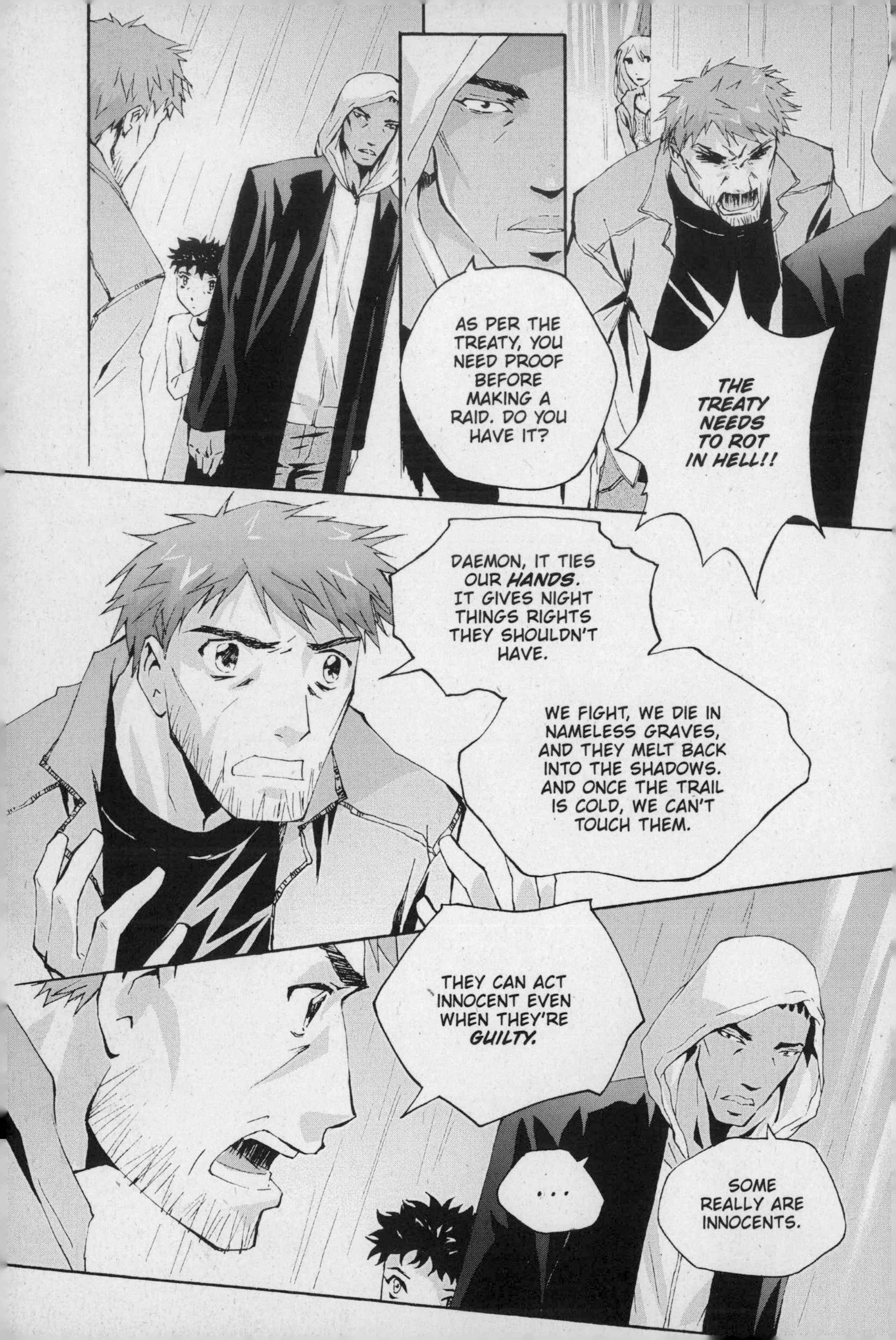
AS PER THE TREATY, YOU NEED PROOF BEFORE MAKING A RAID. DO YOU HAVE IT?
THE TREATY NEEDS TO ROT IN HELL!!
DAEMON, IT TIES OUR HANDS. IT GIVES NIGHT THINGS RIGHTS THEY SHOULDN'T HAVE.
WE FIGHT, WE DIE IN NAMELESS GRAVES, AND THEY MELT BACK INTO THE SHADOWS. AND ONCE THE TRAIL IS COLD, WE CAN'T TOUCH THEM.
THEY CAN ACT INNOCENT EVEN WHEN THEY'RE GUILTY.
...
SOME REALLY ARE INNOCENTS.

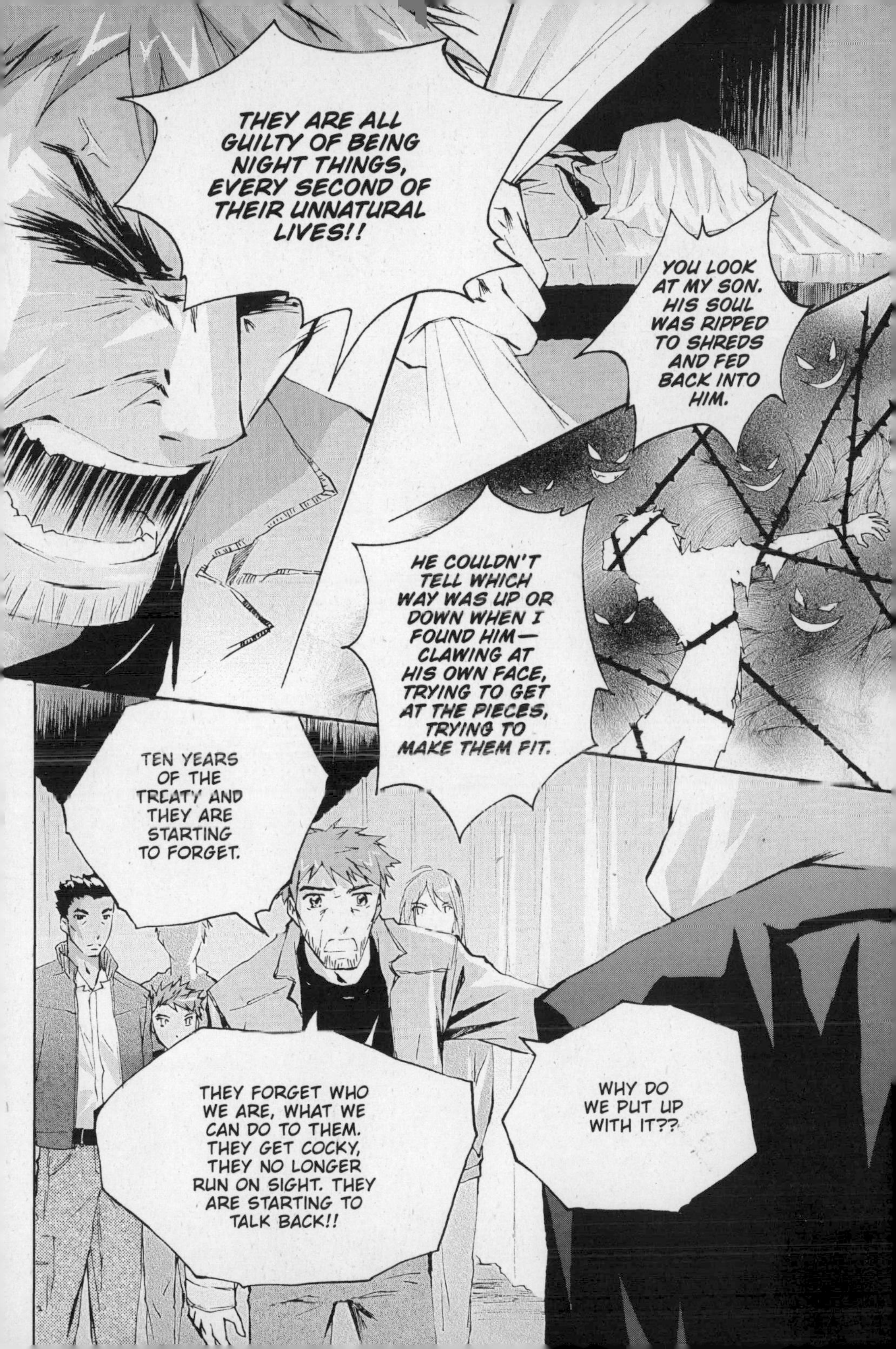
THEY ARE ALL GUILTY OF BEING NIGHT THINGS, EVERY SECOND OF THEIR UNNATURAL LIVES!!
YOU LOOK AT MY SON. HIS SOUL WAS RIPPED TO SHREDS AND FED BACK INTO HIM.
HE COULDN'T TELL WHICH WAY WAS UP OR DOWN WHEN I FOUND HIM—CLAWING AT HIS OWN FACE, TRYING TO GET AT THE PIECES, TRYING TO MAKE THEM FIT.
TEN YEARS OF THE TREATY AND THEY ARE STARTING TO FORGET.
THEY FORGET WHO WE ARE, WHAT WE CAN DO TO THEM. THEY GET COCKY, THEY NO LONGER RUN ON SIGHT. THEY ARE STARTING TO TALK BACK!!
WHY DO WE PUT UP WITH IT??

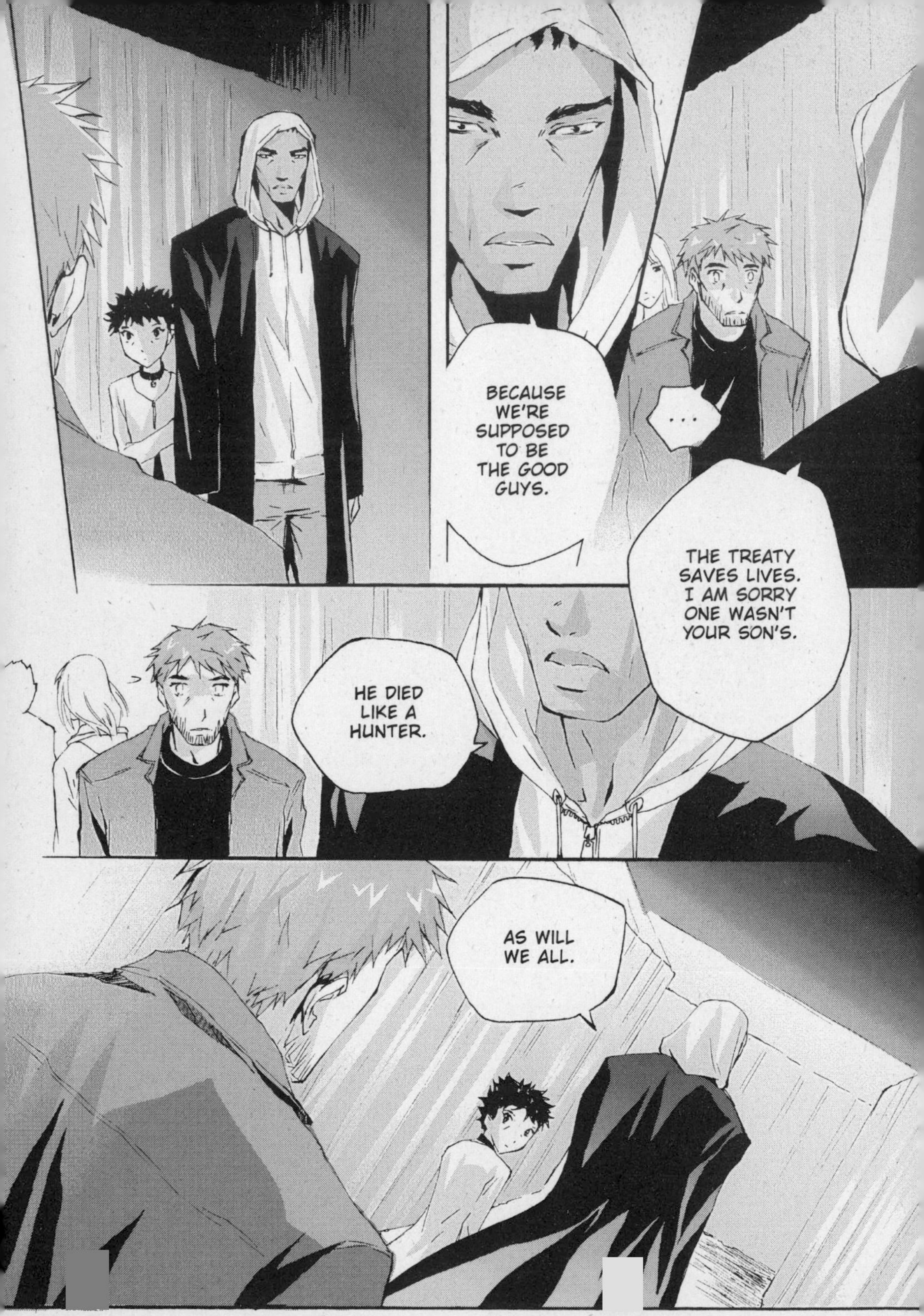
BECAUSE WE'RE SUPPOSED TO BE THE GOOD GUYS.
...
THE TREATY SAVES LIVES. I AM SORRY ONE WASN'T YOUR SON'S.
HE DIED LIKE A HUNTER.
AS WILL WE ALL.

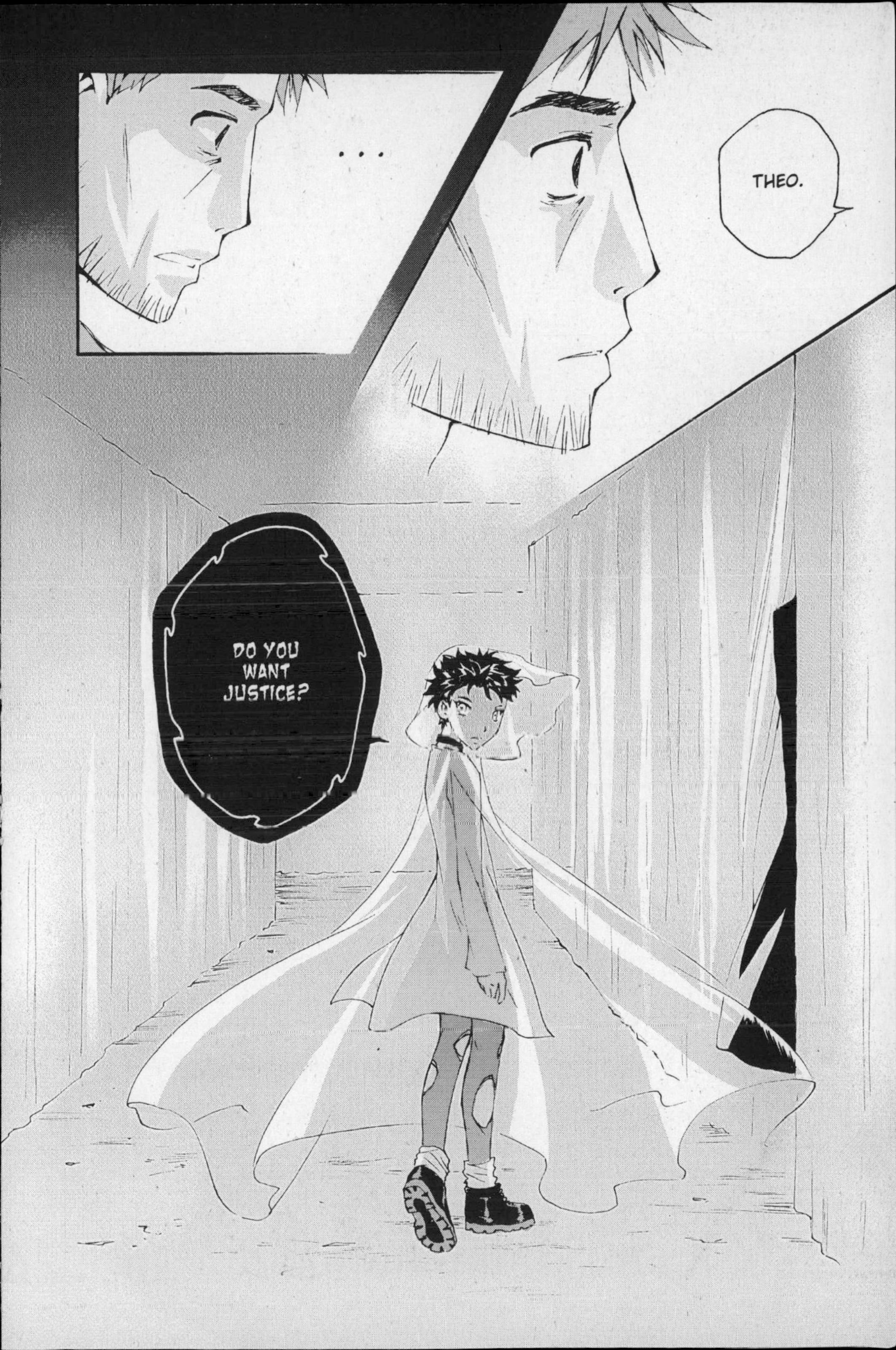
. . .
THEO.
DO YOU WANT JUSTICE?

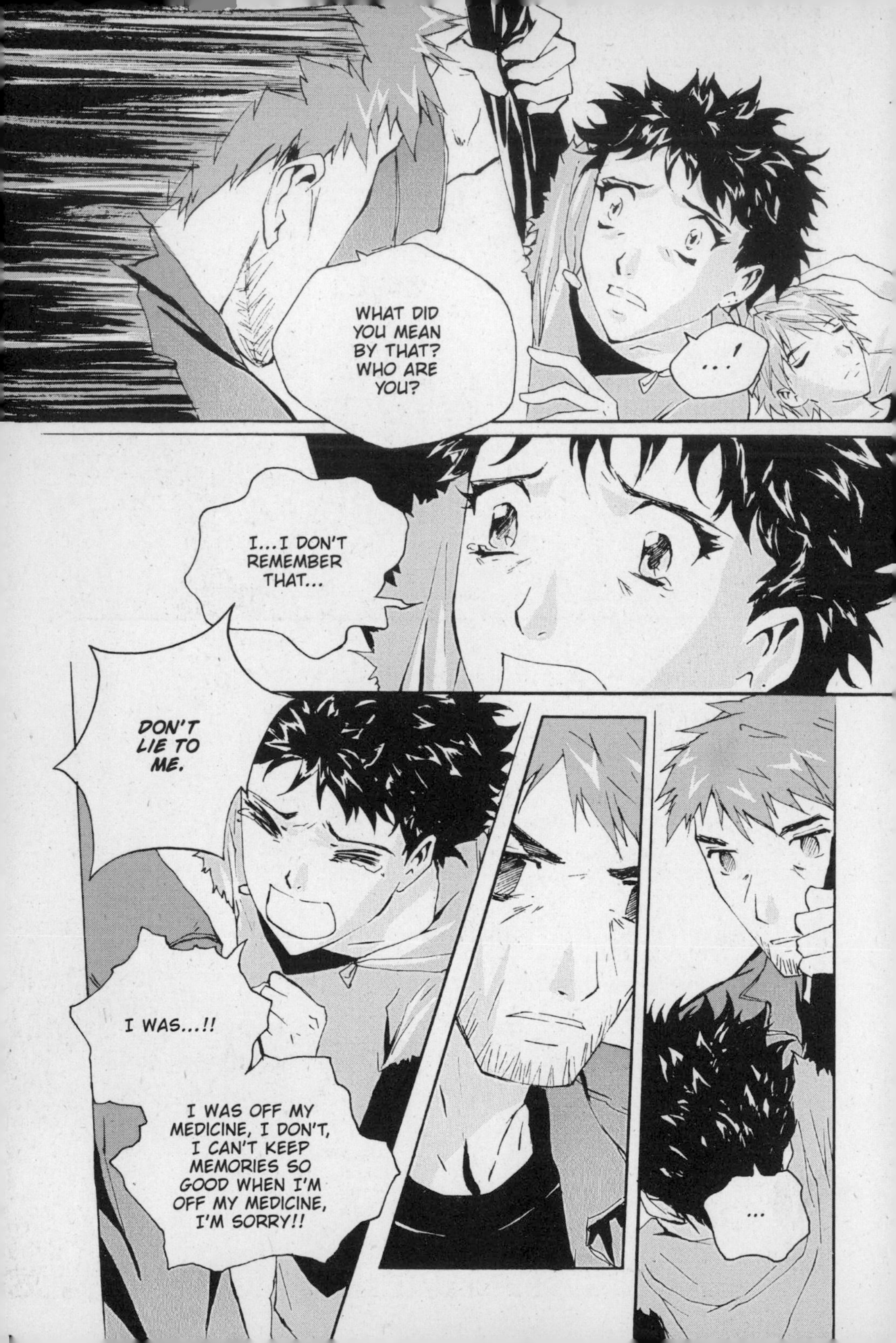
WHAT DID YOU MEAN BY THAT? WHO ARE YOU?
...!
I...I DON'T REMEMBER THAT...
DON'T LIE TO ME.
I WAS...!!
I WAS OFF MY MEDICINE, I DON'T, I CAN'T KEEP MEMORIES SO GOOD WHEN I'M OFF MY MEDICINE, I'M SORRY!!
...

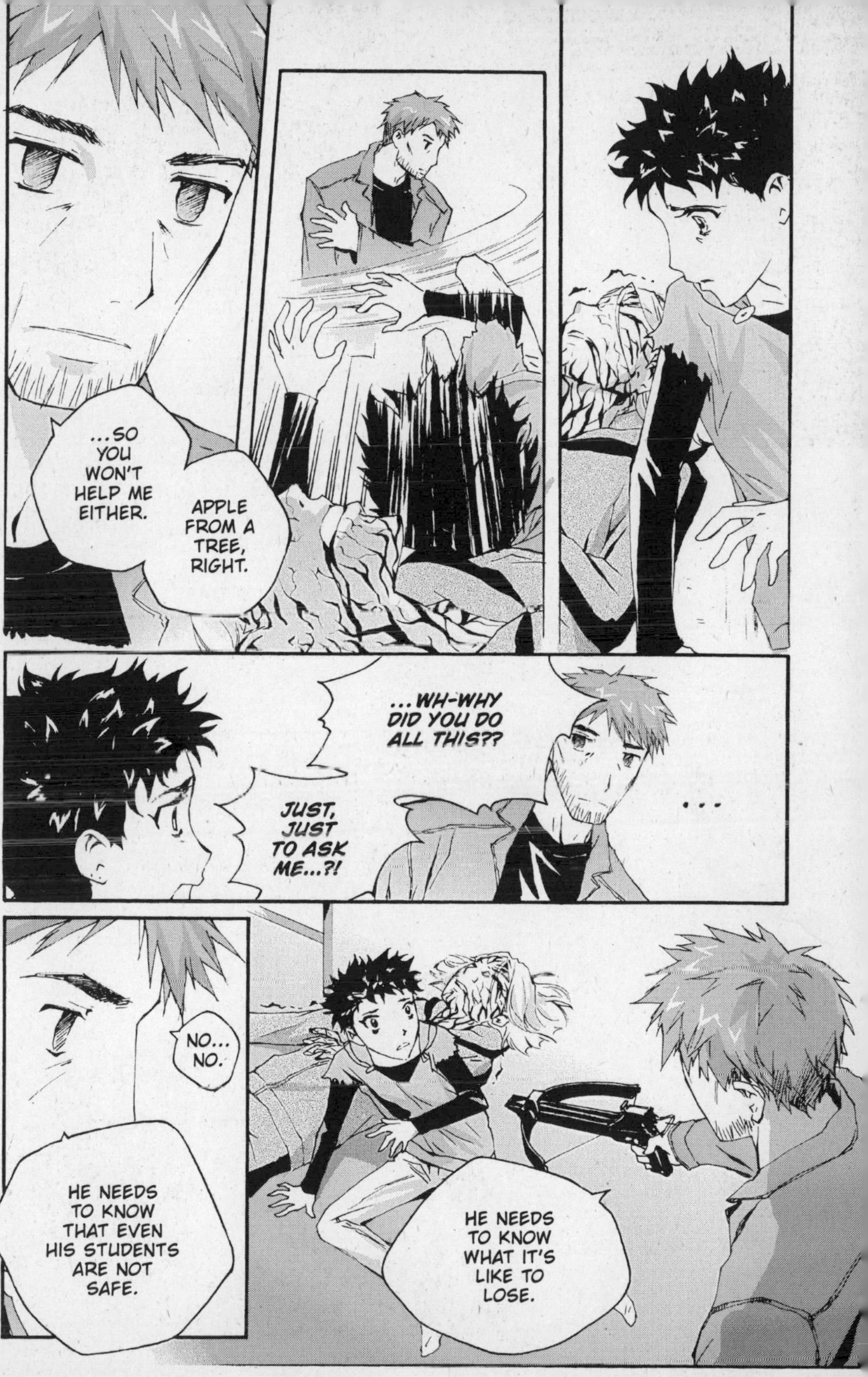
...SO YOU WON'T HELP ME EITHER.
APPLE FROM A TREE, RIGHT.
...WH-WHY DID YOU DO ALL THIS??
JUST, JUST TO ASK ME...?!
...
NO... NO.
HE NEEDS TO KNOW THAT EVEN HIS STUDENTS ARE NOT SAFE.
HE NEEDS TO KNOW WHAT IT'S LIKE TO LOSE.

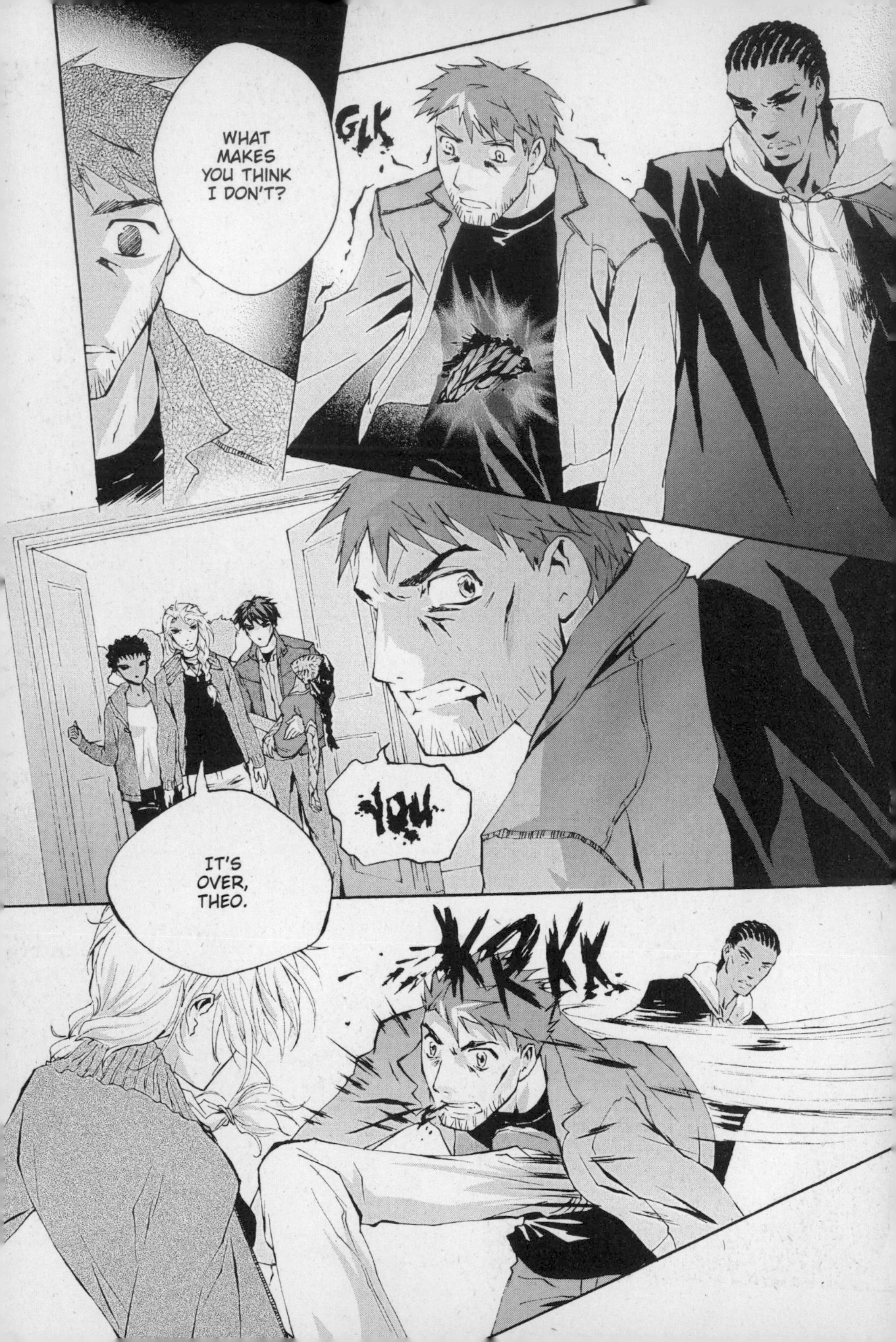
WHAT MAKES YOU THINK I DON'T?
GLK
YOU
IT'S OVER, THEO.
KRKK

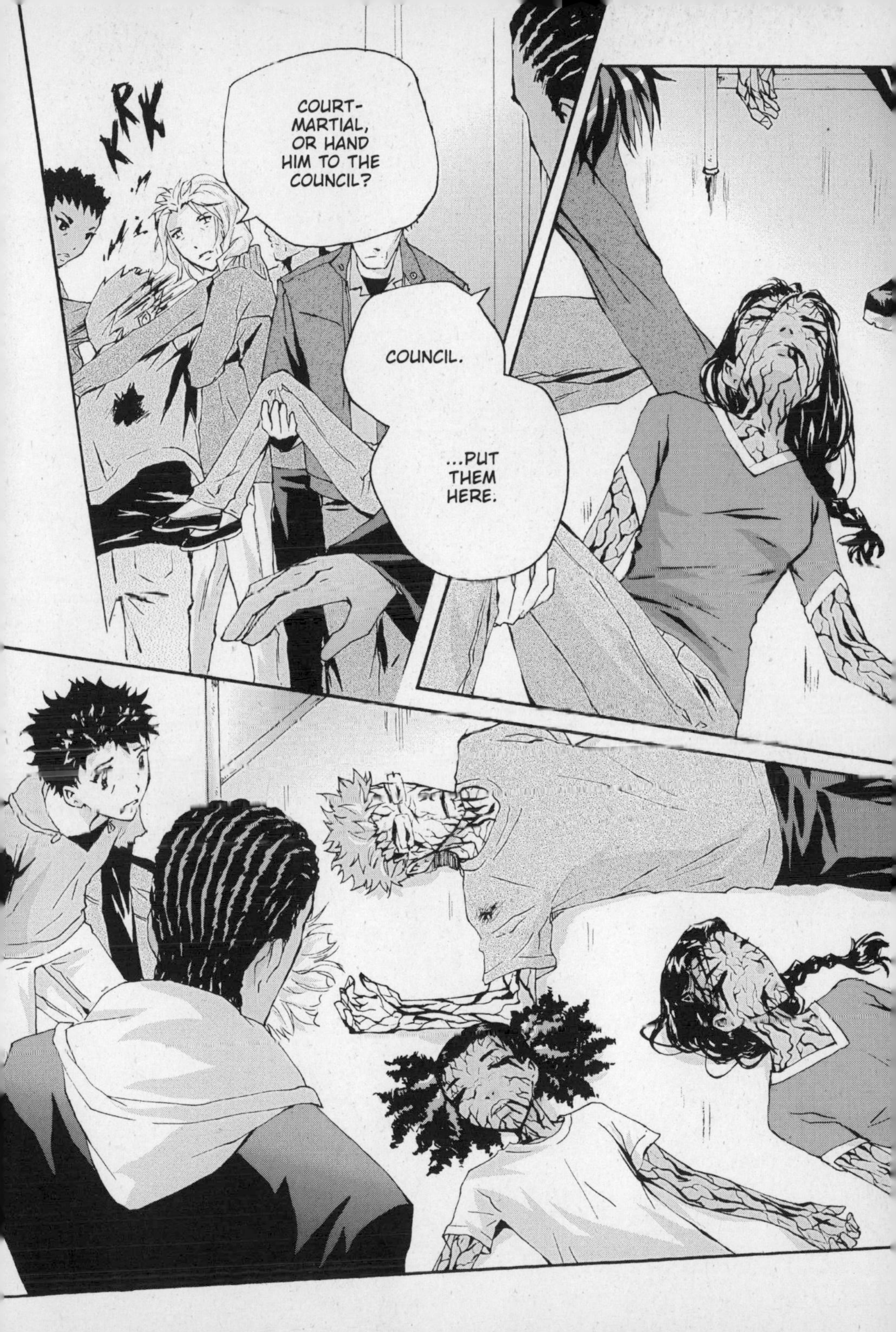
KRK
COURT-MARTIAL, OR HAND HIM TO THE COUNCIL?
COUNCIL.
...PUT THEM HERE.

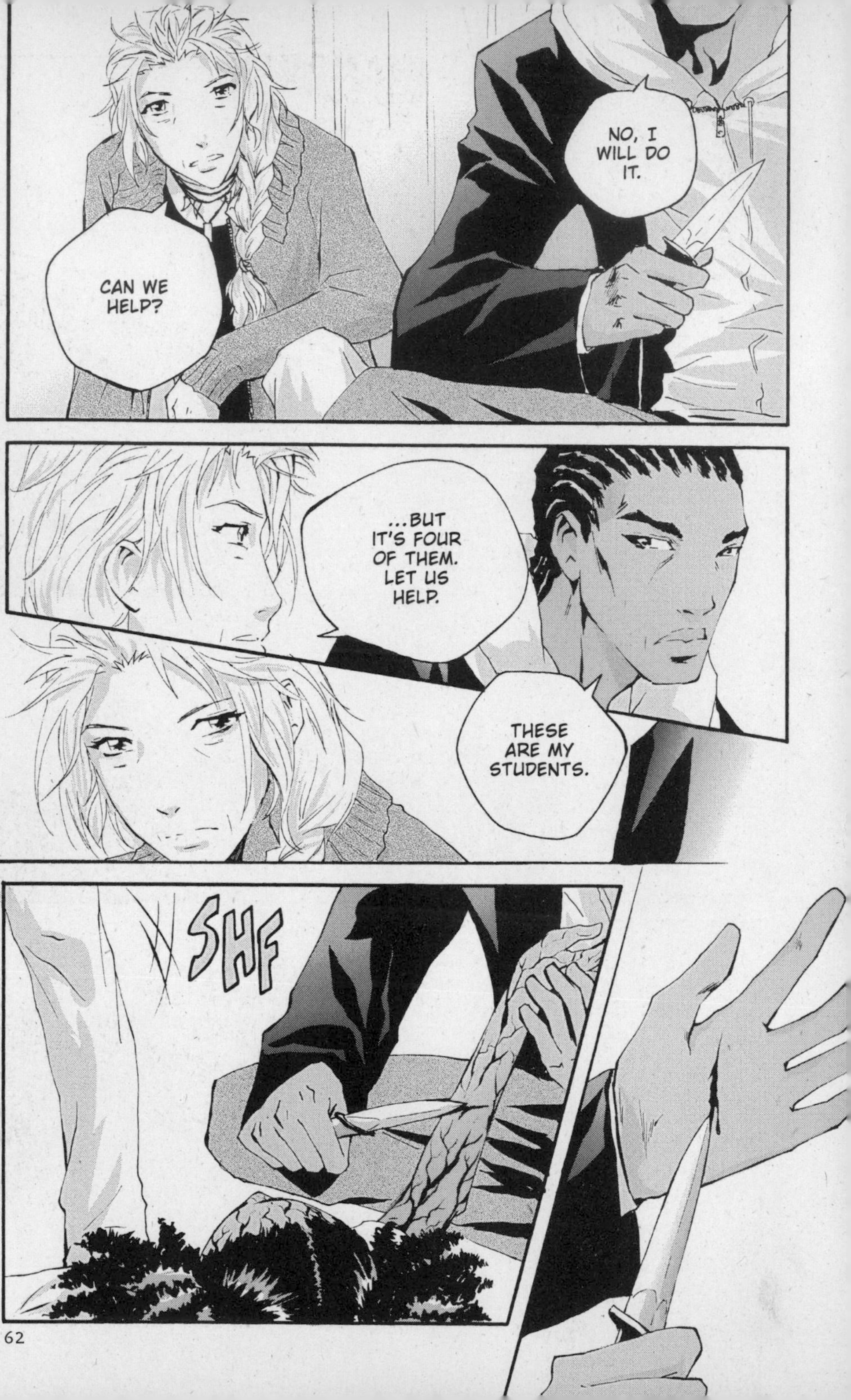
CAN WE HELP?
NO, I WILL DO IT.
...BUT IT'S FOUR OF THEM. LET US HELP.
THESE ARE MY STUDENTS.
SHF

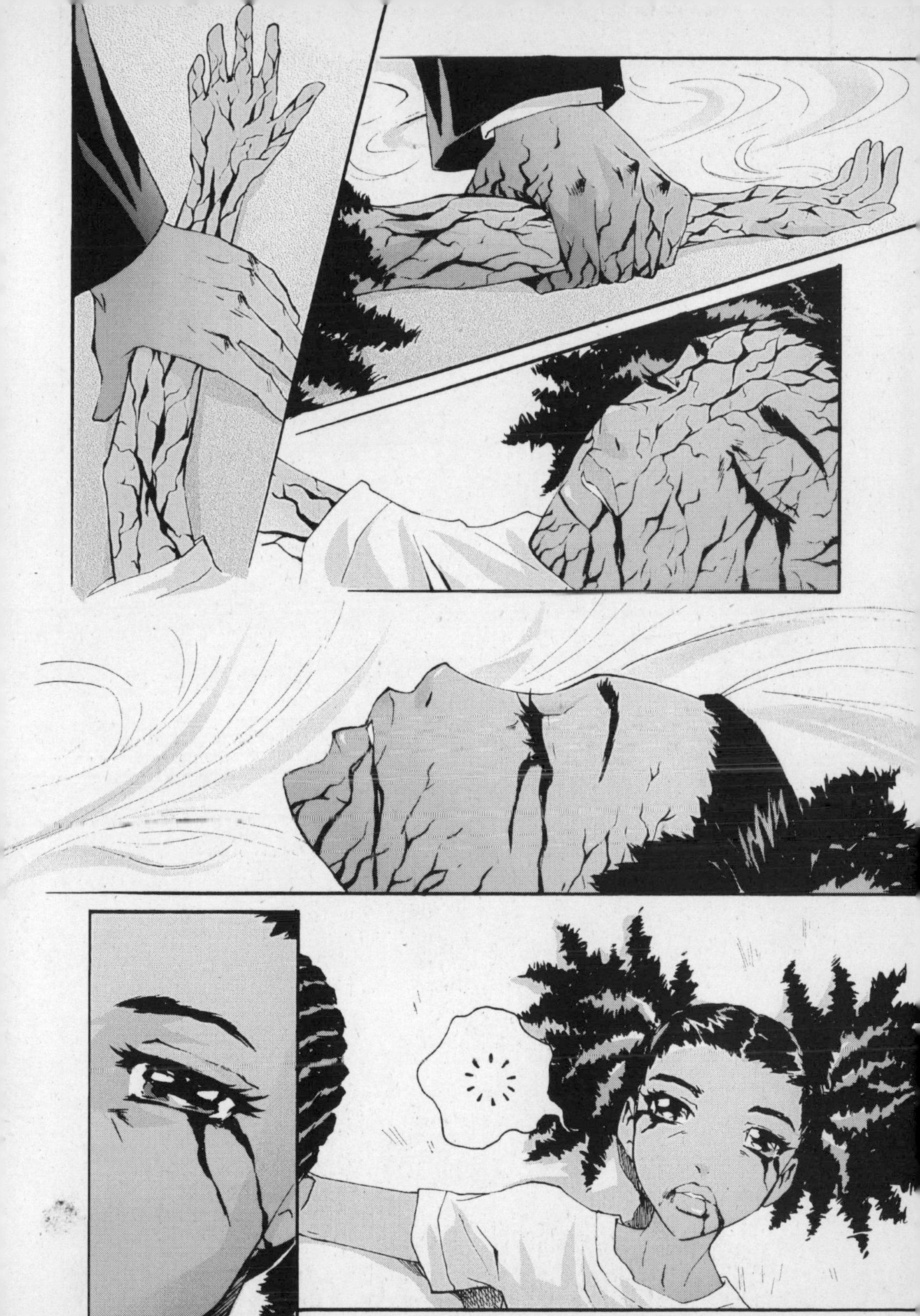

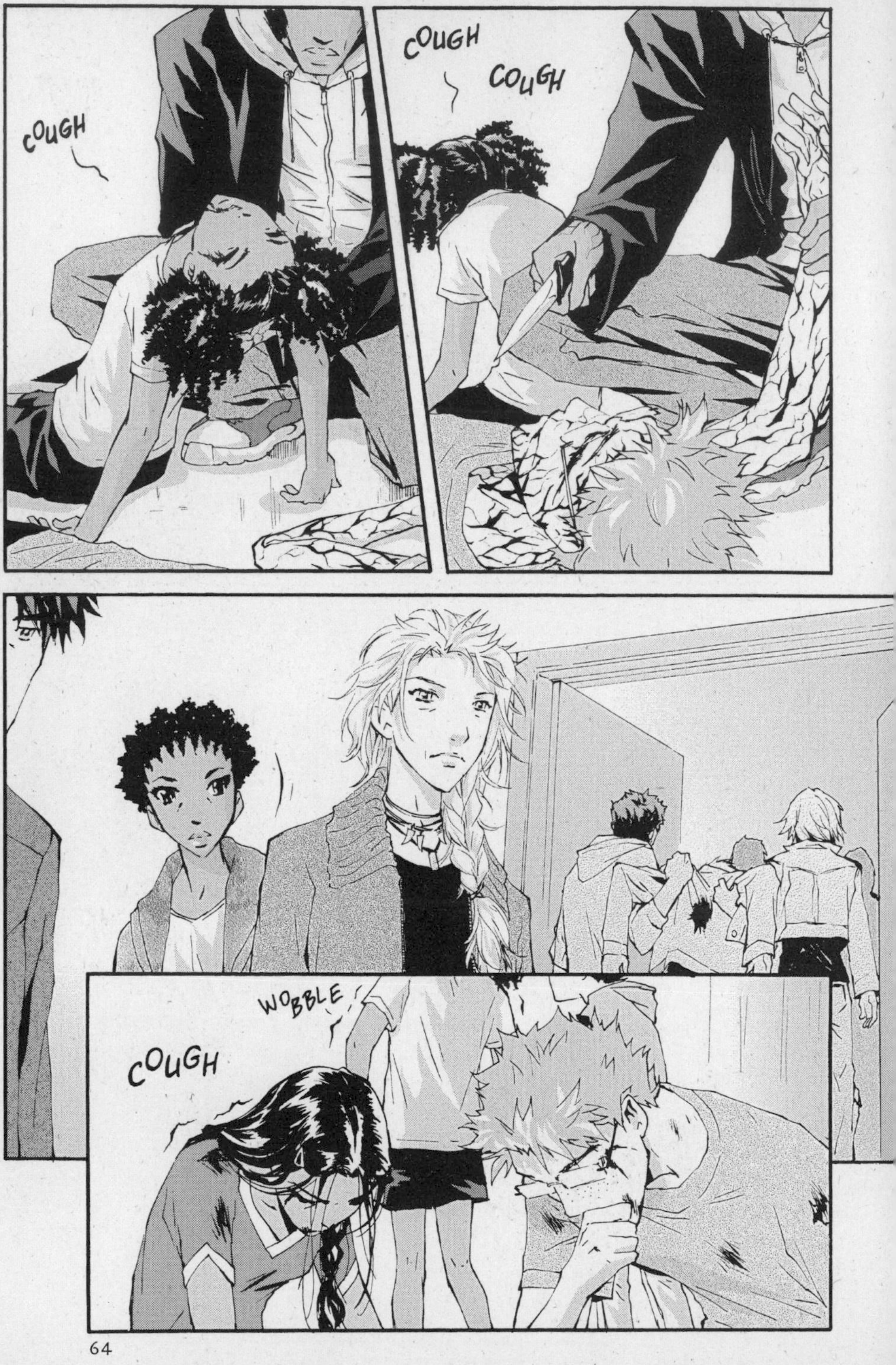
COUGH
COUGH
COUGH
WOBBLE
COUGH

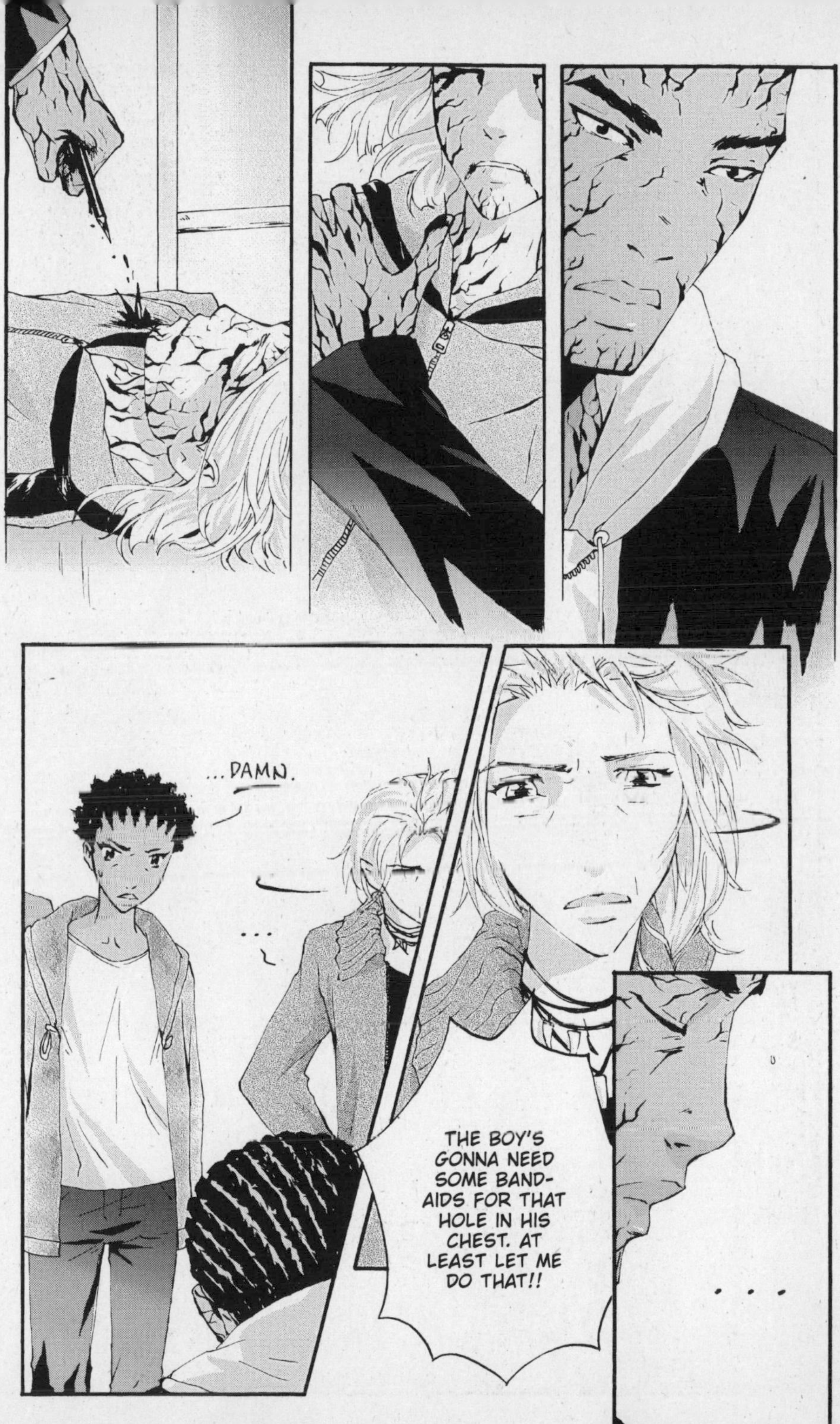
...DAMN.
...
THE BOY'S GONNA NEED SOME BAND-AIDS FOR THAT HOLE IN HIS CHEST. AT LEAST LET ME DO THAT!!
...

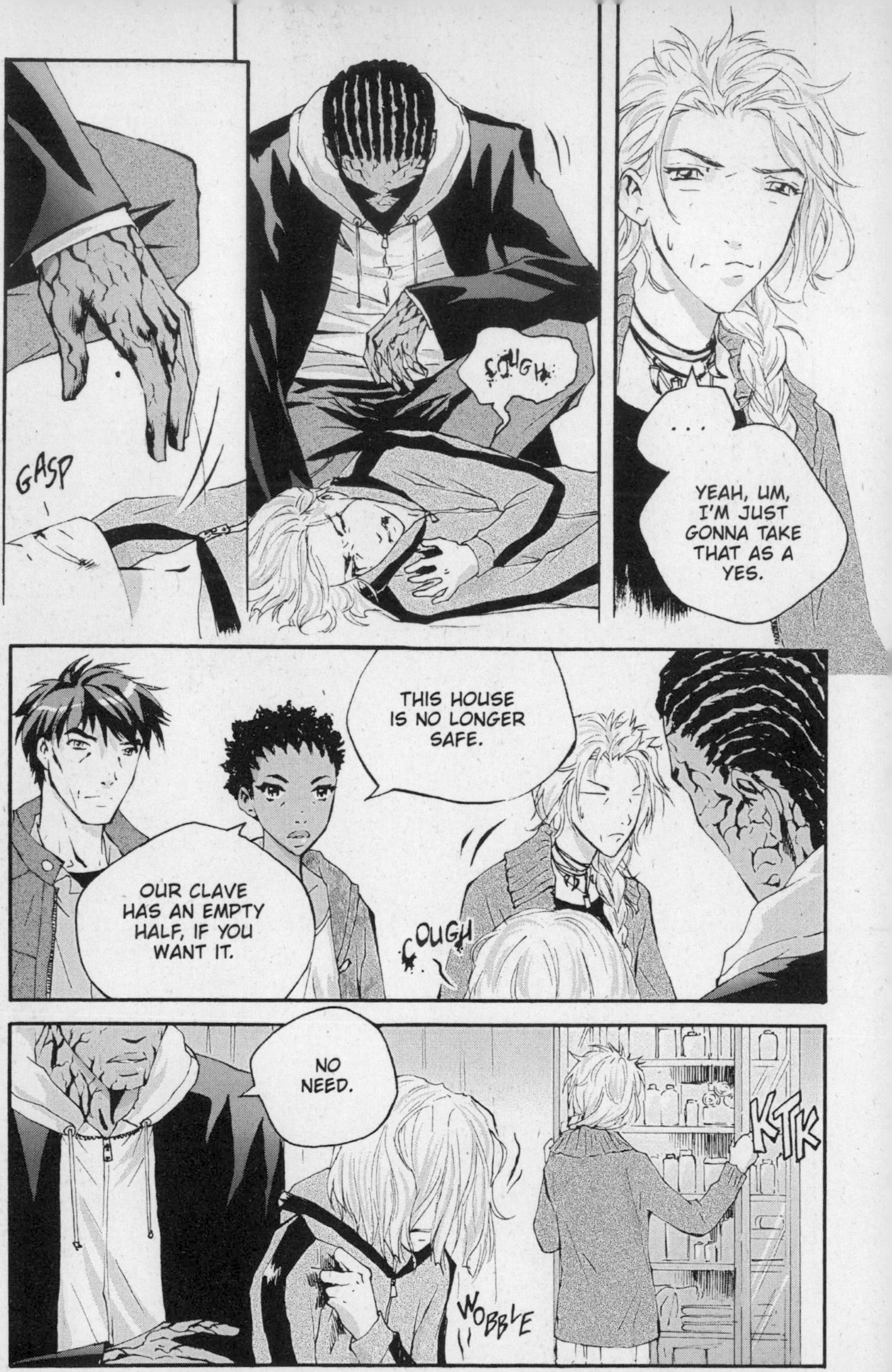

GASP
COUGH
...
YEAH, UM, I'M JUST GONNA TAKE THAT AS A YES.
OUR CLAVE HAS AN EMPTY HALF, IF YOU WANT IT.
THIS HOUSE IS NO LONGER SAFE.
COUGH
NO NEED.
WOBBLE
KTK

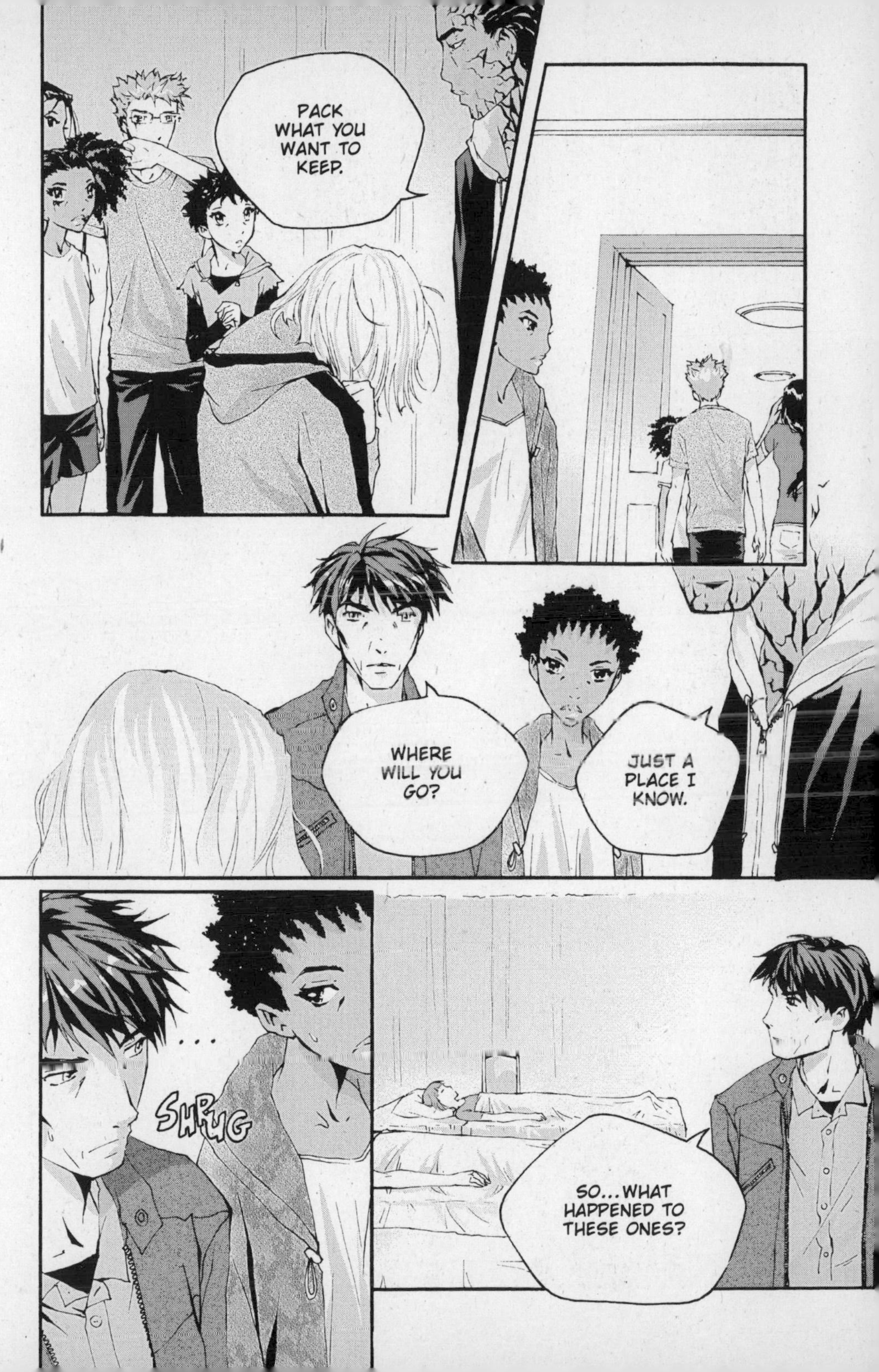
PACK WHAT YOU WANT TO KEEP.
WHERE WILL YOU GO?
JUST A PLACE I KNOW.
...
SHRUG
SO...WHAT HAPPENED TO THESE ONES?

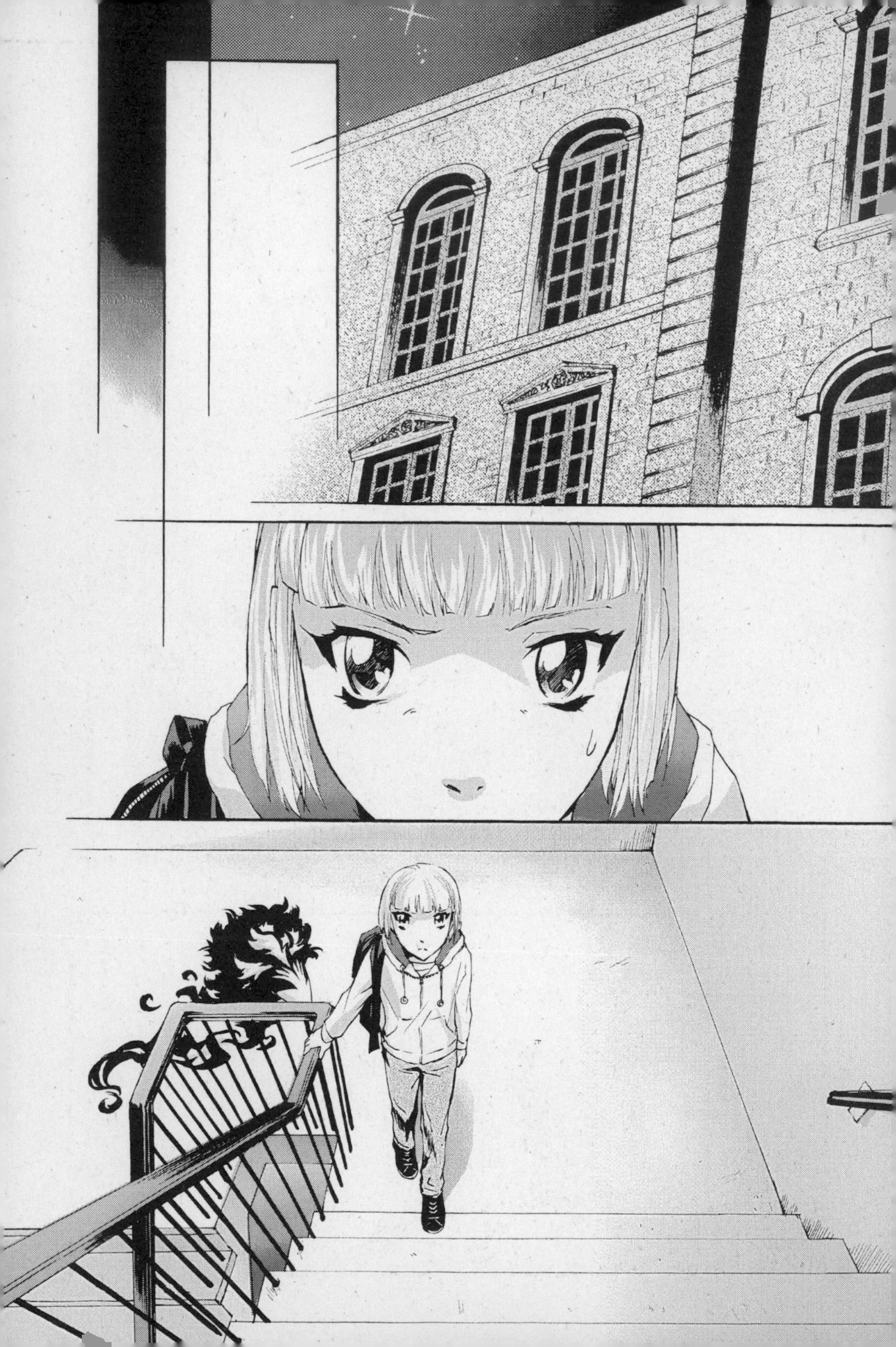

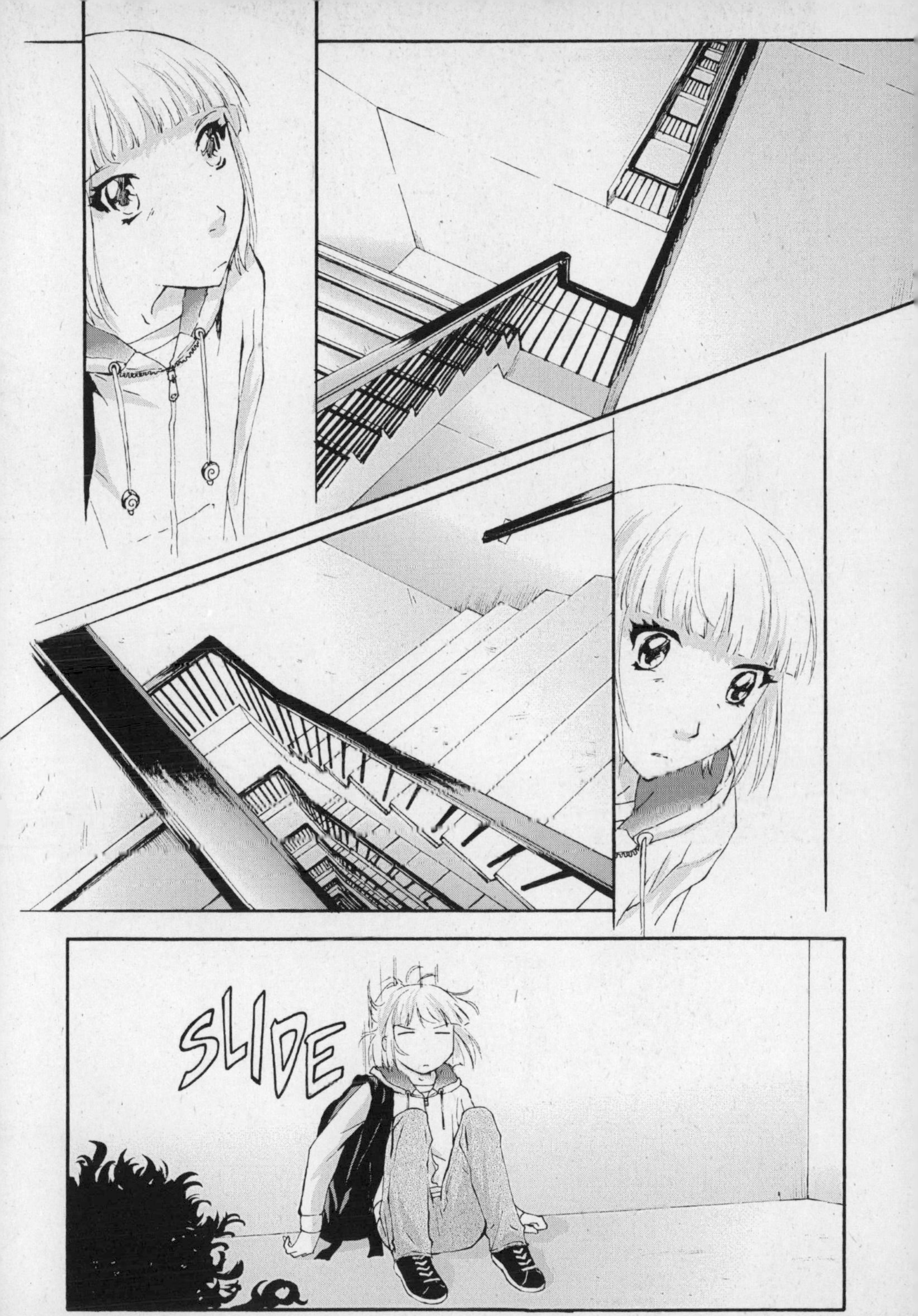
SLIDE

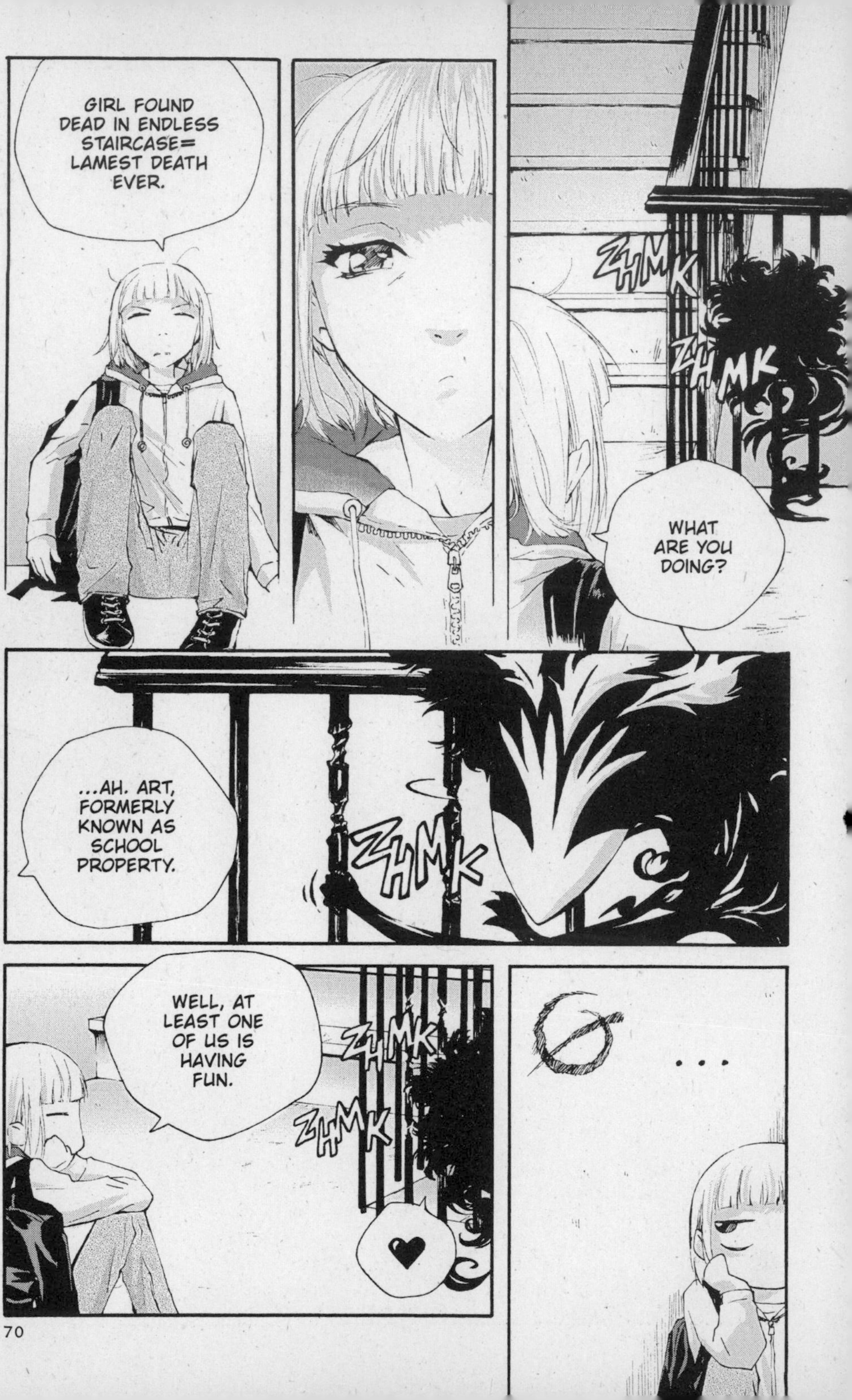
GIRL FOUND DEAD IN ENDLESS STAIRCASE= LAMEST DEATH EVER.
ZHMK
ZHMK
WHAT ARE YOU DOING?
...AH. ART, FORMERLY KNOWN AS SCHOOL PROPERTY.
ZHMK
WELL, AT LEAST ONE OF US IS HAVING FUN.
ZHMK
ZHMK
♥
...

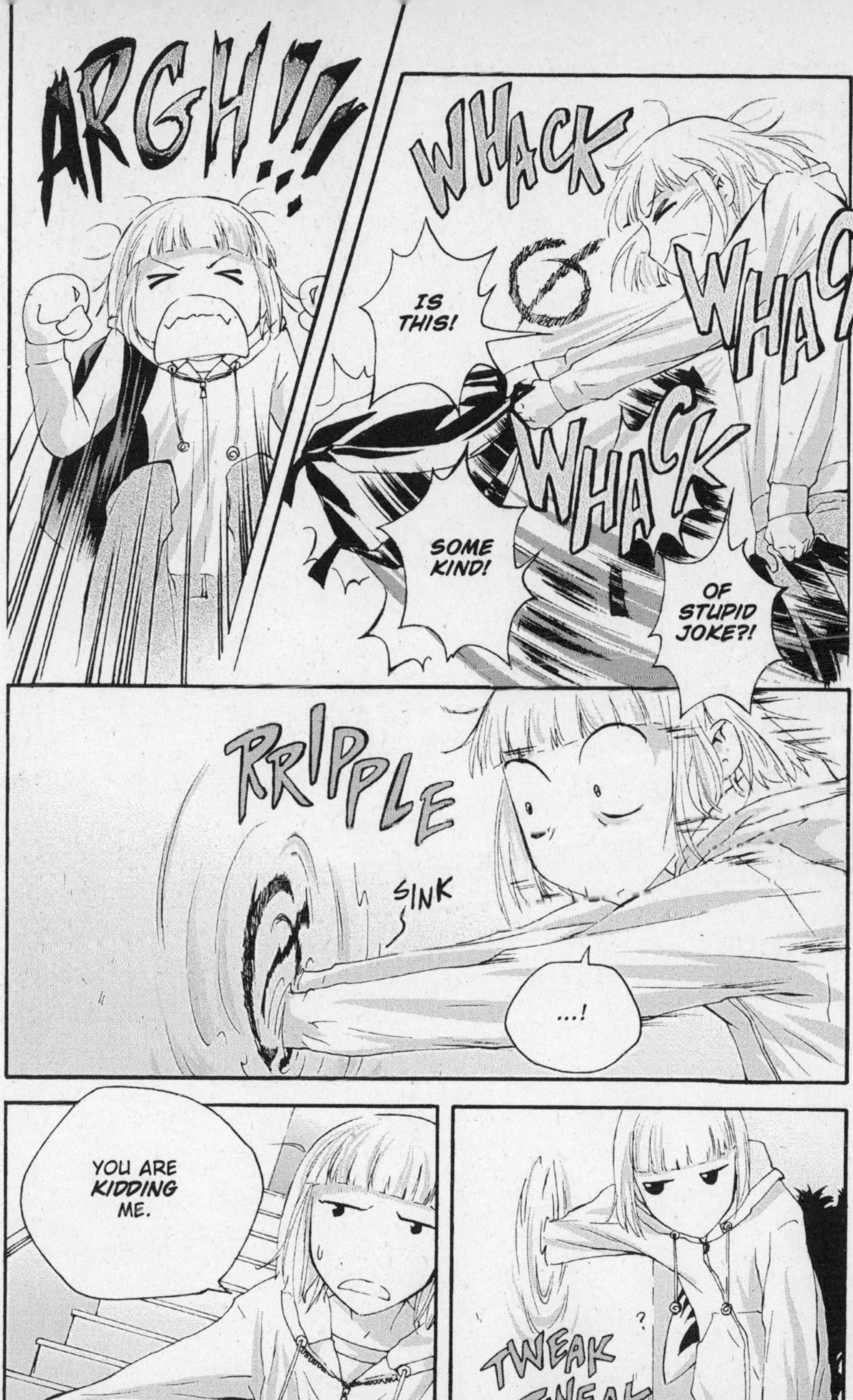
ARGH!!!
WHACK
IS THIS!
WHACK
WHACK
SOME KIND!
OF STUPID JOKE?!
RRIPPLE
SINK
...!
YOU ARE KIDDING ME.
?
TWEAK TWEAK

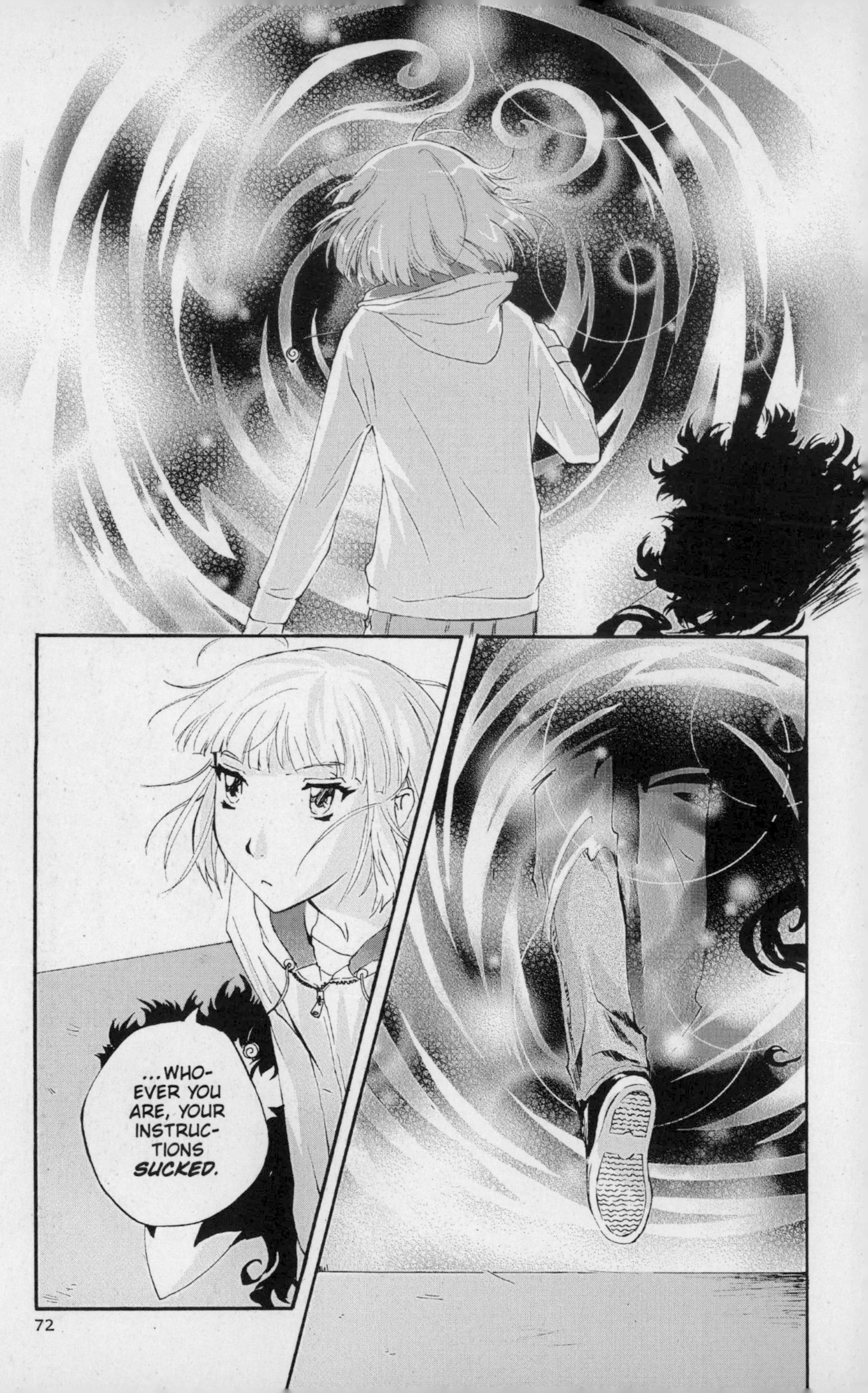
...WHO-EVER YOU ARE, YOUR INSTRUC-TIONS ***SUCKED.***

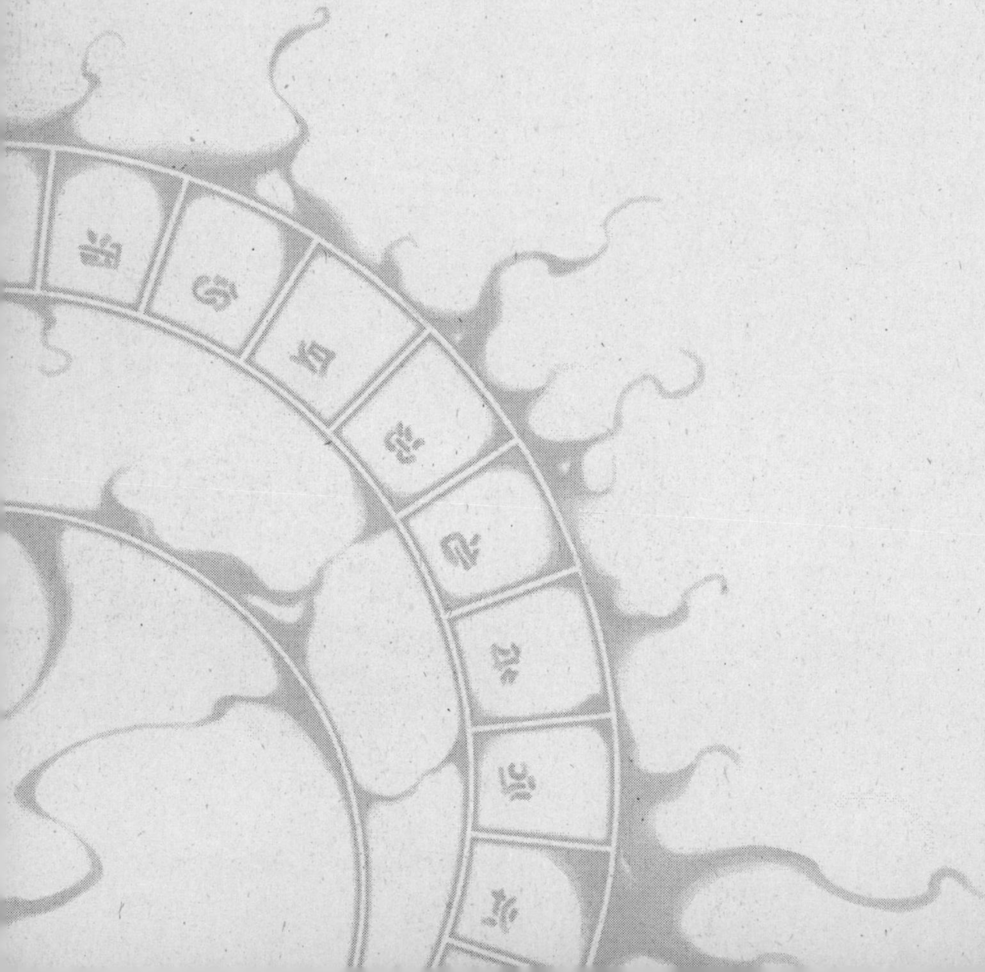

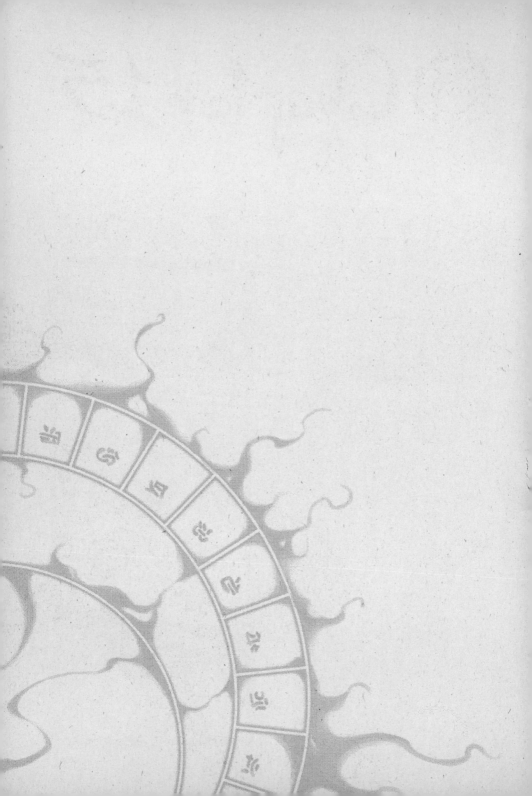

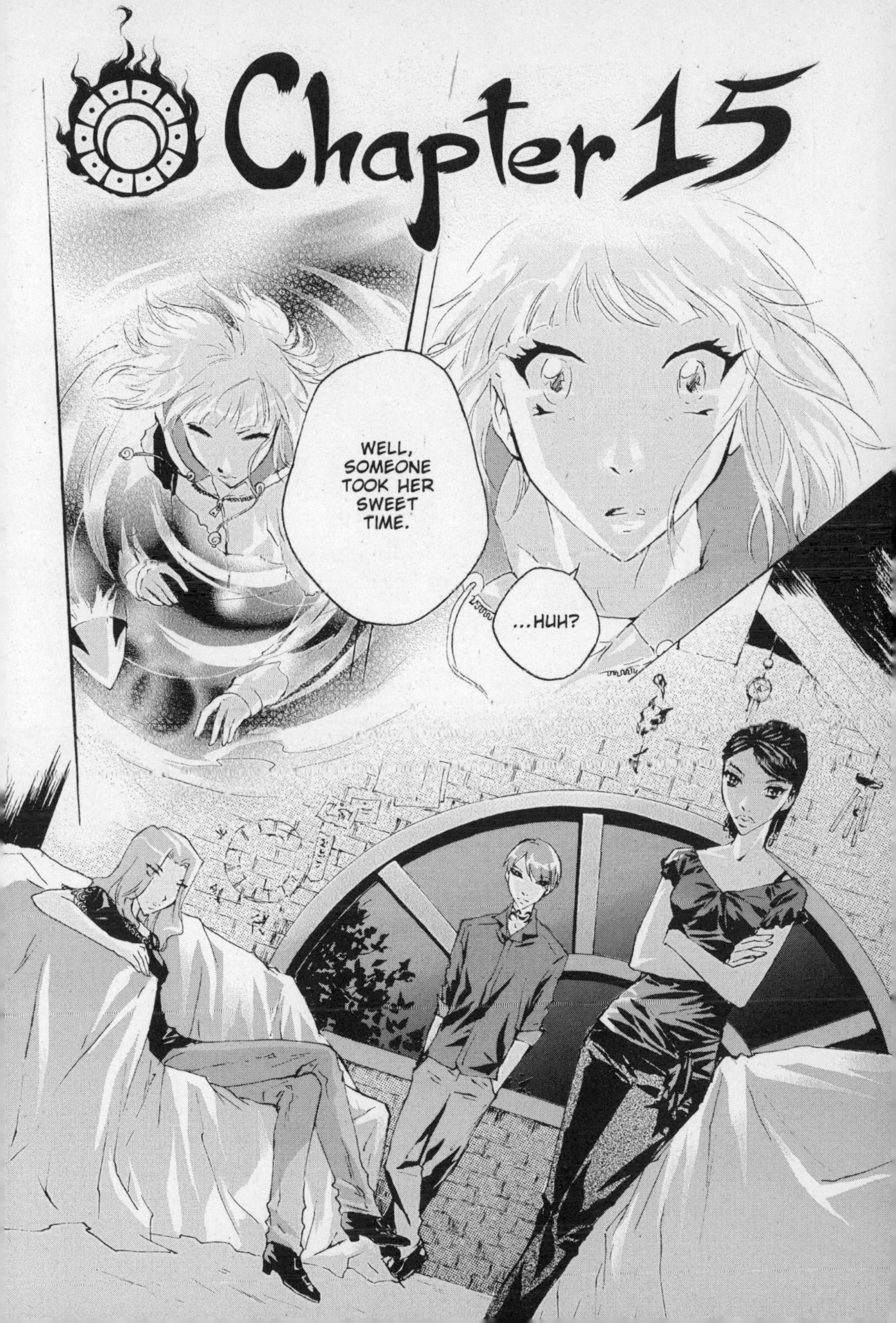
Chapter 15
WELL, SOMEONE TOOK HER SWEET TIME.
...HUH?

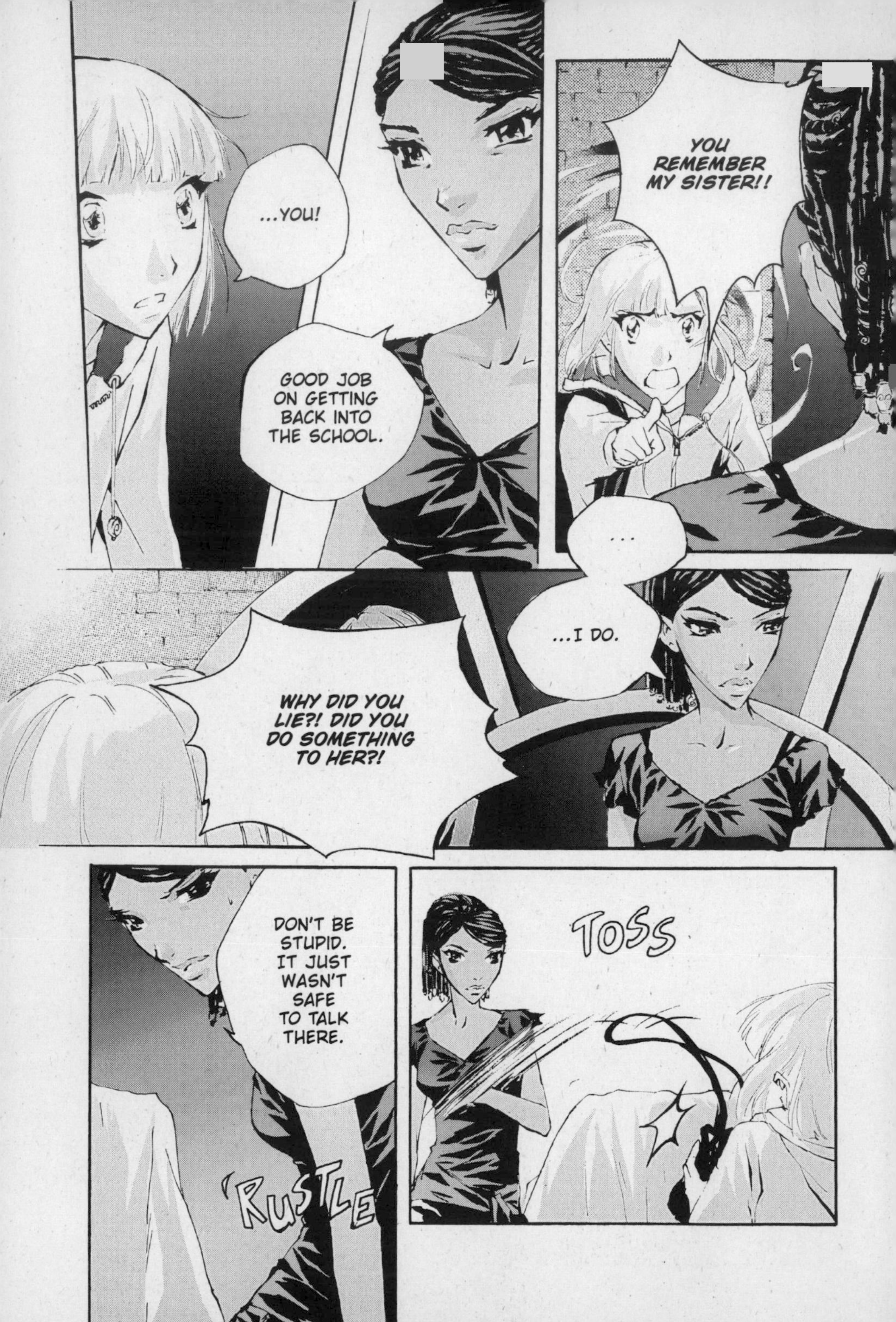
...YOU!
GOOD JOB ON GETTING BACK INTO THE SCHOOL.
YOU REMEMBER MY SISTER!!
...
WHY DID YOU LIE?! DID YOU DO SOMETHING TO HER?!
...I DO.
DON'T BE STUPID. IT JUST WASN'T SAFE TO TALK THERE.
RUSTLE
TOSS

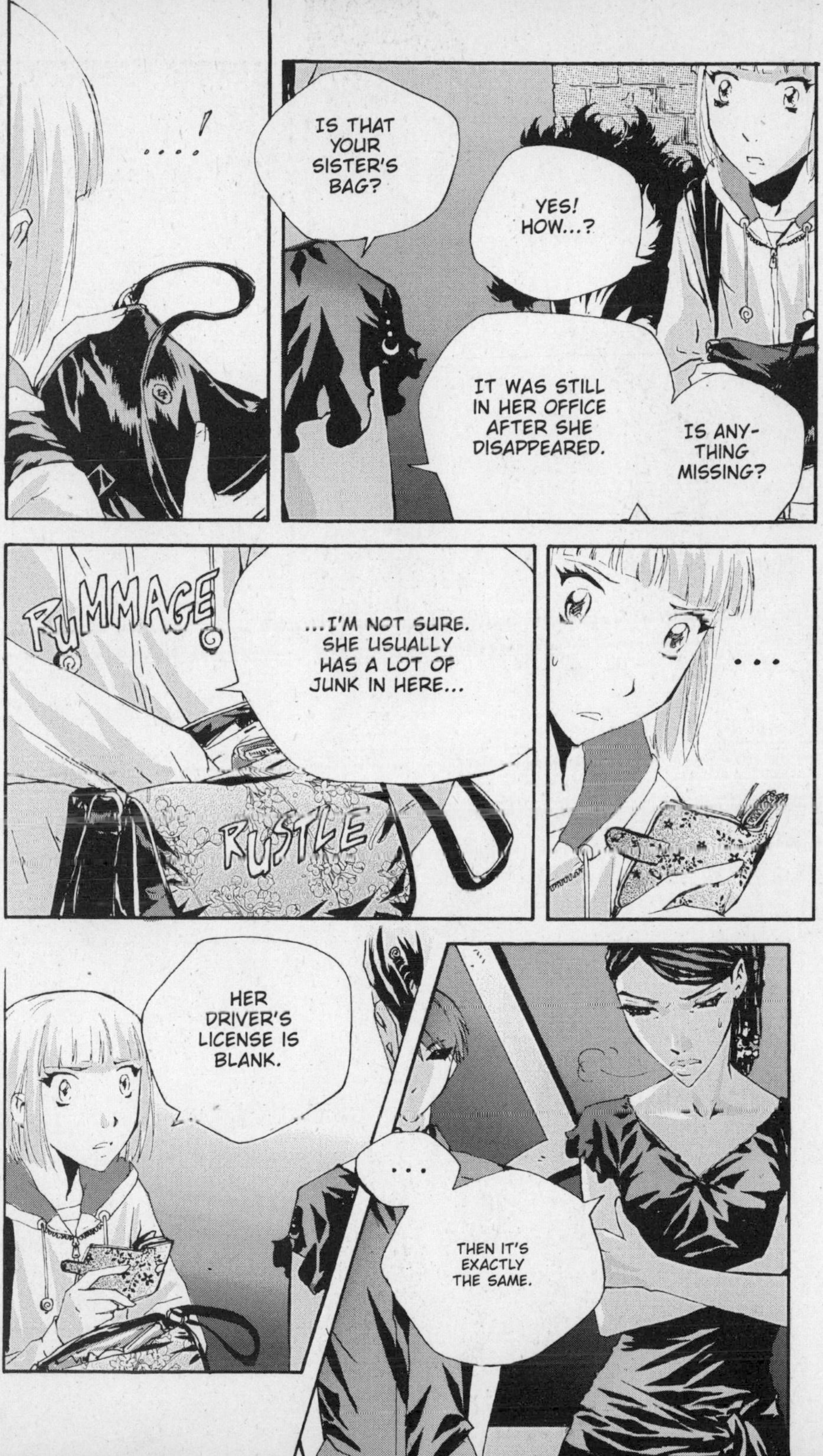
....!
IS THAT YOUR SISTER'S BAG?
YES! HOW...?
IT WAS STILL IN HER OFFICE AFTER SHE DISAPPEARED.
IS ANY-THING MISSING?
RUMMAGE
...I'M NOT SURE. SHE USUALLY HAS A LOT OF JUNK IN HERE...
RUSTLE
...
HER DRIVER'S LICENSE IS BLANK.
...
THEN IT'S EXACTLY THE SAME.

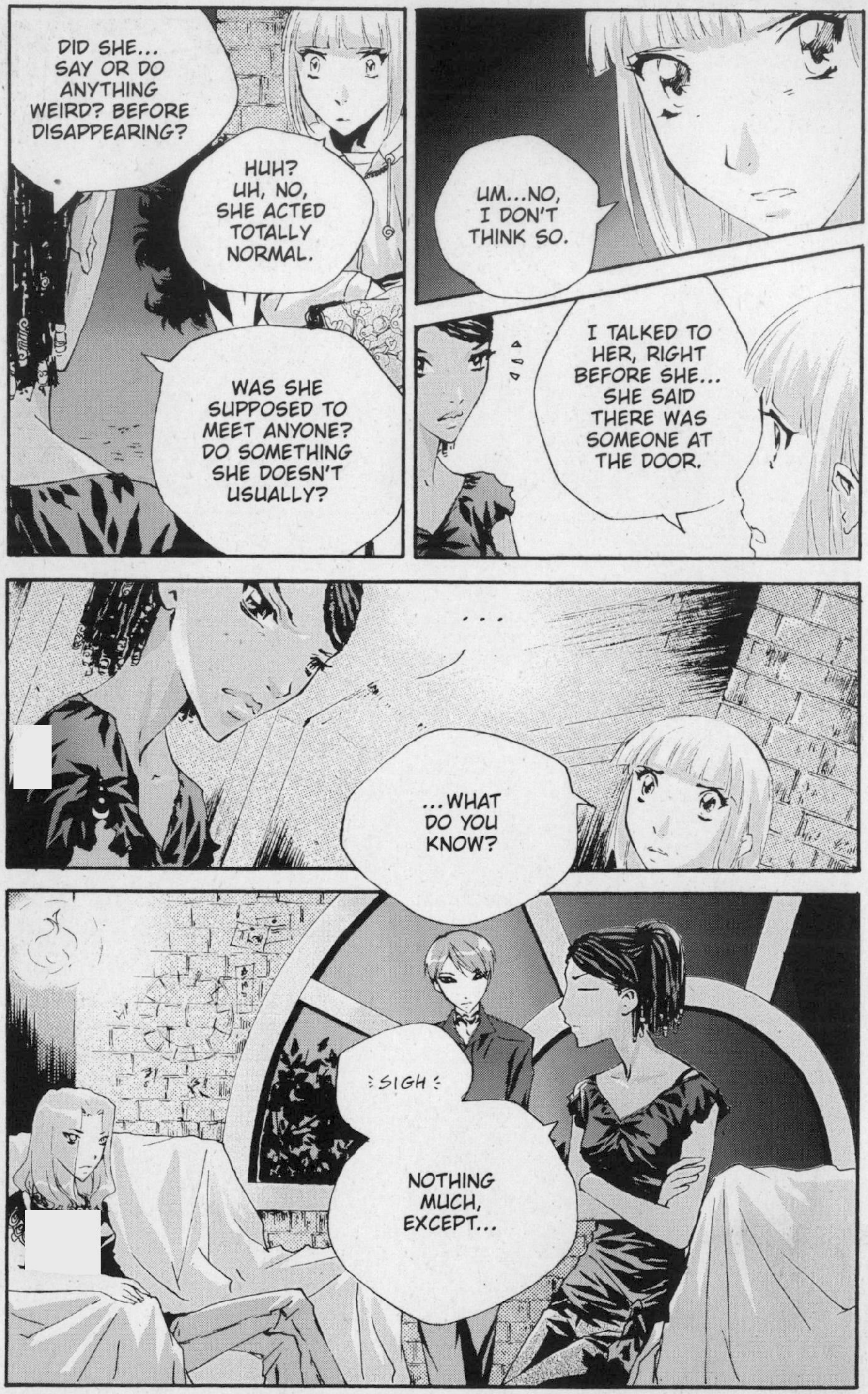
DID SHE... SAY OR DO ANYTHING WEIRD? BEFORE DISAPPEARING?
HUH? UH, NO, SHE ACTED TOTALLY NORMAL.
WAS SHE SUPPOSED TO MEET ANYONE? DO SOMETHING SHE DOESN'T USUALLY?
UM...NO, I DON'T THINK SO.
I TALKED TO HER, RIGHT BEFORE SHE... SHE SAID THERE WAS SOMEONE AT THE DOOR.
...
...WHAT DO YOU KNOW?
SIGH
NOTHING MUCH, EXCEPT...

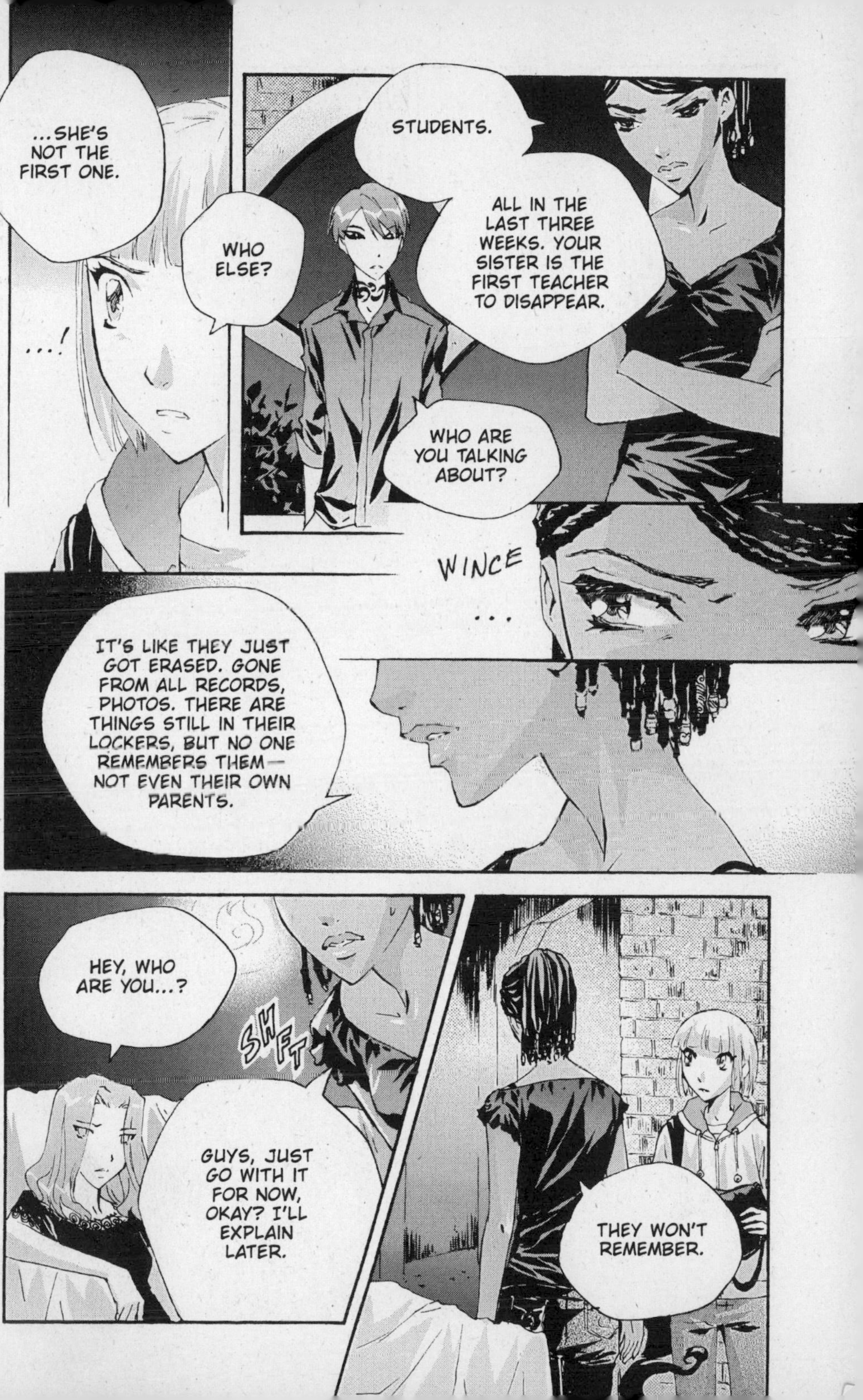
...SHE'S NOT THE FIRST ONE.
...!
WHO ELSE?
STUDENTS.
ALL IN THE LAST THREE WEEKS. YOUR SISTER IS THE FIRST TEACHER TO DISAPPEAR.
WHO ARE YOU TALKING ABOUT?
WINCE
...
IT'S LIKE THEY JUST GOT ERASED. GONE FROM ALL RECORDS, PHOTOS. THERE ARE THINGS STILL IN THEIR LOCKERS, BUT NO ONE REMEMBERS THEM— NOT EVEN THEIR OWN PARENTS.
HEY, WHO ARE YOU...?
SHFT
GUYS, JUST GO WITH IT FOR NOW, OKAY? I'LL EXPLAIN LATER.
THEY WON'T REMEMBER.

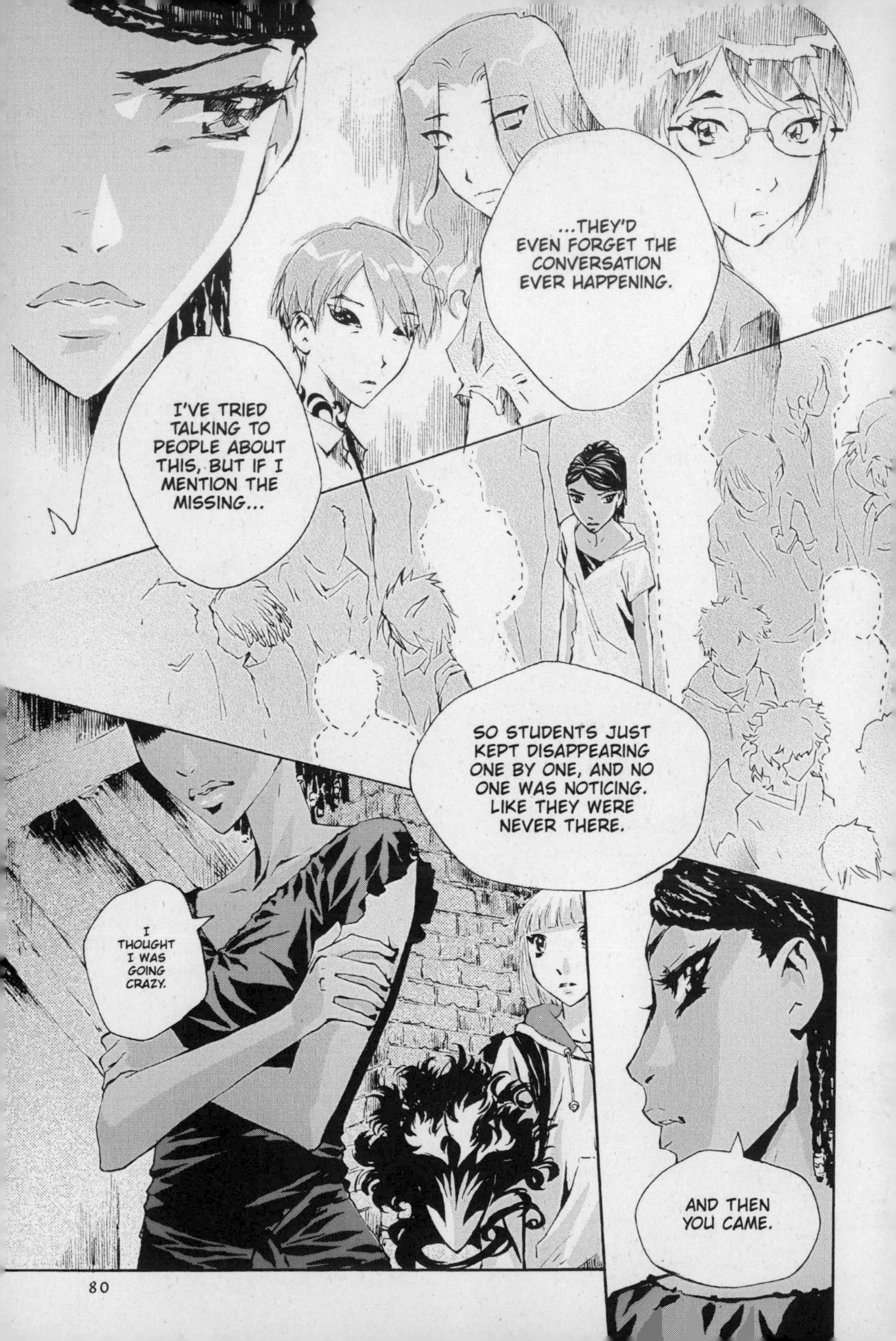
I'VE TRIED TALKING TO PEOPLE ABOUT THIS, BUT IF I MENTION THE MISSING...
...THEY'D EVEN FORGET THE CONVERSATION EVER HAPPENING.
SO STUDENTS JUST KEPT DISAPPEARING ONE BY ONE, AND NO ONE WAS NOTICING. LIKE THEY WERE NEVER THERE.
I THOUGHT I WAS GOING CRAZY.
AND THEN YOU CAME.

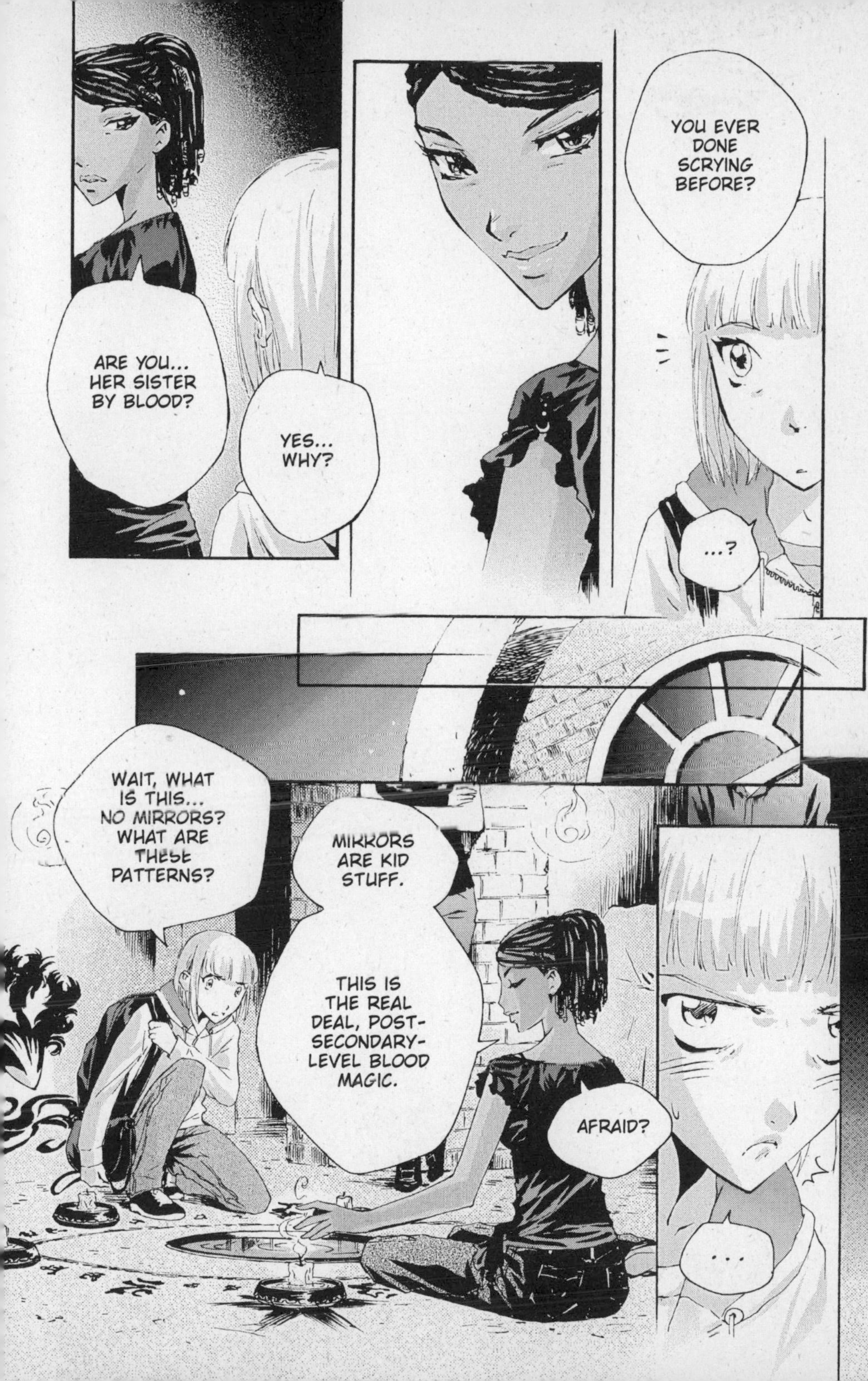

ARE YOU... HER SISTER BY BLOOD?
YES... WHY?
YOU EVER DONE SCRYING BEFORE?
...?
WAIT, WHAT IS THIS... NO MIRRORS? WHAT ARE THESE PATTERNS?
MIRRORS ARE KID STUFF.
THIS IS THE REAL DEAL, POST-SECONDARY-LEVEL BLOOD MAGIC.
AFRAID?
...

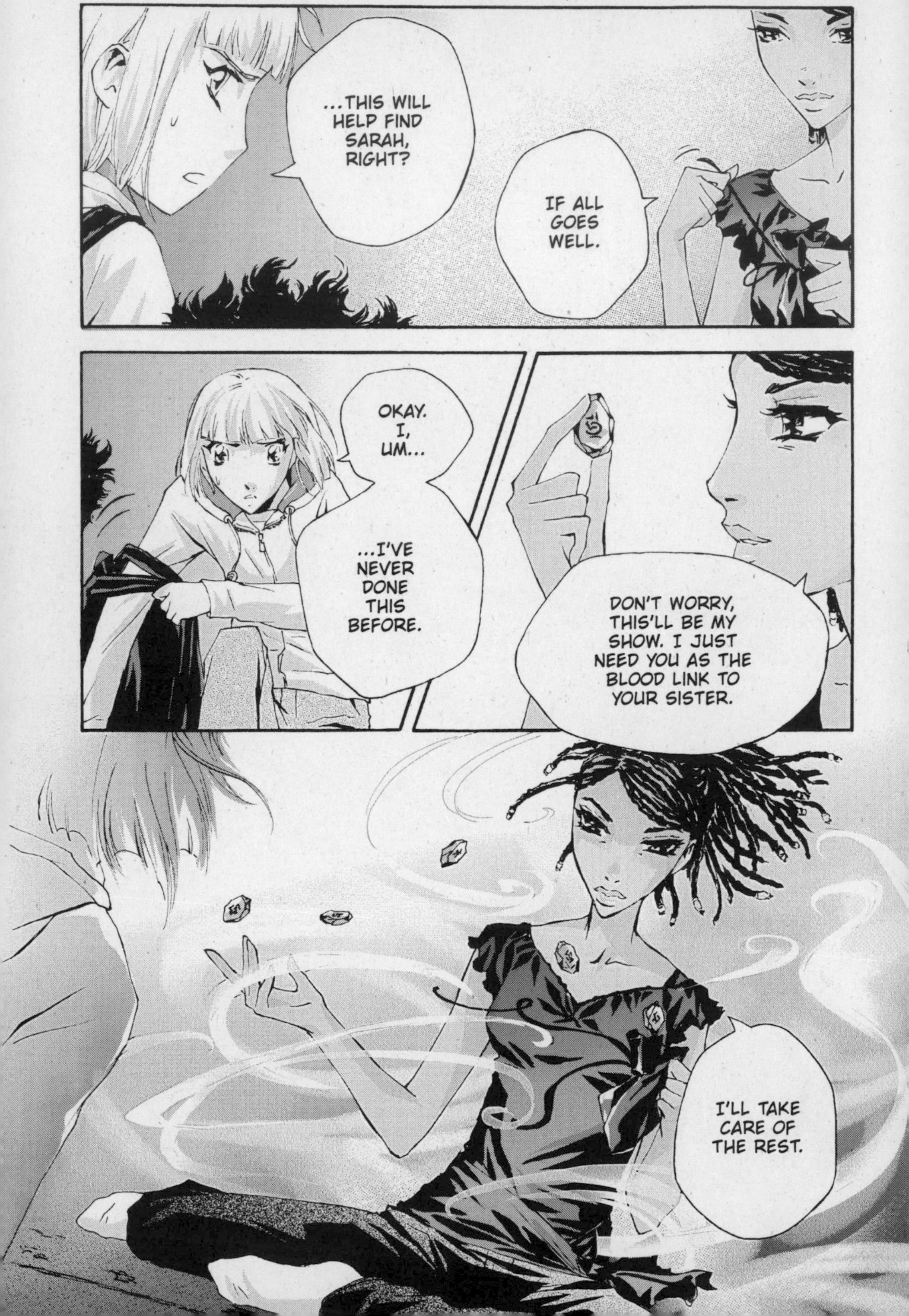
...THIS WILL HELP FIND SARAH, RIGHT?
IF ALL GOES WELL.
OKAY. I, UM...
...I'VE NEVER DONE THIS BEFORE.
DON'T WORRY, THIS'LL BE MY SHOW. I JUST NEED YOU AS THE BLOOD LINK TO YOUR SISTER.
I'LL TAKE CARE OF THE REST.

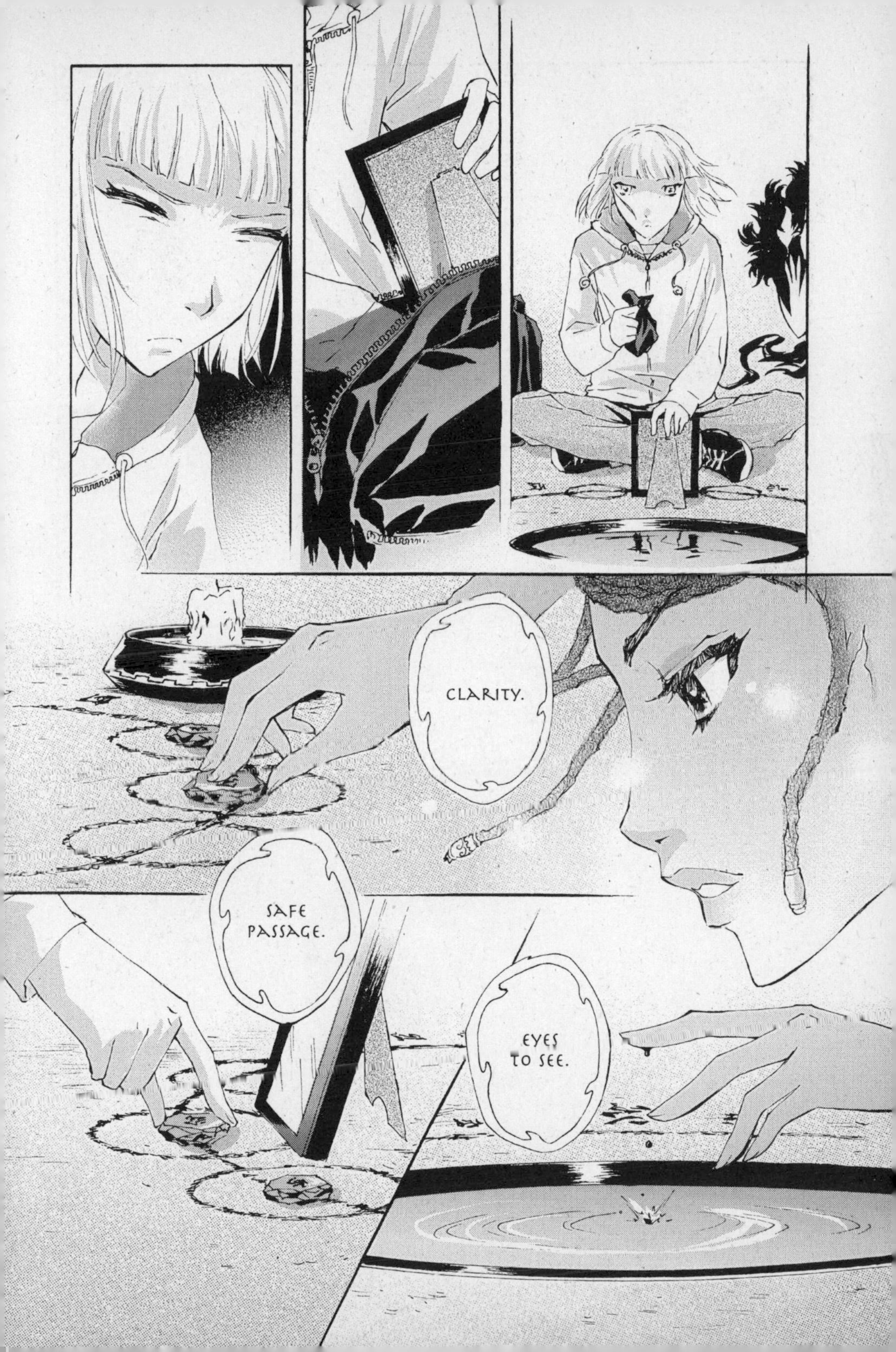
CLARITY.
SAFE PASSAGE.
EYES TO SEE.

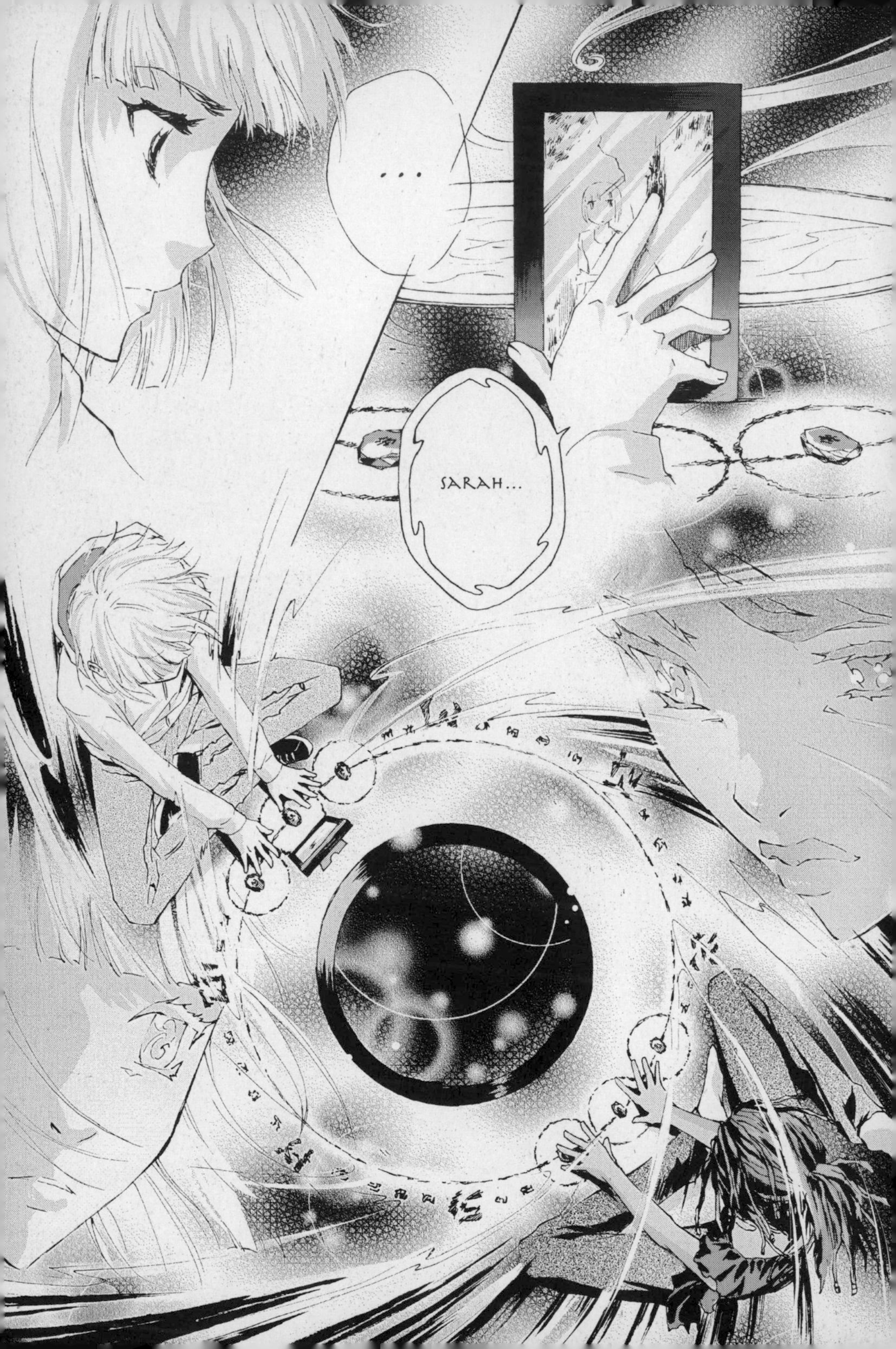
...
SARAH...

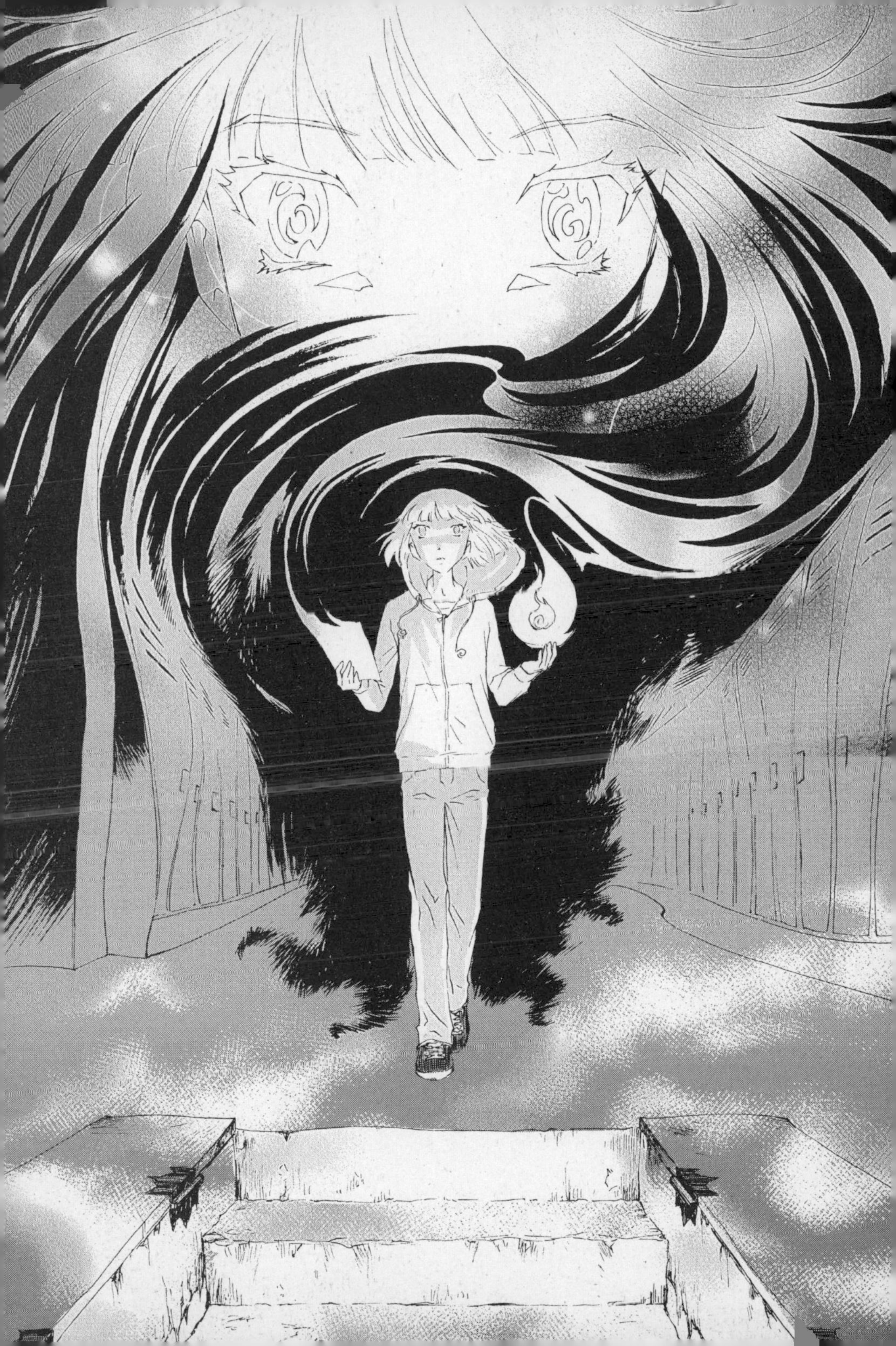

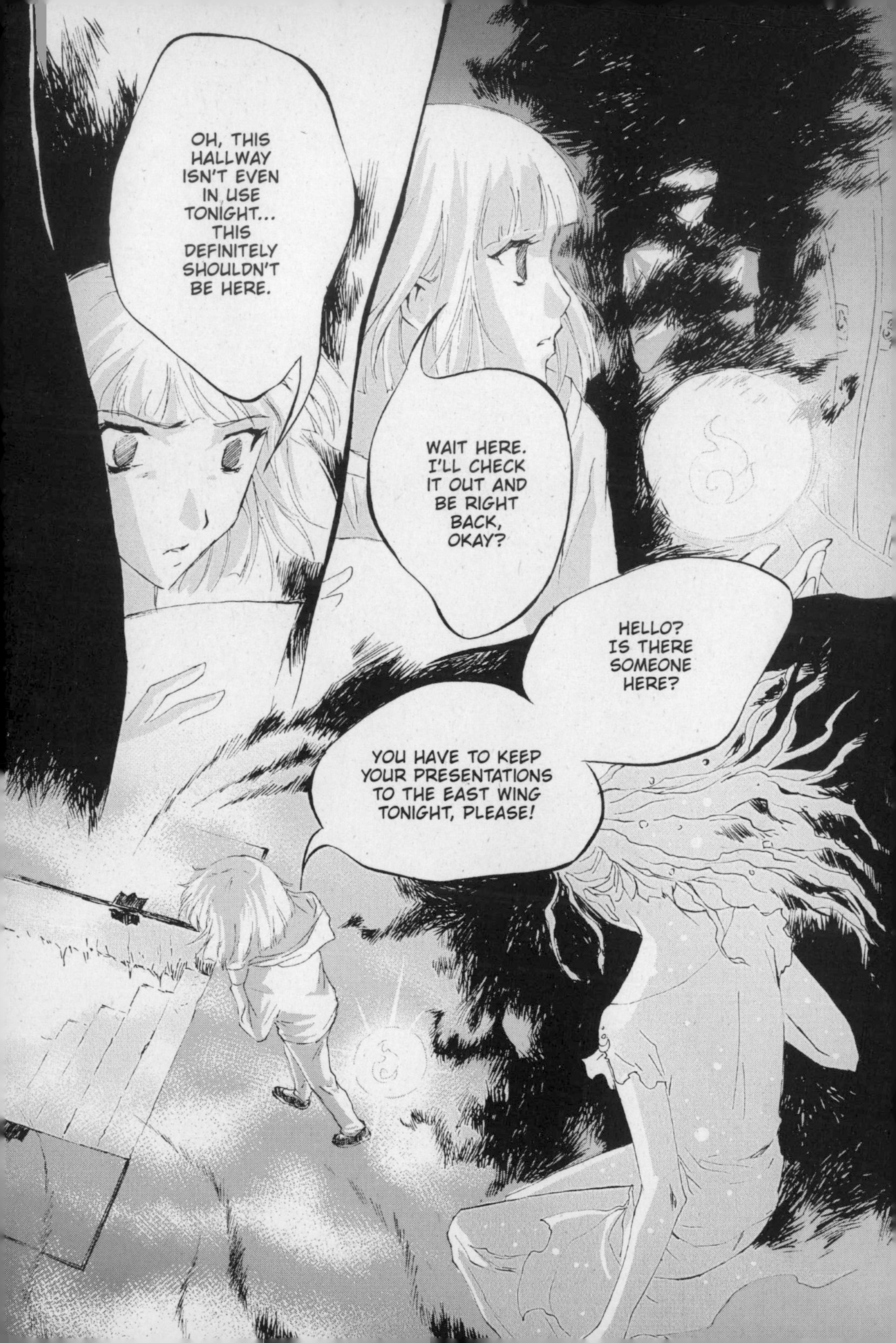
OH, THIS HALLWAY ISN'T EVEN IN USE TONIGHT... THIS DEFINITELY SHOULDN'T BE HERE.
WAIT HERE. I'LL CHECK IT OUT AND BE RIGHT BACK, OKAY?
HELLO? IS THERE SOMEONE HERE?
YOU HAVE TO KEEP YOUR PRESENTATIONS TO THE EAST WING TONIGHT, PLEASE!

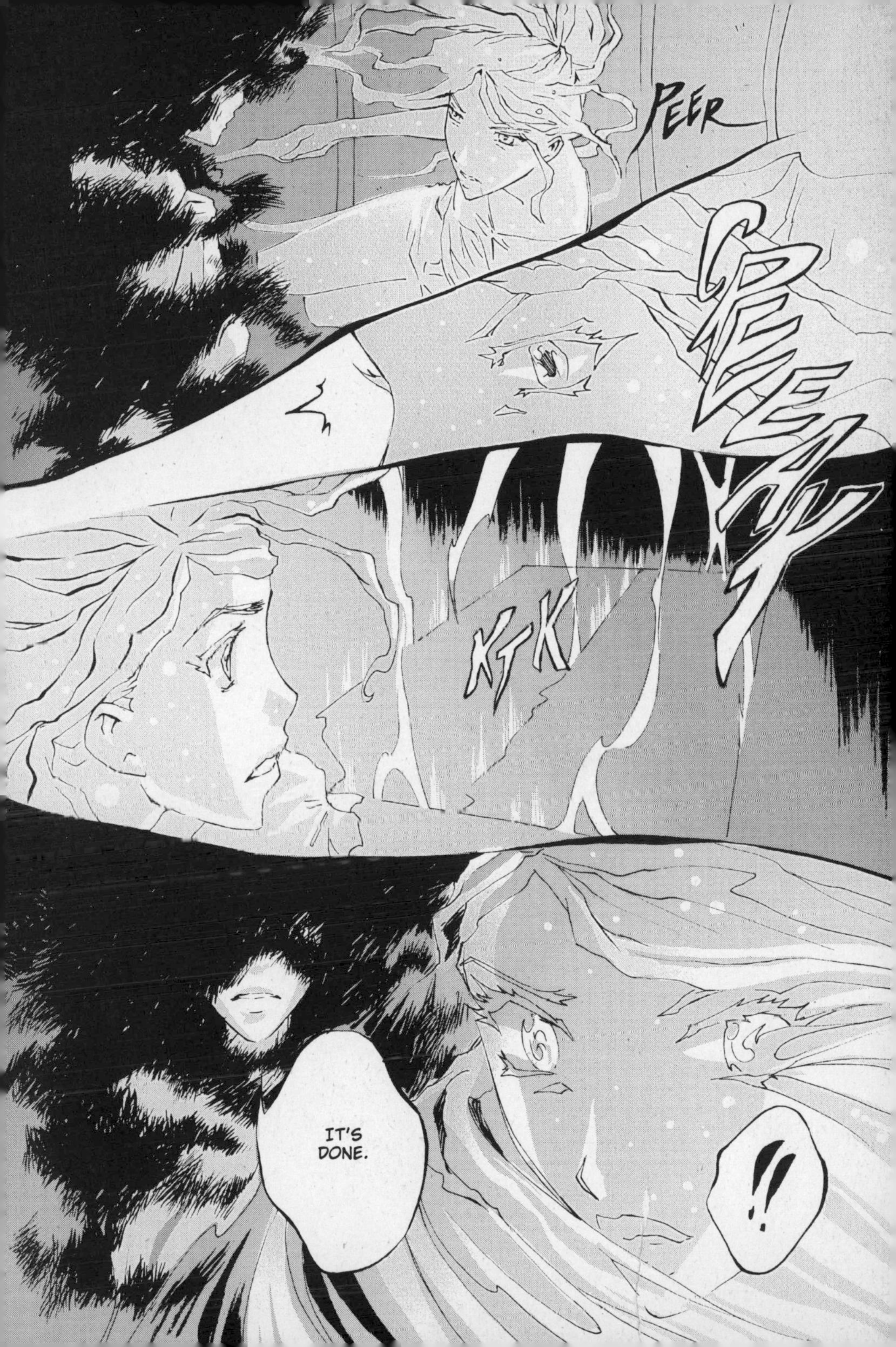
PEER
CREEAK
KT-K
IT'S DONE.
!!

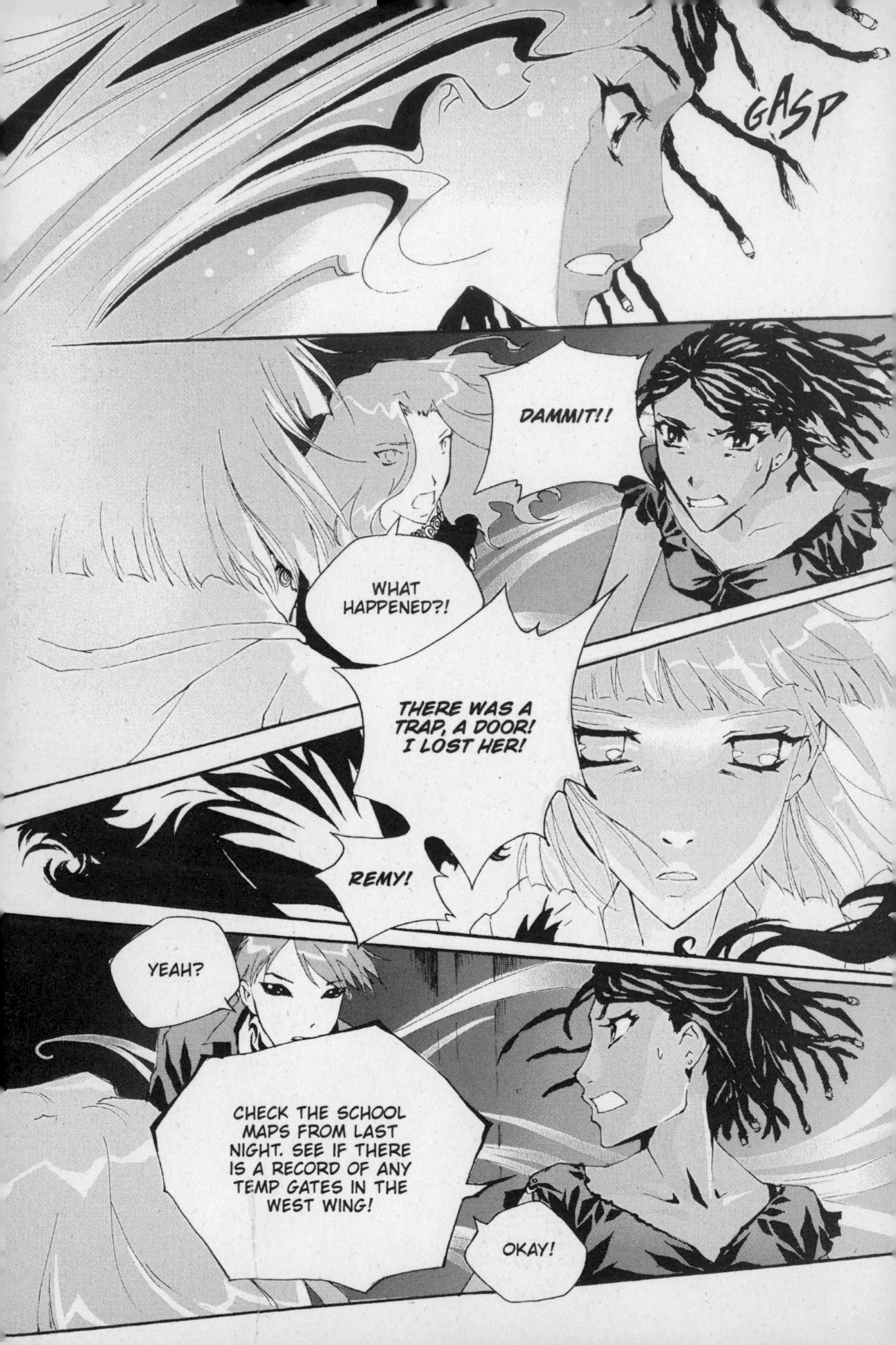
GASP
DAMMIT!!
WHAT HAPPENED?!
THERE WAS A TRAP, A DOOR! I LOST HER!
REMY!
YEAH?
CHECK THE SCHOOL MAPS FROM LAST NIGHT. SEE IF THERE IS A RECORD OF ANY TEMP GATES IN THE WEST WING!
OKAY!

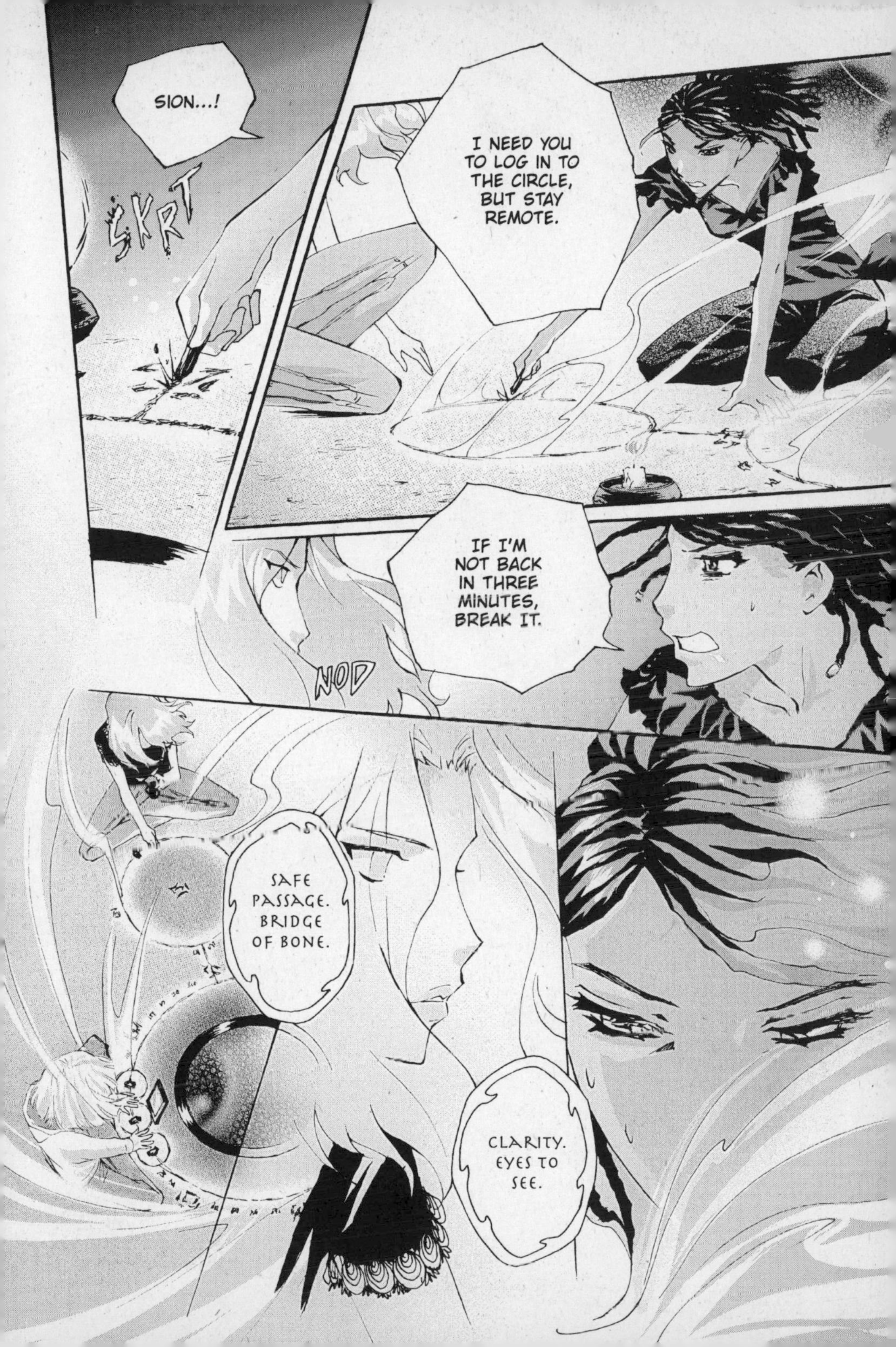
SION...!
SKRT
I NEED YOU TO LOG IN TO THE CIRCLE, BUT STAY REMOTE.
IF I'M NOT BACK IN THREE MINUTES, BREAK IT.
NOD
SAFE PASSAGE. BRIDGE OF BONE.
CLARITY. EYES TO SEE.

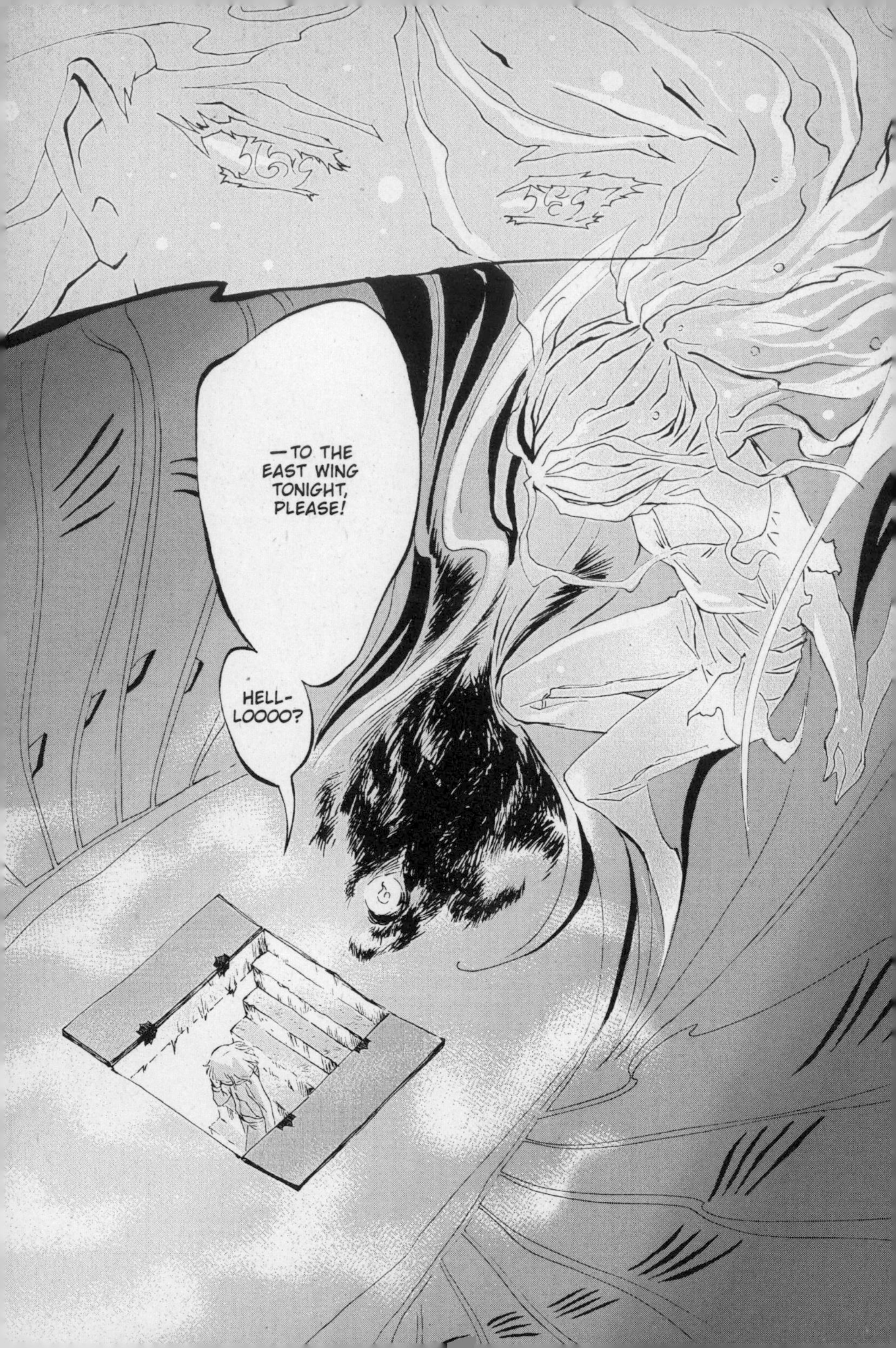
—TO THE EAST WING TONIGHT, PLEASE!
HELL-LOOOO?

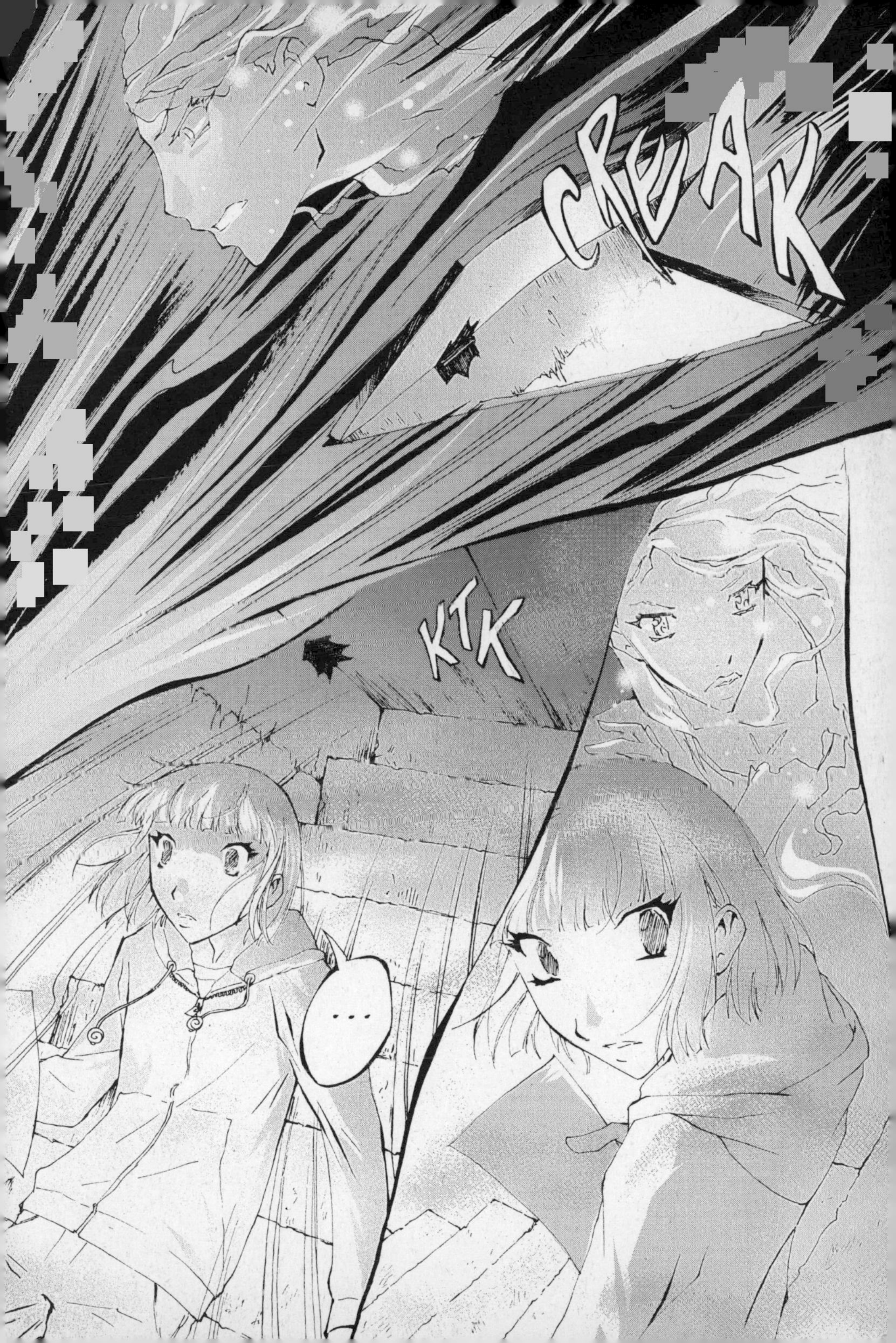
CREAK
KTK
...

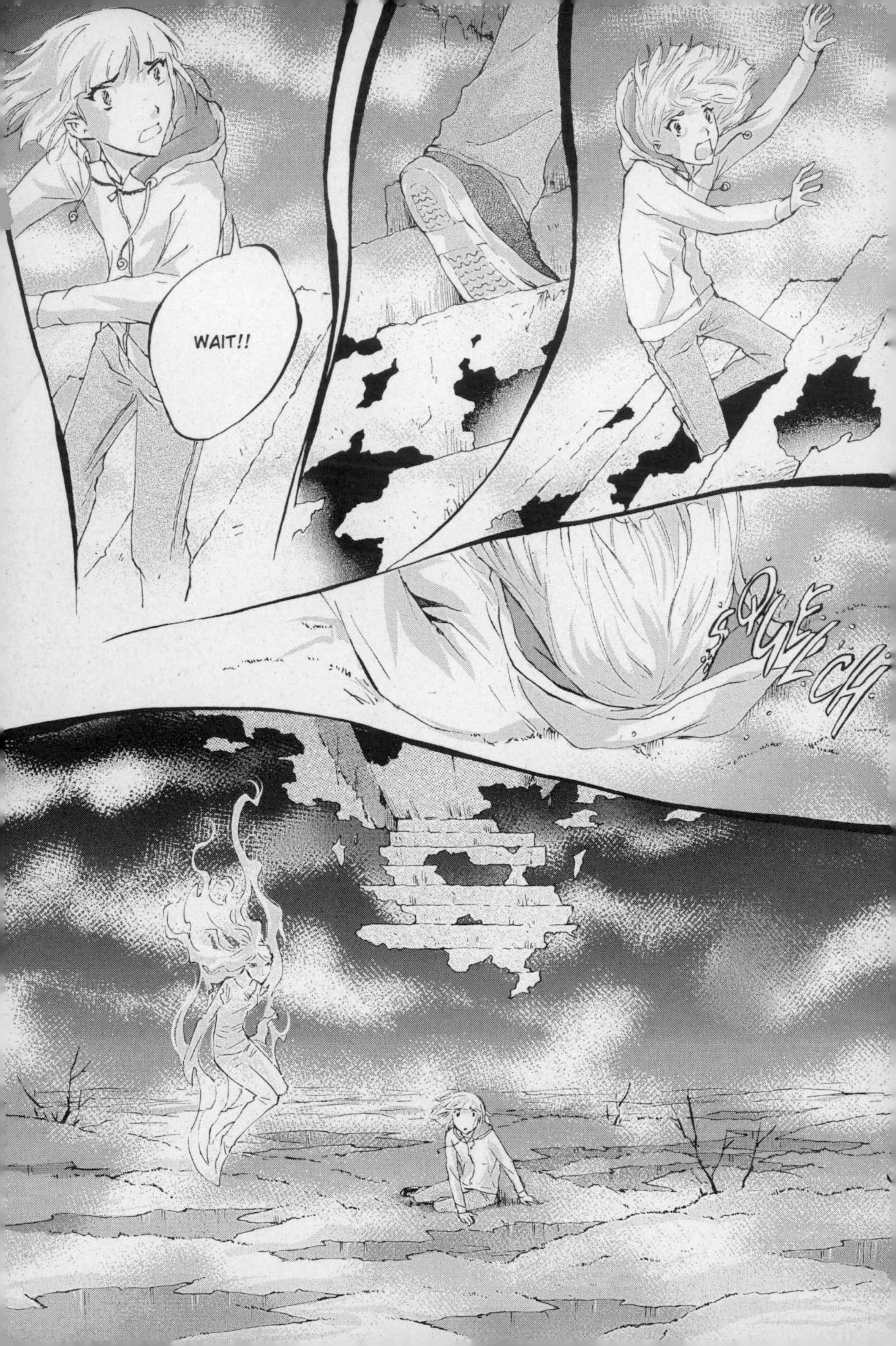
WAIT!!
SQUELCH

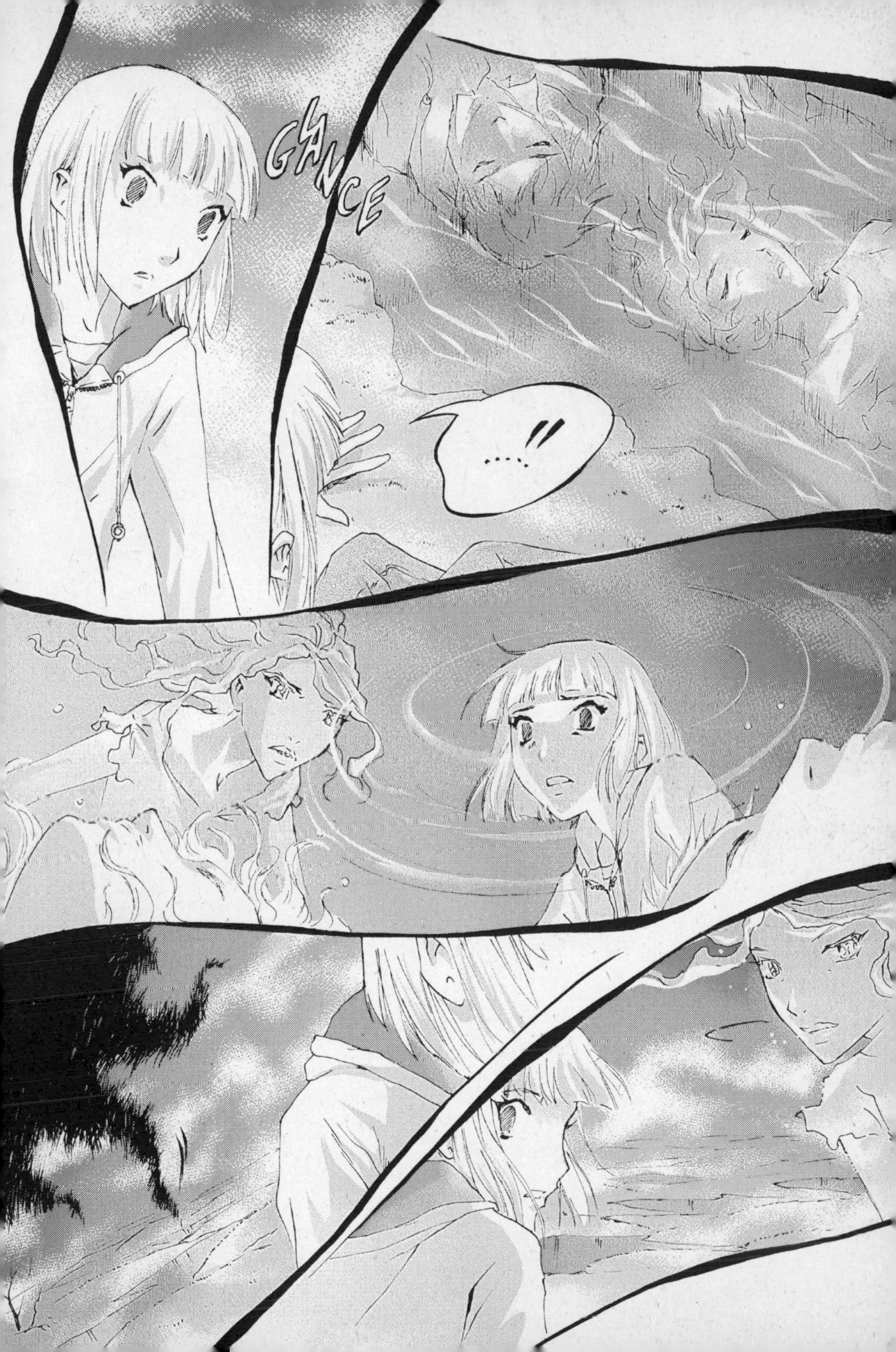
GLANCE
...!!

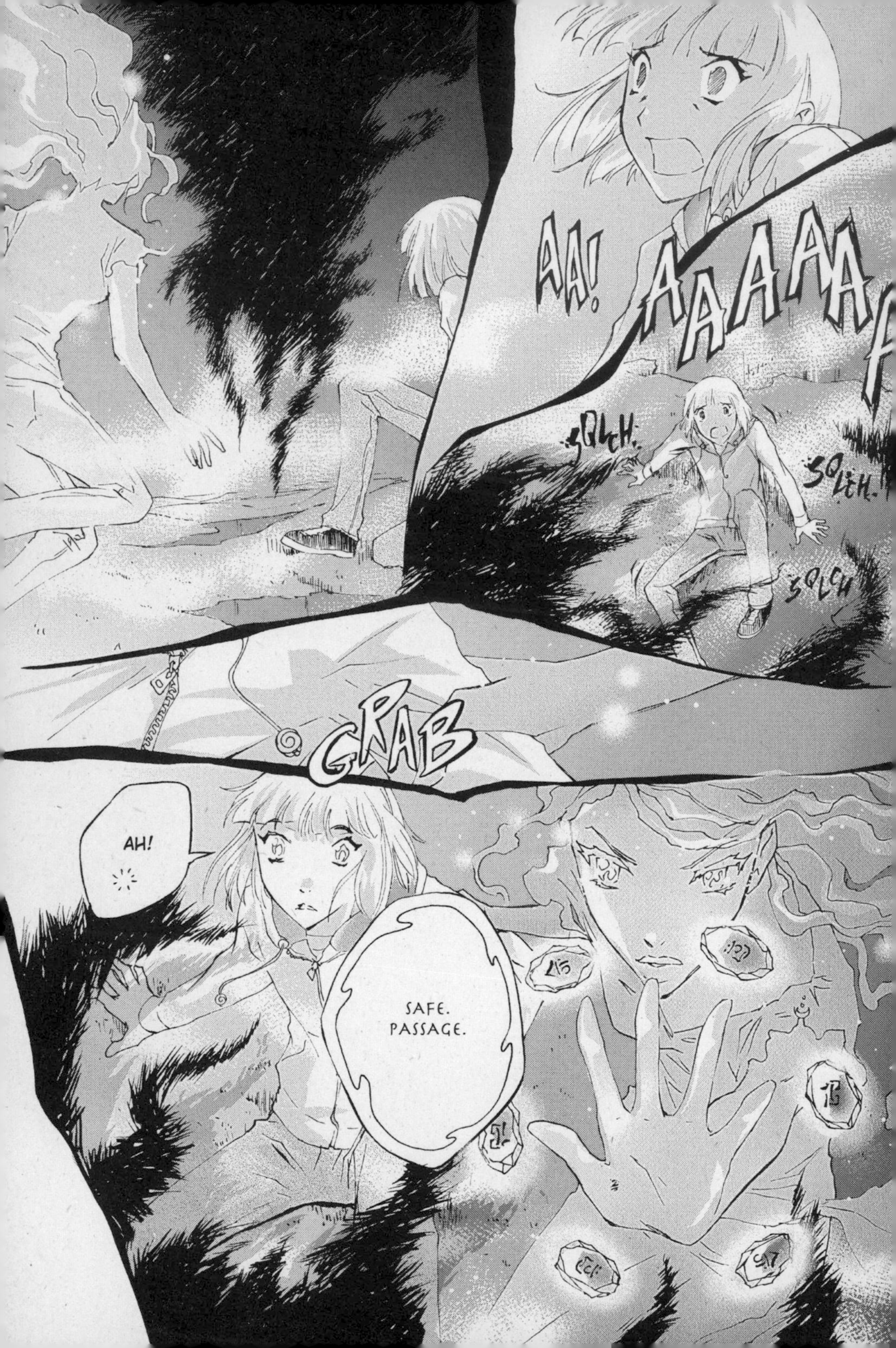
AA! AAAAA
SQLCH
SQLCH
SQLCH
GRAB
AH!
SAFE. PASSAGE.

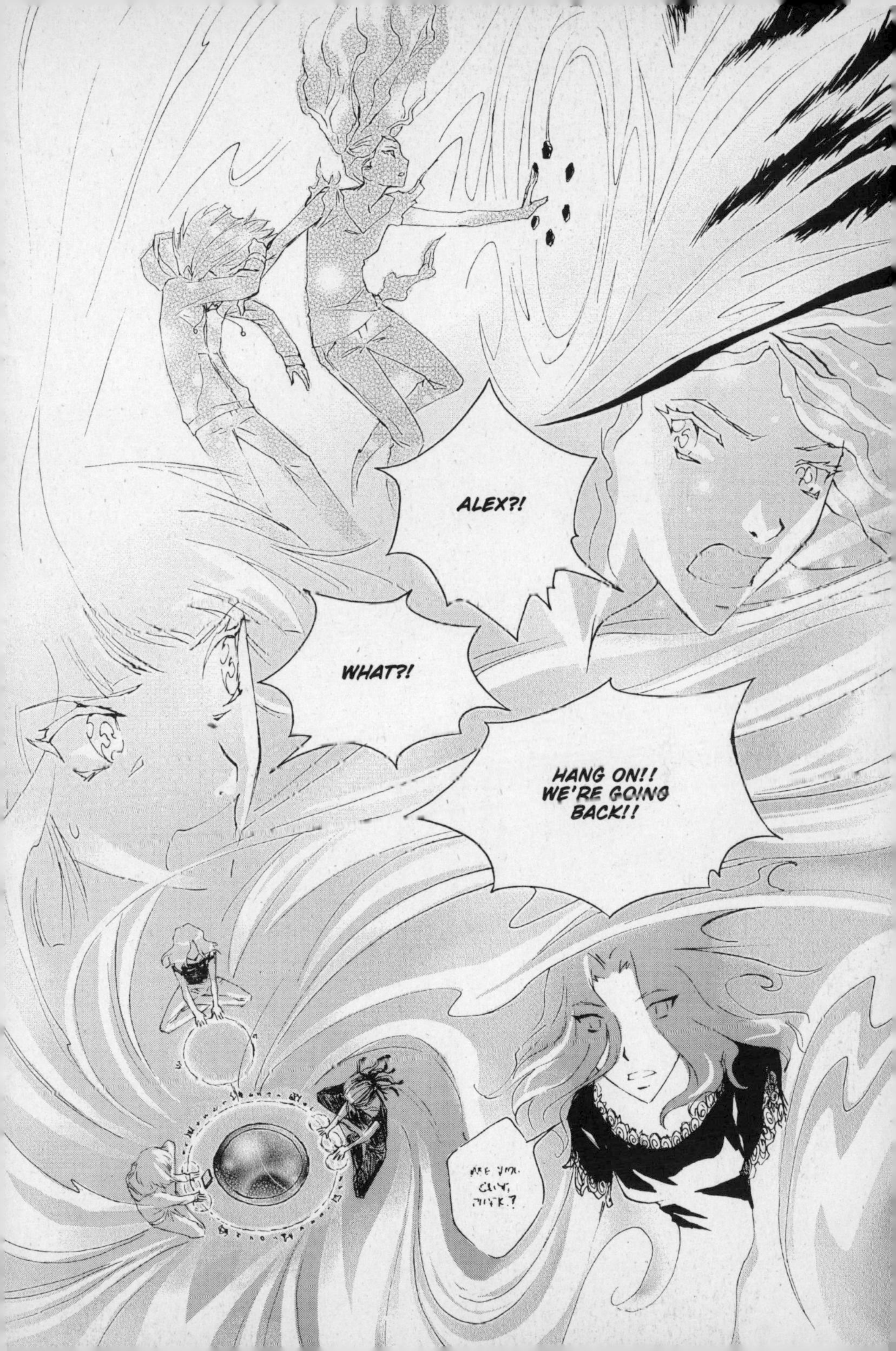
ALEX?!
WHAT?!
HANG ON!! WE'RE GOING BACK!!

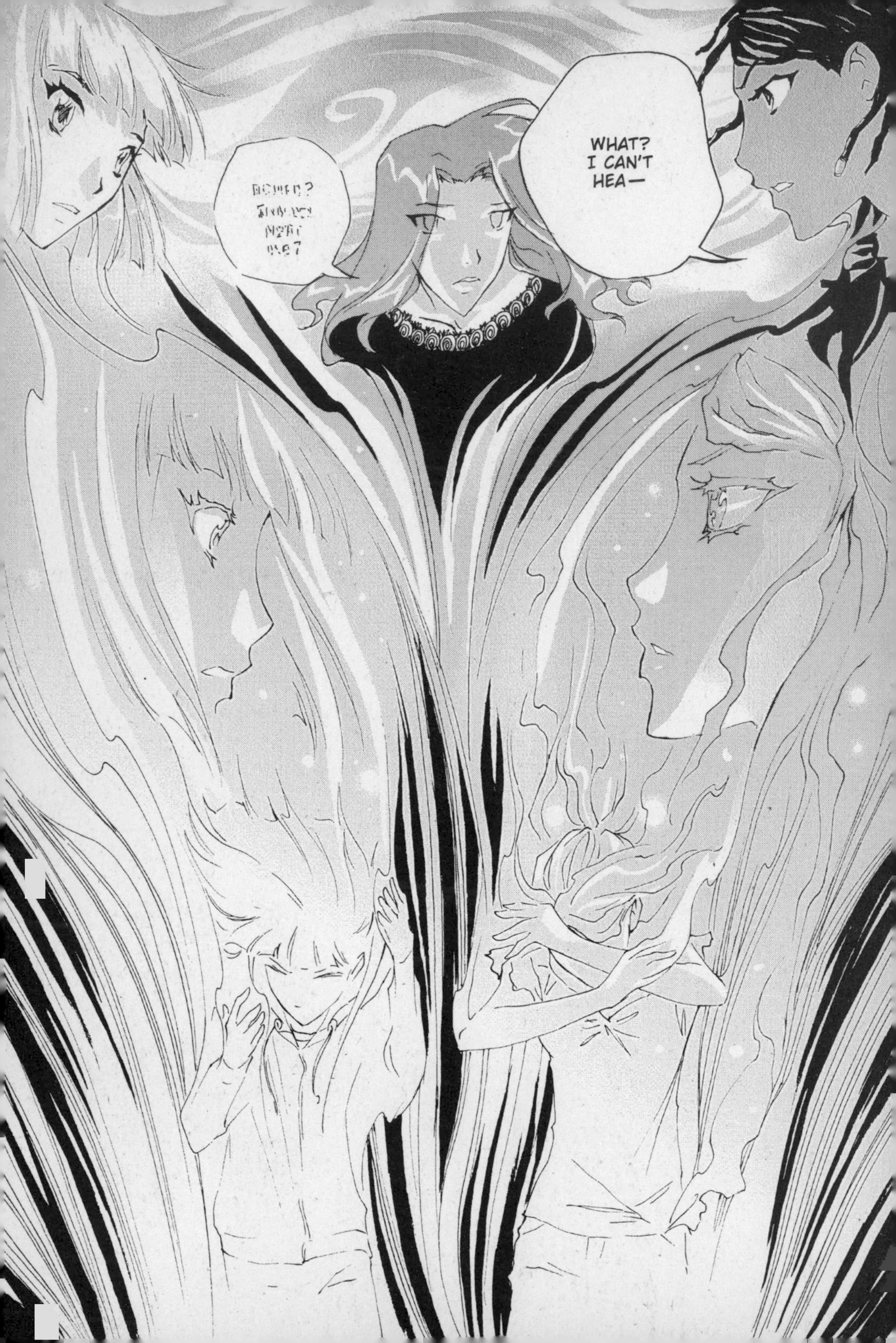
WHAT? I CAN'T HEA—

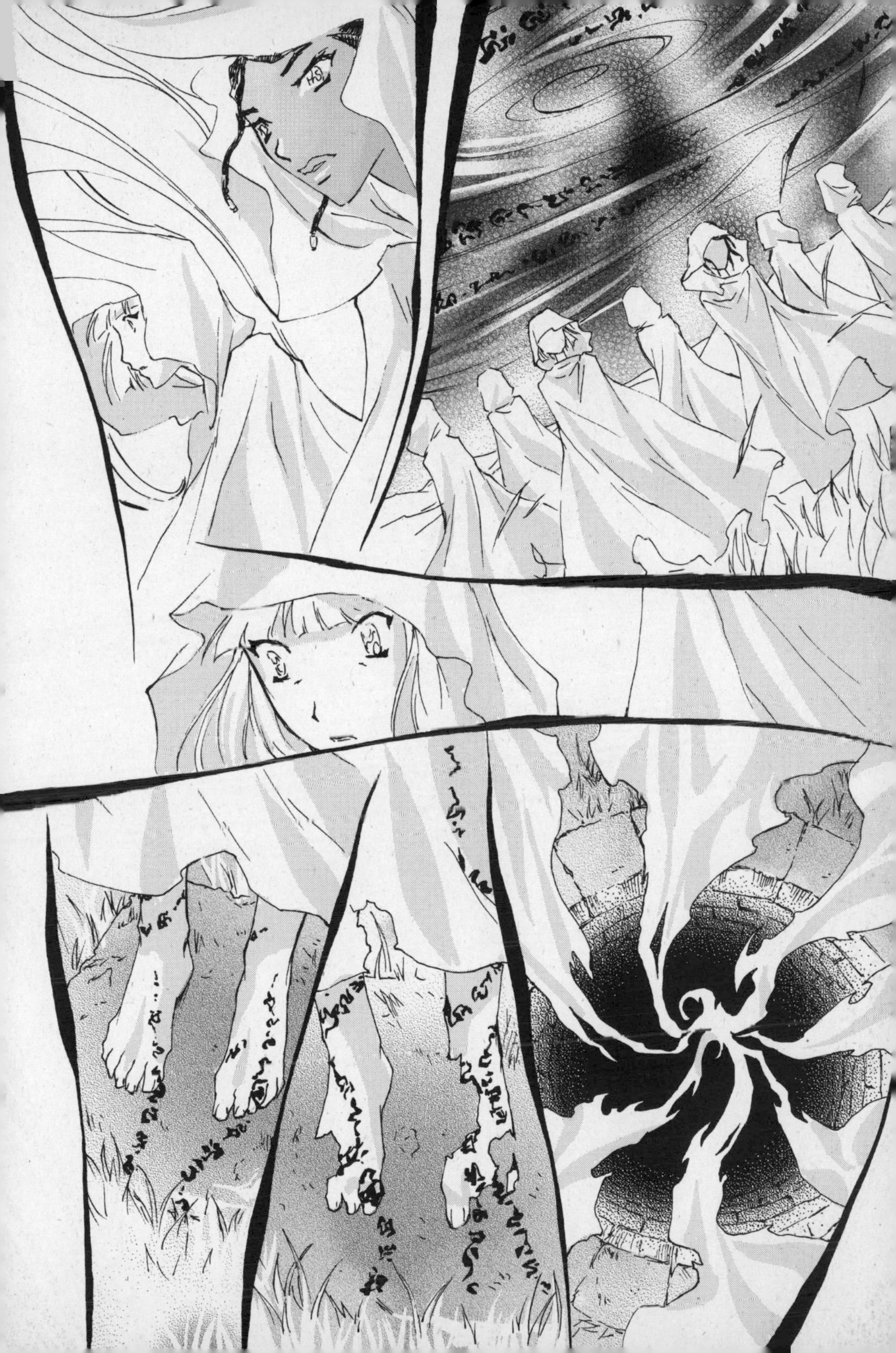

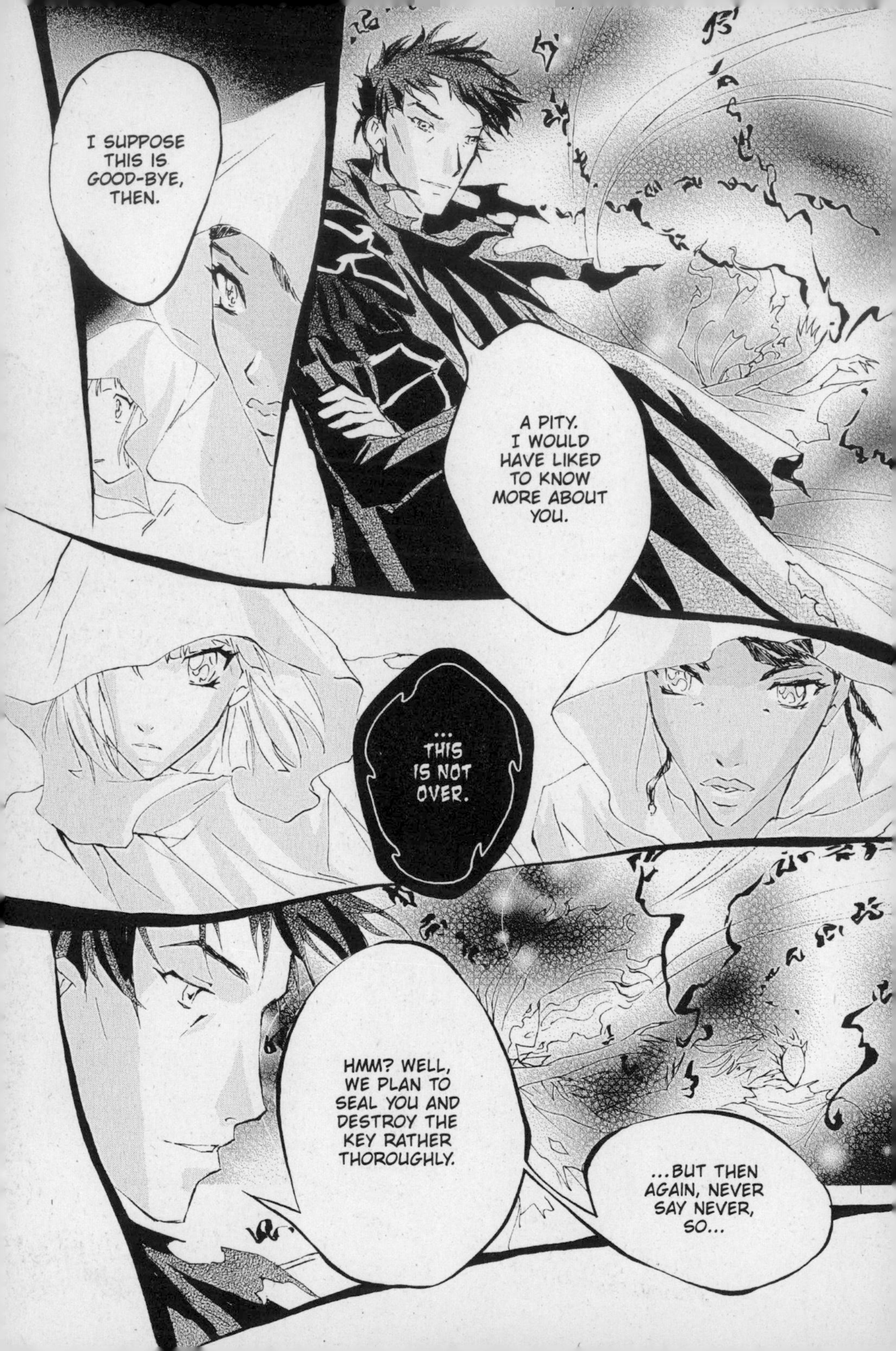
I SUPPOSE THIS IS GOOD-BYE, THEN.
A PITY. I WOULD HAVE LIKED TO KNOW MORE ABOUT YOU.
... THIS IS NOT OVER.
HMM? WELL, WE PLAN TO SEAL YOU AND DESTROY THE KEY RATHER THOROUGHLY.
...BUT THEN AGAIN, NEVER SAY NEVER, SO...

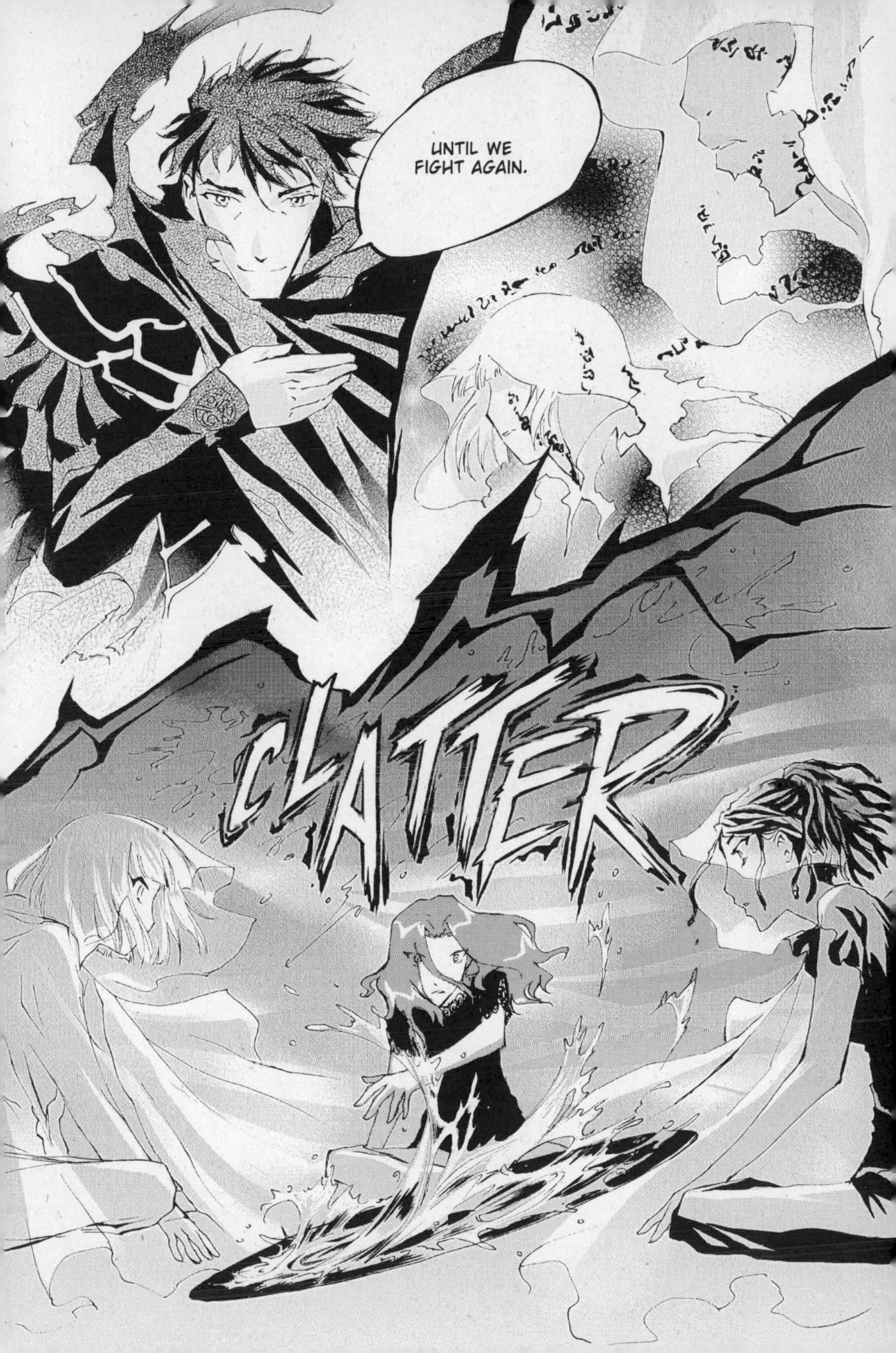
UNTIL WE FIGHT AGAIN.
CLATTER

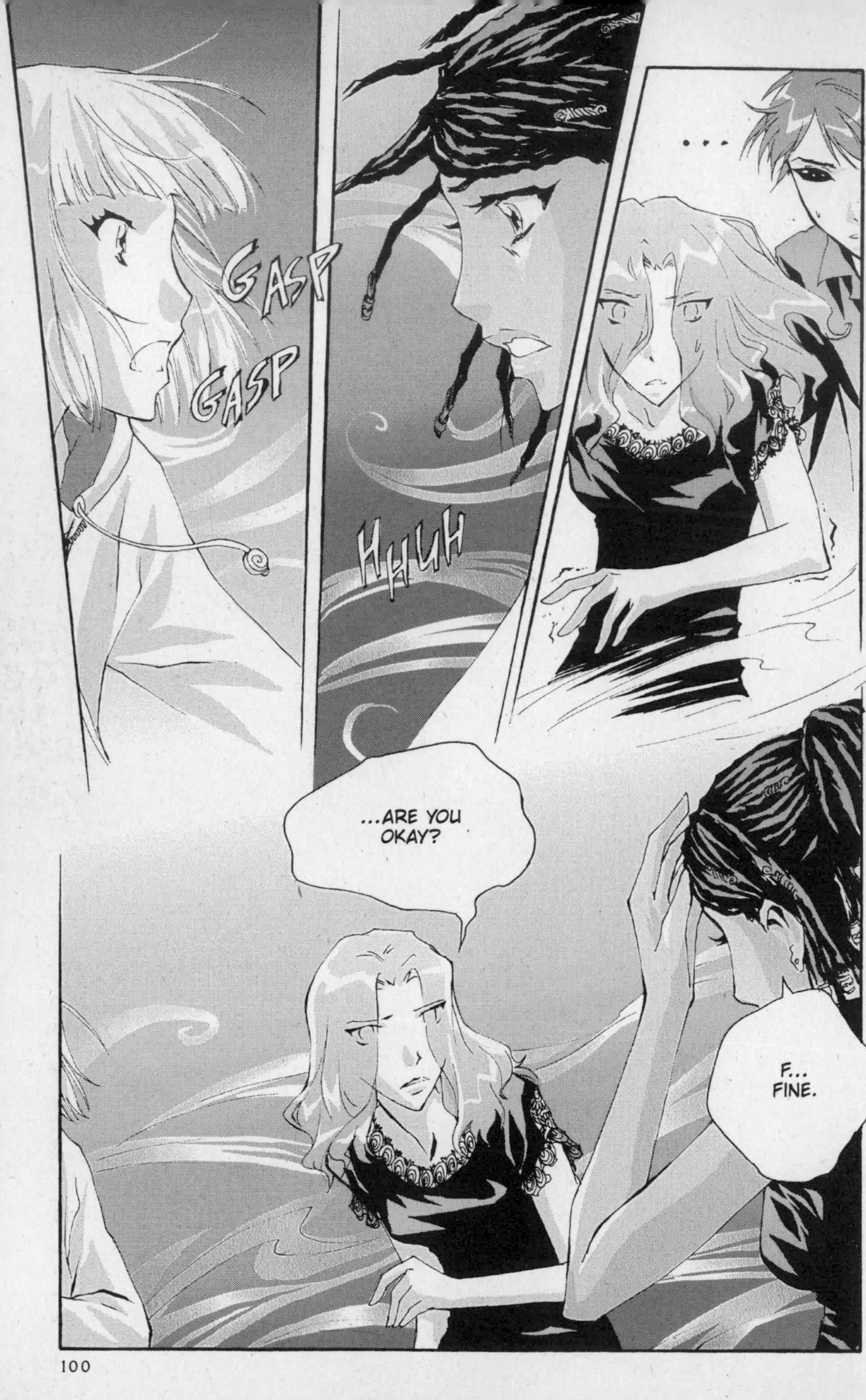
GASP
GASP
HHUH
...
...ARE YOU OKAY?
F... FINE.

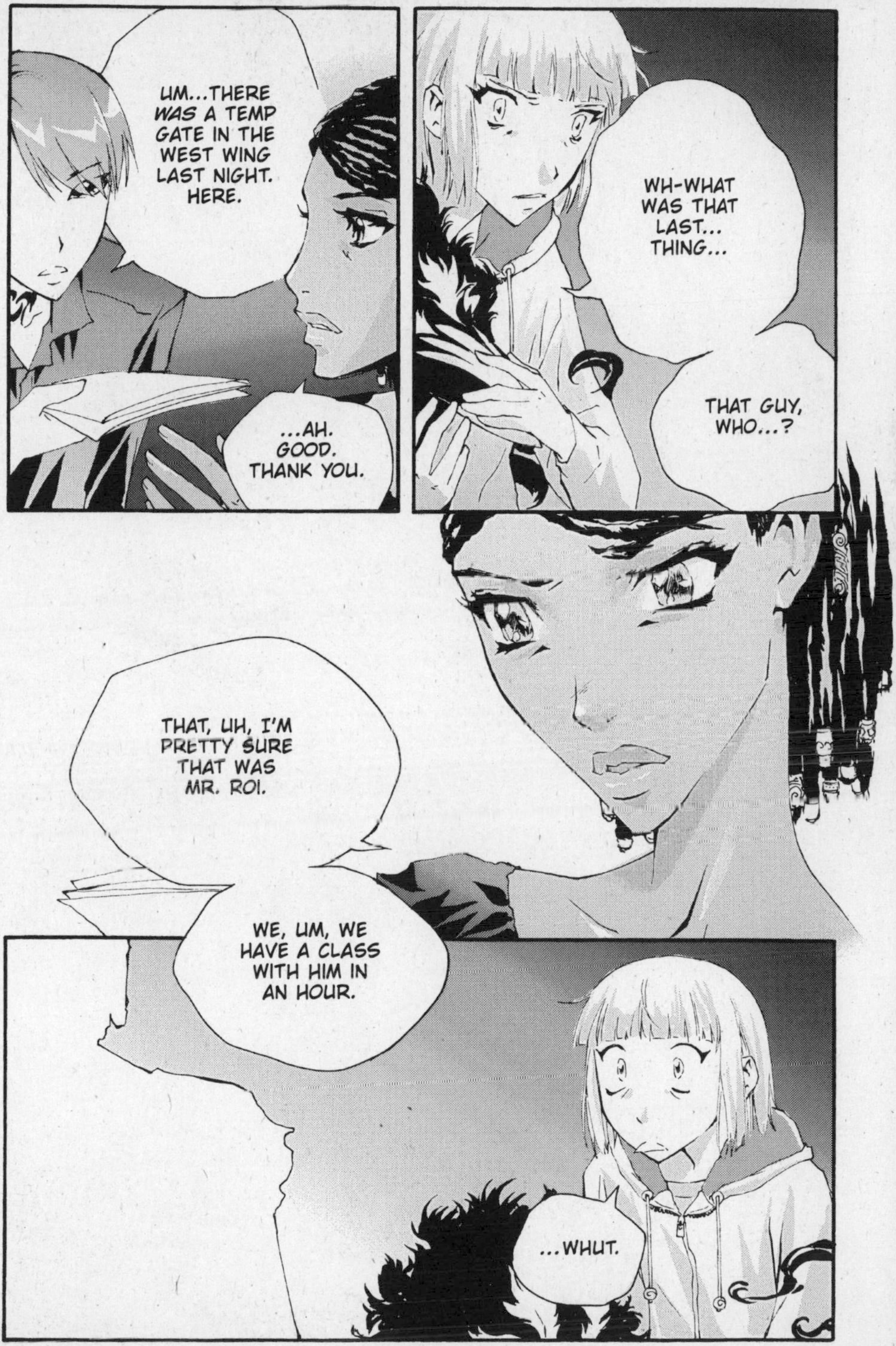
UM...THERE WAS A TEMP GATE IN THE WEST WING LAST NIGHT. HERE.
...AH. GOOD. THANK YOU.
WH-WHAT WAS THAT LAST... THING...
THAT GUY, WHO...?
THAT, UH, I'M PRETTY SURE THAT WAS MR. ROI.
WE, UM, WE HAVE A CLASS WITH HIM IN AN HOUR.
...WHUT.

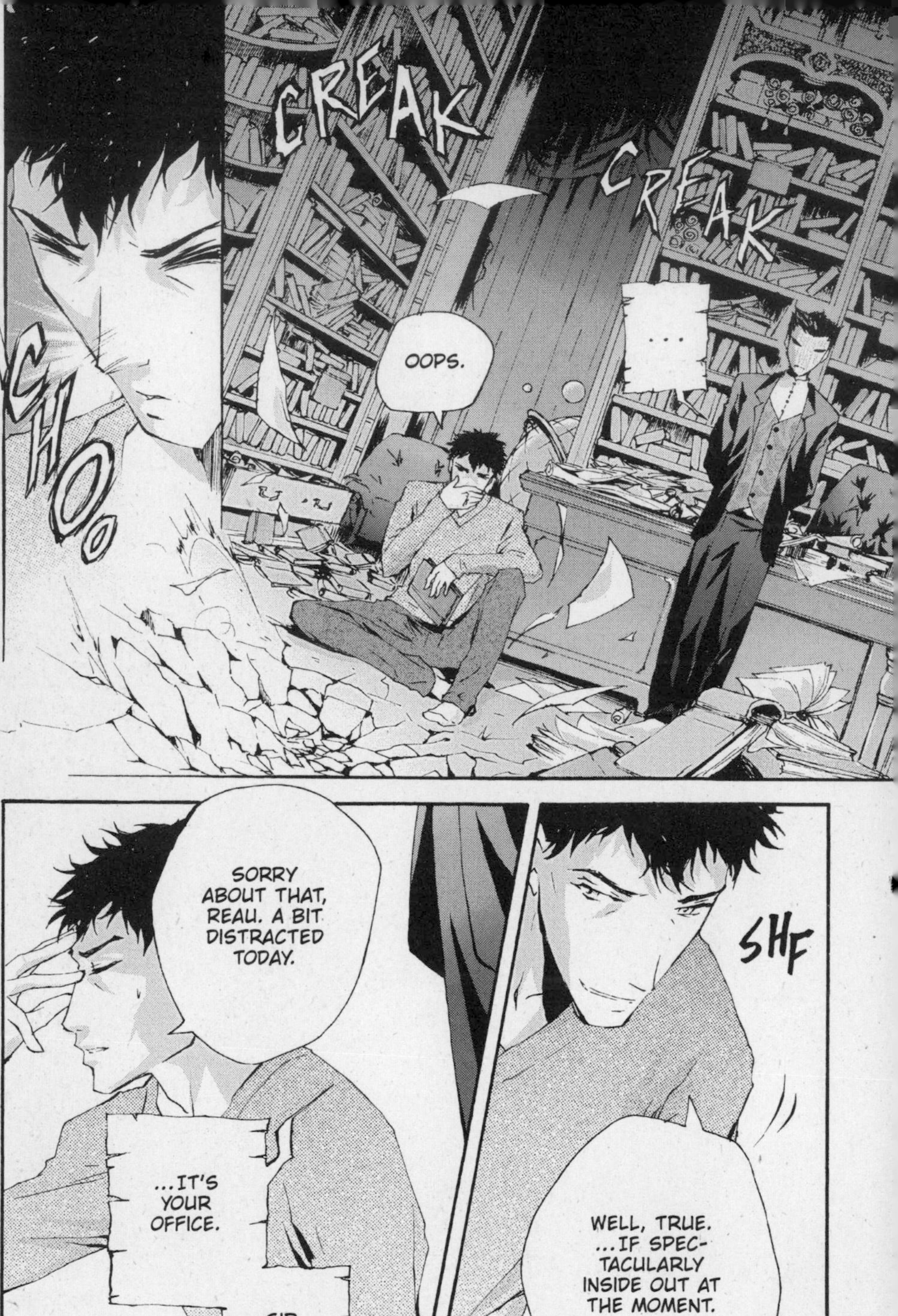
ACHOO
CREAK
CREAK
OOPS.
. . .
SORRY ABOUT THAT, REAU. A BIT DISTRACTED TODAY.
...IT'S YOUR OFFICE.
SIR.
SHF
WELL, TRUE. ...IF SPEC-TACULARLY INSIDE OUT AT THE MOMENT.

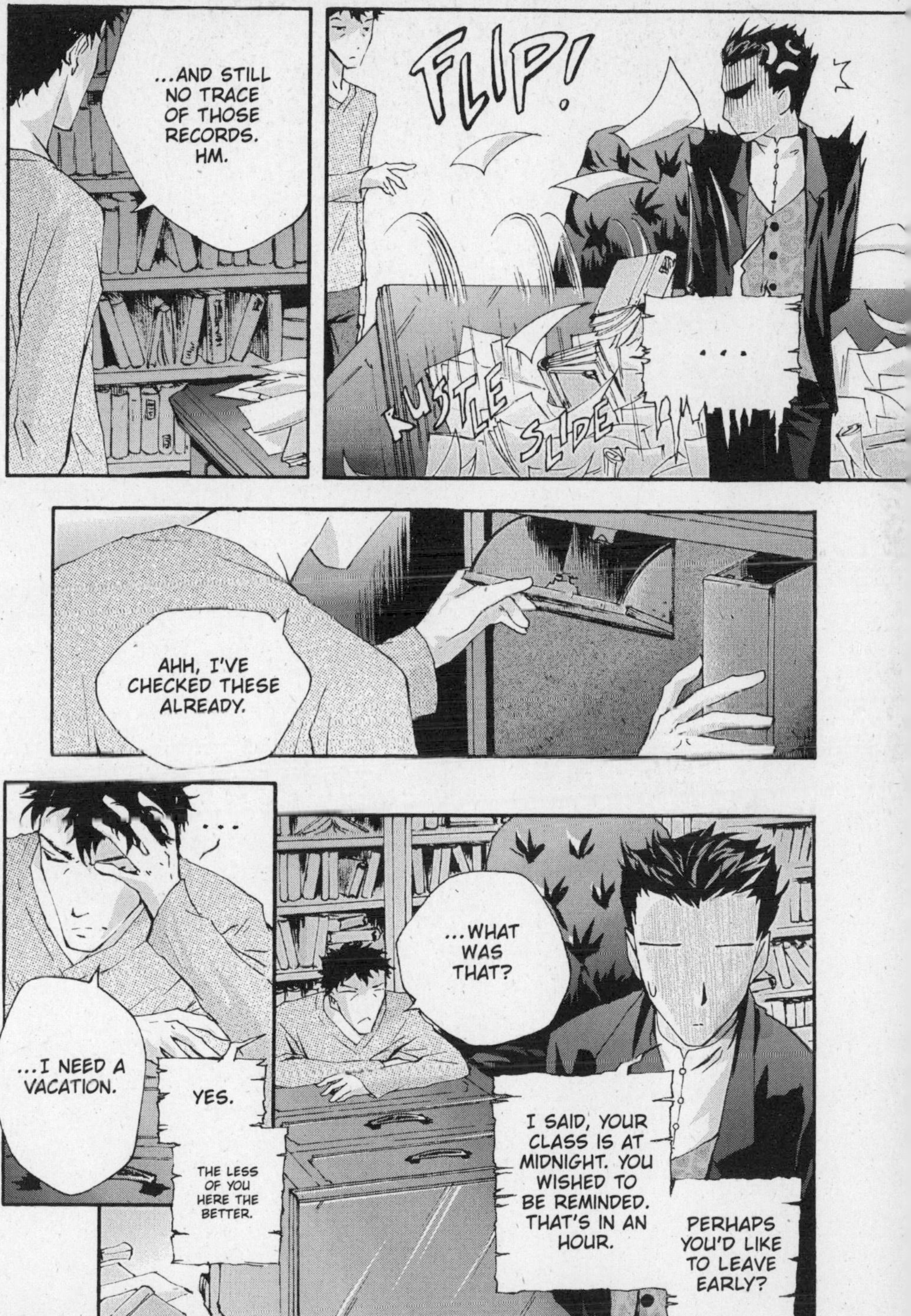
...AND STILL NO TRACE OF THOSE RECORDS. HM.
FLIP!
...
RUSTLE
SLIDE
AHH, I'VE CHECKED THESE ALREADY.
...
...I NEED A VACATION.
YES.
THE LESS OF YOU HERE THE BETTER.
...WHAT WAS THAT?
I SAID, YOUR CLASS IS AT MIDNIGHT. YOU WISHED TO BE REMINDED. THAT'S IN AN HOUR.
PERHAPS YOU'D LIKE TO LEAVE EARLY?

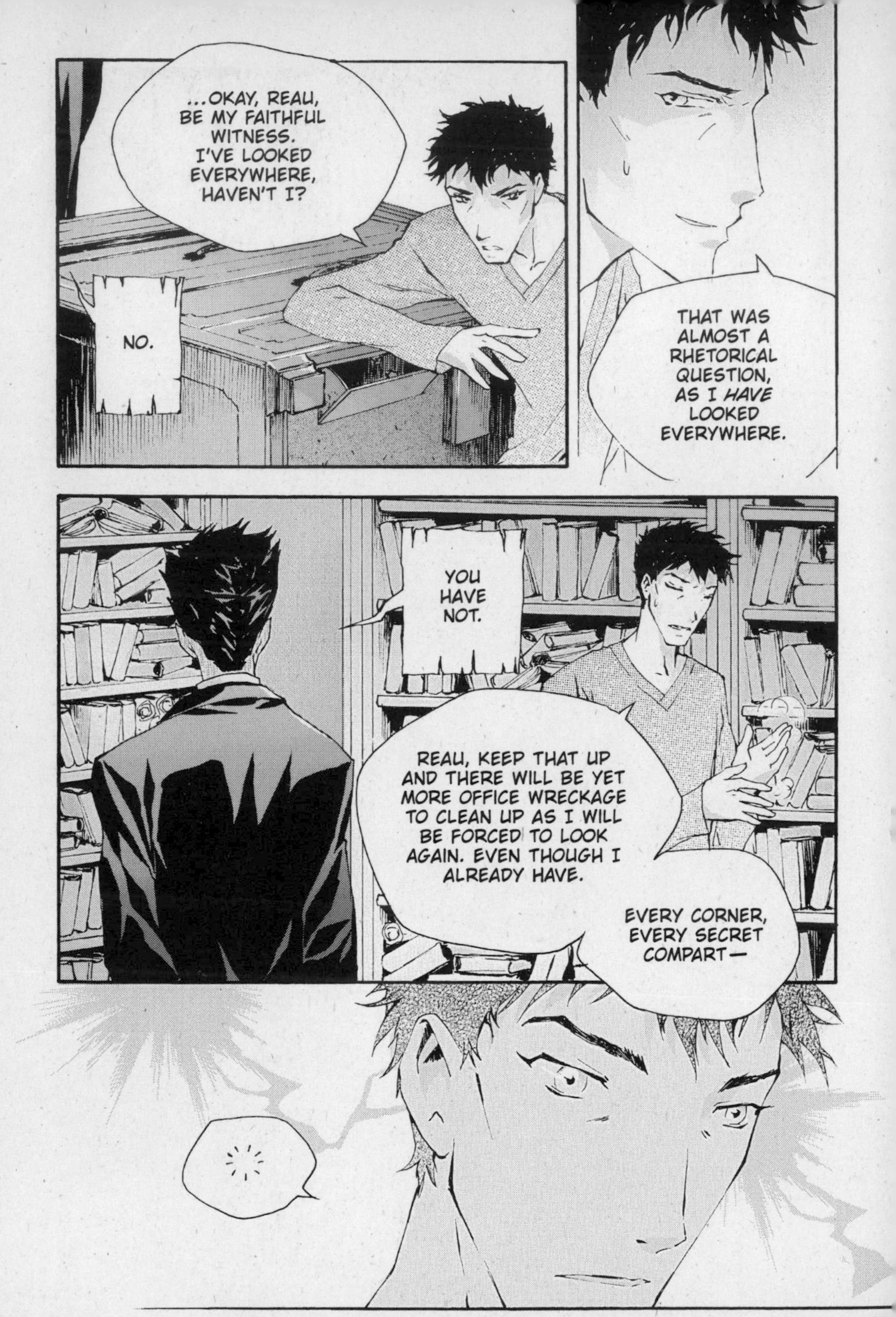
...OKAY, REAU, BE MY FAITHFUL WITNESS. I'VE LOOKED EVERYWHERE, HAVEN'T I?
NO.
THAT WAS ALMOST A RHETORICAL QUESTION, AS I *HAVE* LOOKED EVERYWHERE.
YOU HAVE NOT.
REAU, KEEP THAT UP AND THERE WILL BE YET MORE OFFICE WRECKAGE TO CLEAN UP AS I WILL BE FORCED TO LOOK AGAIN. EVEN THOUGH I ALREADY HAVE.
EVERY CORNER, EVERY SECRET COMPART—

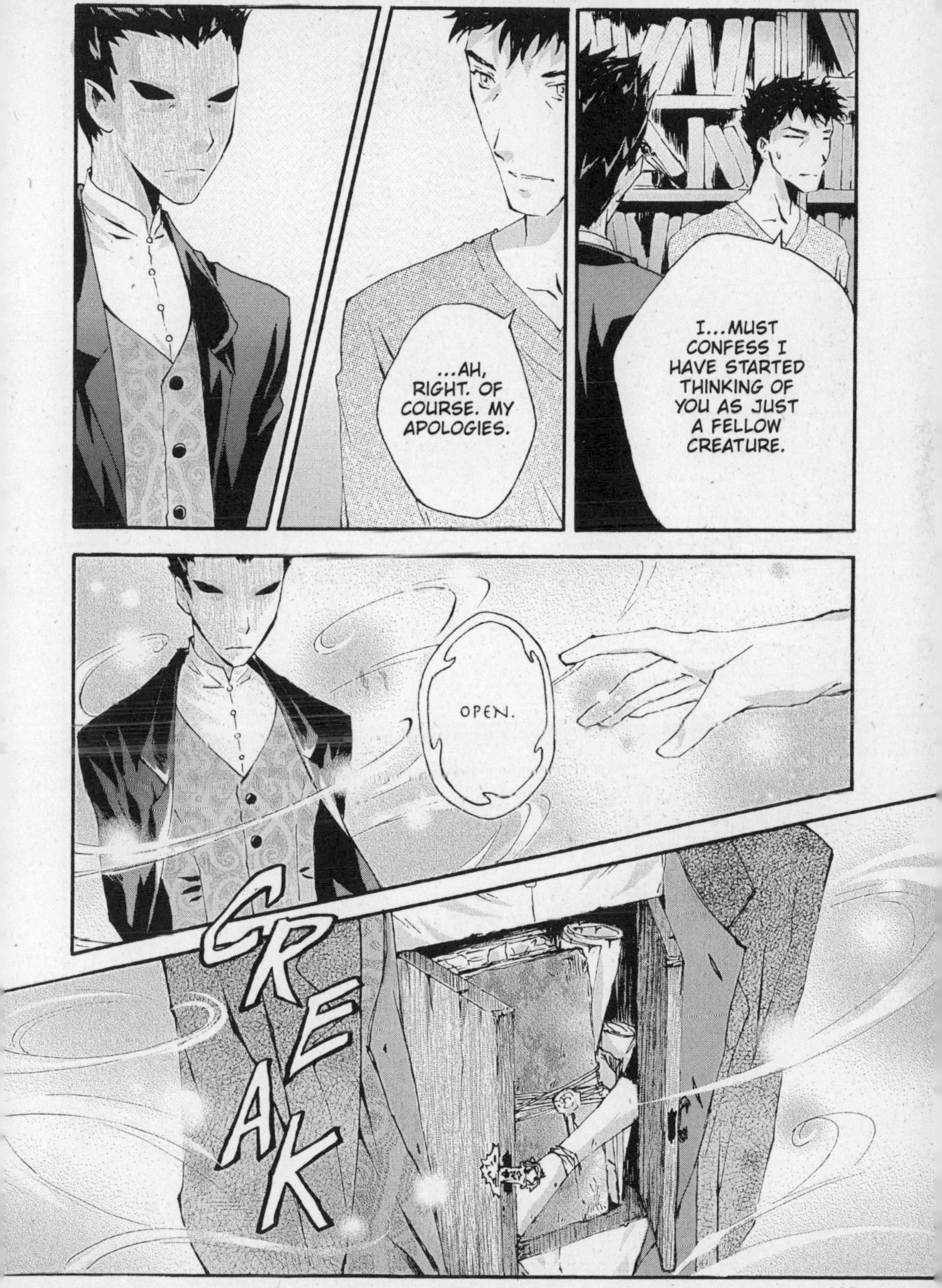
...AH, RIGHT. OF COURSE. MY APOLOGIES.
I...MUST CONFESS I HAVE STARTED THINKING OF YOU AS JUST A FELLOW CREATURE.
OPEN.
CREAK

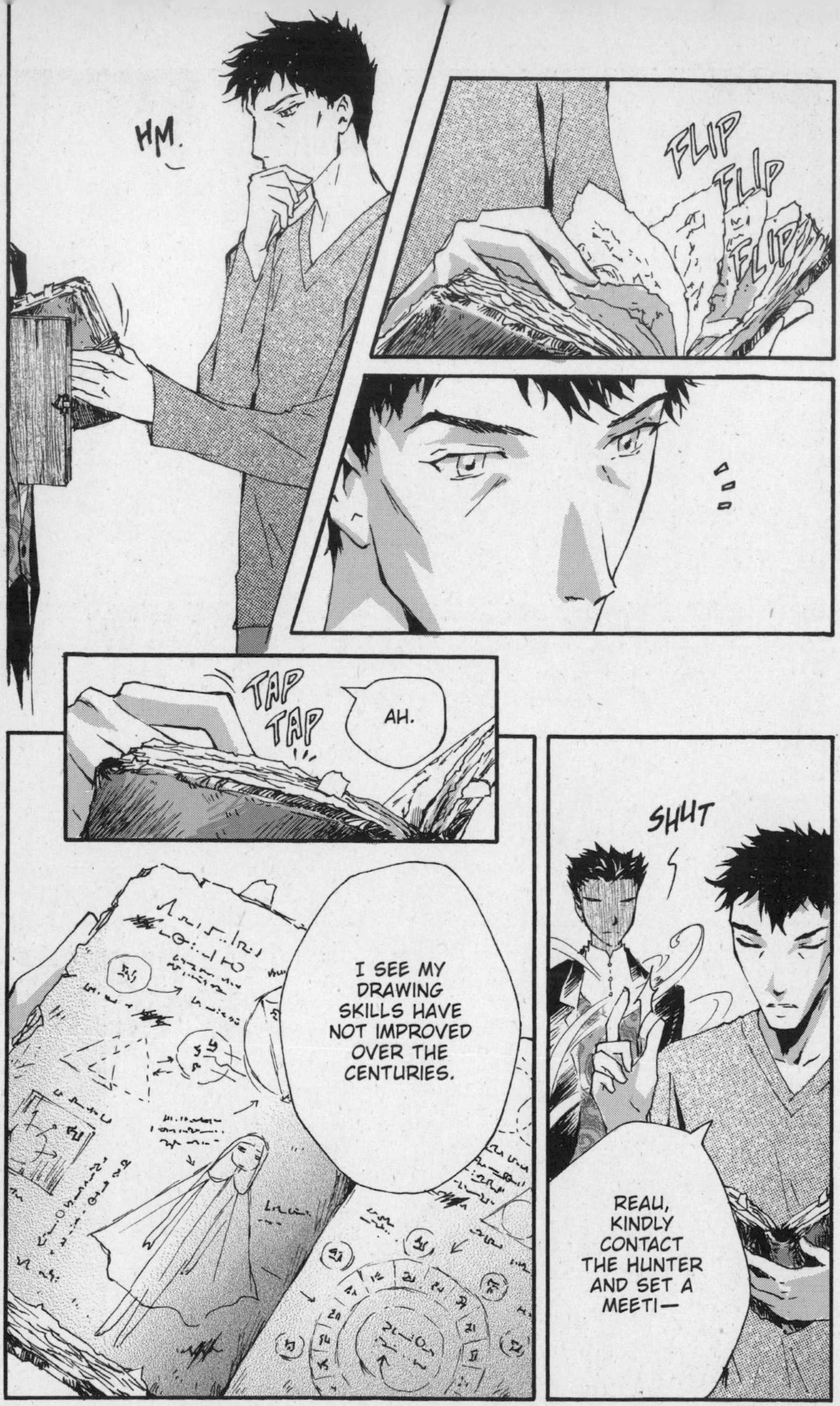

HM.
FLIP FLIP FLIP
TAP TAP
AH.
I SEE MY DRAWING SKILLS HAVE NOT IMPROVED OVER THE CENTURIES.
SHUT
REAU, KINDLY CONTACT THE HUNTER AND SET A MEETI—

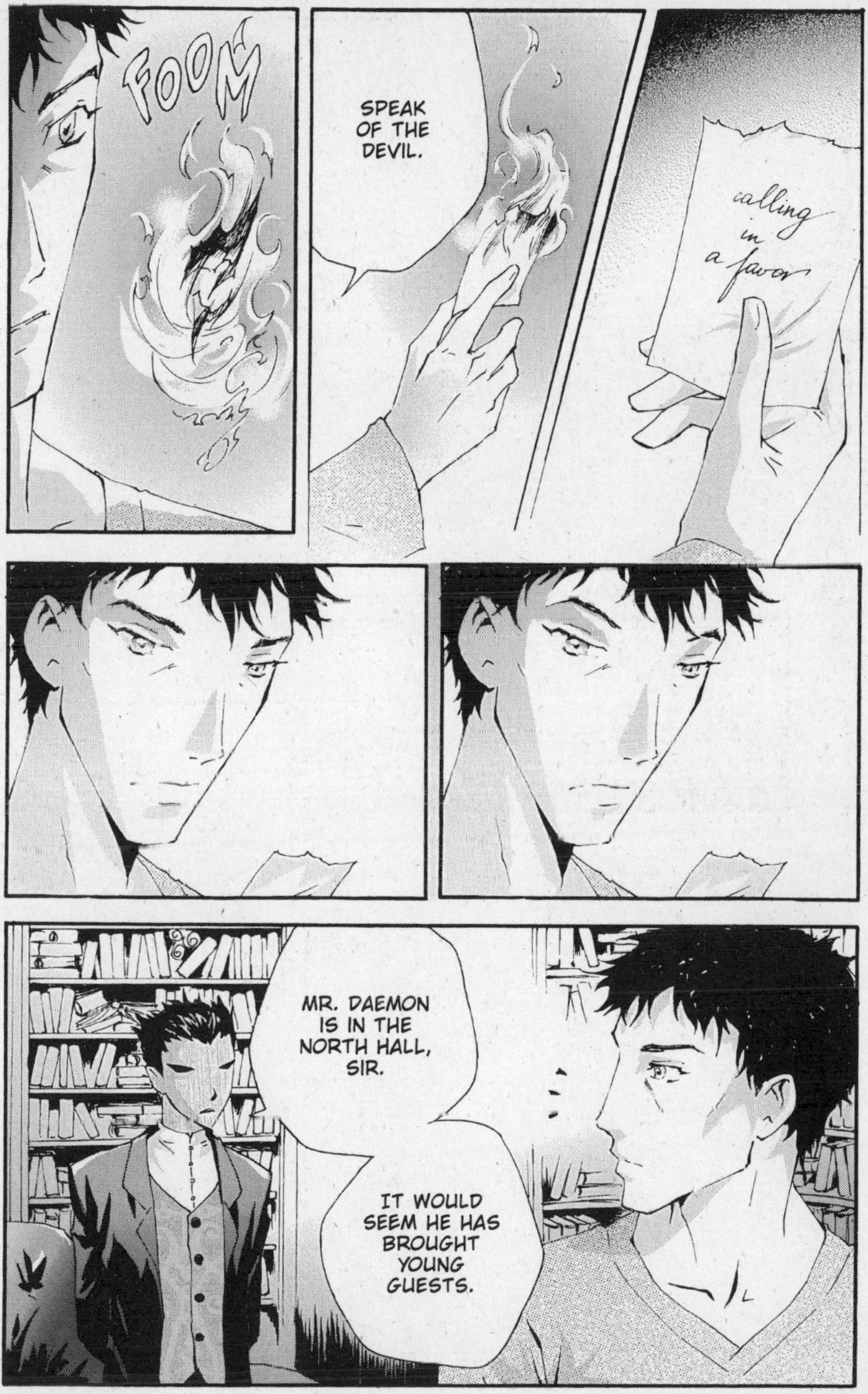
FOOM
SPEAK OF THE DEVIL.
calling in a favor
MR. DAEMON IS IN THE NORTH HALL, SIR.
IT WOULD SEEM HE HAS BROUGHT YOUNG GUESTS.

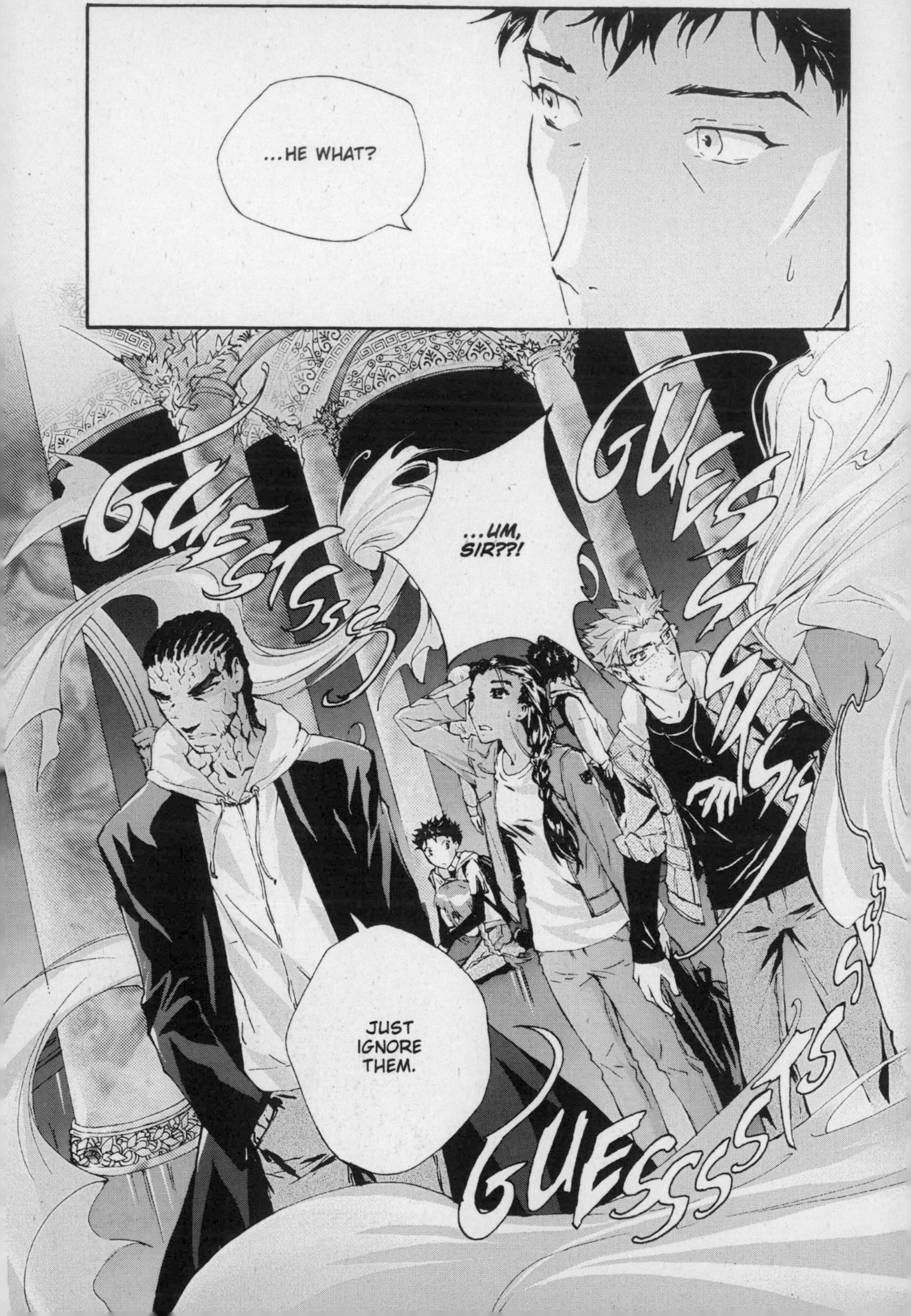
...HE WHAT?
...UM, SIR??!
JUST IGNORE THEM.
GUESSSSTS

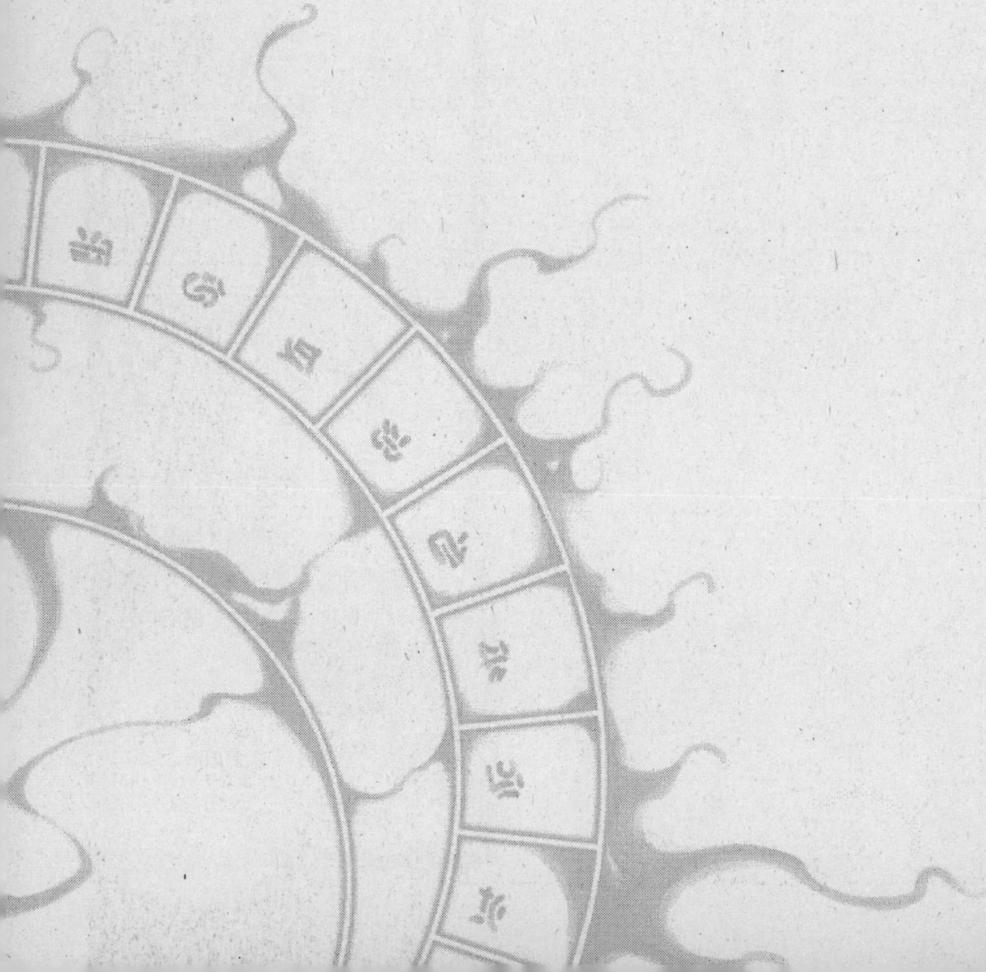

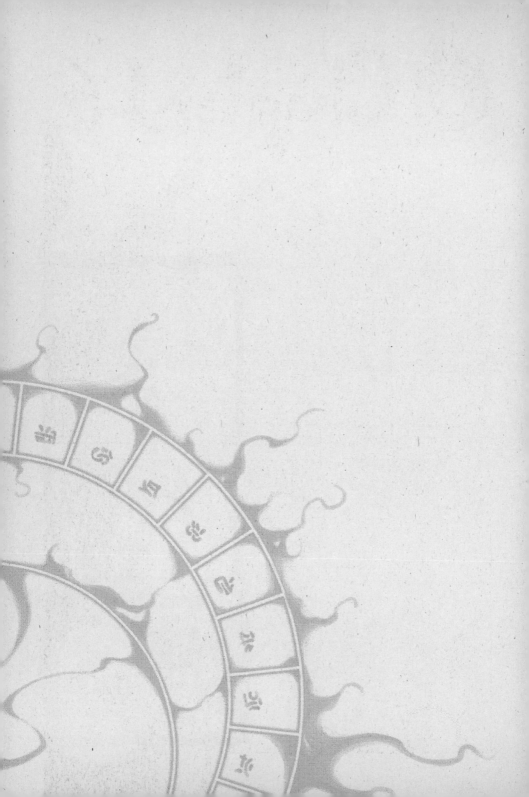

Chapter 16

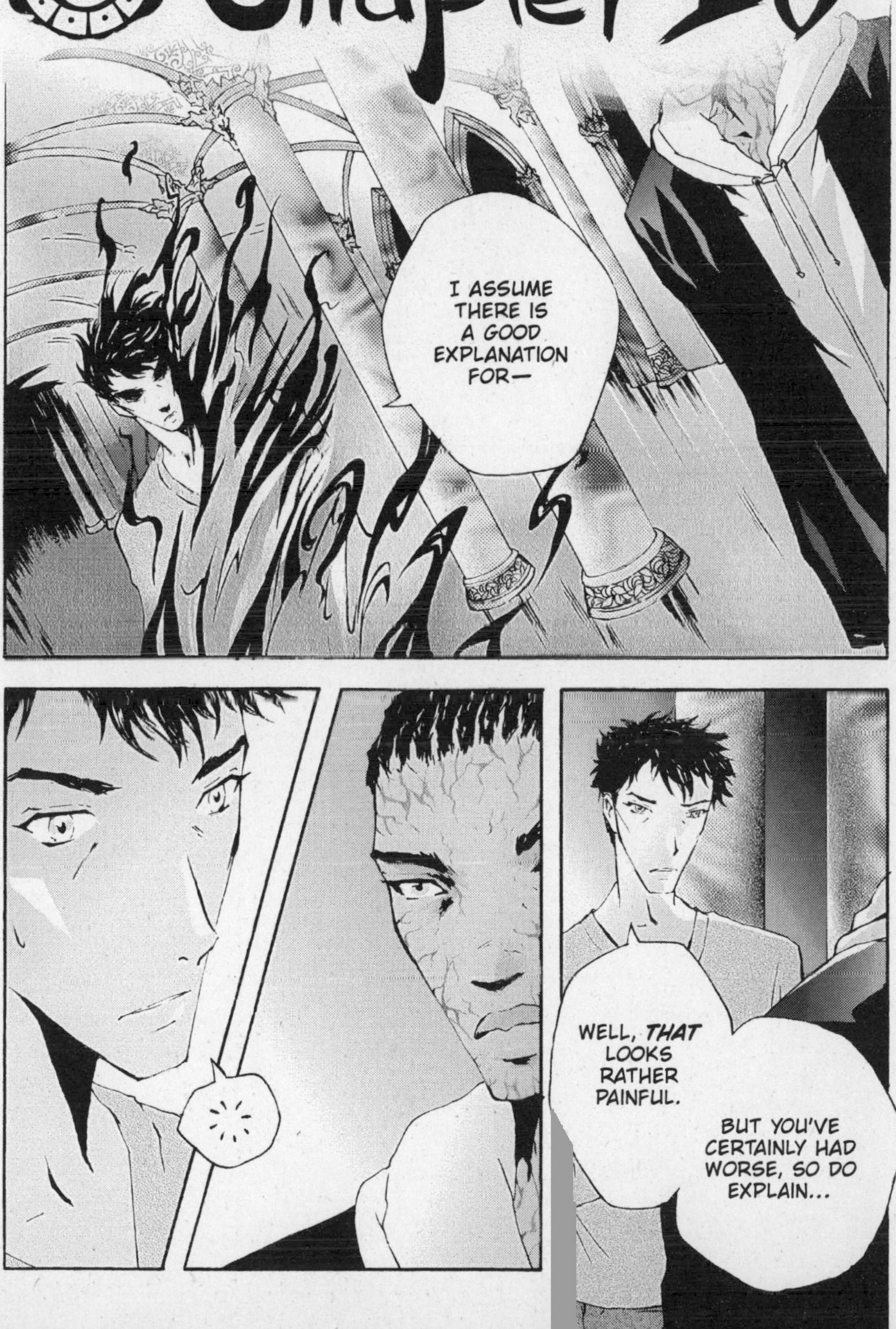
I ASSUME THERE IS A GOOD EXPLANATION FOR—
WELL, *THAT* LOOKS RATHER PAINFUL.
BUT YOU'VE CERTAINLY HAD WORSE, SO DO EXPLAIN...

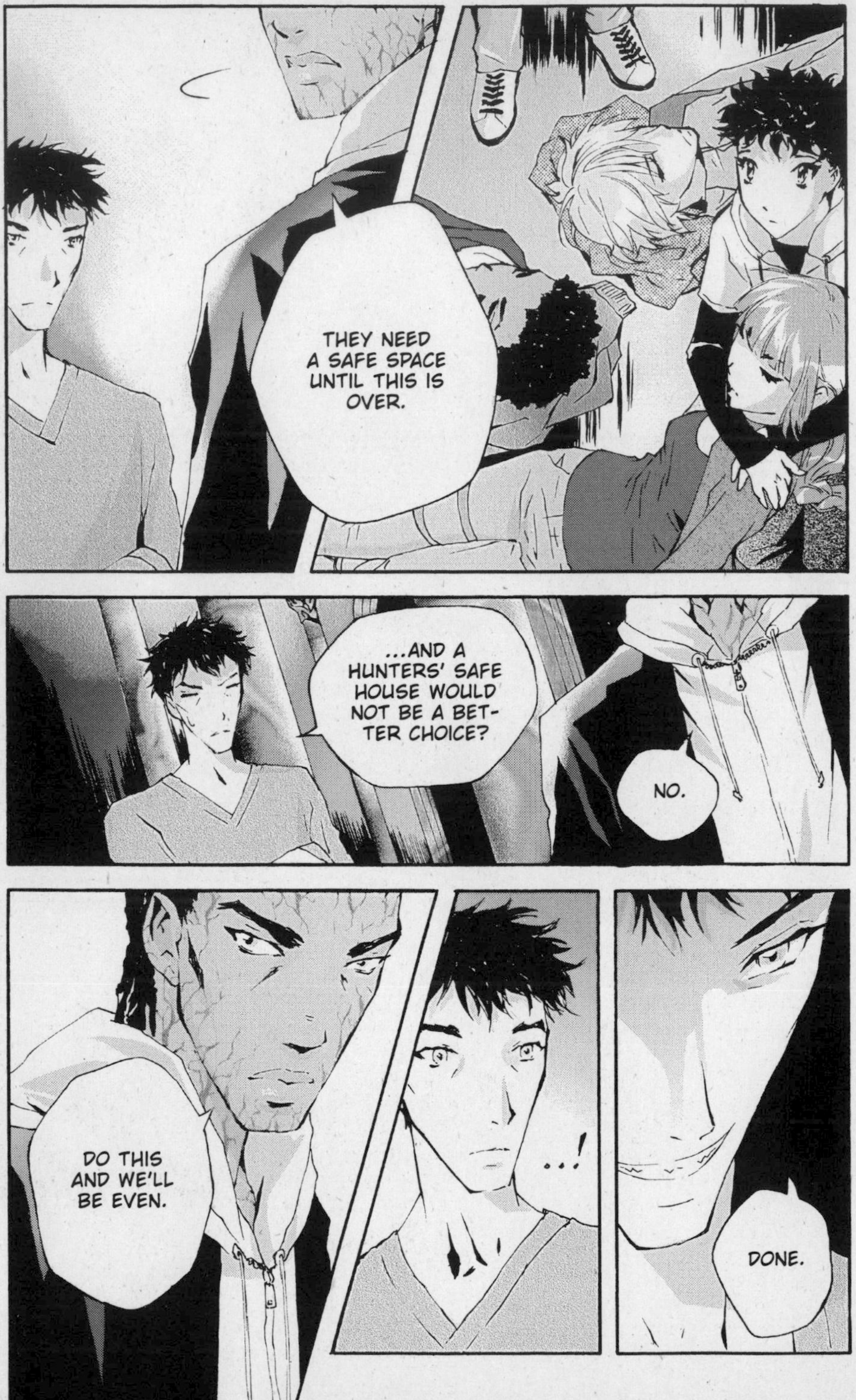
THEY NEED A SAFE SPACE UNTIL THIS IS OVER.
...AND A HUNTERS' SAFE HOUSE WOULD NOT BE A BET-TER CHOICE?
NO.
DO THIS AND WE'LL BE EVEN.
...!
DONE.

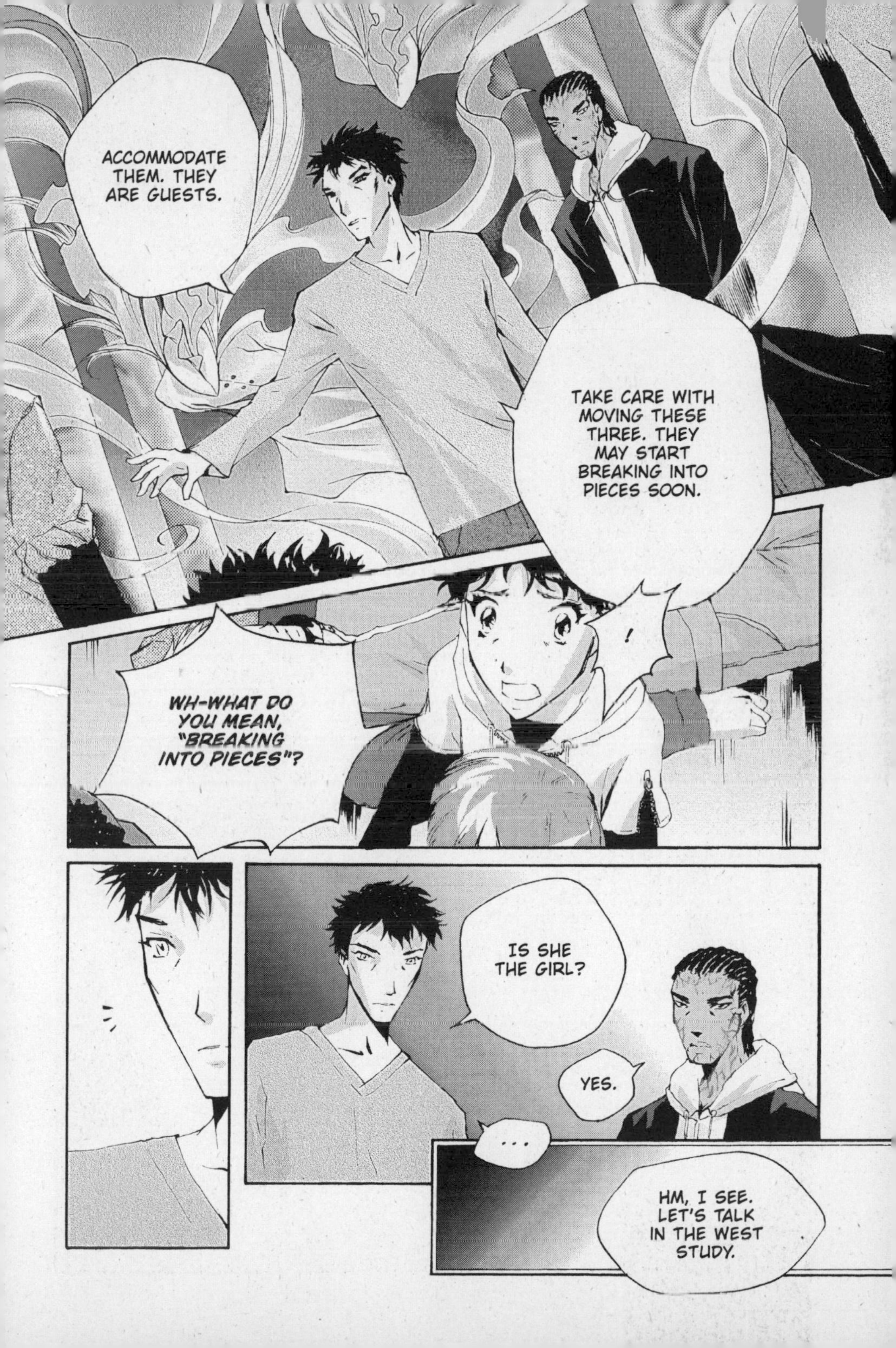
ACCOMMODATE THEM. THEY ARE GUESTS.
TAKE CARE WITH MOVING THESE THREE. THEY MAY START BREAKING INTO PIECES SOON.
!
WH-WHAT DO YOU MEAN, "BREAKING INTO PIECES"?
IS SHE THE GIRL?
YES.
...
HM, I SEE. LET'S TALK IN THE WEST STUDY.

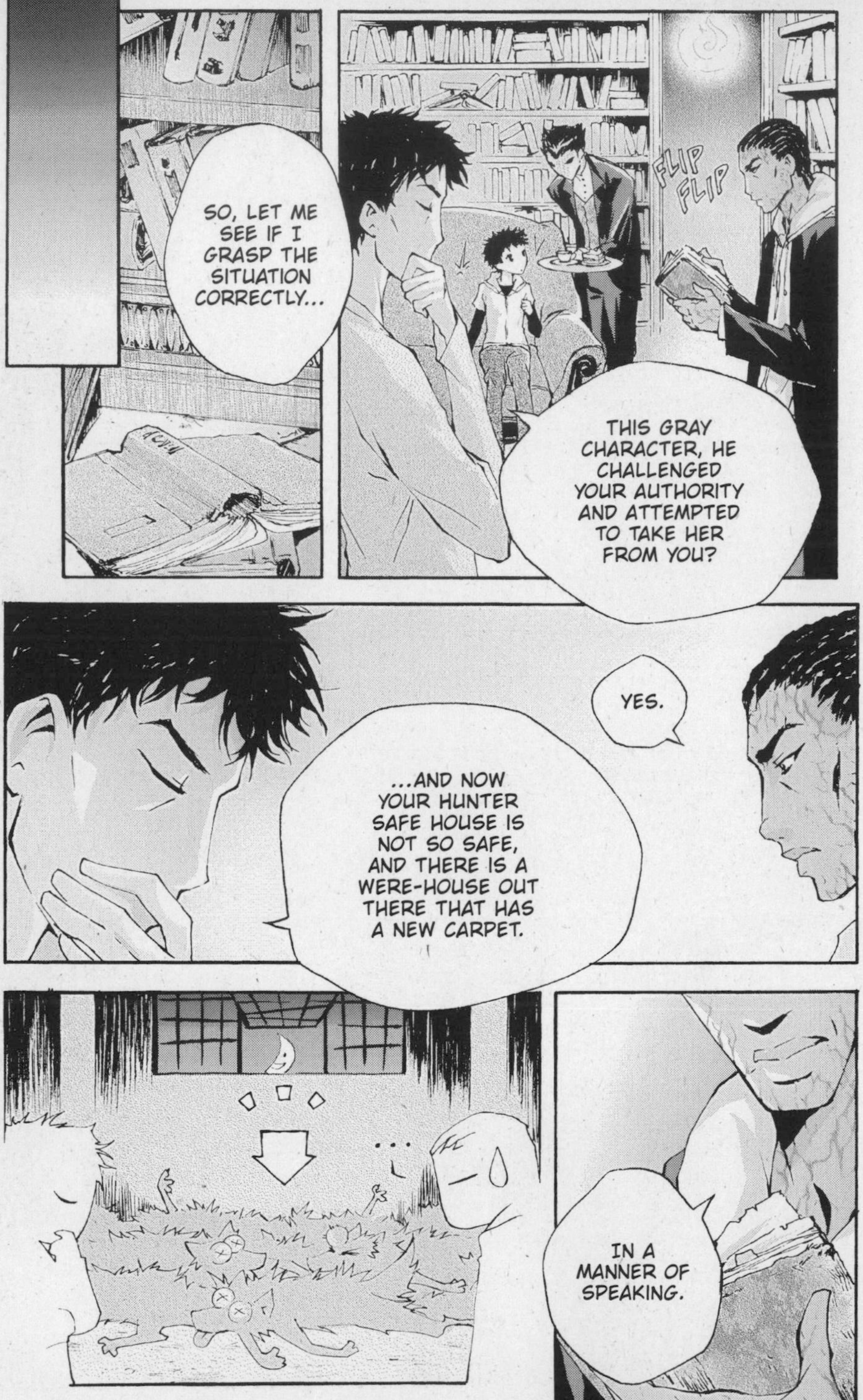
SO, LET ME SEE IF I GRASP THE SITUATION CORRECTLY...
FLIP FLIP
THIS GRAY CHARACTER, HE CHALLENGED YOUR AUTHORITY AND ATTEMPTED TO TAKE HER FROM YOU?
YES.
...AND NOW YOUR HUNTER SAFE HOUSE IS NOT SO SAFE, AND THERE IS A WERE-HOUSE OUT THERE THAT HAS A NEW CARPET.
...
IN A MANNER OF SPEAKING.

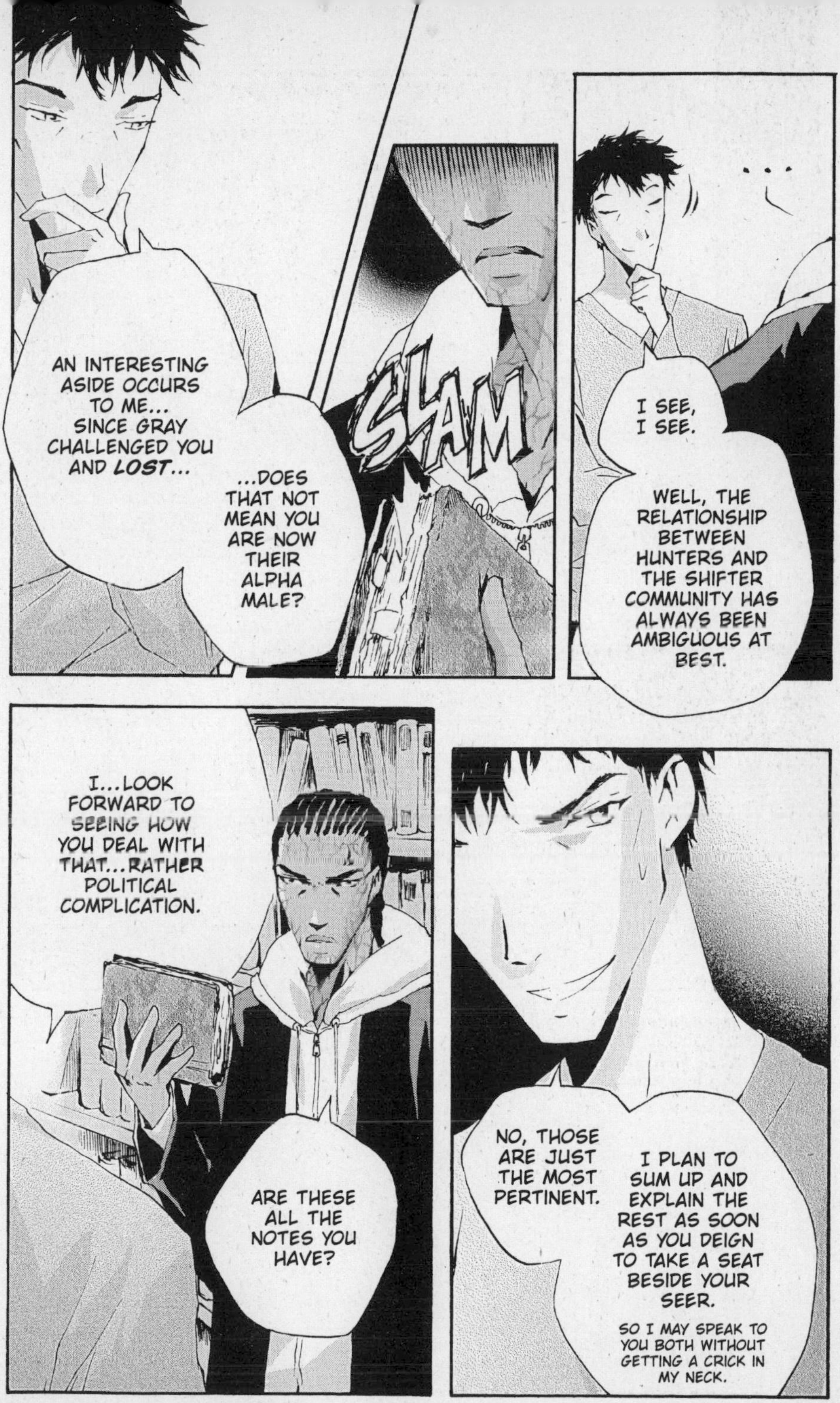
AN INTERESTING ASIDE OCCURS TO ME... SINCE GRAY CHALLENGED YOU AND LOST...
...DOES THAT NOT MEAN YOU ARE NOW THEIR ALPHA MALE?
SLAM
...
I SEE, I SEE.
WELL, THE RELATIONSHIP BETWEEN HUNTERS AND THE SHIFTER COMMUNITY HAS ALWAYS BEEN AMBIGUOUS AT BEST.
I...LOOK FORWARD TO SEEING HOW YOU DEAL WITH THAT...RATHER POLITICAL COMPLICATION.
ARE THESE ALL THE NOTES YOU HAVE?
NO, THOSE ARE JUST THE MOST PERTINENT.
I PLAN TO SUM UP AND EXPLAIN THE REST AS SOON AS YOU DEIGN TO TAKE A SEAT BESIDE YOUR SEER.
SO I MAY SPEAK TO YOU BOTH WITHOUT GETTING A CRICK IN MY NECK.

EVER THE WARY HUNTER.

MAY I REMIND— YOU HAVE BEEN WELCOMED AS GUESTS INTO MY HOME, AND THERE ARE RULES ABOUT THAT.

CHEW CHEW

DO SIT. YOU LOOK LIKE YOU HAVEN'T SLEPT IN A YEAR.

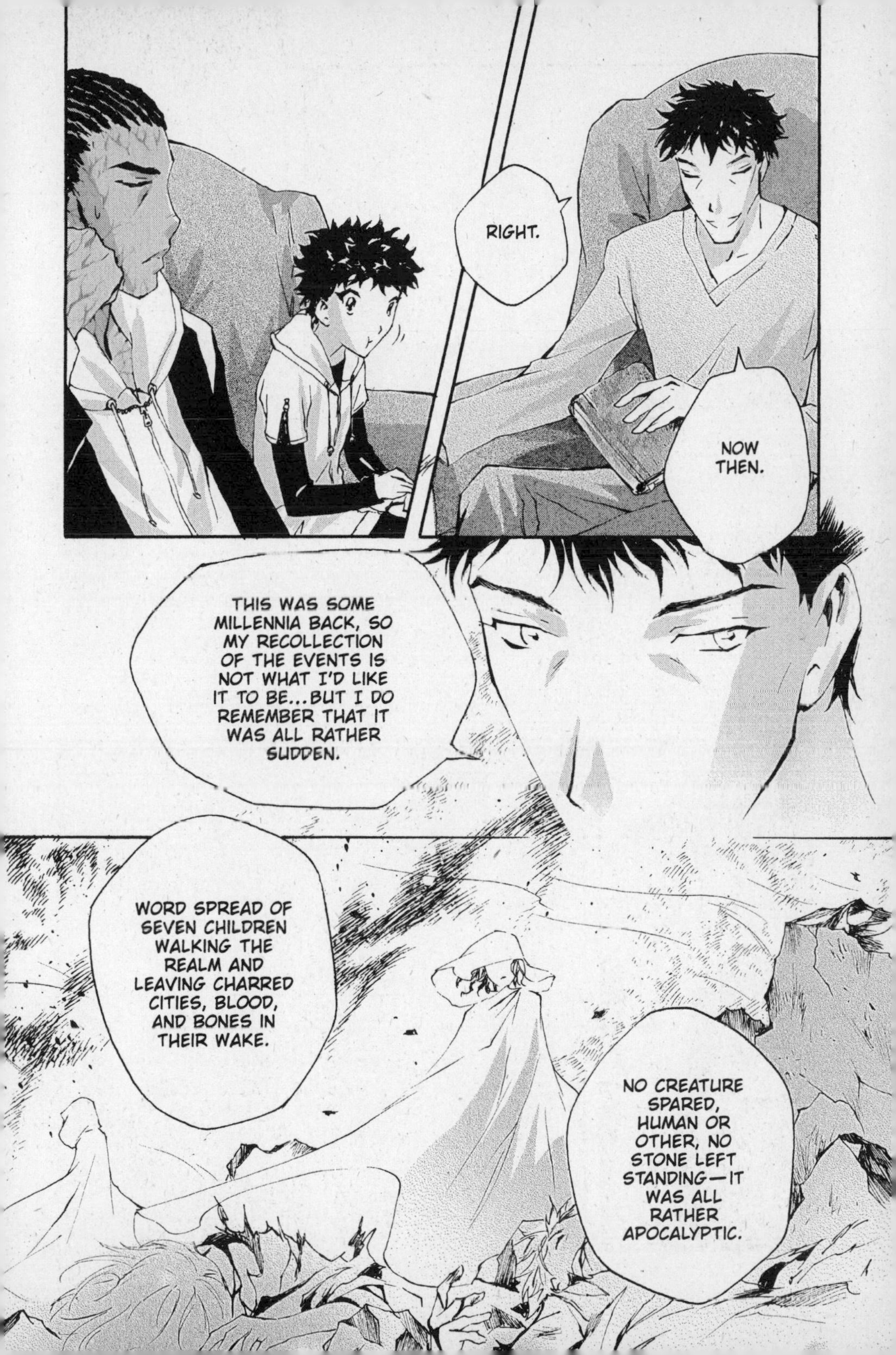
RIGHT.
NOW THEN.
THIS WAS SOME MILLENNIA BACK, SO MY RECOLLECTION OF THE EVENTS IS NOT WHAT I'D LIKE IT TO BE...BUT I DO REMEMBER THAT IT WAS ALL RATHER SUDDEN.
WORD SPREAD OF SEVEN CHILDREN WALKING THE REALM AND LEAVING CHARRED CITIES, BLOOD, AND BONES IN THEIR WAKE.
NO CREATURE SPARED, HUMAN OR OTHER, NO STONE LEFT STANDING—IT WAS ALL RATHER APOCALYPTIC.

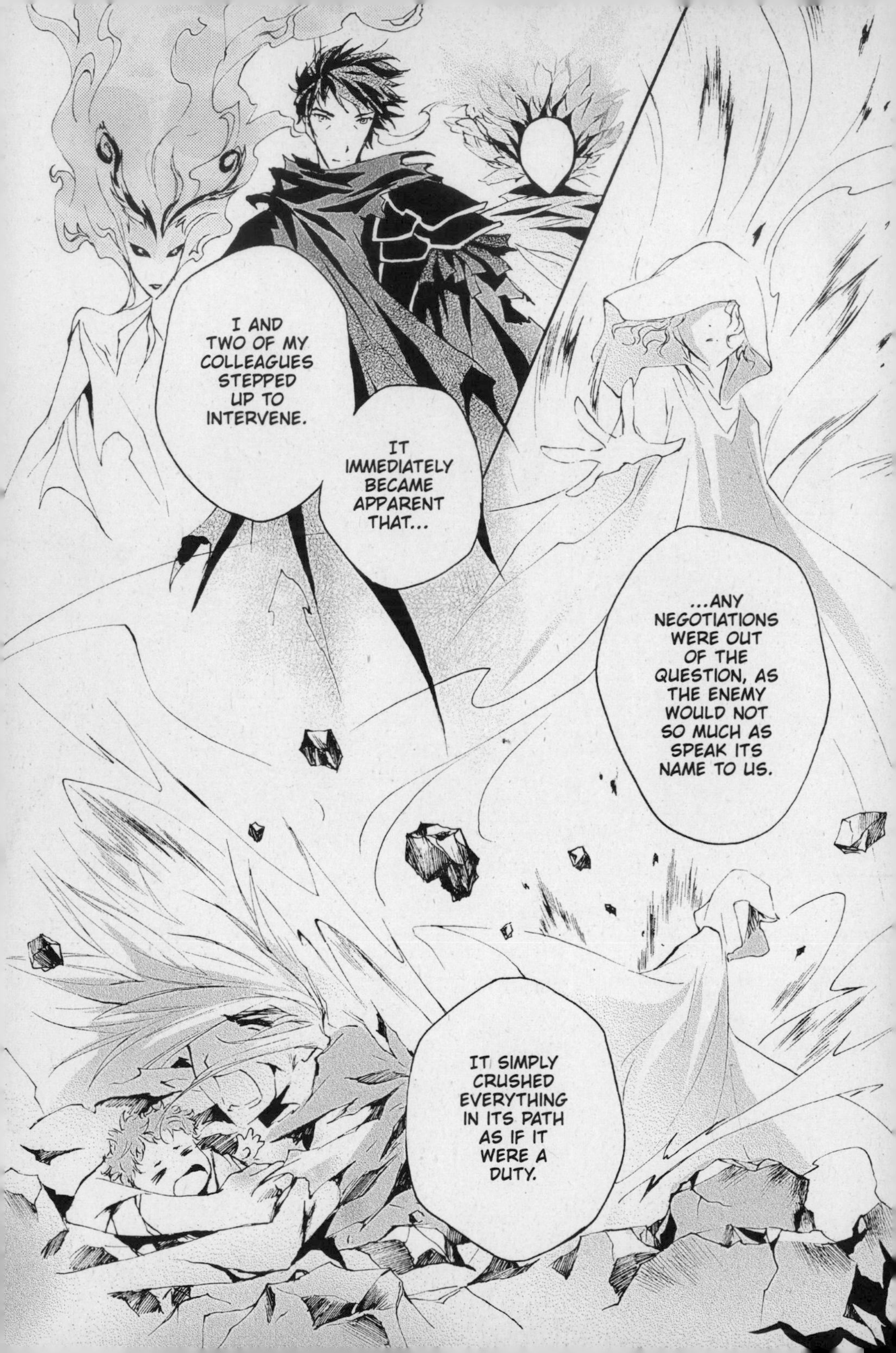
I AND TWO OF MY COLLEAGUES STEPPED UP TO INTERVENE.
IT IMMEDIATELY BECAME APPARENT THAT...
...ANY NEGOTIATIONS WERE OUT OF THE QUESTION, AS THE ENEMY WOULD NOT SO MUCH AS SPEAK ITS NAME TO US.
IT SIMPLY CRUSHED EVERYTHING IN ITS PATH AS IF IT WERE A DUTY.

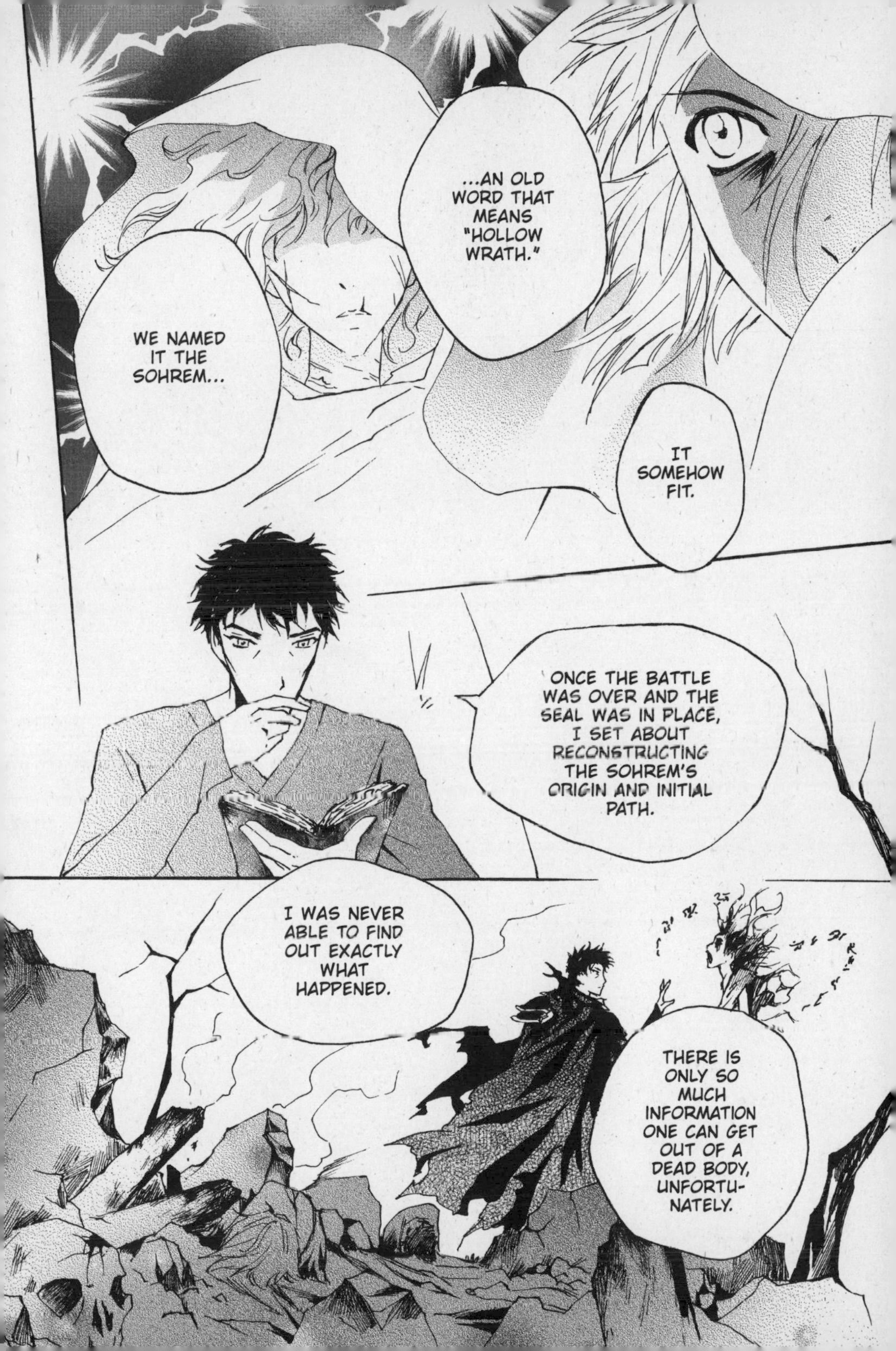
WE NAMED IT THE SOHREM...
...AN OLD WORD THAT MEANS "HOLLOW WRATH."
IT SOMEHOW FIT.
ONCE THE BATTLE WAS OVER AND THE SEAL WAS IN PLACE, I SET ABOUT RECONSTRUCTING THE SOHREM'S ORIGIN AND INITIAL PATH.
I WAS NEVER ABLE TO FIND OUT EXACTLY WHAT HAPPENED.
THERE IS ONLY SO MUCH INFORMATION ONE CAN GET OUT OF A DEAD BODY, UNFORTUNATELY.

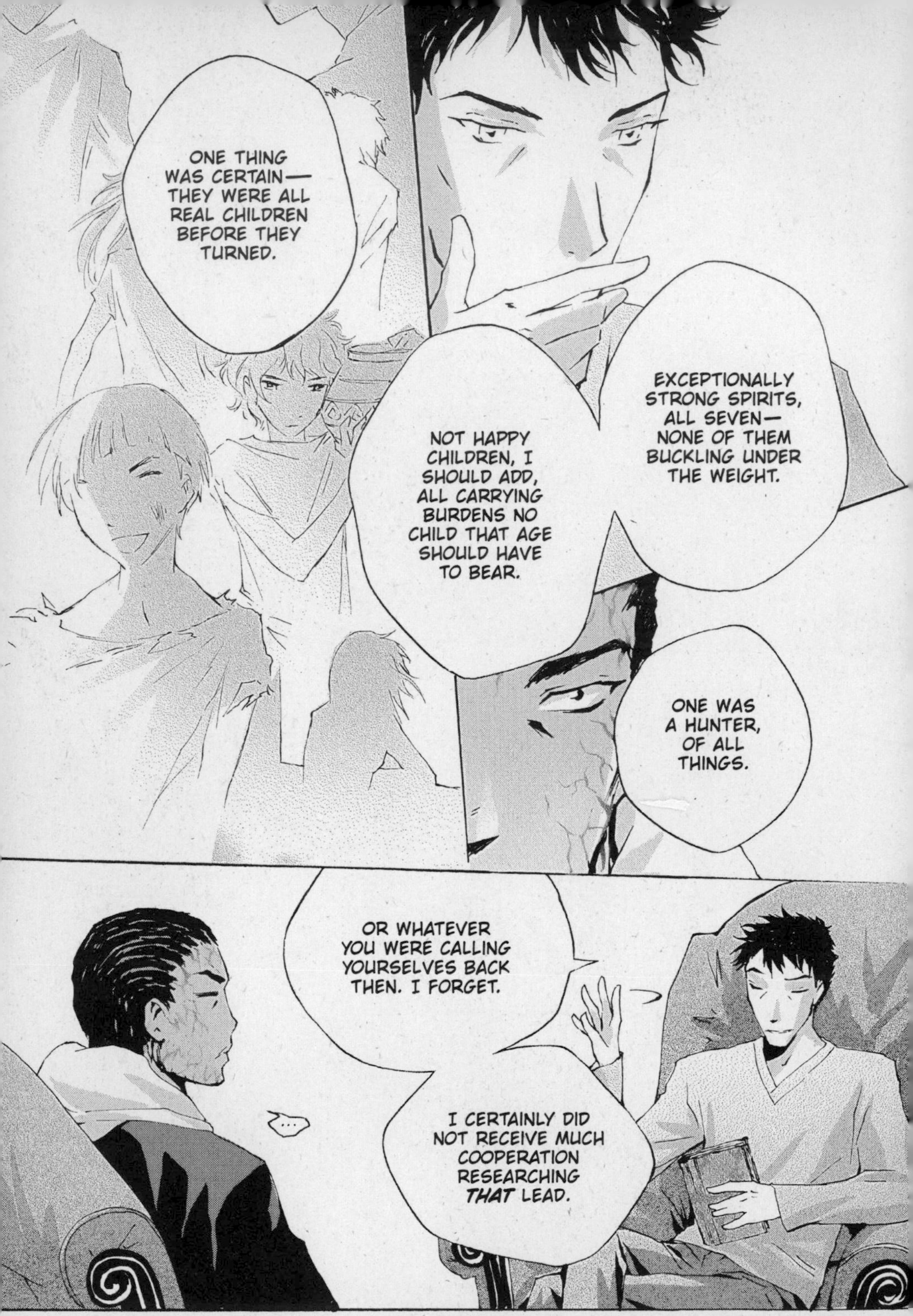

ONE THING WAS CERTAIN—THEY WERE ALL REAL CHILDREN BEFORE THEY TURNED.
NOT HAPPY CHILDREN, I SHOULD ADD, ALL CARRYING BURDENS NO CHILD THAT AGE SHOULD HAVE TO BEAR.
EXCEPTIONALLY STRONG SPIRITS, ALL SEVEN—NONE OF THEM BUCKLING UNDER THE WEIGHT.
ONE WAS A HUNTER, OF ALL THINGS.
OR WHATEVER YOU WERE CALLING YOURSELVES BACK THEN. I FORGET.
...
I CERTAINLY DID NOT RECEIVE MUCH COOPERATION RESEARCHING *THAT* LEAD.

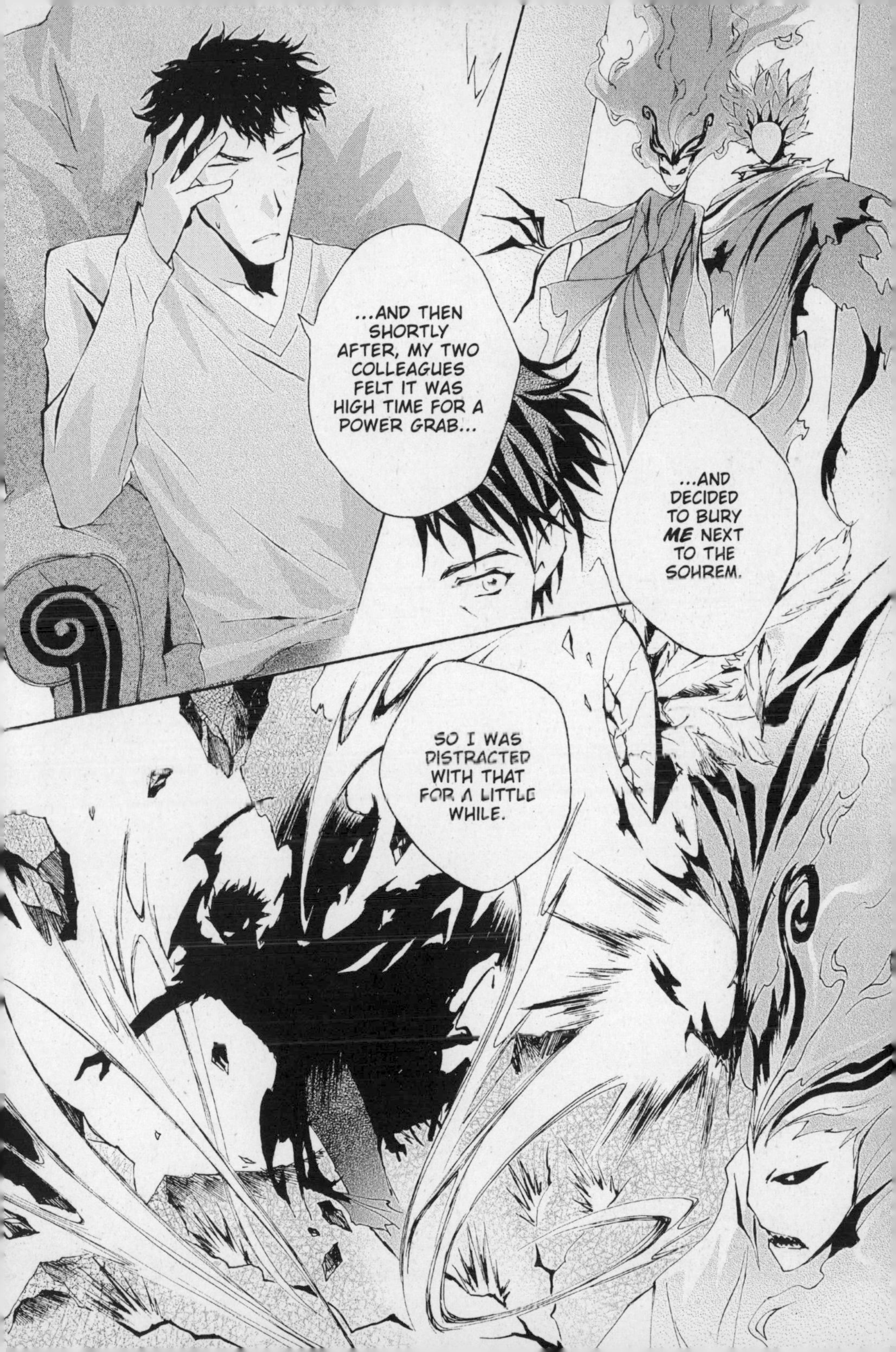
...AND THEN SHORTLY AFTER, MY TWO COLLEAGUES FELT IT WAS HIGH TIME FOR A POWER GRAB...
...AND DECIDED TO BURY *ME* NEXT TO THE SOHREM.
SO I WAS DISTRACTED WITH THAT FOR A LITTLE WHILE.

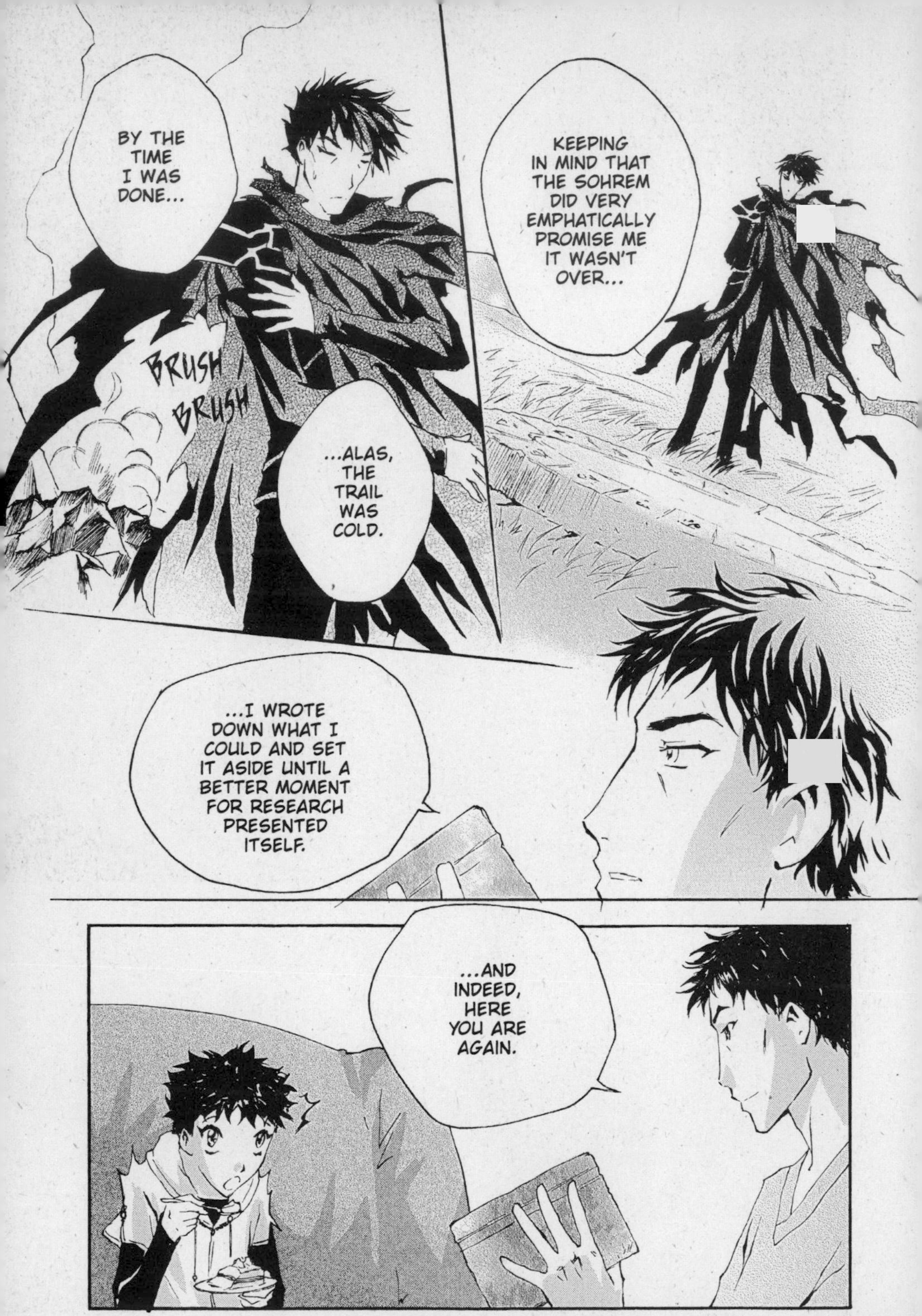
BY THE TIME I WAS DONE...
BRUSH
BRUSH
...ALAS, THE TRAIL WAS COLD.
KEEPING IN MIND THAT THE SOHREM DID VERY EMPHATICALLY PROMISE ME IT WASN'T OVER...
...I WROTE DOWN WHAT I COULD AND SET IT ASIDE UNTIL A BETTER MOMENT FOR RESEARCH PRESENTED ITSELF.
...AND INDEED, HERE YOU ARE AGAIN.

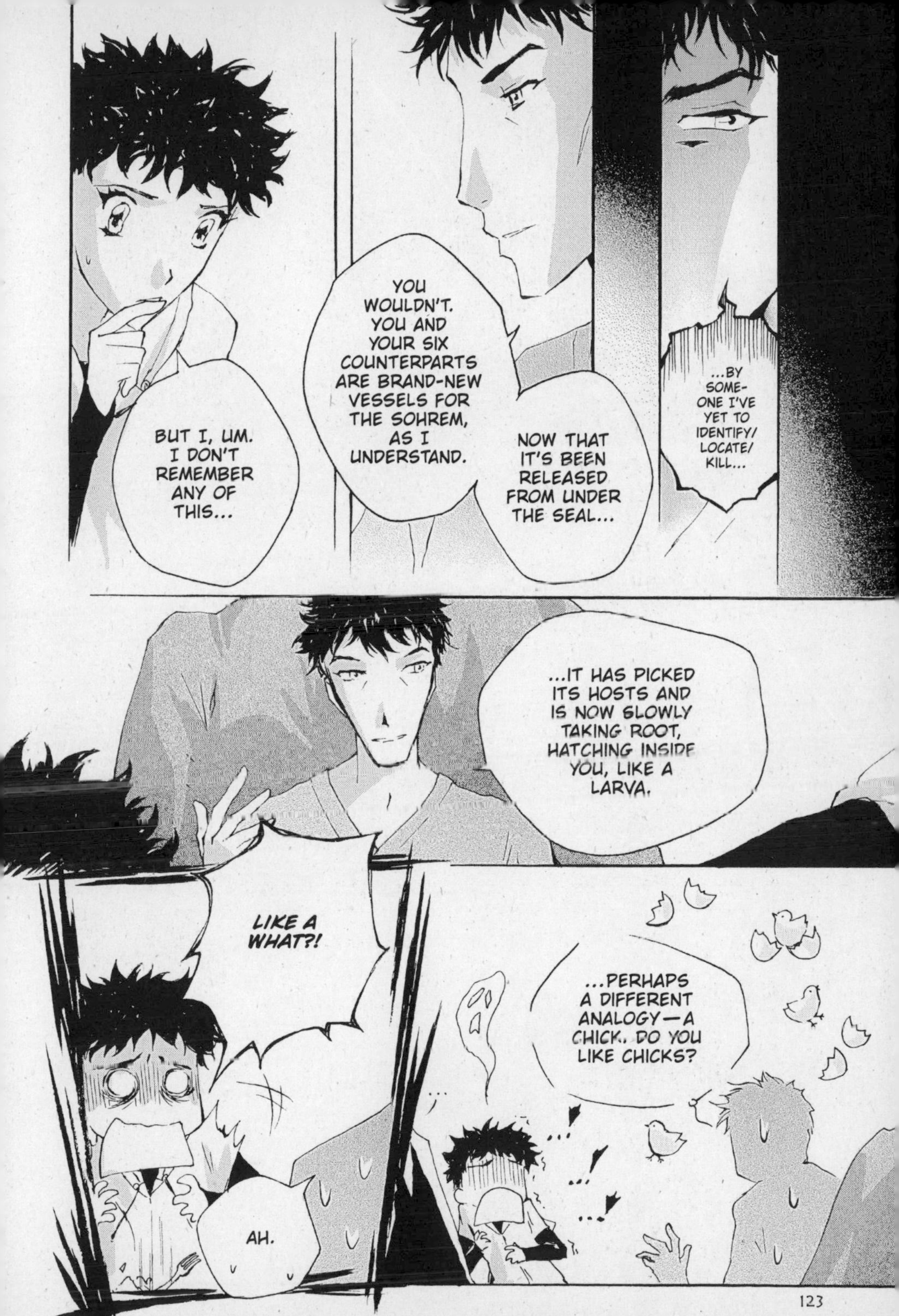
BUT I, UM. I DON'T REMEMBER ANY OF THIS...
YOU WOULDN'T. YOU AND YOUR SIX COUNTERPARTS ARE BRAND-NEW VESSELS FOR THE SOHREM, AS I UNDERSTAND.
NOW THAT IT'S BEEN RELEASED FROM UNDER THE SEAL...
...BY SOME-ONE I'VE YET TO IDENTIFY/ LOCATE/ KILL...
...IT HAS PICKED ITS HOSTS AND IS NOW SLOWLY TAKING ROOT, HATCHING INSIDE YOU, LIKE A LARVA.
LIKE A WHAT?!
AH.
...PERHAPS A DIFFERENT ANALOGY—A CHICK.. DO YOU LIKE CHICKS?
...
...!
...!
...!

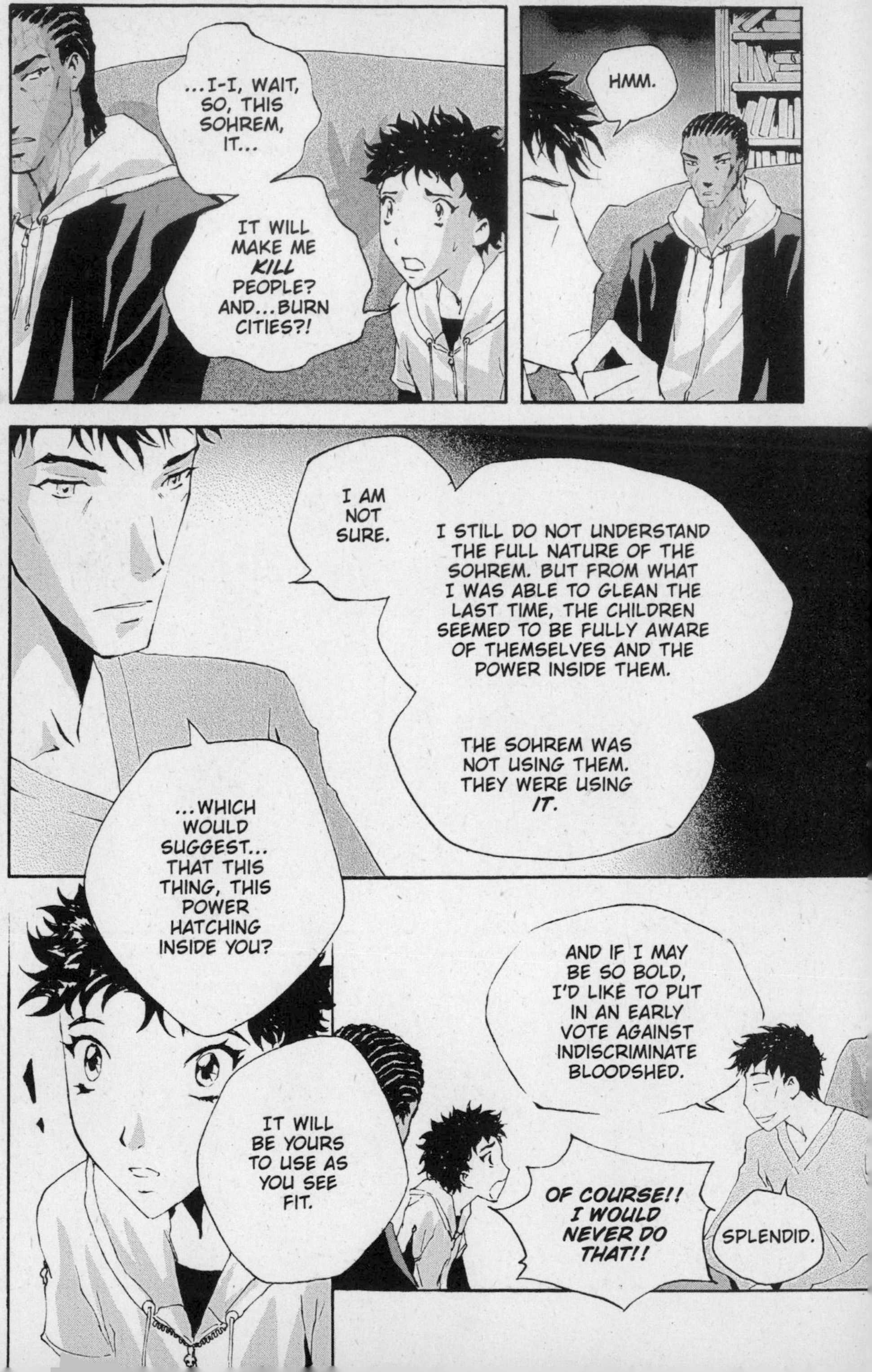
...I-I, WAIT, SO, THIS SOHREM, IT...
IT WILL MAKE ME *KILL* PEOPLE? AND...BURN CITIES?!
HMM.
I AM NOT SURE.
I STILL DO NOT UNDERSTAND THE FULL NATURE OF THE SOHREM. BUT FROM WHAT I WAS ABLE TO GLEAN THE LAST TIME, THE CHILDREN SEEMED TO BE FULLY AWARE OF THEMSELVES AND THE POWER INSIDE THEM.
THE SOHREM WAS NOT USING THEM. THEY WERE USING *IT*.
...WHICH WOULD SUGGEST... THAT THIS THING, THIS POWER HATCHING INSIDE YOU?
IT WILL BE YOURS TO USE AS YOU SEE FIT.
AND IF I MAY BE SO BOLD, I'D LIKE TO PUT IN AN EARLY VOTE AGAINST INDISCRIMINATE BLOODSHED.
OF COURSE!! I WOULD NEVER DO THAT!!
SPLENDID.

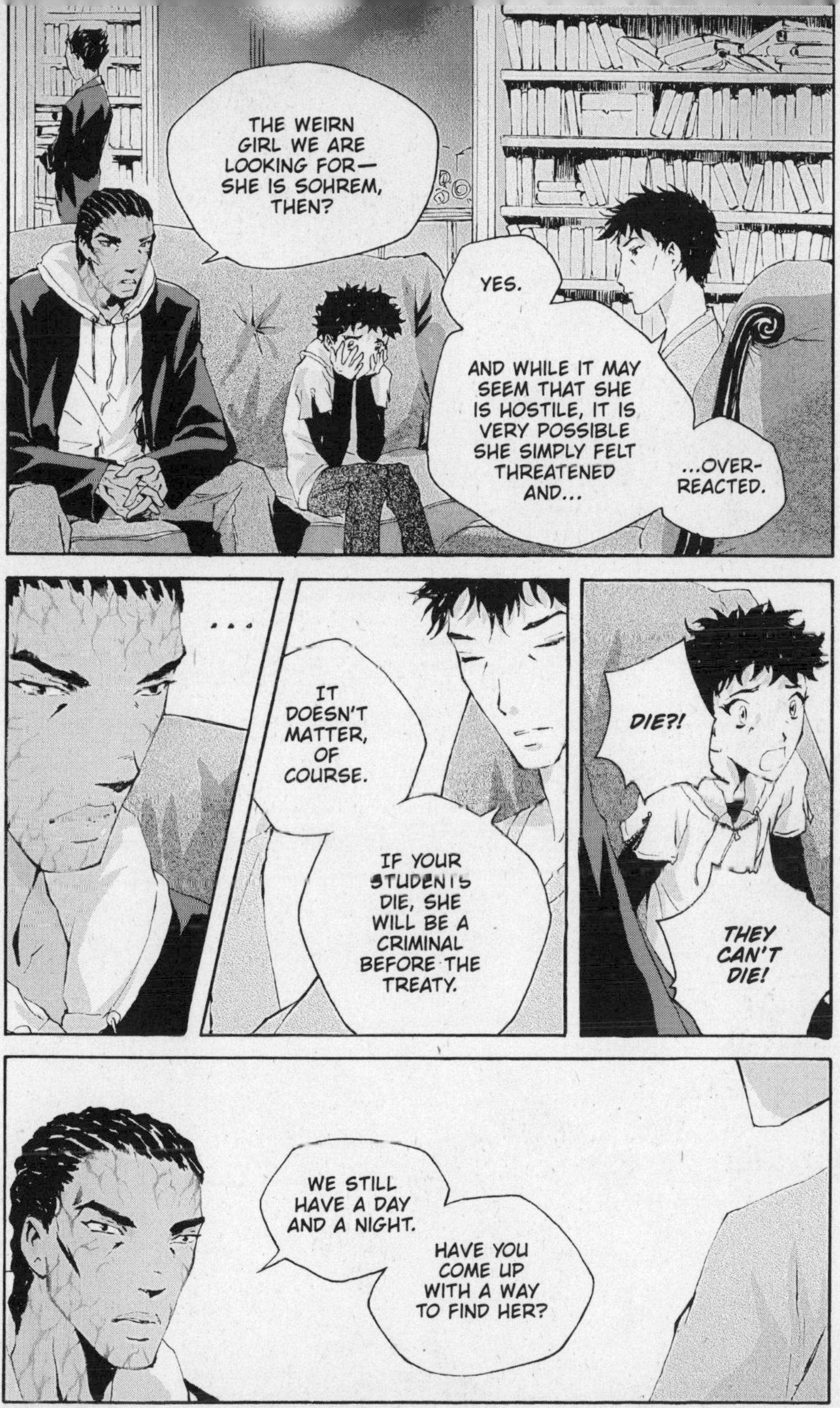
THE WEIRN GIRL WE ARE LOOKING FOR—SHE IS SOHREM, THEN?
YES.
AND WHILE IT MAY SEEM THAT SHE IS HOSTILE, IT IS VERY POSSIBLE SHE SIMPLY FELT THREATENED AND...
...OVER-REACTED.
...
IT DOESN'T MATTER, OF COURSE.
IF YOUR STUDENTS DIE, SHE WILL BE A CRIMINAL BEFORE THE TREATY.
DIE?!
THEY CAN'T DIE!
WE STILL HAVE A DAY AND A NIGHT.
HAVE YOU COME UP WITH A WAY TO FIND HER?

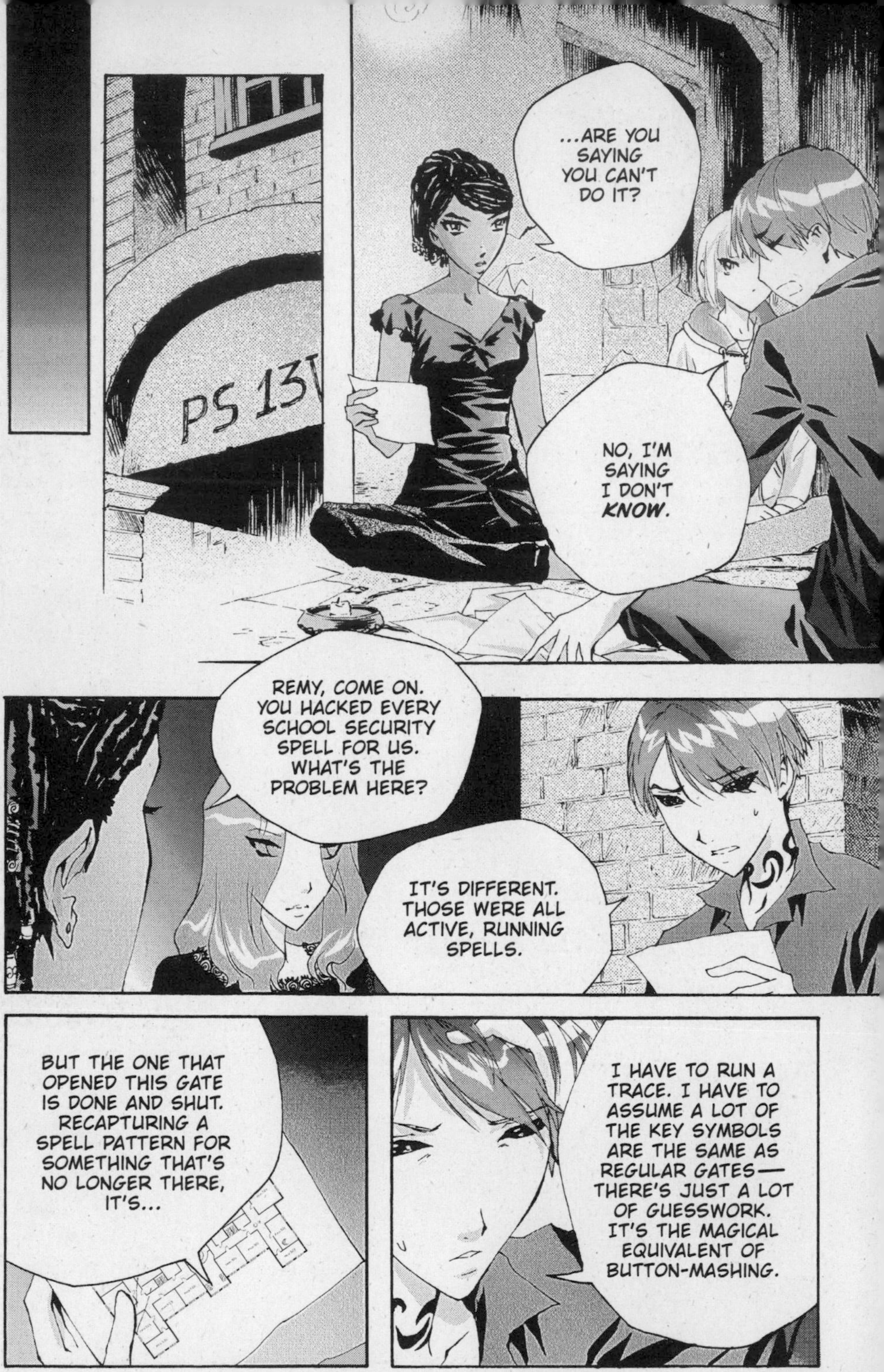
PS 13
...ARE YOU SAYING YOU CAN'T DO IT?
NO, I'M SAYING I DON'T **KNOW**.
REMY, COME ON. YOU HACKED EVERY SCHOOL SECURITY SPELL FOR US. WHAT'S THE PROBLEM HERE?
IT'S DIFFERENT. THOSE WERE ALL ACTIVE, RUNNING SPELLS.
BUT THE ONE THAT OPENED THIS GATE IS DONE AND SHUT. RECAPTURING A SPELL PATTERN FOR SOMETHING THAT'S NO LONGER THERE, IT'S...
I HAVE TO RUN A TRACE. I HAVE TO ASSUME A LOT OF THE KEY SYMBOLS ARE THE SAME AS REGULAR GATES— THERE'S JUST A LOT OF GUESSWORK. IT'S THE MAGICAL EQUIVALENT OF BUTTON-MASHING.

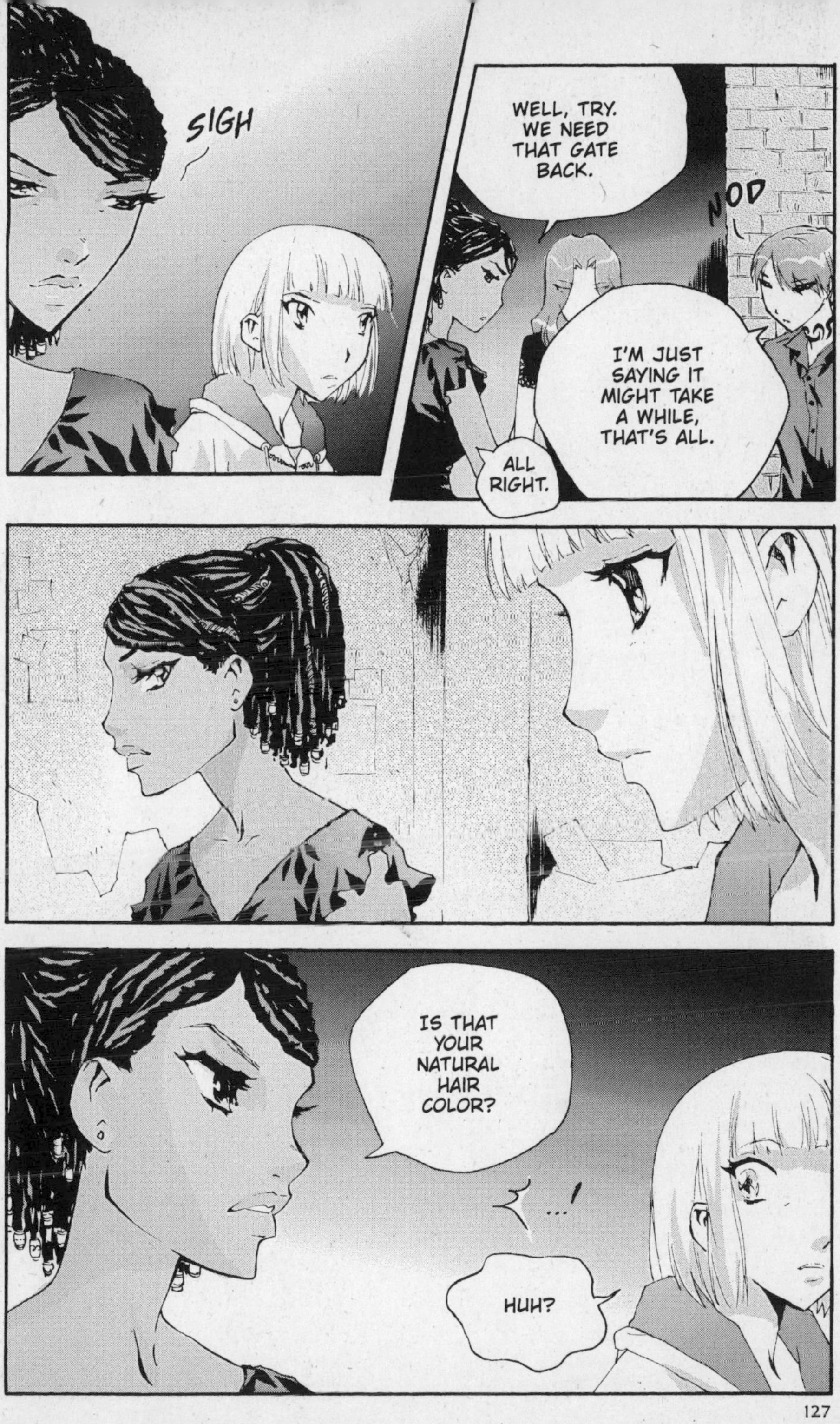
SIGH
WELL, TRY. WE NEED THAT GATE BACK.
NOD
I'M JUST SAYING IT MIGHT TAKE A WHILE, THAT'S ALL.
ALL RIGHT.
IS THAT YOUR NATURAL HAIR COLOR?
...!
HUH?

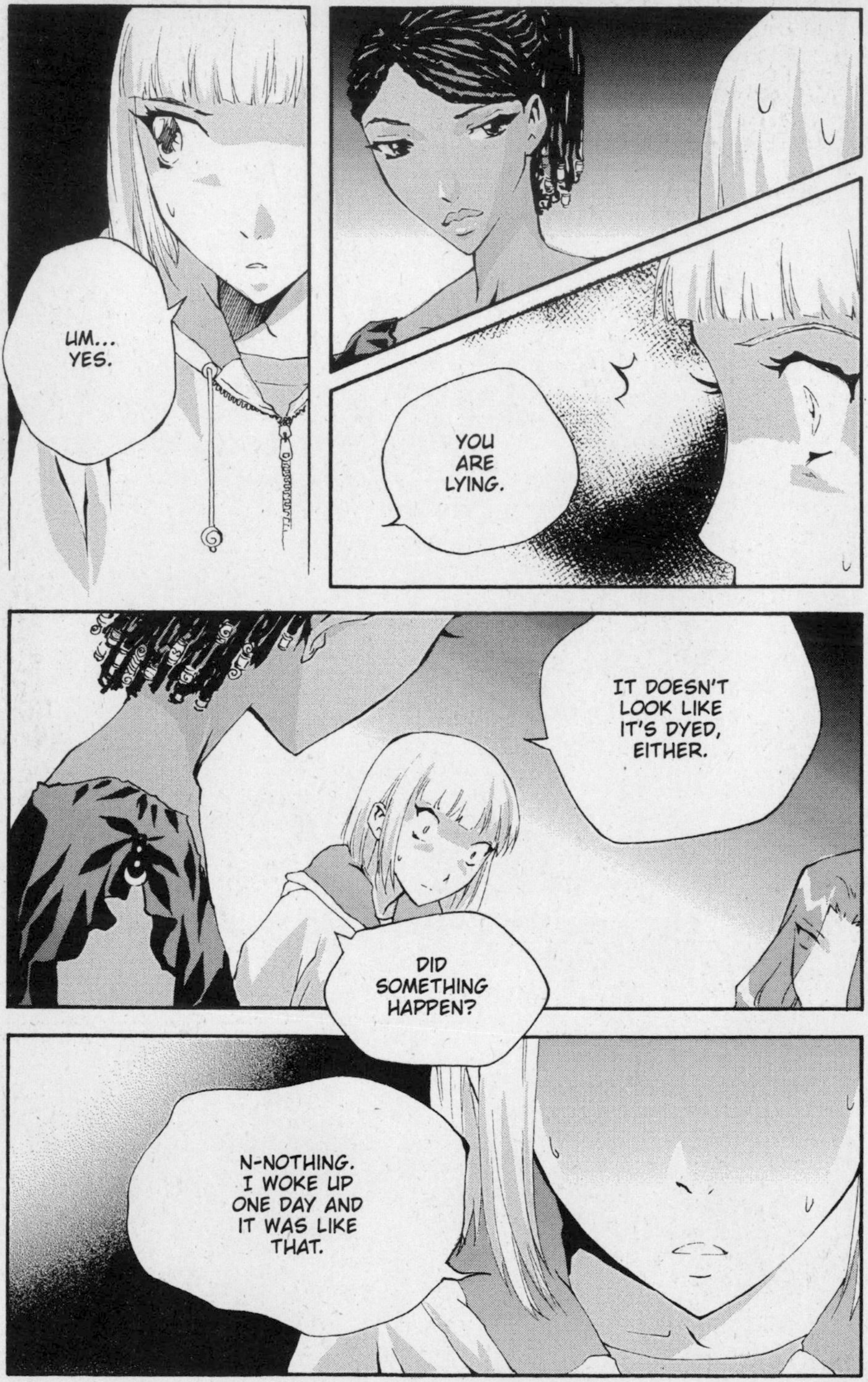
UM... YES.
YOU ARE LYING.
IT DOESN'T LOOK LIKE IT'S DYED, EITHER.
DID SOMETHING HAPPEN?
N-NOTHING. I WOKE UP ONE DAY AND IT WAS LIKE THAT.

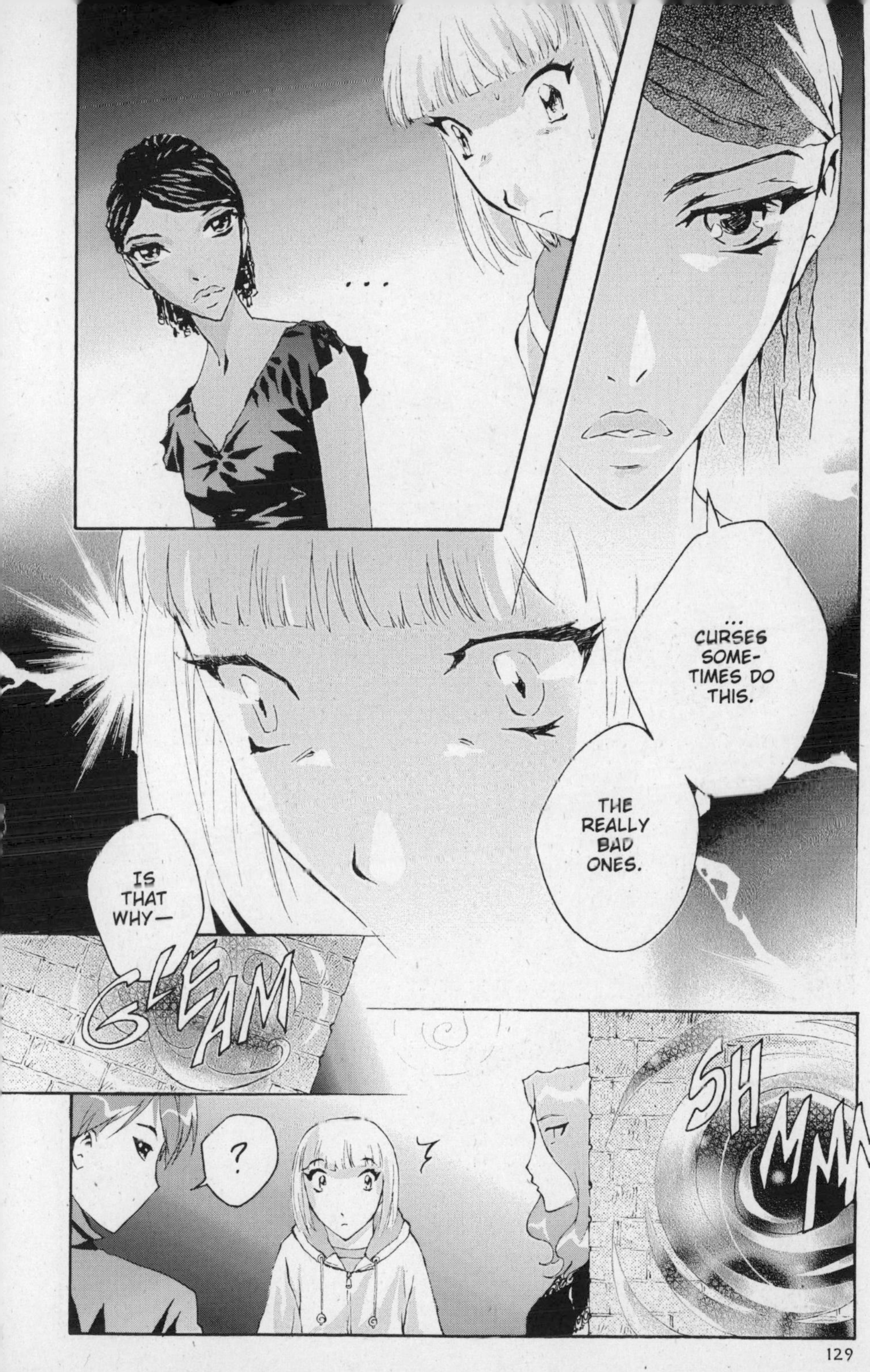
...
... CURSES SOME- TIMES DO THIS.
THE REALLY BAD ONES.
IS THAT WHY—
GLEAM
?
SHMMMM

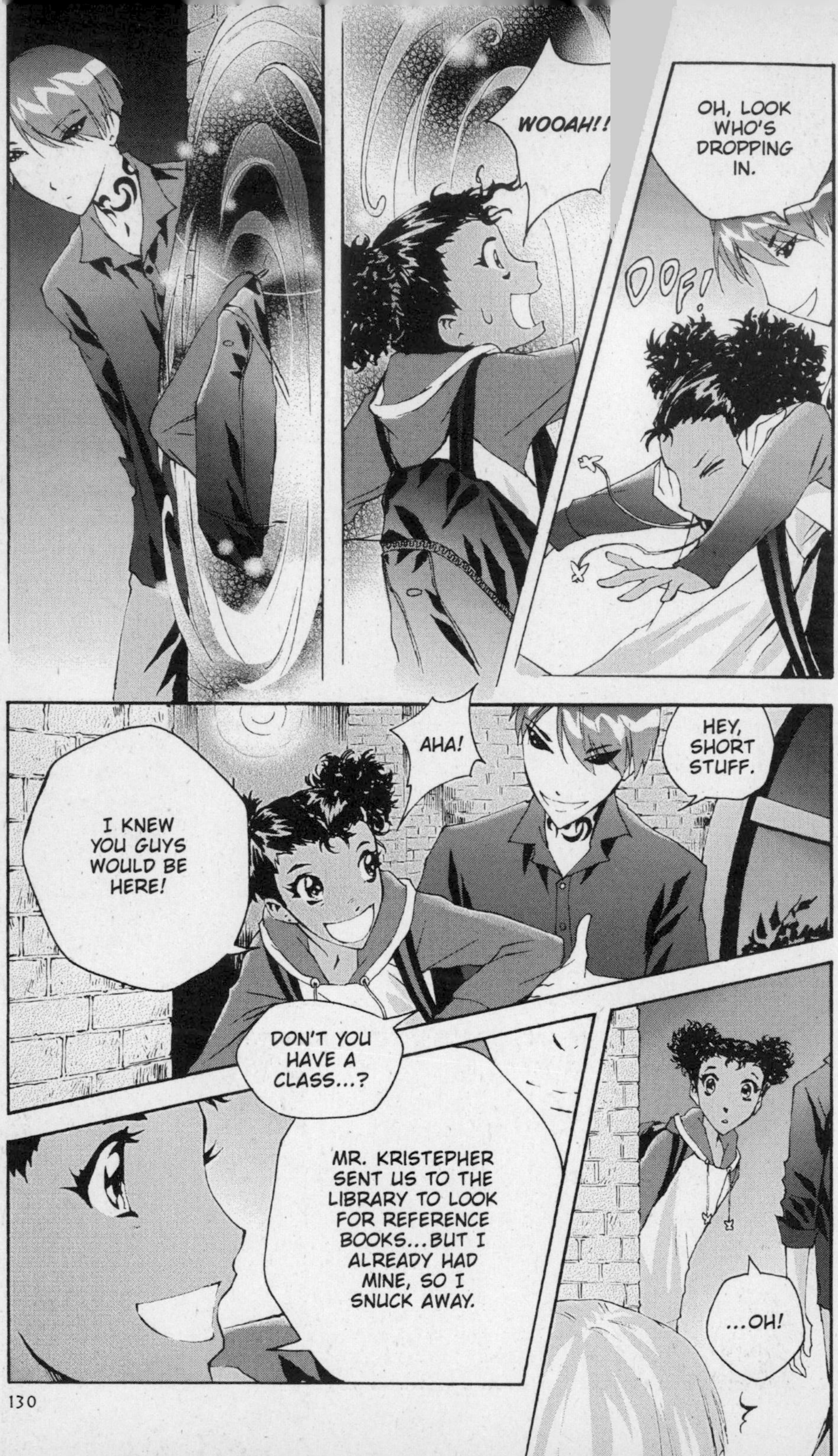
WOOAH!!
OH, LOOK WHO'S DROPPING IN.
OOF!
I KNEW YOU GUYS WOULD BE HERE!
AHA!
HEY, SHORT STUFF.
DON'T YOU HAVE A CLASS...?
MR. KRISTEPHER SENT US TO THE LIBRARY TO LOOK FOR REFERENCE BOOKS...BUT I ALREADY HAD MINE, SO I SNUCK AWAY.
...OH!

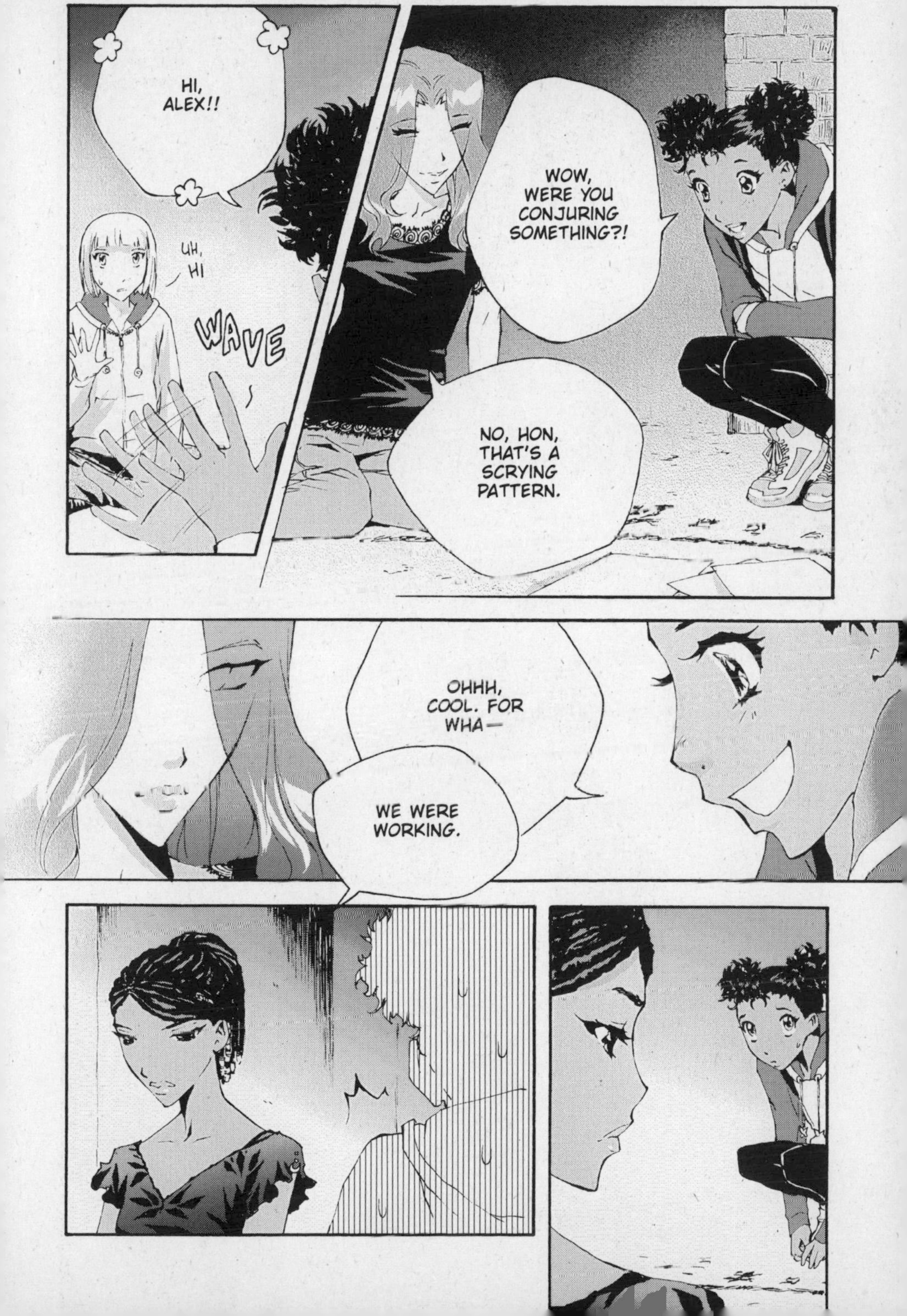
HI, ALEX!!
UH, HI
WAVE
WOW, WERE YOU CONJURING SOMETHING?!
NO, HON, THAT'S A SCRYING PATTERN.
OHHH, COOL. FOR WHA—
WE WERE WORKING.

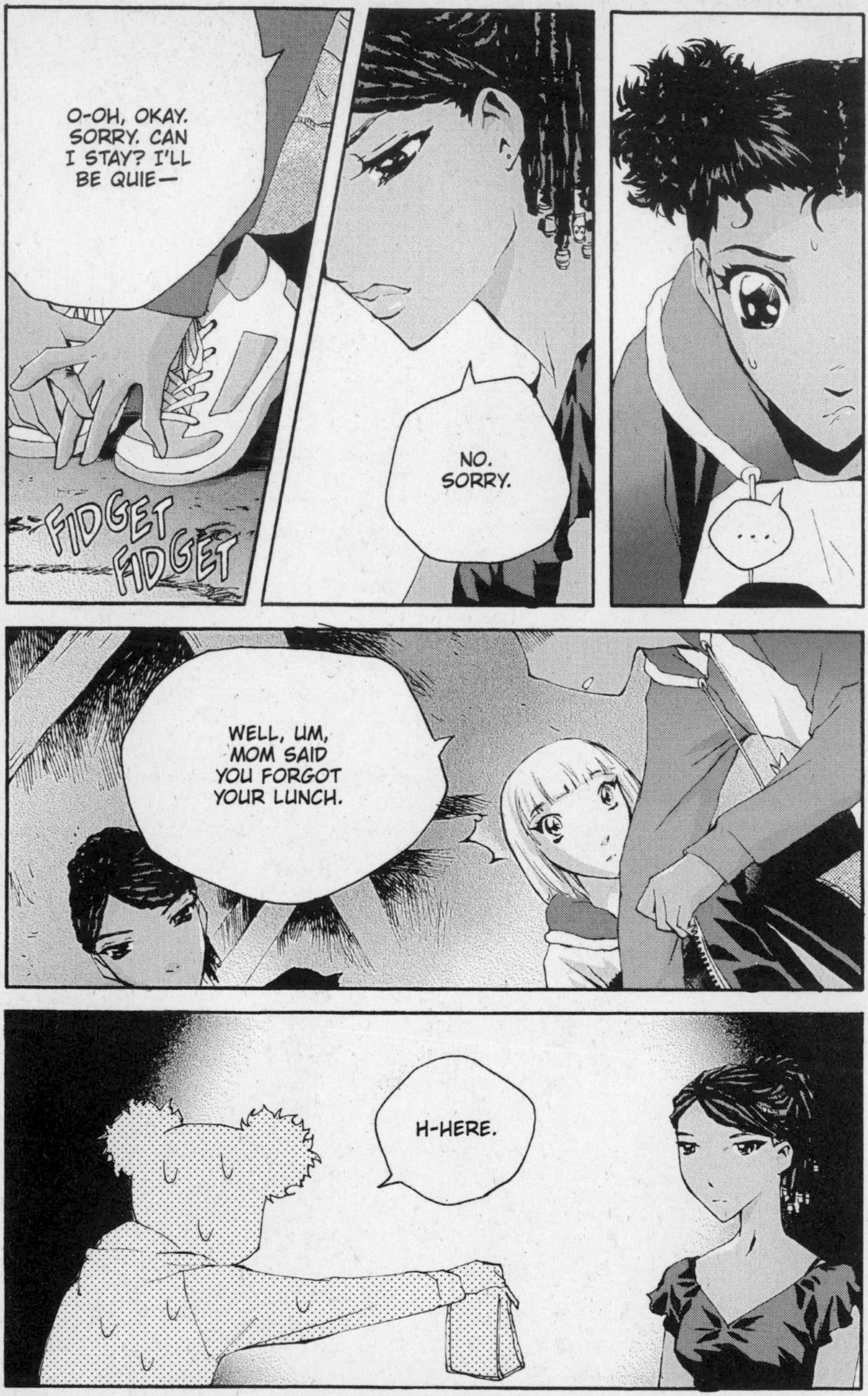
O-OH, OKAY. SORRY. CAN I STAY? I'LL BE QUIE—
FIDGET FIDGET
NO. SORRY.
...
WELL, UM, MOM SAID YOU FORGOT YOUR LUNCH.
H-HERE.

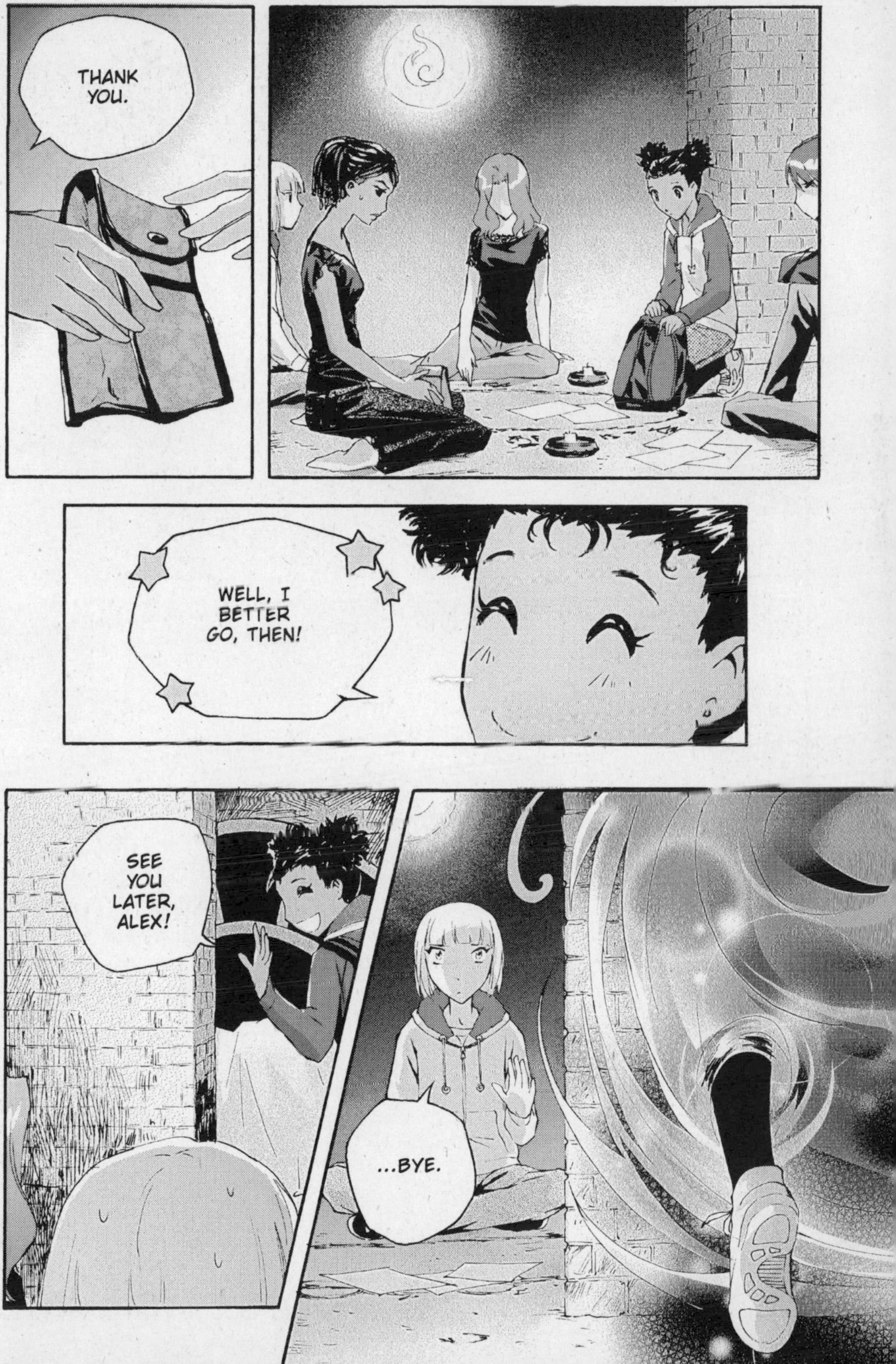

THANK YOU.
WELL, I BETTER GO, THEN!
SEE YOU LATER, ALEX!
...BYE.

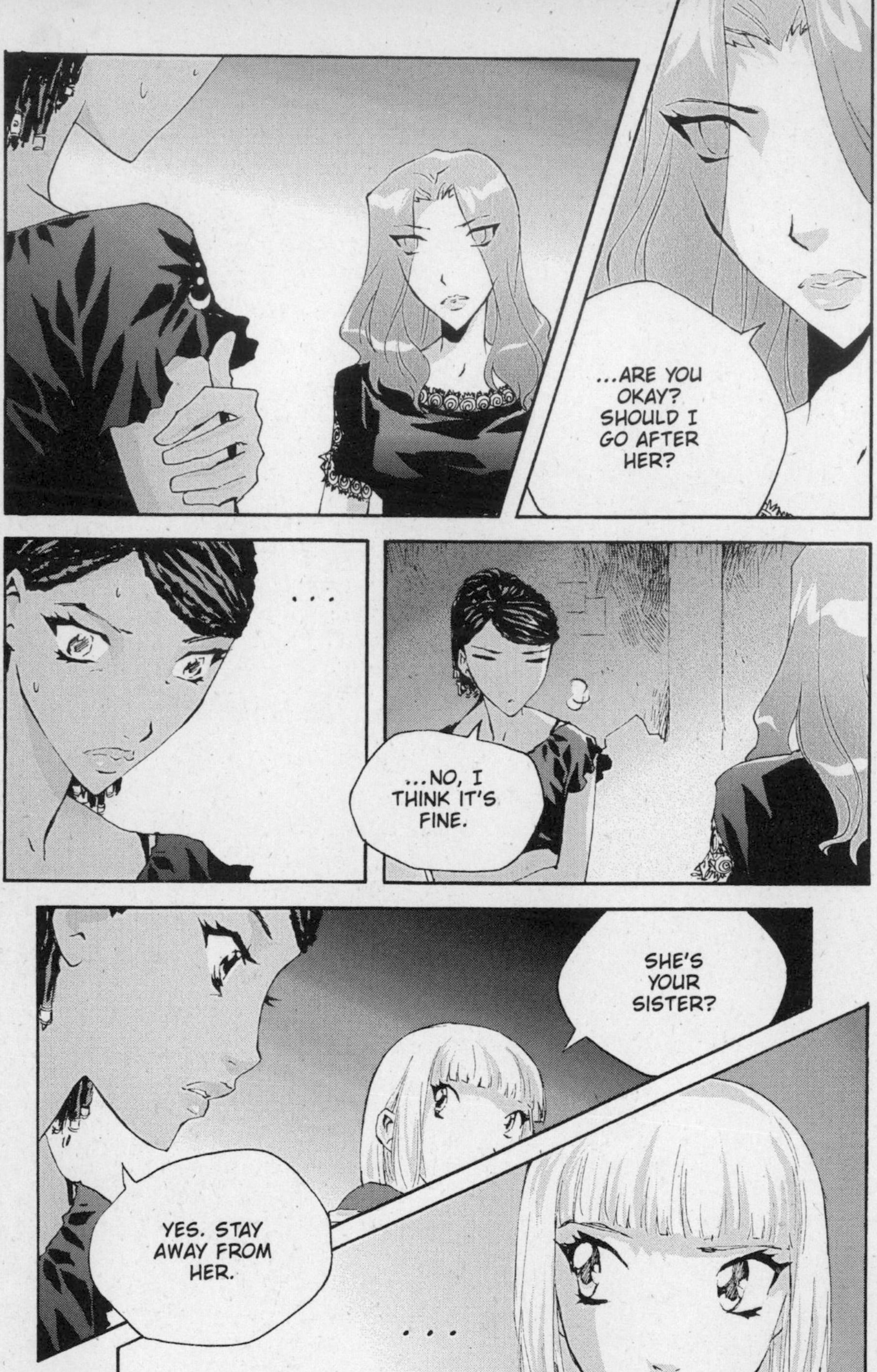
...ARE YOU OKAY? SHOULD I GO AFTER HER?
...
...NO, I THINK IT'S FINE.
SHE'S YOUR SISTER?
YES. STAY AWAY FROM HER.
...

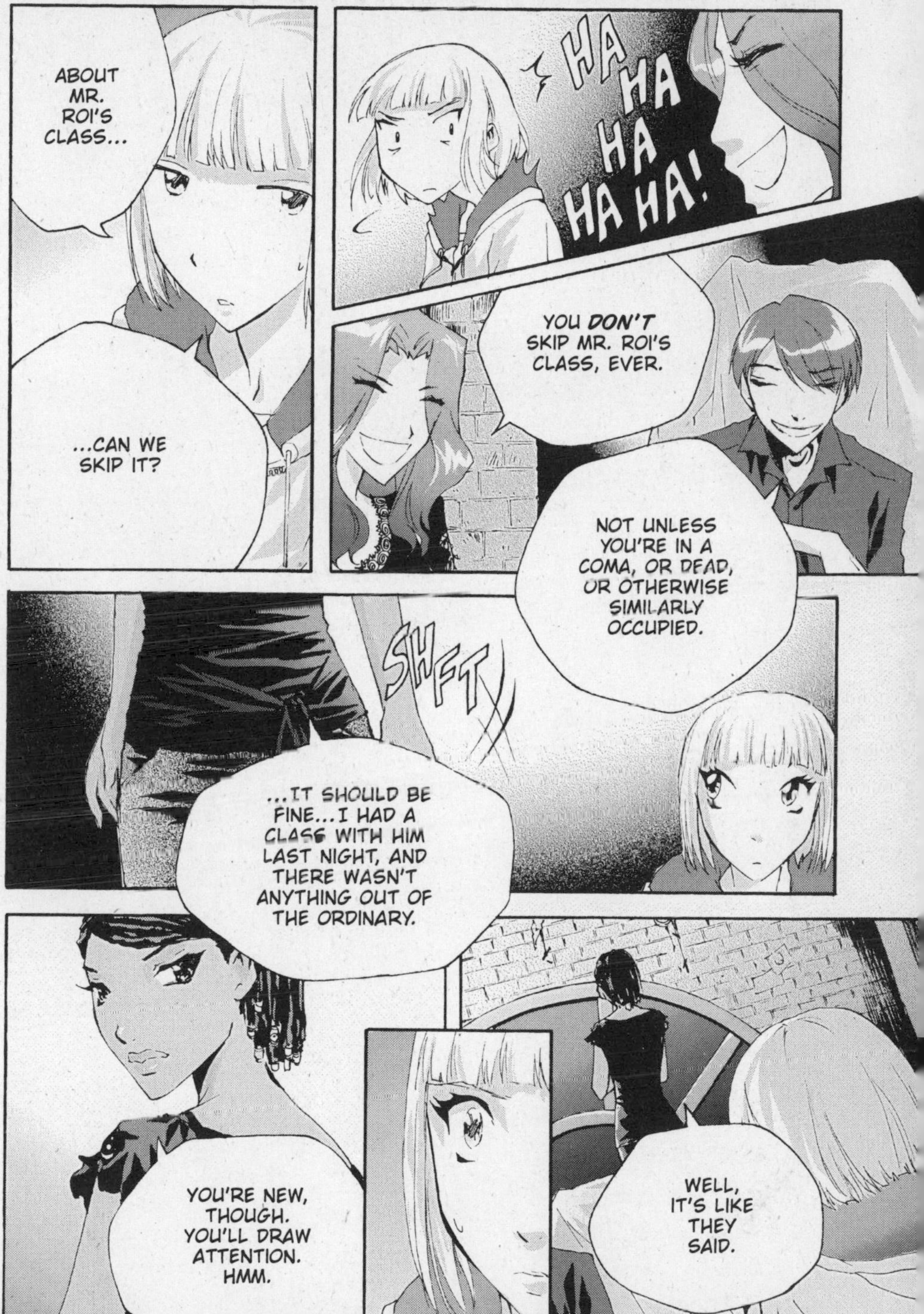
ABOUT MR. ROI'S CLASS...
...CAN WE SKIP IT?
HA HA HA HA HA HA!
YOU *DON'T* SKIP MR. ROI'S CLASS, EVER.
NOT UNLESS YOU'RE IN A COMA, OR DEAD, OR OTHERWISE SIMILARLY OCCUPIED.
SHFT
...IT SHOULD BE FINE...I HAD A CLASS WITH HIM LAST NIGHT, AND THERE WASN'T ANYTHING OUT OF THE ORDINARY.
YOU'RE NEW, THOUGH. YOU'LL DRAW ATTENTION. HMM.
WELL, IT'S LIKE THEY SAID.

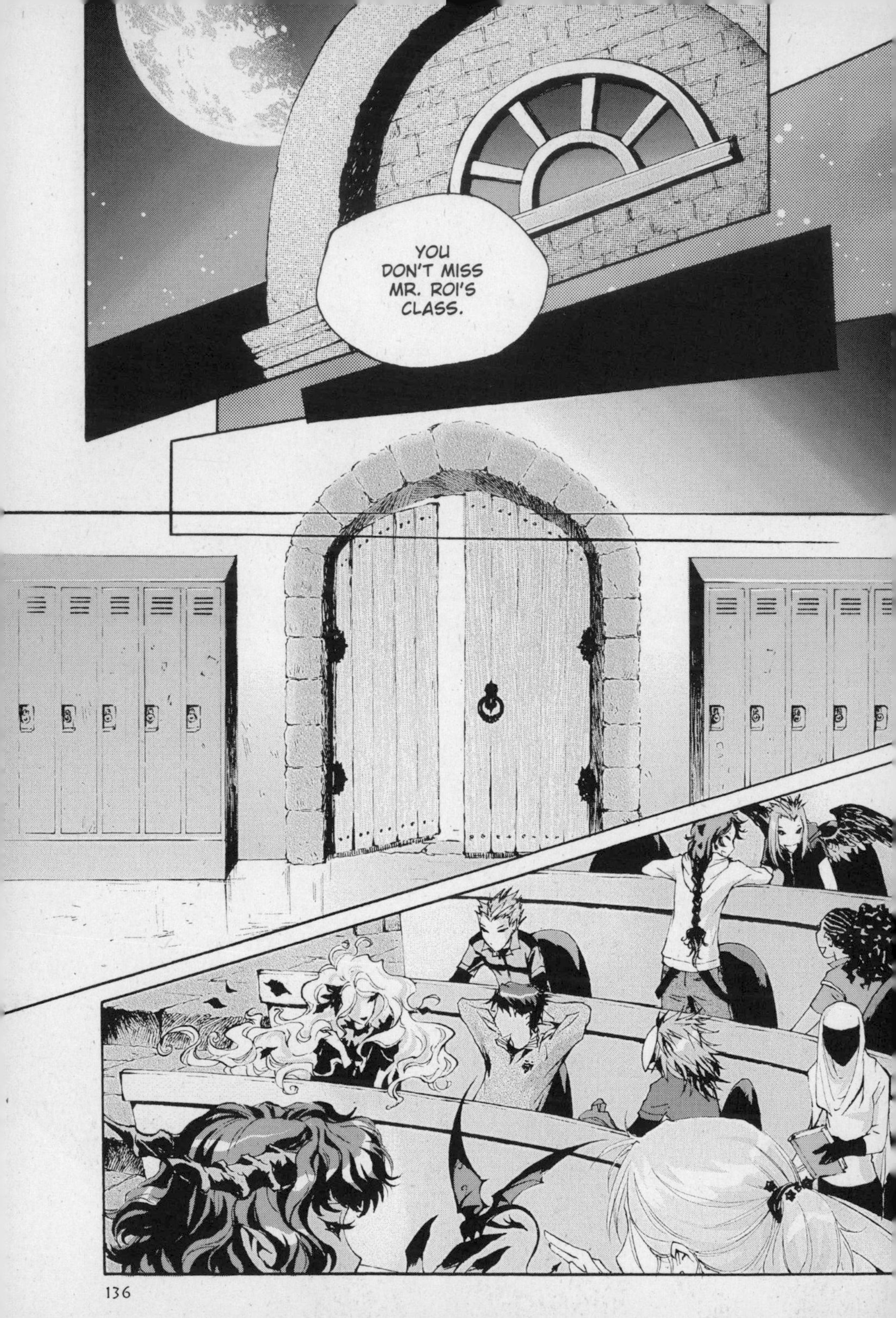
YOU DON'T MISS MR. ROI'S CLASS.

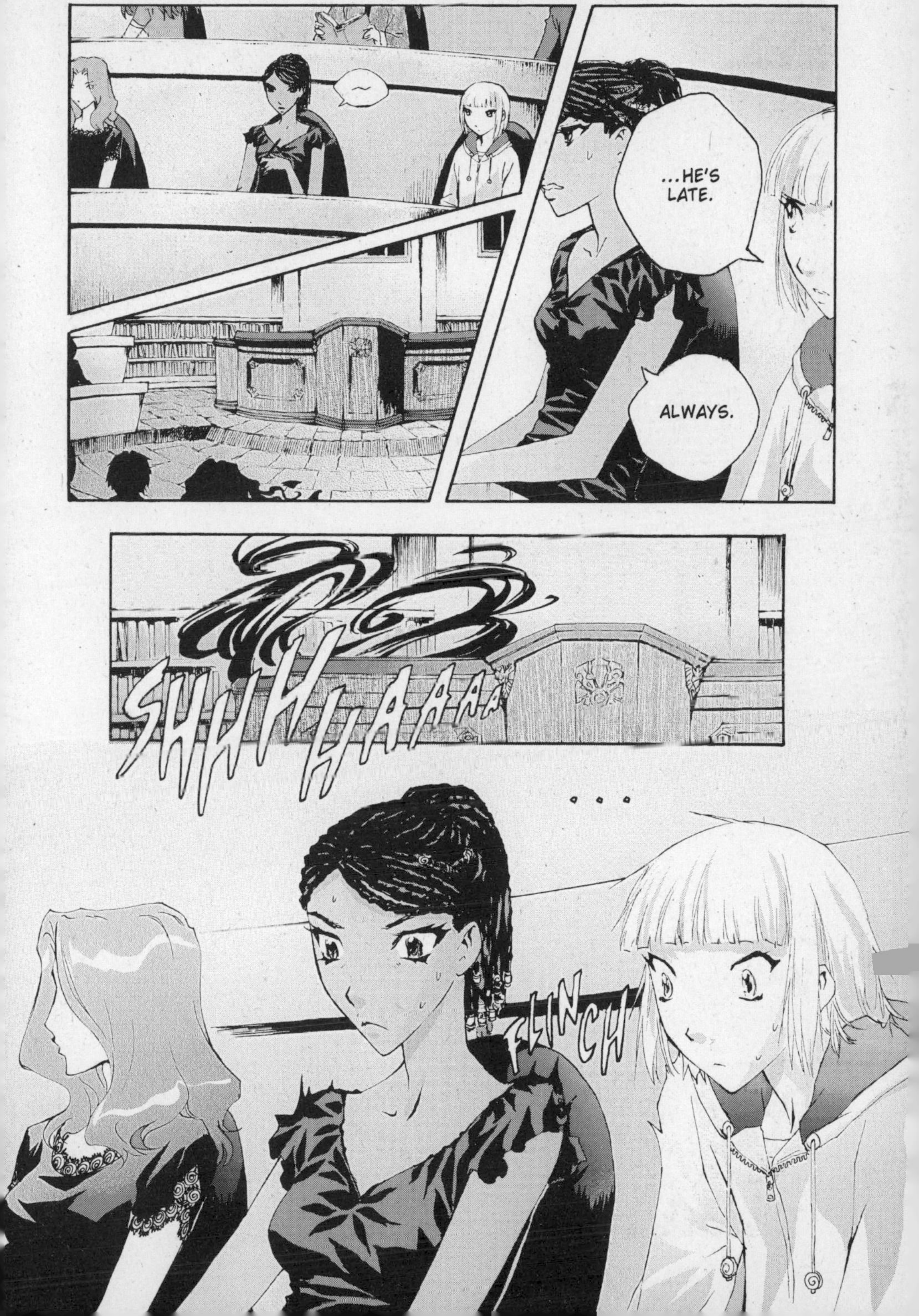
~
...HE'S LATE.
ALWAYS.
SHHHHAAAAA
...
FLINCH

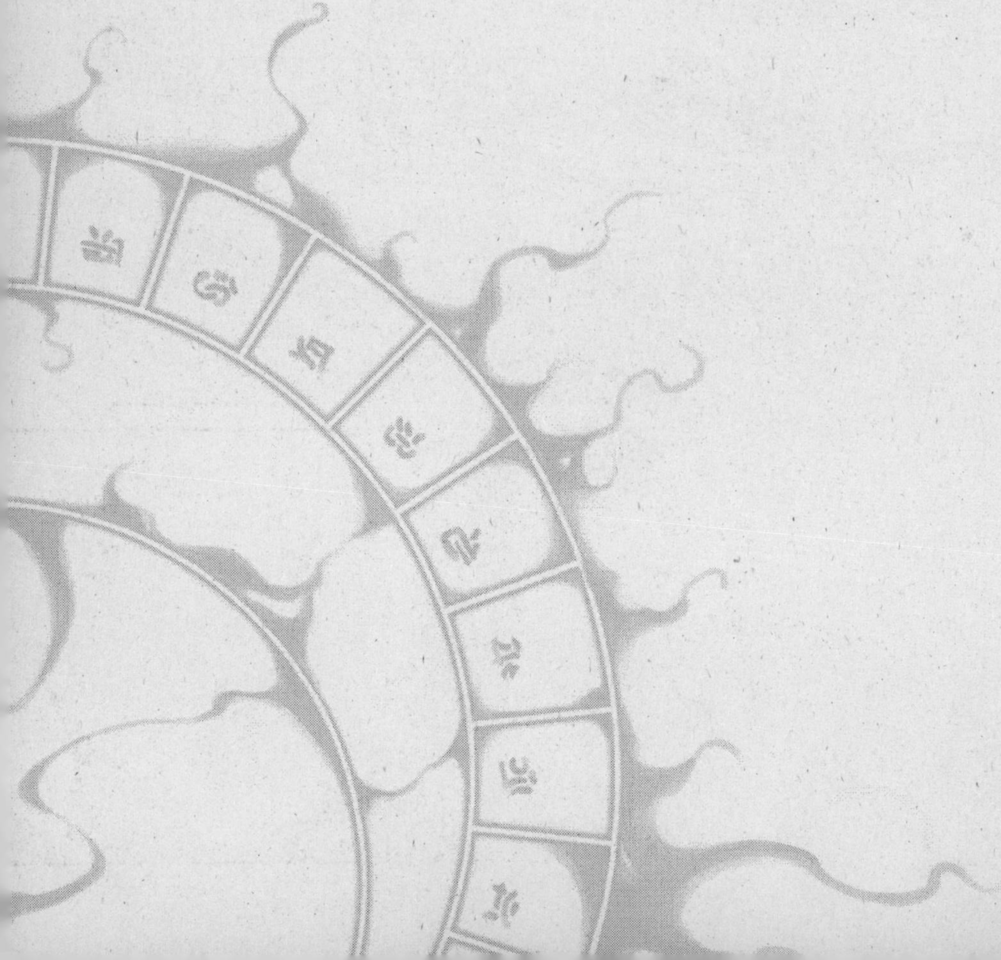

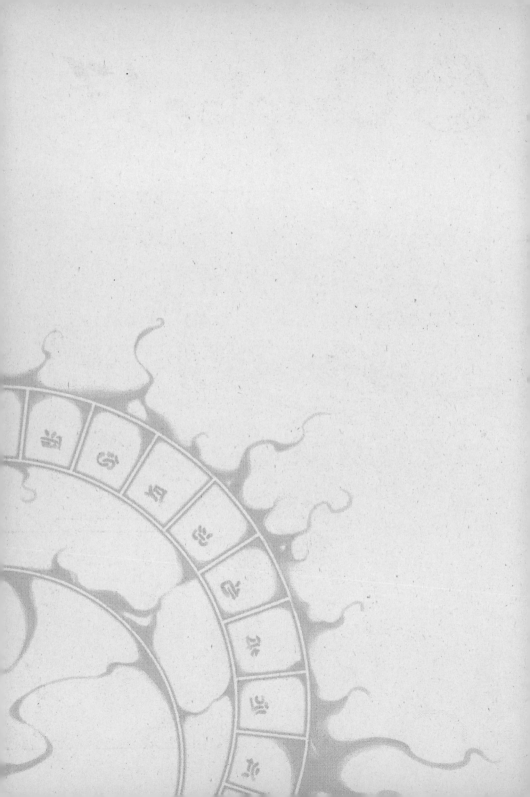

Chapter 17

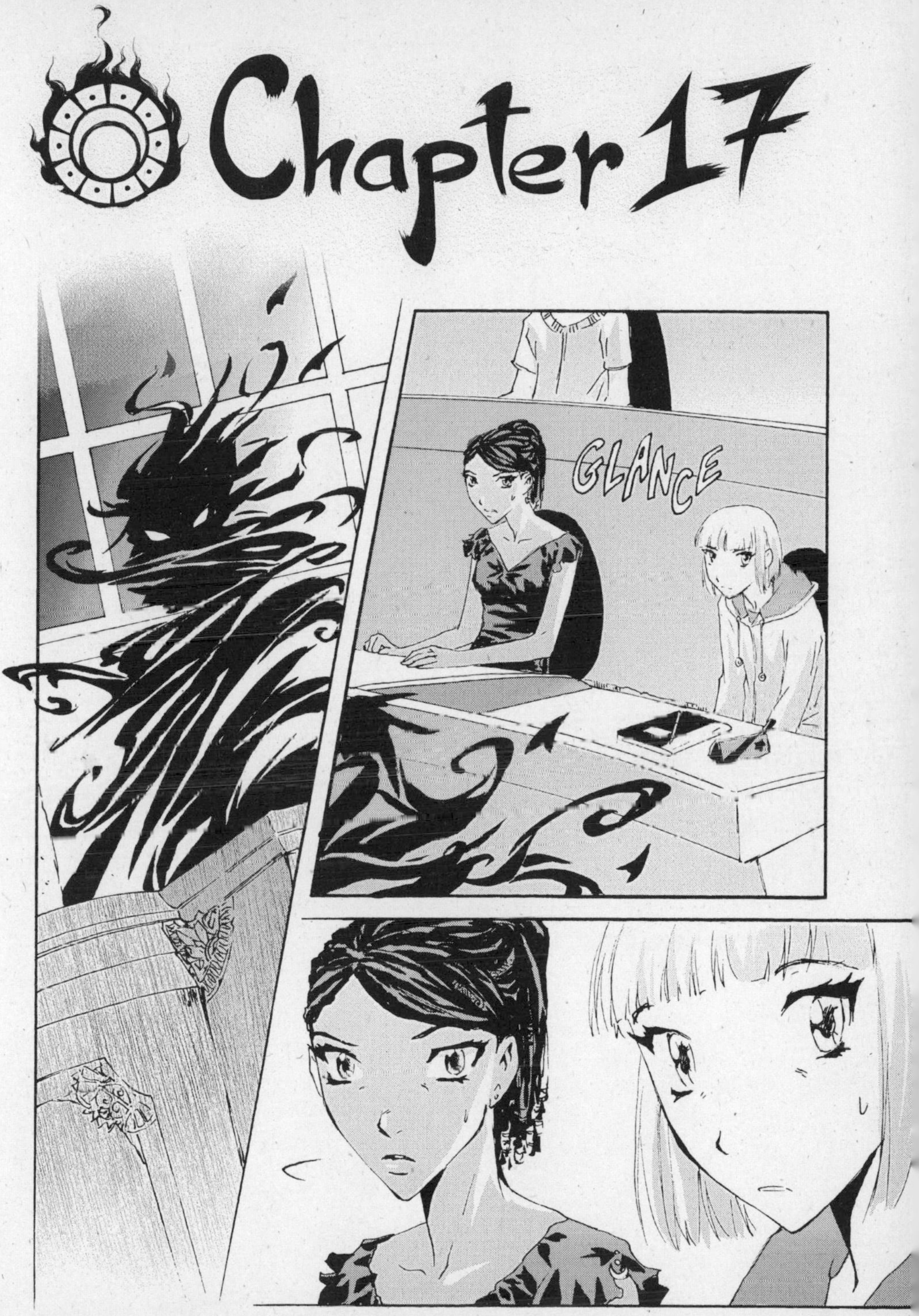
GLANCE

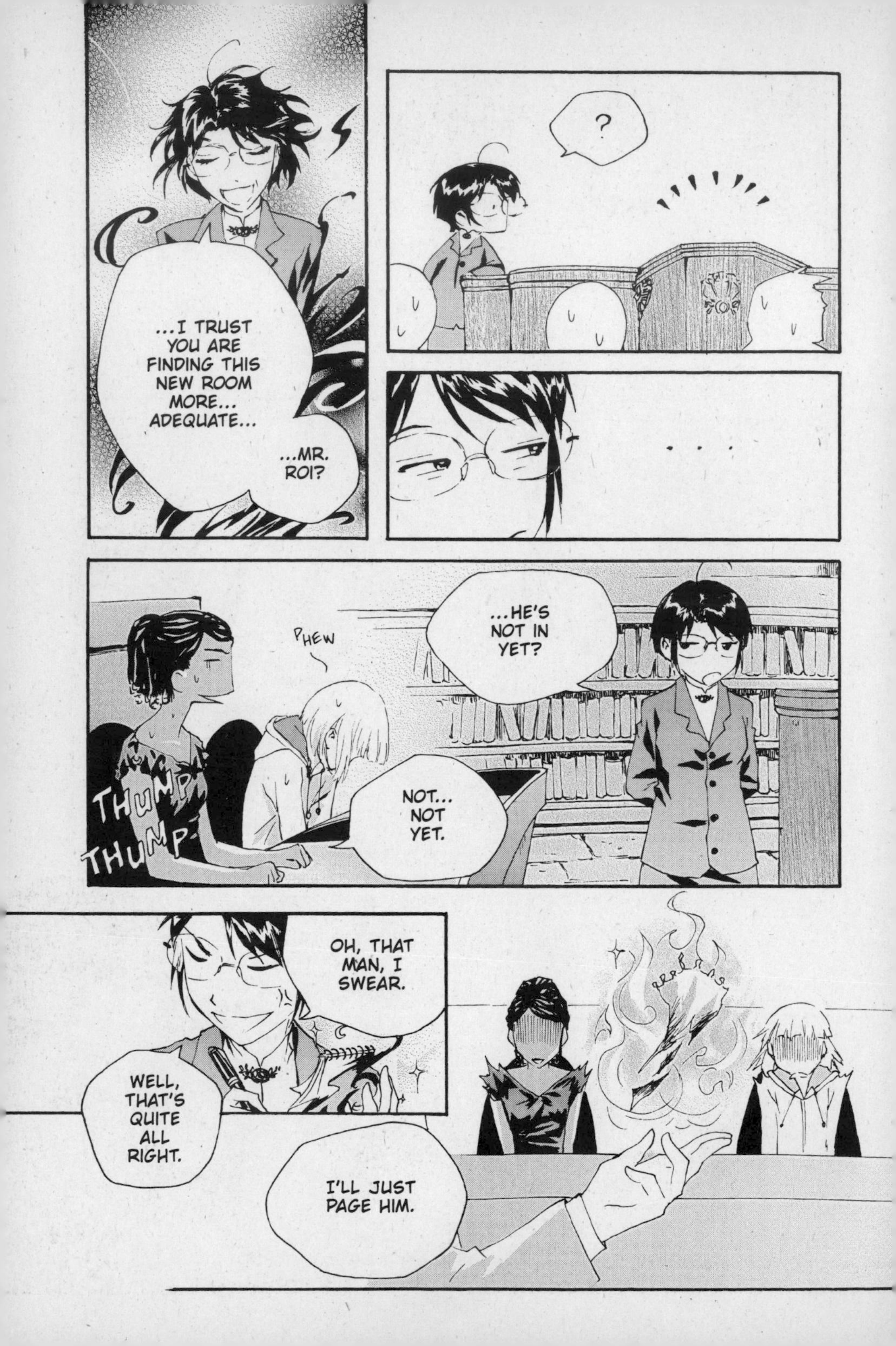

...I TRUST YOU ARE FINDING THIS NEW ROOM MORE... ADEQUATE...
...MR. ROI?
?
. . .
...HE'S NOT IN YET?
PHEW
NOT... NOT YET.
THUMP THUMP
OH, THAT MAN, I SWEAR.
WELL, THAT'S QUITE ALL RIGHT.
I'LL JUST PAGE HIM.

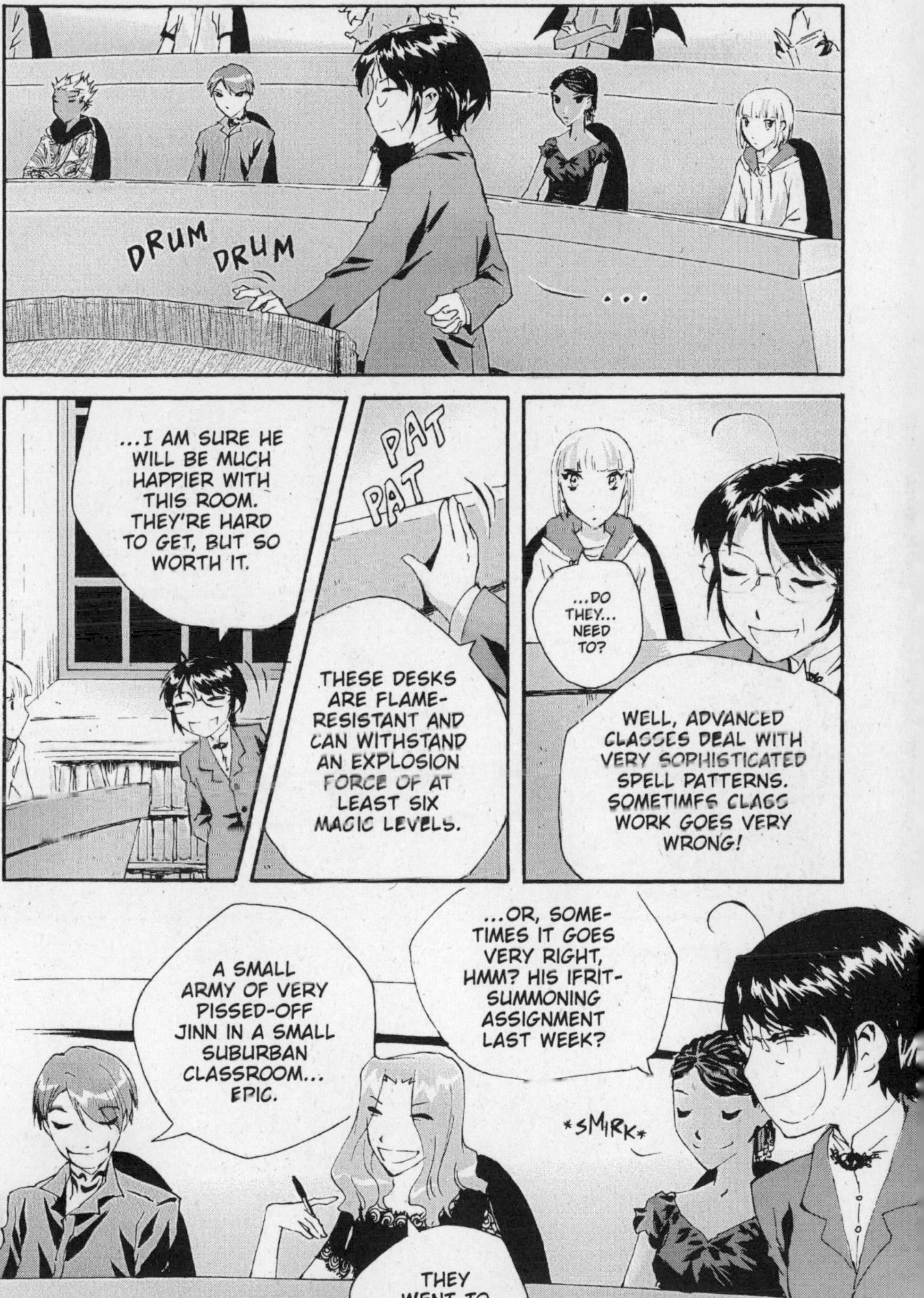
DRUM DRUM
...
...I AM SURE HE WILL BE MUCH HAPPIER WITH THIS ROOM. THEY'RE HARD TO GET, BUT SO WORTH IT.
PAT PAT
THESE DESKS ARE FLAME-RESISTANT AND CAN WITHSTAND AN EXPLOSION FORCE OF AT LEAST SIX MAGIC LEVELS.
...DO THEY... NEED TO?
WELL, ADVANCED CLASSES DEAL WITH VERY SOPHISTICATED SPELL PATTERNS. SOMETIMES CLASS WORK GOES VERY WRONG!
...OR, SOME-TIMES IT GOES VERY RIGHT, HMM? HIS IFRIT-SUMMONING ASSIGNMENT LAST WEEK?
A SMALL ARMY OF VERY PISSED-OFF JINN IN A SMALL SUBURBAN CLASSROOM... EPIC.
SMIRK
THEY WENT TO *TOWN*.

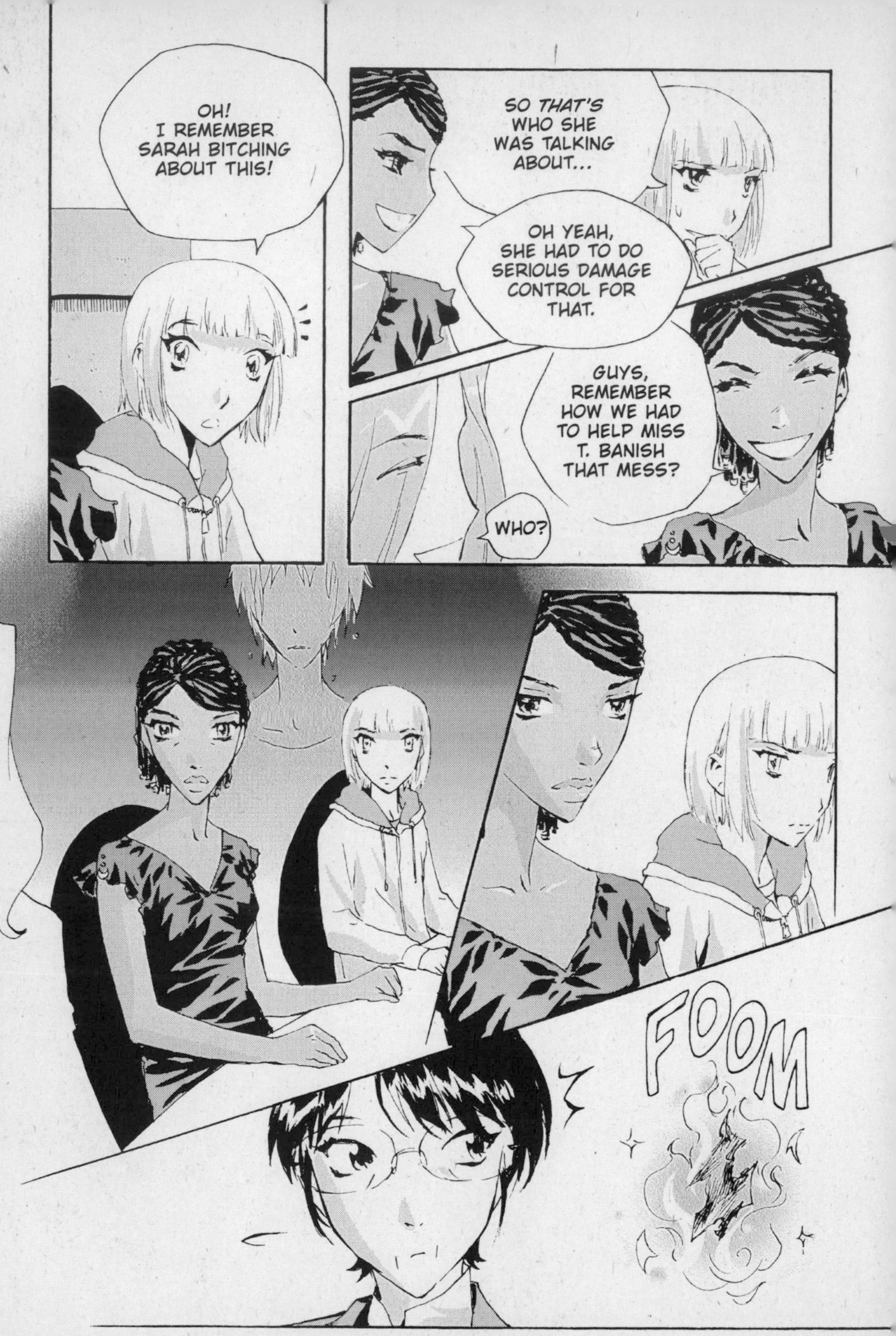
OH! I REMEMBER SARAH BITCHING ABOUT THIS!
SO THAT'S WHO SHE WAS TALKING ABOUT...
OH YEAH, SHE HAD TO DO SERIOUS DAMAGE CONTROL FOR THAT.
WHO?
GUYS, REMEMBER HOW WE HAD TO HELP MISS T. BANISH THAT MESS?
FOOM

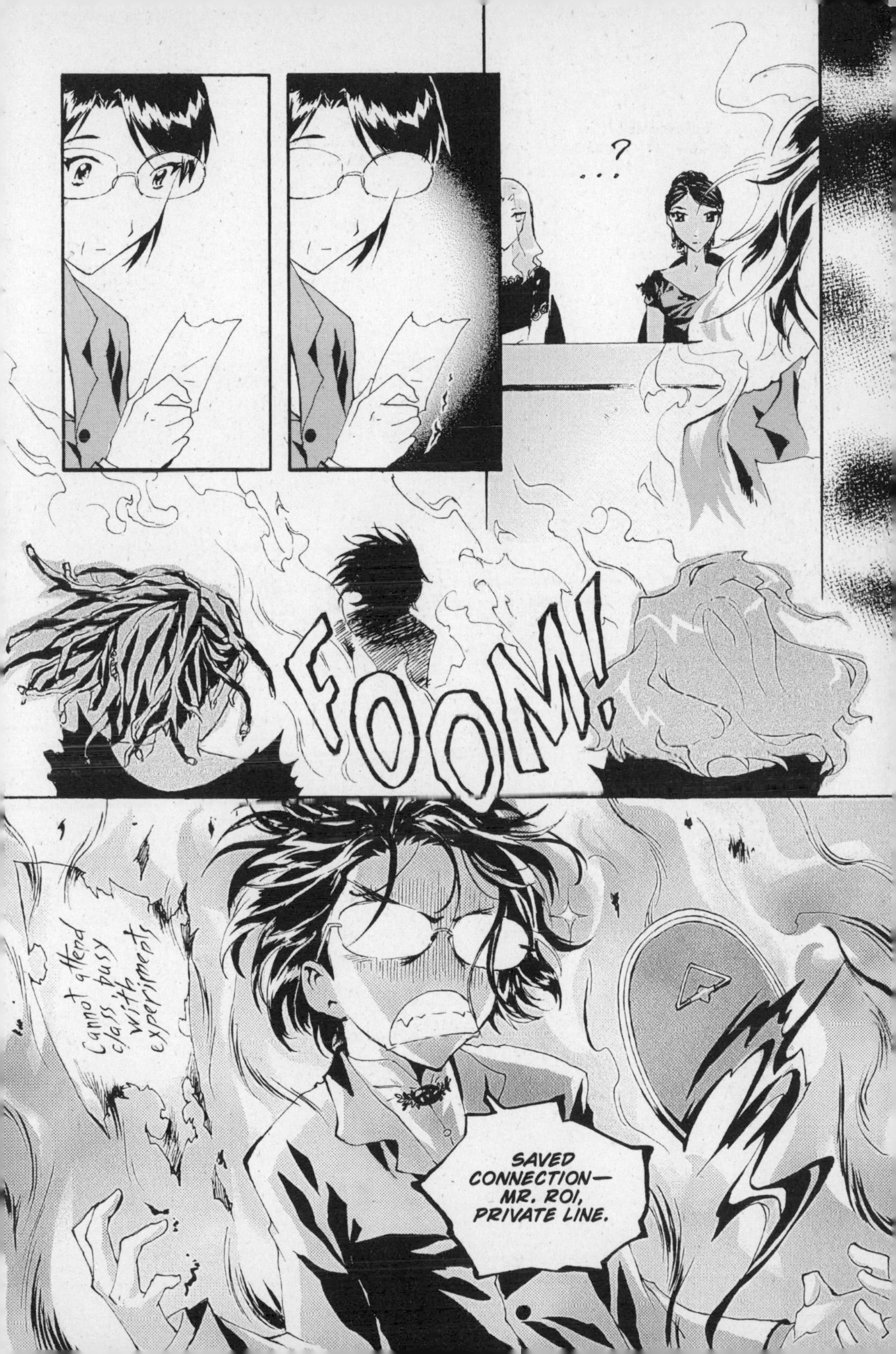

...?
FOOM!
Cannot attend class, busy with experiments
SAVED CONNECTION— MR. ROI, PRIVATE LINE.

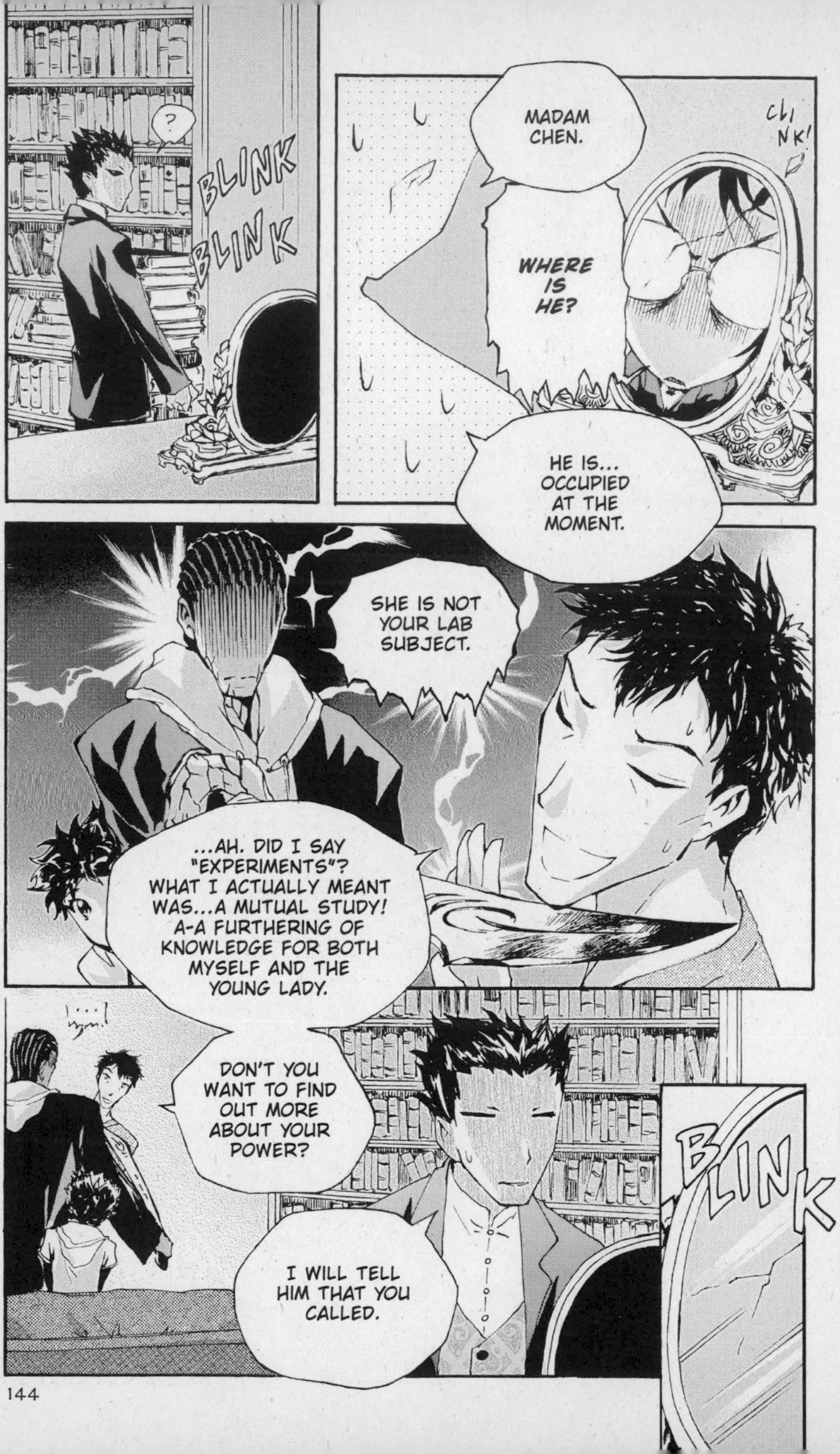
?
BLINK BLINK
MADAM CHEN.
CLINK!
WHERE IS HE?
HE IS... OCCUPIED AT THE MOMENT.
SHE IS NOT YOUR LAB SUBJECT.
...AH. DID I SAY "EXPERIMENTS"? WHAT I ACTUALLY MEANT WAS...A MUTUAL STUDY! A-A FURTHERING OF KNOWLEDGE FOR BOTH MYSELF AND THE YOUNG LADY.
DON'T YOU WANT TO FIND OUT MORE ABOUT YOUR POWER?
I WILL TELL HIM THAT YOU CALLED.
BLINK

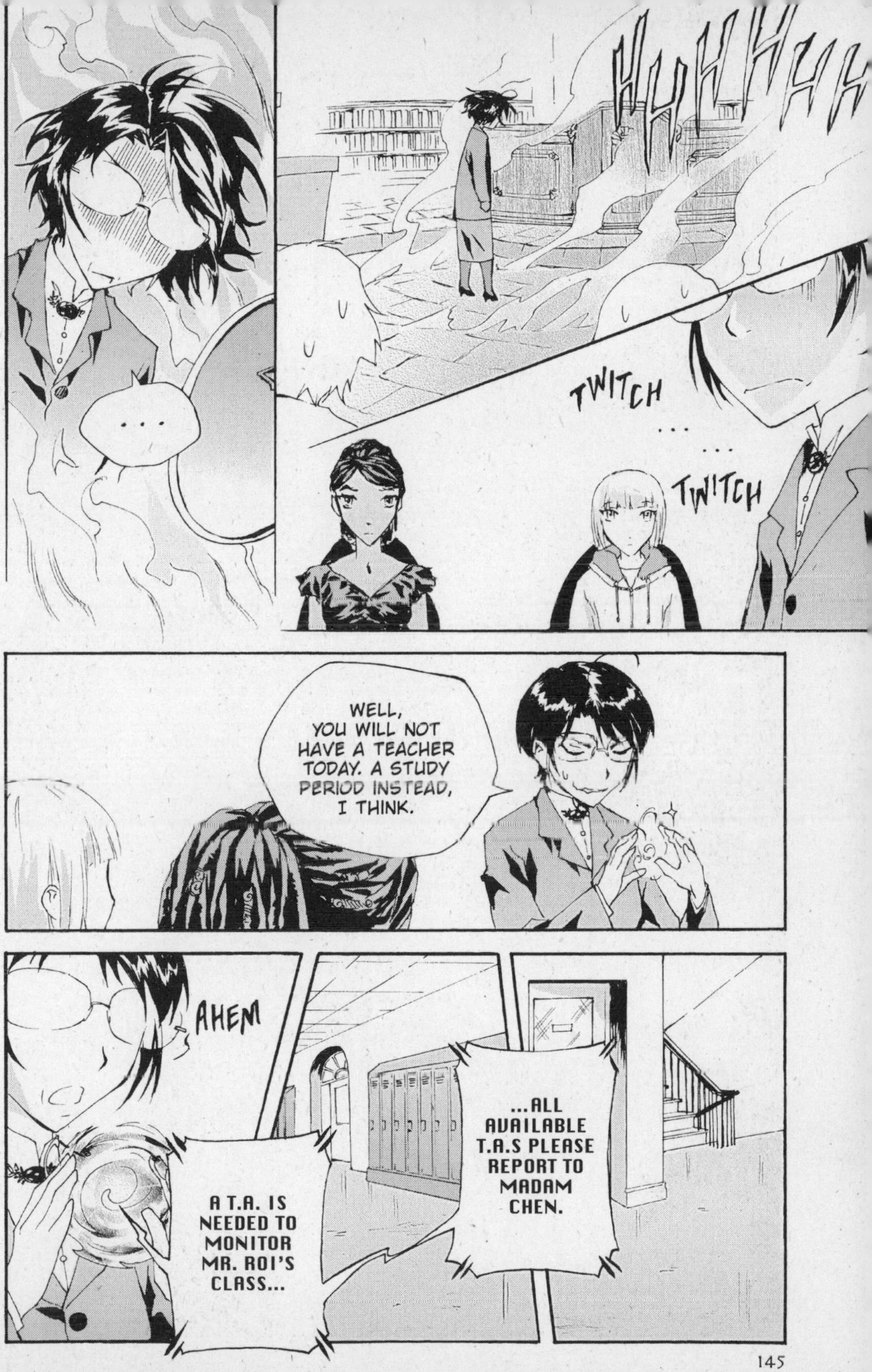
...
HUHHHHH
TWITCH
...
...
TWITCH
WELL, YOU WILL NOT HAVE A TEACHER TODAY. A STUDY PERIOD INSTEAD, I THINK.
AHEM
A T.A. IS NEEDED TO MONITOR MR. ROI'S CLASS...
...ALL AVAILABLE T.A.S PLEASE REPORT TO MADAM CHEN.

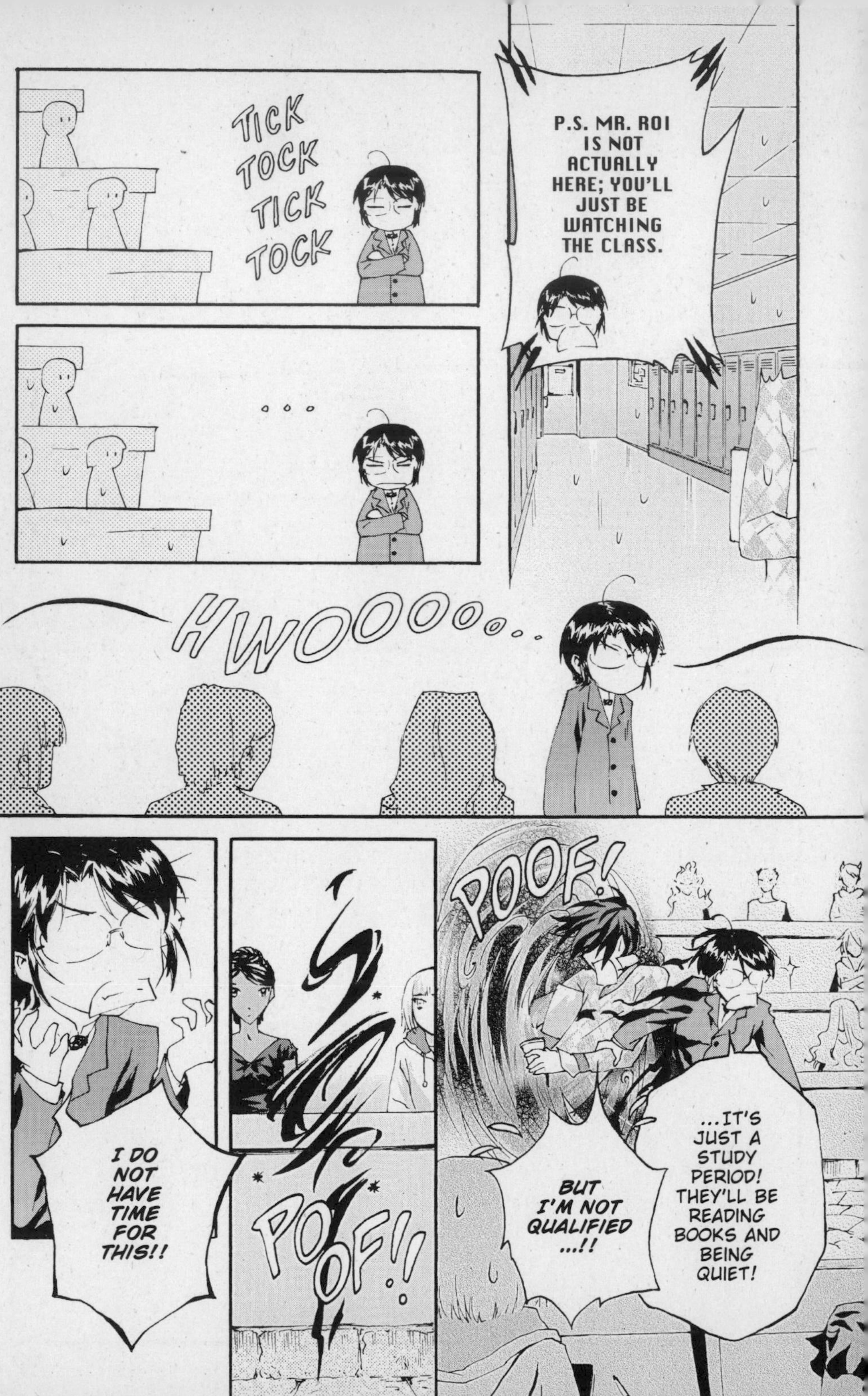
TICK TOCK TICK TOCK
...
P.S. MR. ROI IS NOT ACTUALLY HERE; YOU'LL JUST BE WATCHING THE CLASS.
HWOOOOO...
I DO NOT HAVE TIME FOR THIS!!
POOF!!
POOF!
BUT I'M NOT QUALIFIED ...!!
...IT'S JUST A STUDY PERIOD! THEY'LL BE READING BOOKS AND BEING QUIET!

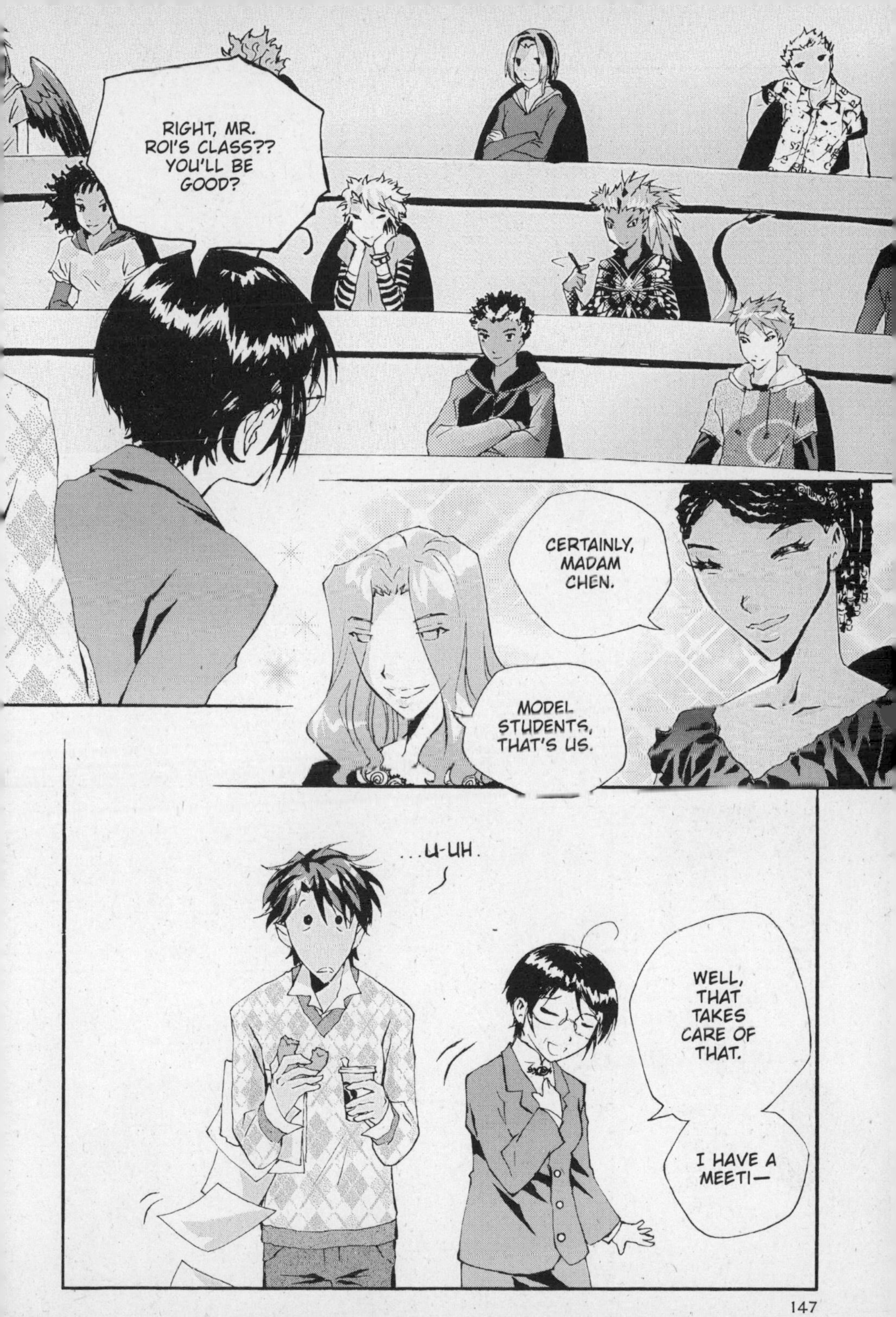
RIGHT, MR. ROI'S CLASS?? YOU'LL BE GOOD?
CERTAINLY, MADAM CHEN.
MODEL STUDENTS, THAT'S US.
...U-UH.
WELL, THAT TAKES CARE OF THAT.
I HAVE A MEETI—

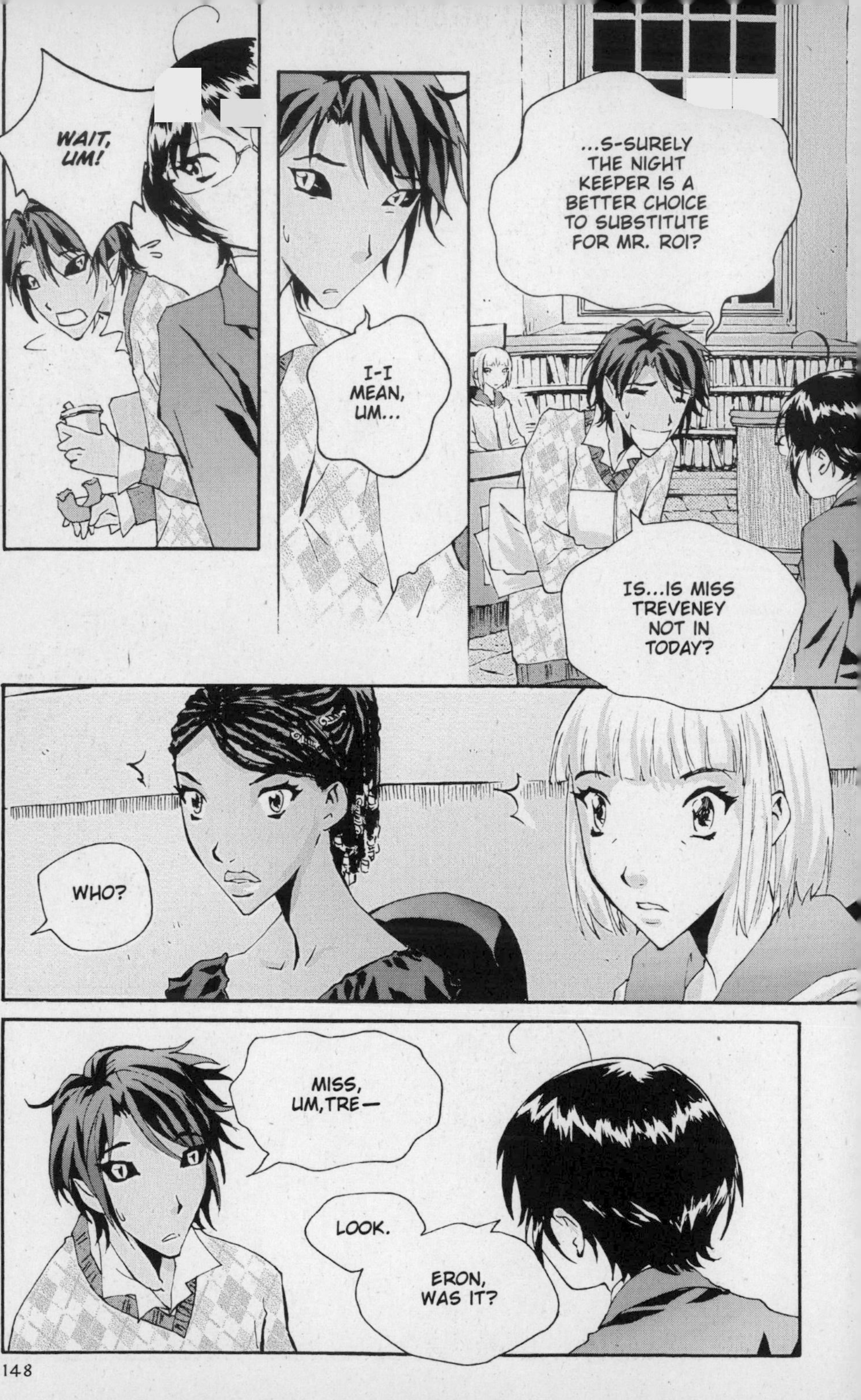
WAIT, UM!
I-I MEAN, UM...
...S-SURELY THE NIGHT KEEPER IS A BETTER CHOICE TO SUBSTITUTE FOR MR. ROI?
IS...IS MISS TREVENEY NOT IN TODAY?
WHO?
MISS, UM, TRE—
LOOK.
ERON, WAS IT?

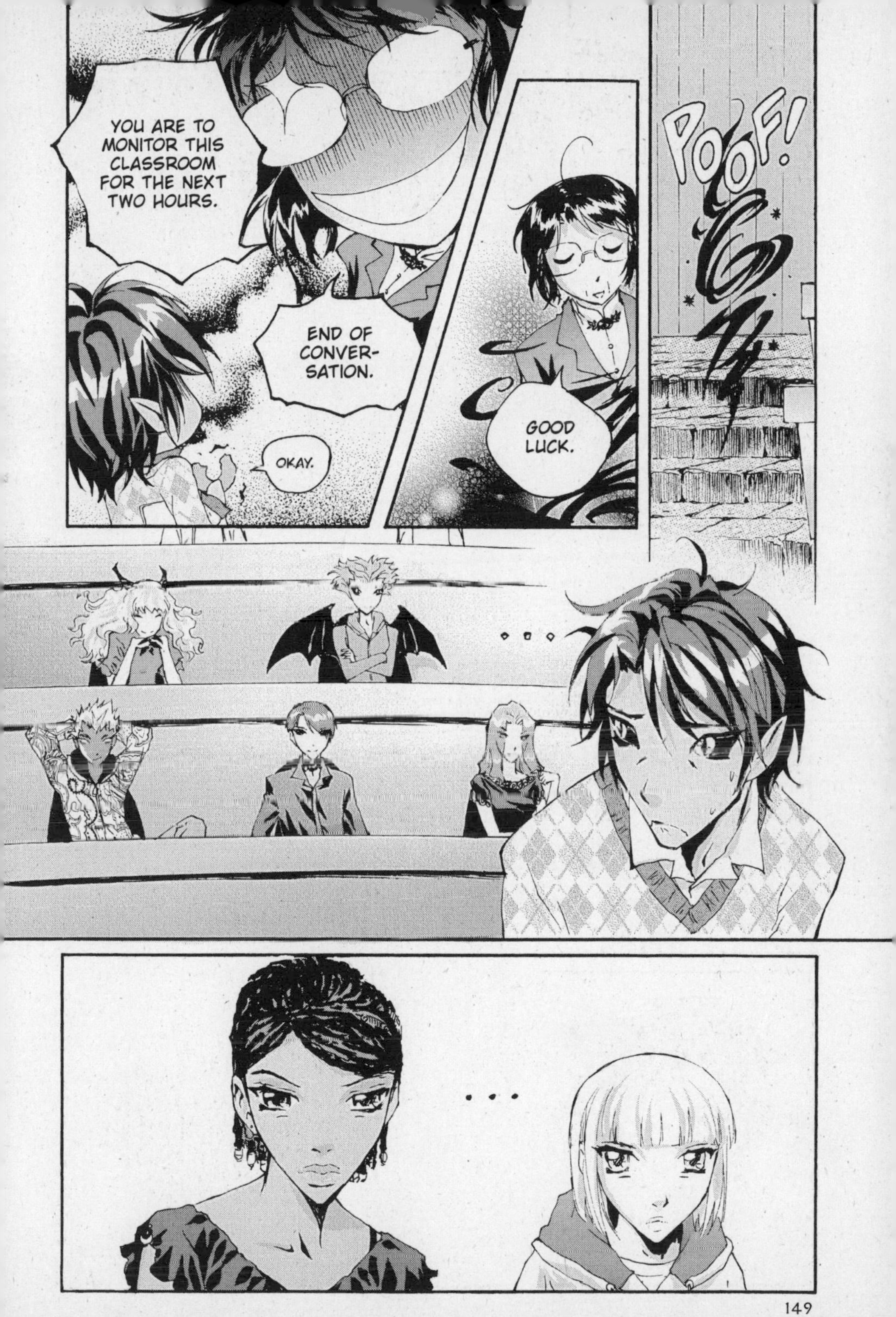
YOU ARE TO MONITOR THIS CLASSROOM FOR THE NEXT TWO HOURS.
END OF CONVERSATION.
OKAY.
GOOD LUCK.
POOF!
...
...

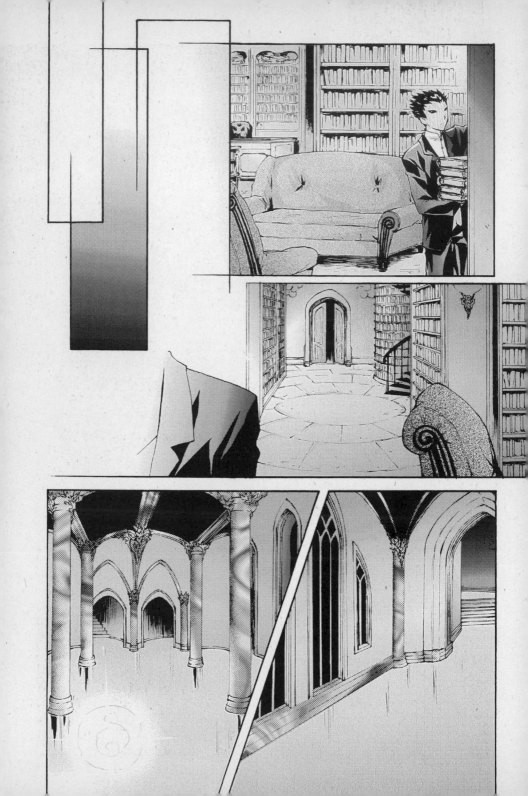

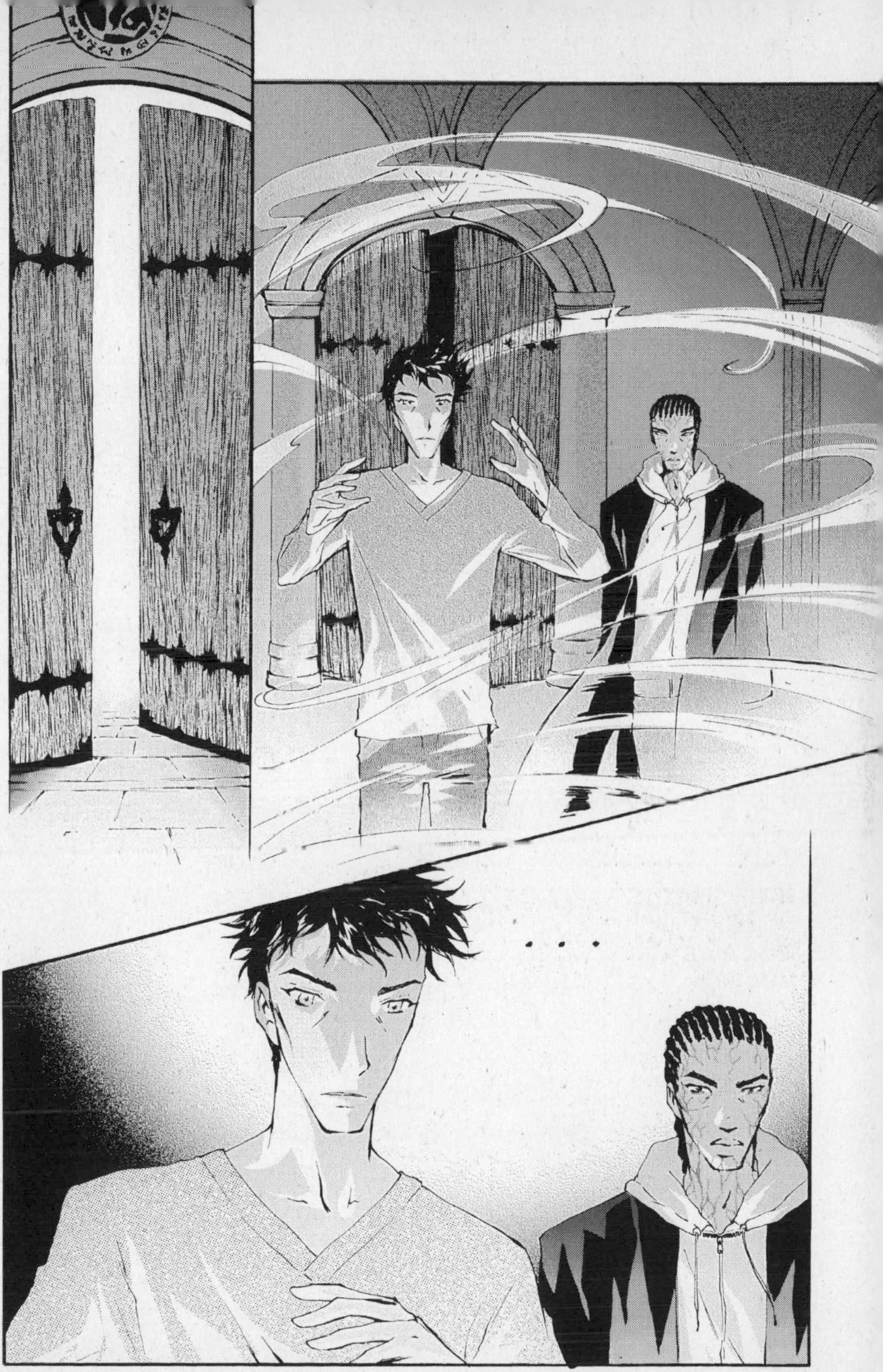
...

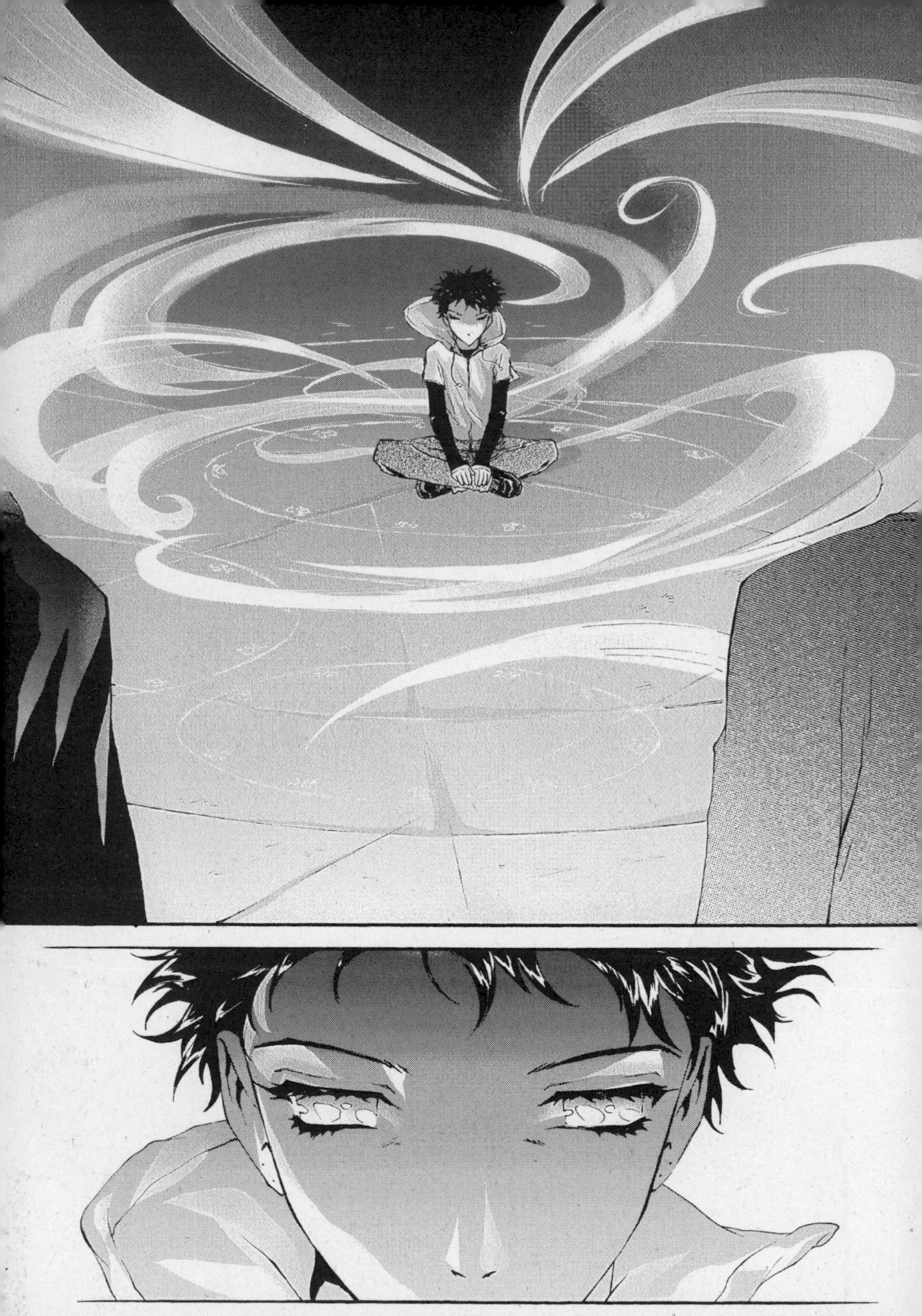

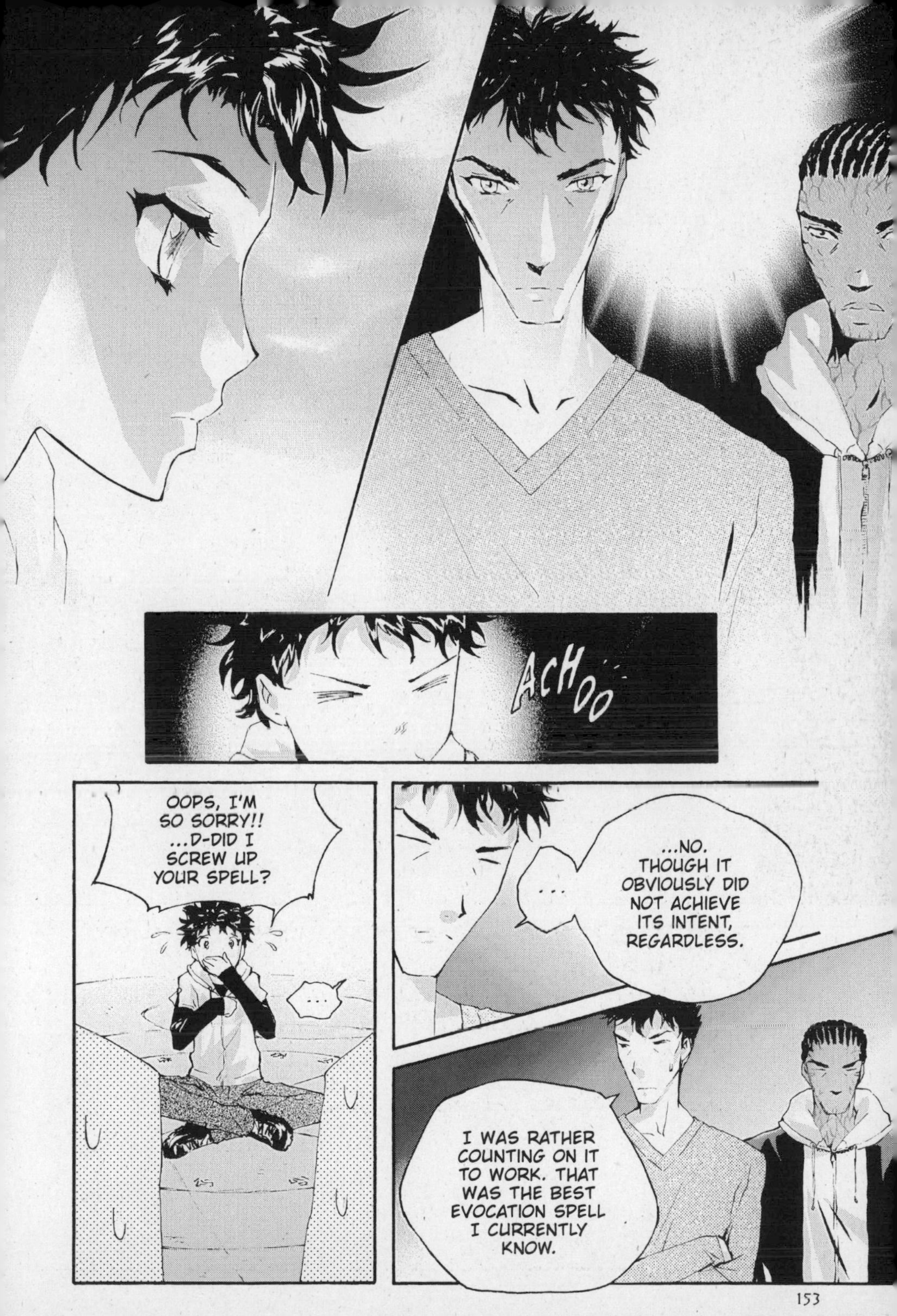
ACHOO
OOPS, I'M SO SORRY!! ...D-DID I SCREW UP YOUR SPELL?
...
...
...NO. THOUGH IT OBVIOUSLY DID NOT ACHIEVE ITS INTENT, REGARDLESS.
I WAS RATHER COUNTING ON IT TO WORK. THAT WAS THE BEST EVOCATION SPELL I CURRENTLY KNOW.

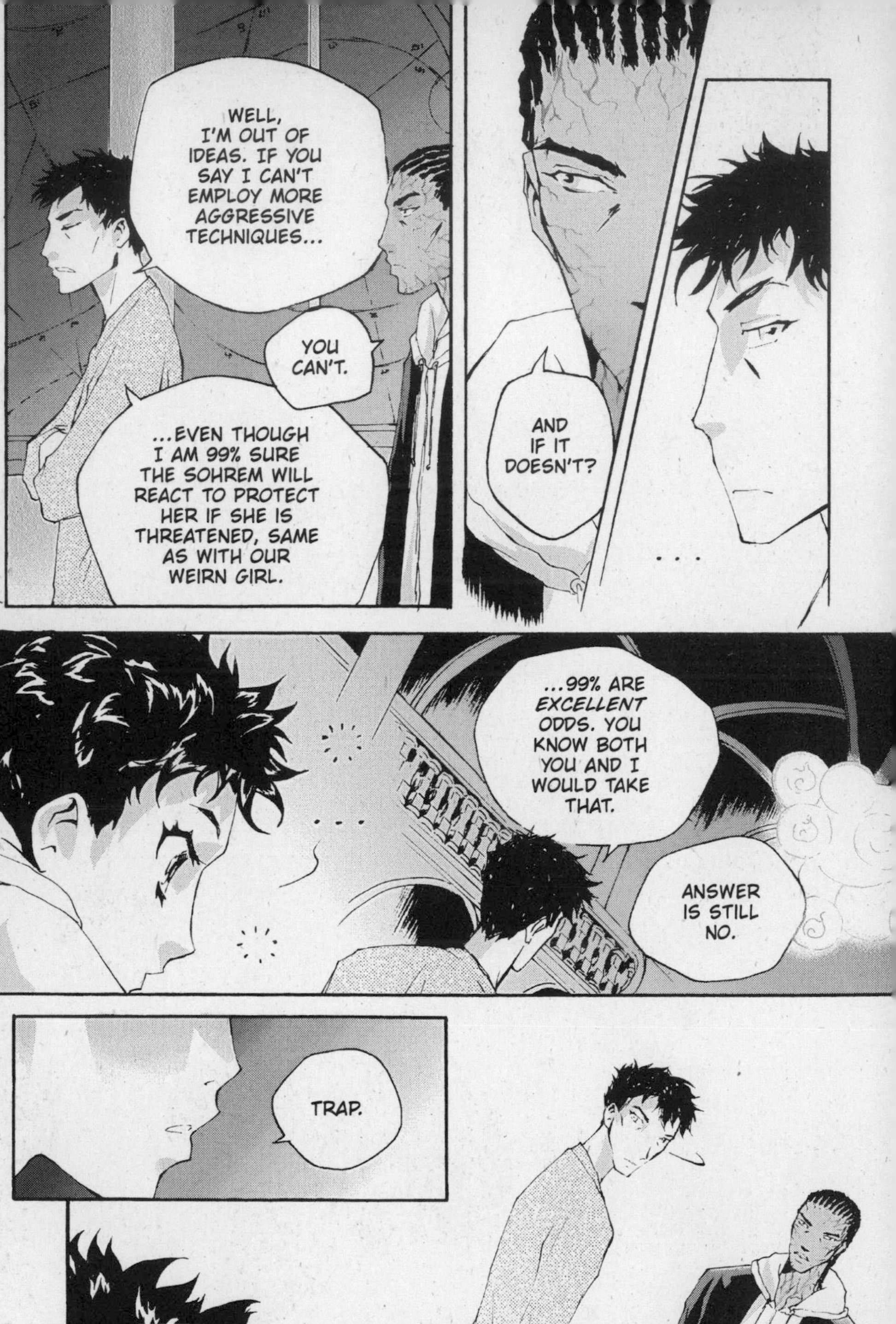
WELL, I'M OUT OF IDEAS. IF YOU SAY I CAN'T EMPLOY MORE AGGRESSIVE TECHNIQUES...
YOU CAN'T.
...EVEN THOUGH I AM 99% SURE THE SOHREM WILL REACT TO PROTECT HER IF SHE IS THREATENED, SAME AS WITH OUR WEIRN GIRL.
AND IF IT DOESN'T?
...
...
...99% ARE *EXCELLENT* ODDS. YOU KNOW BOTH YOU AND I WOULD TAKE THAT.
ANSWER IS STILL NO.
TRAP.

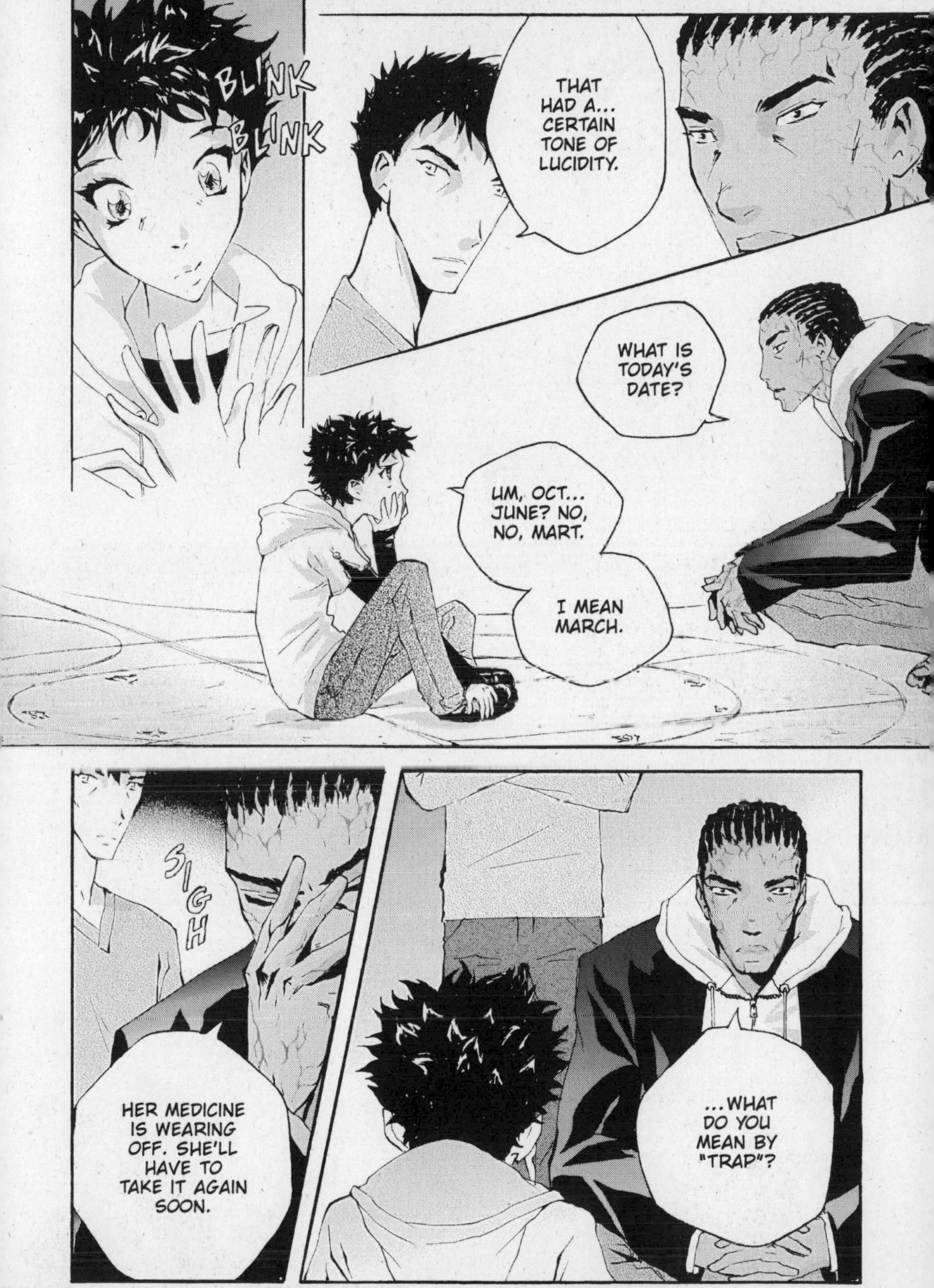
BLINK BLINK
THAT HAD A... CERTAIN TONE OF LUCIDITY.
WHAT IS TODAY'S DATE?
UM, OCT... JUNE? NO, NO, MART.
I MEAN MARCH.
SIGH
HER MEDICINE IS WEARING OFF. SHE'LL HAVE TO TAKE IT AGAIN SOON.
...WHAT DO YOU MEAN BY "TRAP"?

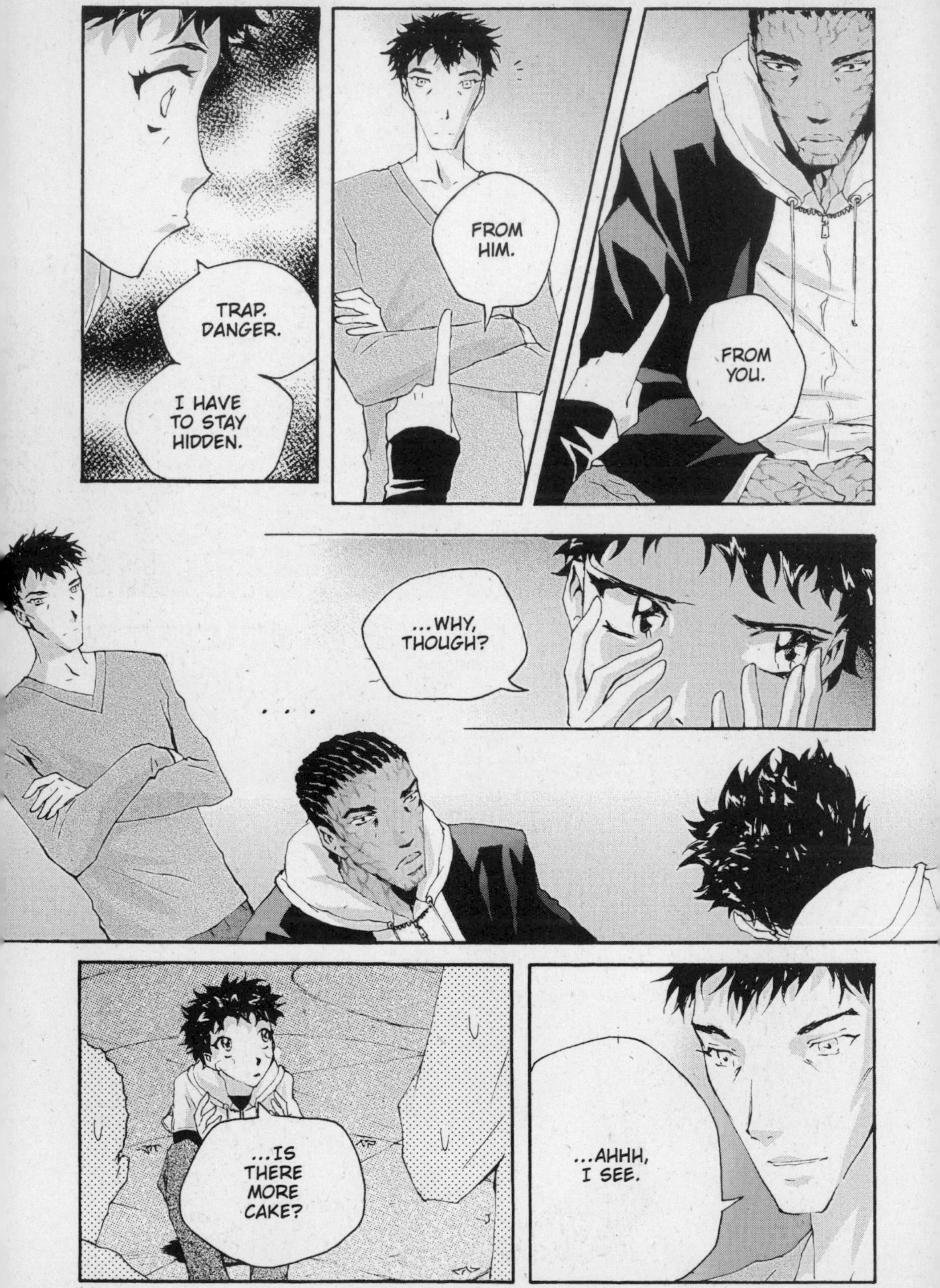
TRAP. DANGER.
I HAVE TO STAY HIDDEN.
FROM HIM.
FROM YOU.
...WHY, THOUGH?
. . .
...IS THERE MORE CAKE?
...AHHH, I SEE.

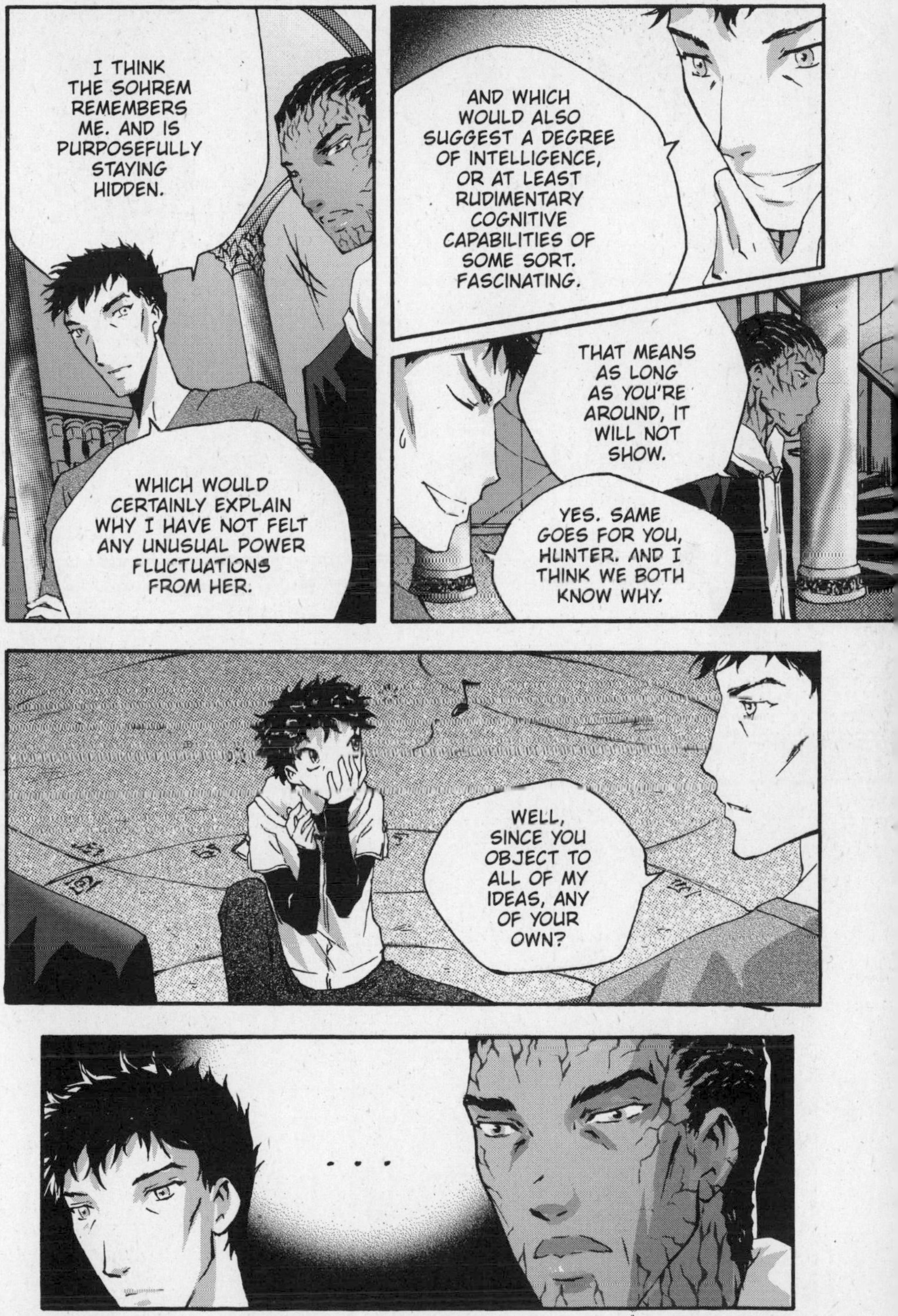
I THINK THE SOHREM REMEMBERS ME. AND IS PURPOSEFULLY STAYING HIDDEN.
WHICH WOULD CERTAINLY EXPLAIN WHY I HAVE NOT FELT ANY UNUSUAL POWER FLUCTUATIONS FROM HER.
AND WHICH WOULD ALSO SUGGEST A DEGREE OF INTELLIGENCE, OR AT LEAST RUDIMENTARY COGNITIVE CAPABILITIES OF SOME SORT. FASCINATING.
THAT MEANS AS LONG AS YOU'RE AROUND, IT WILL NOT SHOW.
YES. SAME GOES FOR YOU, HUNTER. AND I THINK WE BOTH KNOW WHY.
WELL, SINCE YOU OBJECT TO ALL OF MY IDEAS, ANY OF YOUR OWN?
...

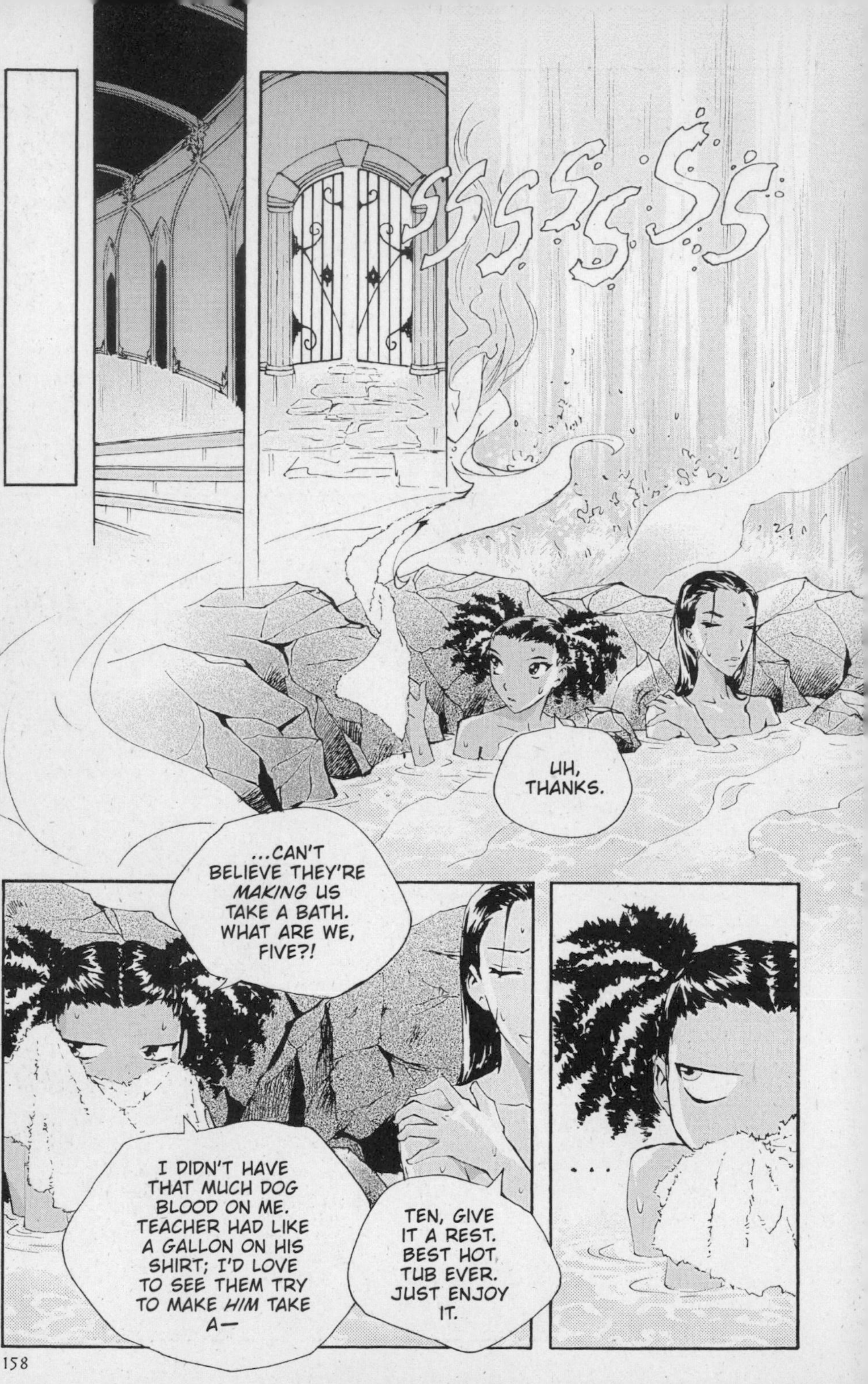
SSSSSSS
UH, THANKS.
...CAN'T BELIEVE THEY'RE *MAKING* US TAKE A BATH. WHAT ARE WE, FIVE?!
I DIDN'T HAVE THAT MUCH DOG BLOOD ON ME. TEACHER HAD LIKE A GALLON ON HIS SHIRT; I'D LOVE TO SEE THEM TRY TO MAKE *HIM* TAKE A—
TEN, GIVE IT A REST. BEST HOT TUB EVER. JUST ENJOY IT.
...

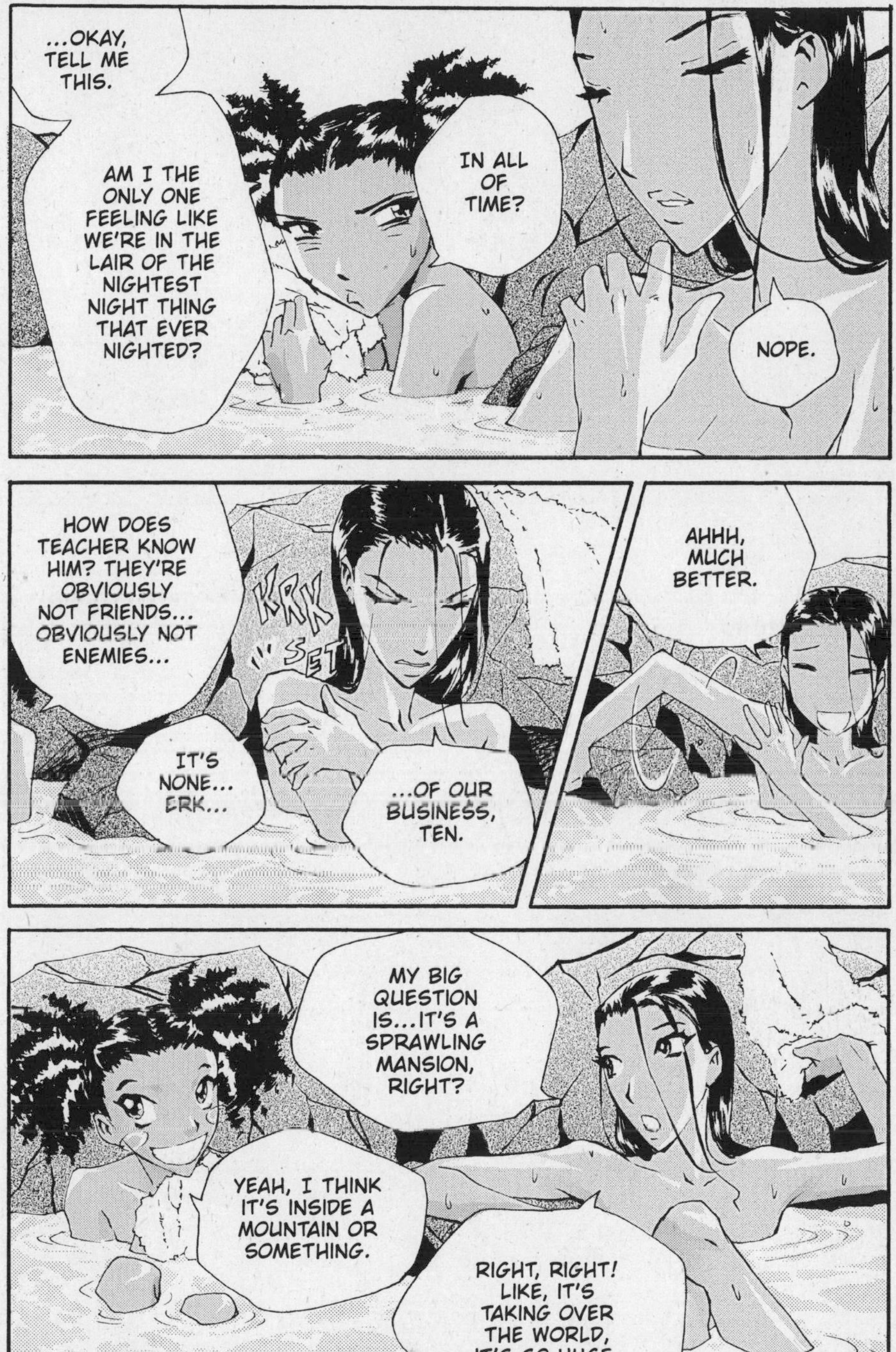
...OKAY, TELL ME THIS.
AM I THE ONLY ONE FEELING LIKE WE'RE IN THE LAIR OF THE NIGHTEST NIGHT THING THAT EVER NIGHTED?
IN ALL OF TIME?
NOPE.
HOW DOES TEACHER KNOW HIM? THEY'RE OBVIOUSLY NOT FRIENDS... OBVIOUSLY NOT ENEMIES...
KRK SET
IT'S NONE... ERK...
...OF OUR BUSINESS, TEN.
AHHH, MUCH BETTER.
MY BIG QUESTION IS...IT'S A SPRAWLING MANSION, RIGHT?
YEAH, I THINK IT'S INSIDE A MOUNTAIN OR SOMETHING.
RIGHT, RIGHT! LIKE, IT'S TAKING OVER THE WORLD, IT'S SO HUGE.

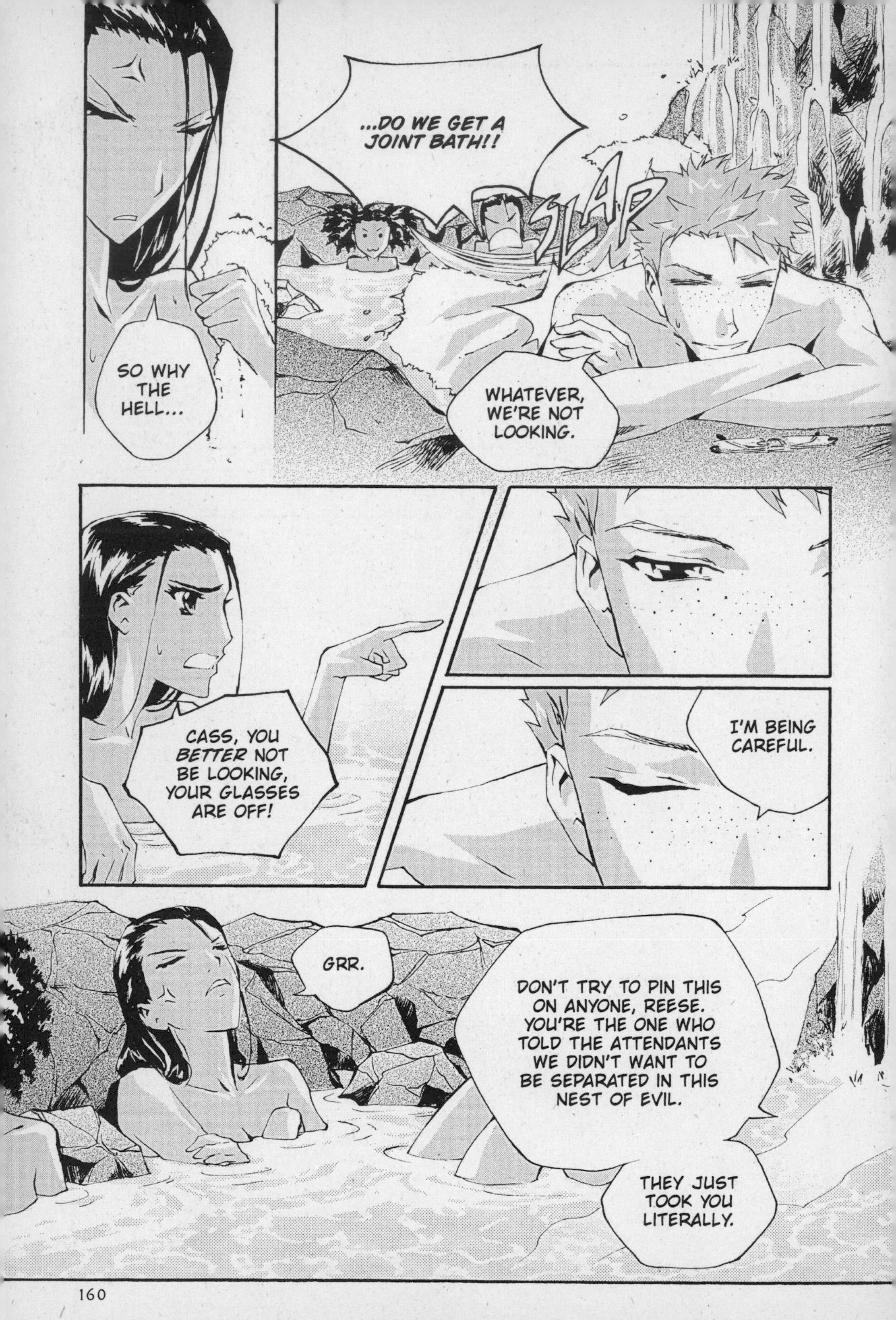
SO WHY THE HELL...
...DO WE GET A JOINT BATH!!
SLAP
WHATEVER, WE'RE NOT LOOKING.
CASS, YOU *BETTER* NOT BE LOOKING, YOUR GLASSES ARE OFF!
I'M BEING CAREFUL.
GRR.
DON'T TRY TO PIN THIS ON ANYONE, REESE. YOU'RE THE ONE WHO TOLD THE ATTENDANTS WE DIDN'T WANT TO BE SEPARATED IN THIS NEST OF EVIL.
THEY JUST TOOK YOU LITERALLY.

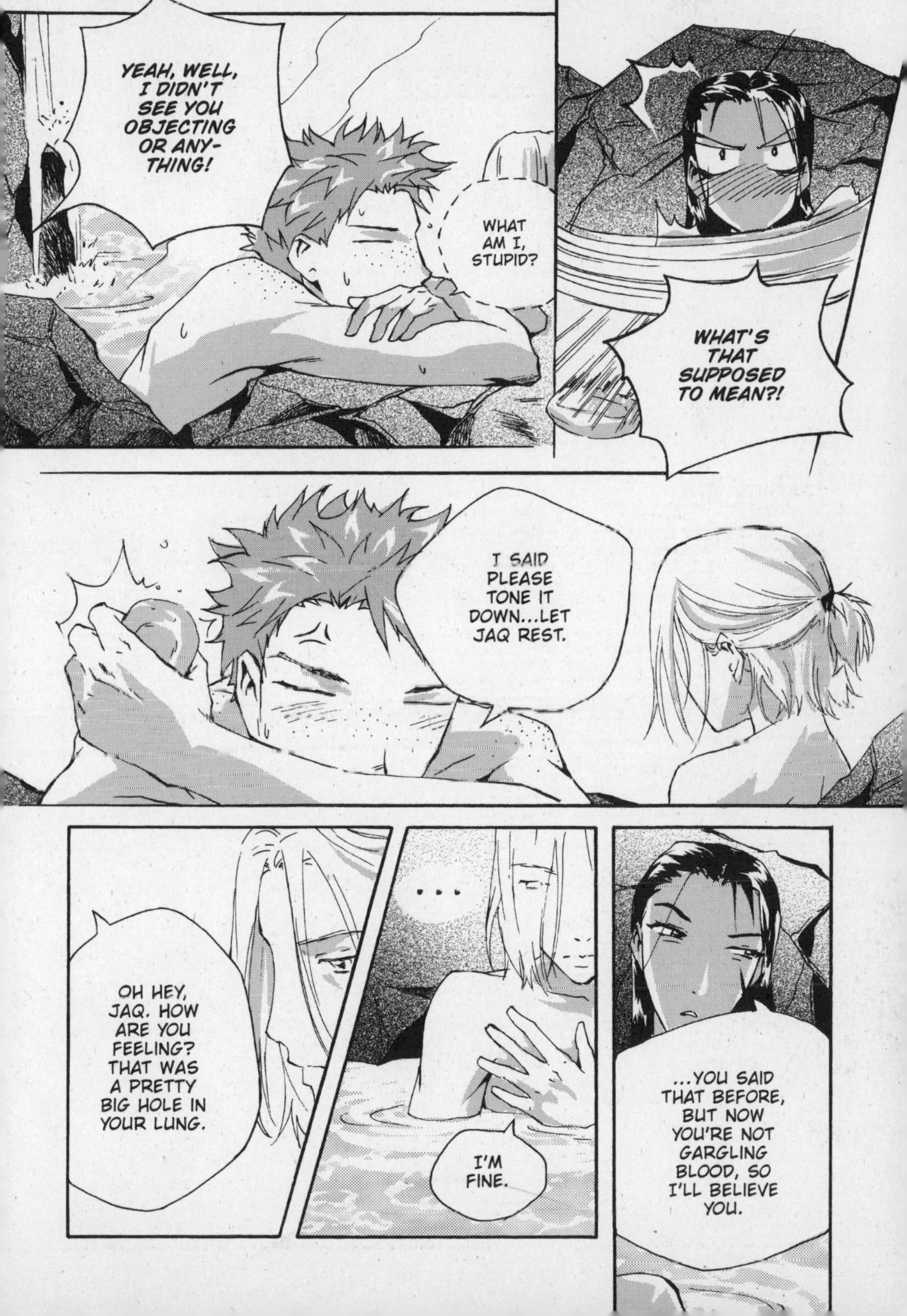
YEAH, WELL, I DIDN'T SEE YOU OBJECTING OR ANY-THING!
WHAT AM I, STUPID?
WHAT'S THAT SUPPOSED TO MEAN?!
I SAID PLEASE TONE IT DOWN...LET JAQ REST.
OH HEY, JAQ. HOW ARE YOU FEELING? THAT WAS A PRETTY BIG HOLE IN YOUR LUNG.
...
I'M FINE.
...YOU SAID THAT BEFORE, BUT NOW YOU'RE NOT GARGLING BLOOD, SO I'LL BELIEVE YOU.

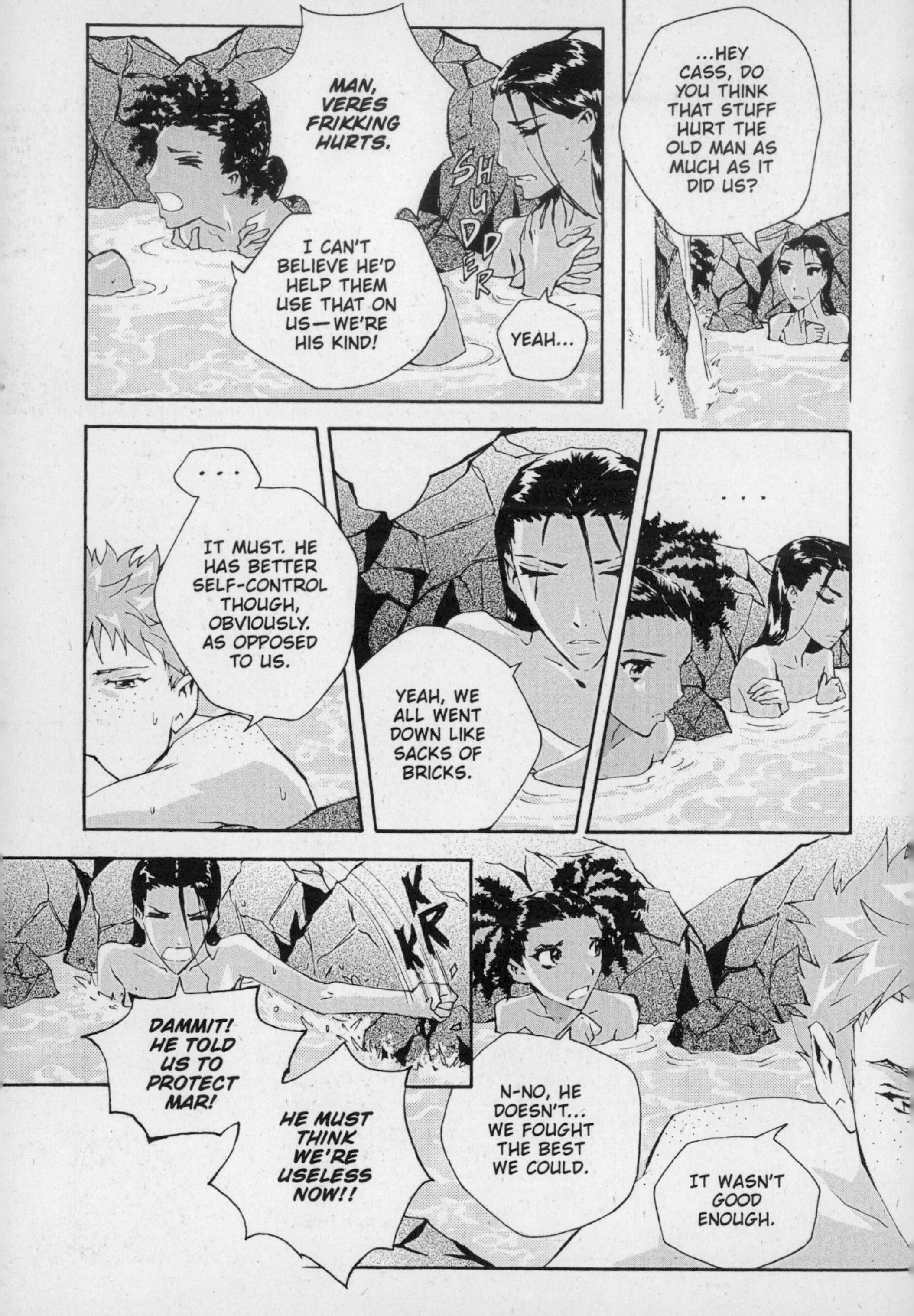
MAN, VERES FRIKKING HURTS.
SHUDDER
I CAN'T BELIEVE HE'D HELP THEM USE THAT ON US—WE'RE HIS KIND!
YEAH...
...HEY CASS, DO YOU THINK THAT STUFF HURT THE OLD MAN AS MUCH AS IT DID US?
...
IT MUST. HE HAS BETTER SELF-CONTROL THOUGH, OBVIOUSLY. AS OPPOSED TO US.
YEAH, WE ALL WENT DOWN LIKE SACKS OF BRICKS.
...
KRK
DAMMIT! HE TOLD US TO PROTECT MAR!
HE MUST THINK WE'RE USELESS NOW!!
N-NO, HE DOESN'T... WE FOUGHT THE BEST WE COULD.
IT WASN'T GOOD ENOUGH.

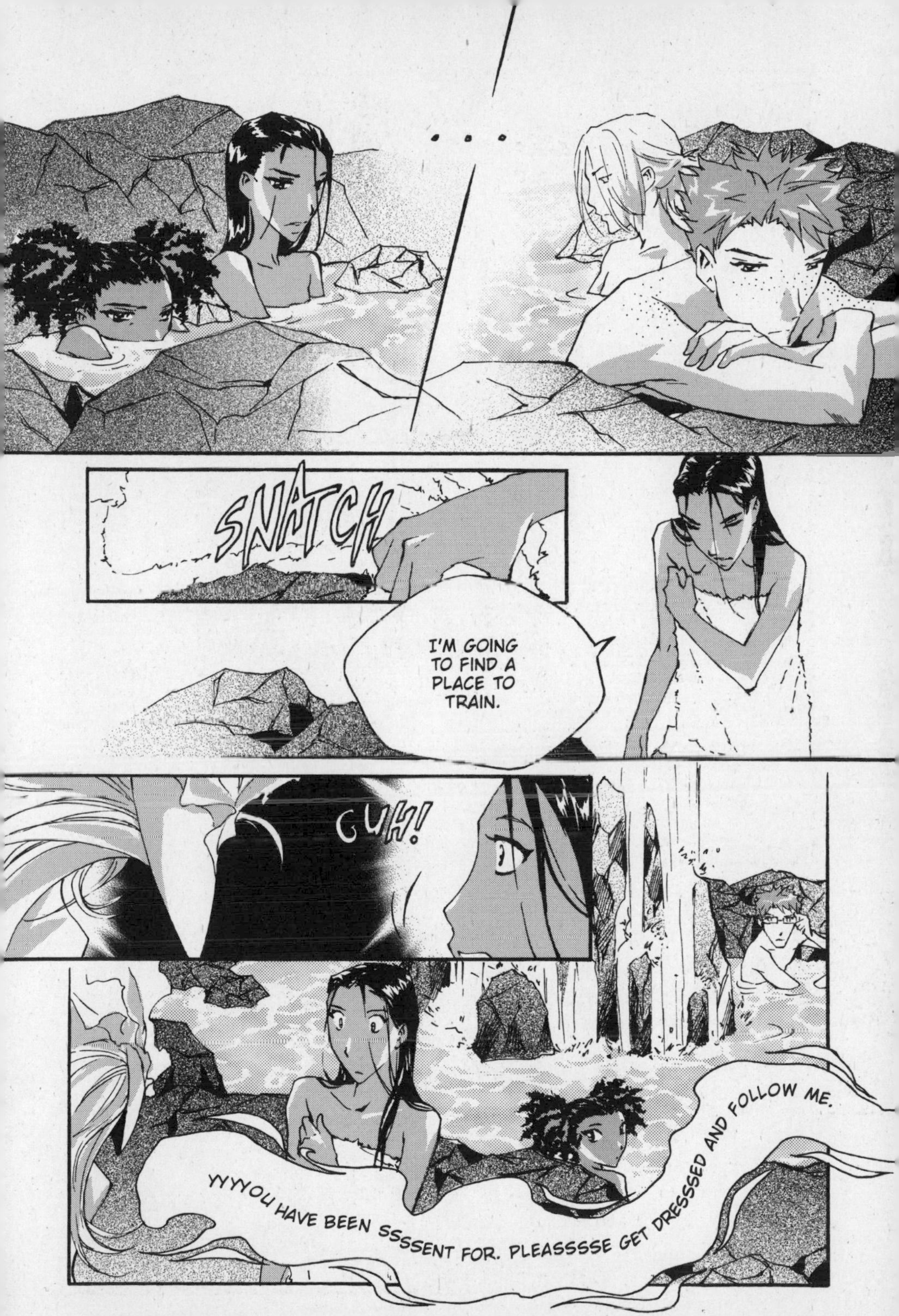
. . .
SNATCH
I'M GOING TO FIND A PLACE TO TRAIN.
GUH!
YYYYOU HAVE BEEN SSSSENT FOR. PLEASSSSE GET DRESSSED AND FOLLOW ME.

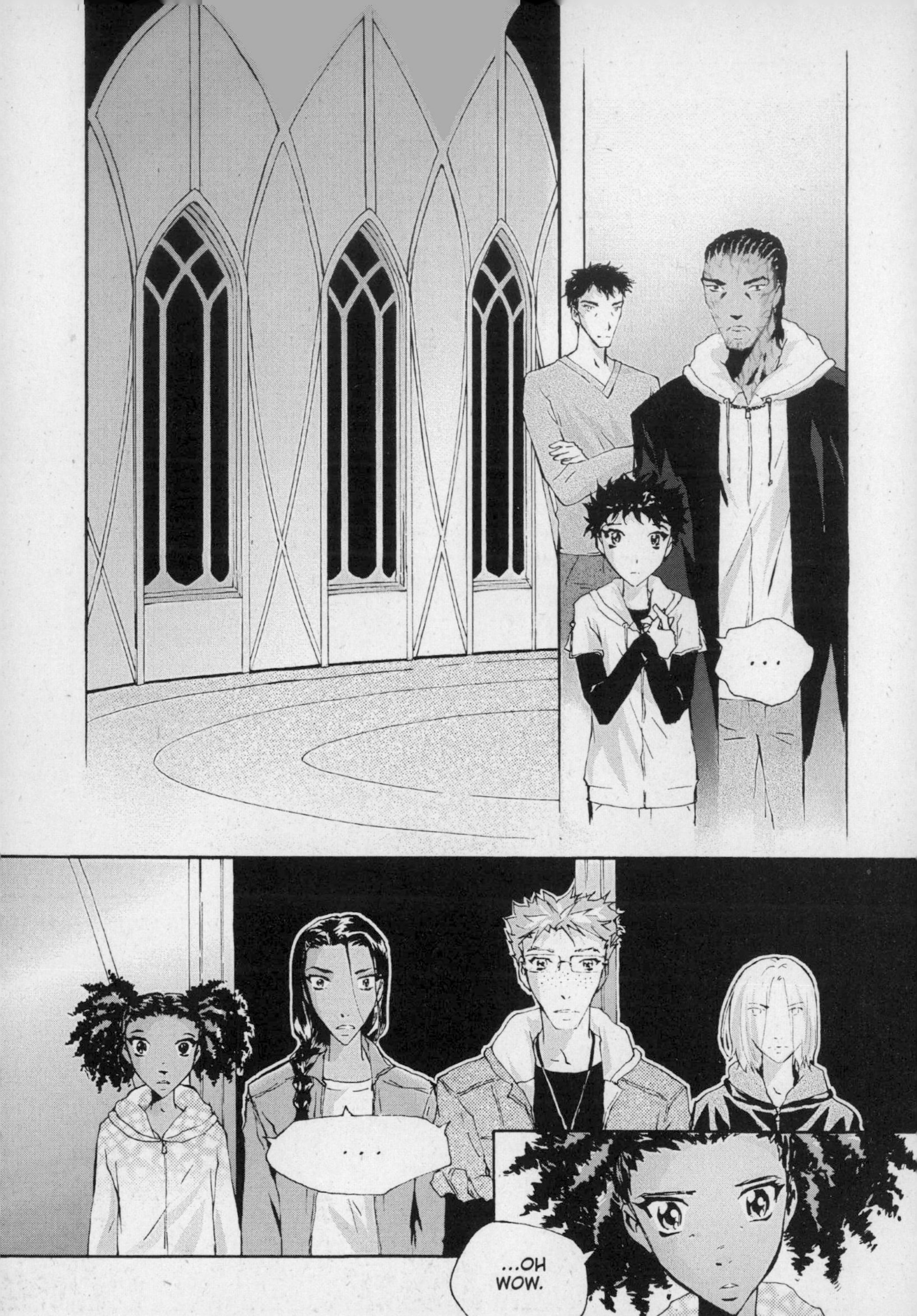
...
...
...OH WOW.

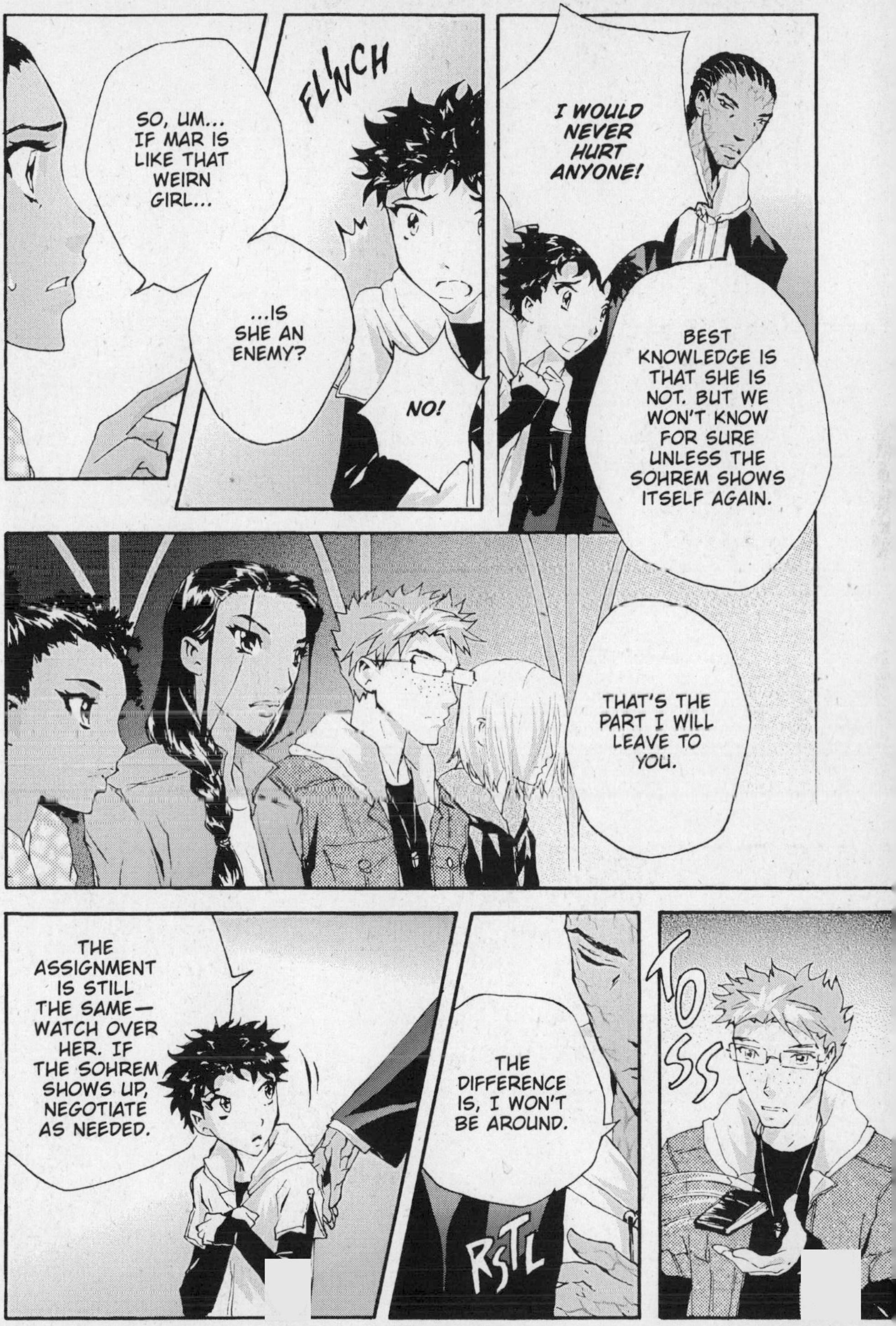
SO, UM... IF MAR IS LIKE THAT WEIRN GIRL...
...IS SHE AN ENEMY?
FLINCH
NO!
I WOULD NEVER HURT ANYONE!
BEST KNOWLEDGE IS THAT SHE IS NOT. BUT WE WON'T KNOW FOR SURE UNLESS THE SOHREM SHOWS ITSELF AGAIN.
THAT'S THE PART I WILL LEAVE TO YOU.
THE ASSIGNMENT IS STILL THE SAME—WATCH OVER HER. IF THE SOHREM SHOWS UP, NEGOTIATE AS NEEDED.
THE DIFFERENCE IS, I WON'T BE AROUND.
RSTL
TOSSS

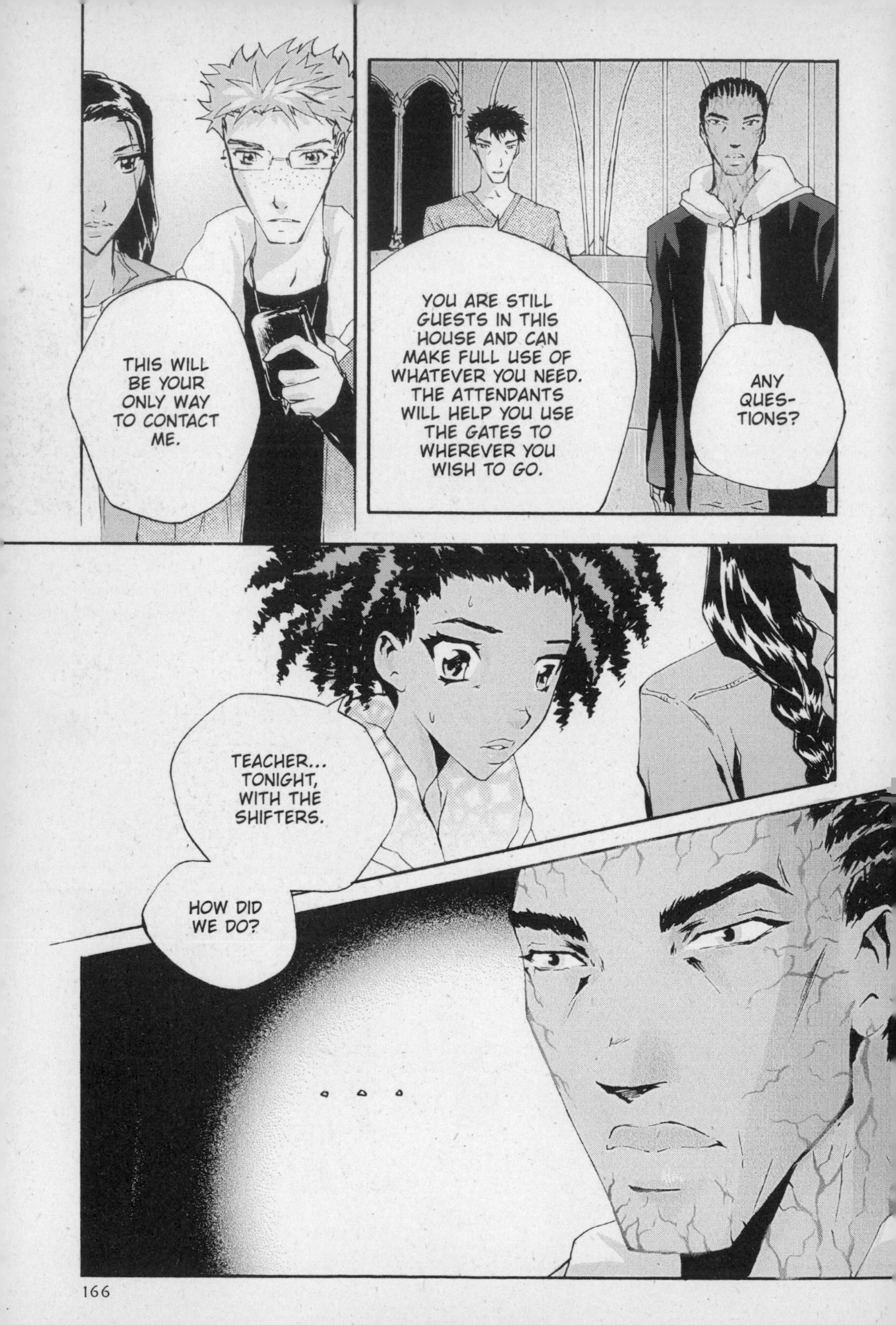
THIS WILL BE YOUR ONLY WAY TO CONTACT ME.
YOU ARE STILL GUESTS IN THIS HOUSE AND CAN MAKE FULL USE OF WHATEVER YOU NEED. THE ATTENDANTS WILL HELP YOU USE THE GATES TO WHEREVER YOU WISH TO GO.
ANY QUES-TIONS?
TEACHER... TONIGHT, WITH THE SHIFTERS.
HOW DID WE DO?
. . .

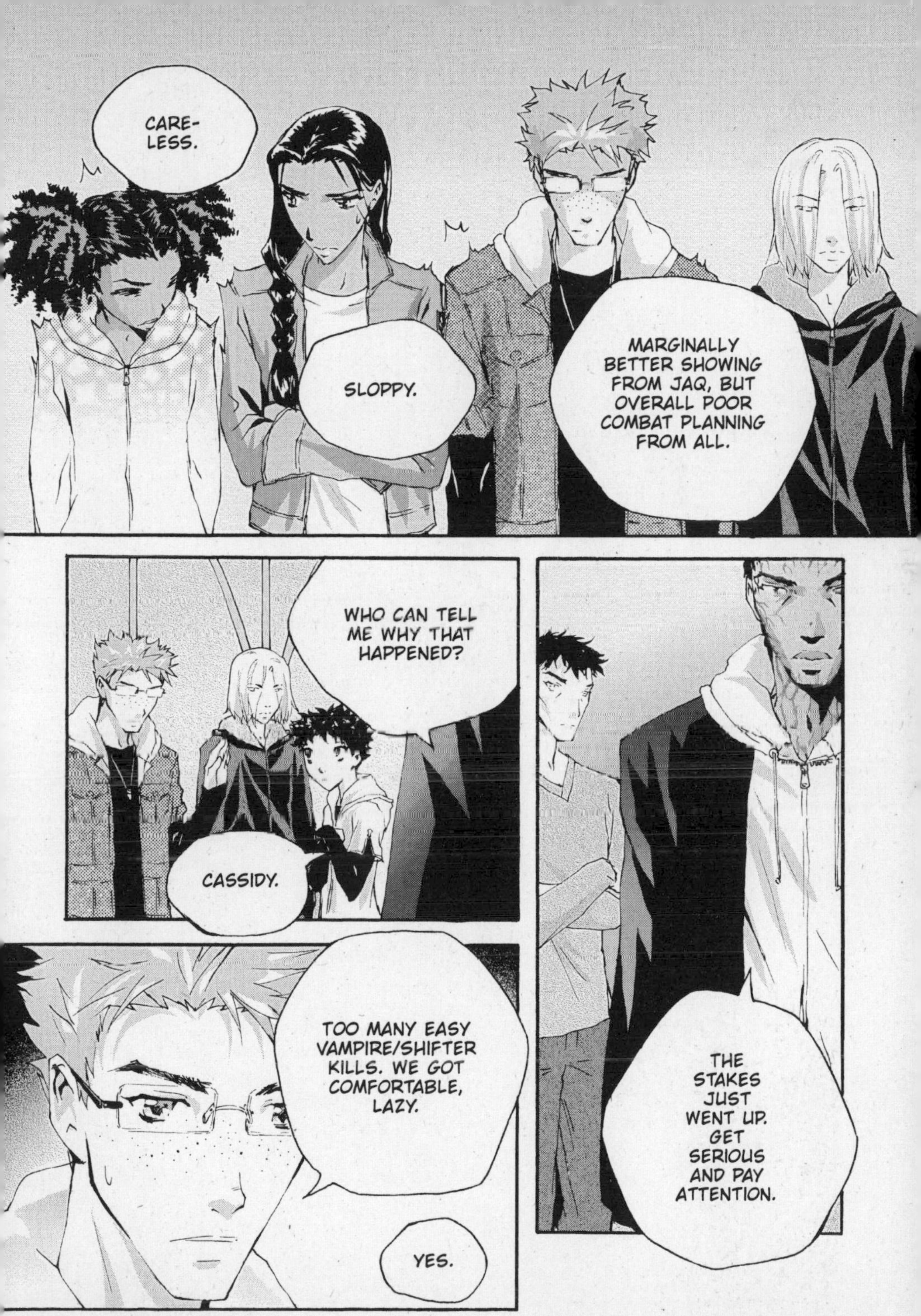
CARE-LESS.
SLOPPY.
MARGINALLY BETTER SHOWING FROM JAQ, BUT OVERALL POOR COMBAT PLANNING FROM ALL.
WHO CAN TELL ME WHY THAT HAPPENED?
CASSIDY.
TOO MANY EASY VAMPIRE/SHIFTER KILLS. WE GOT COMFORTABLE, LAZY.
YES.
THE STAKES JUST WENT UP. GET SERIOUS AND PAY ATTENTION.

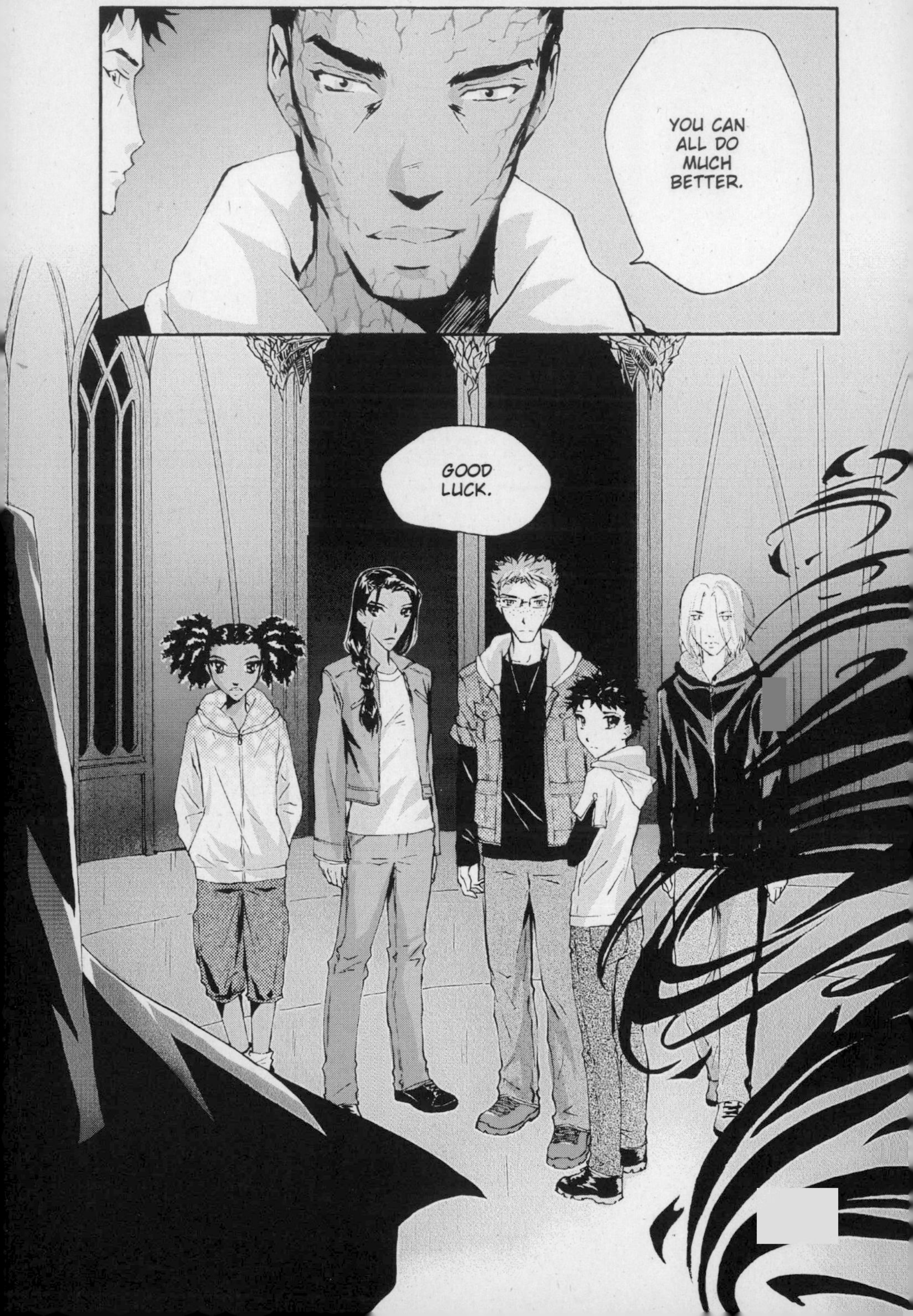
YOU CAN ALL DO MUCH BETTER.
GOOD LUCK.

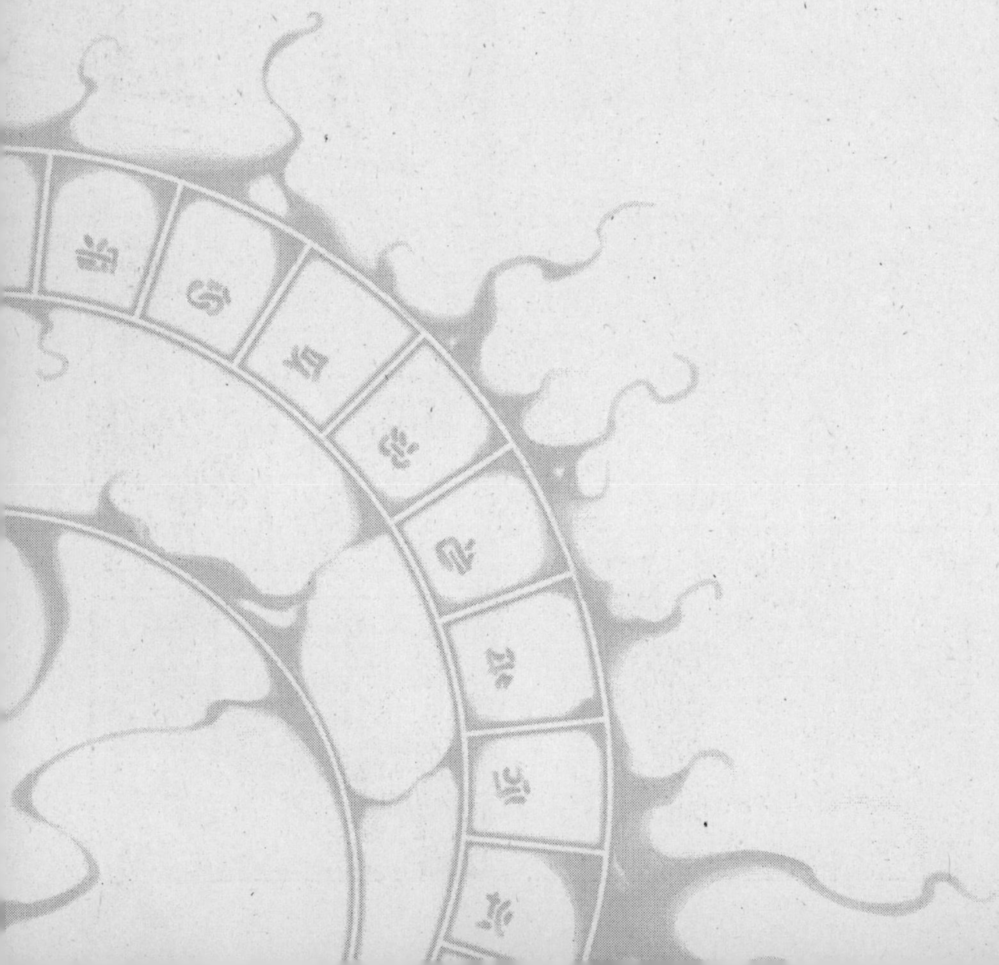

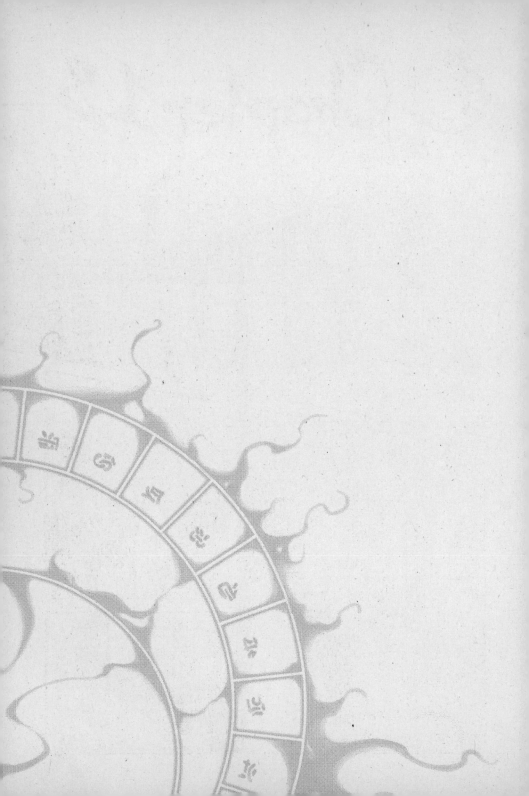

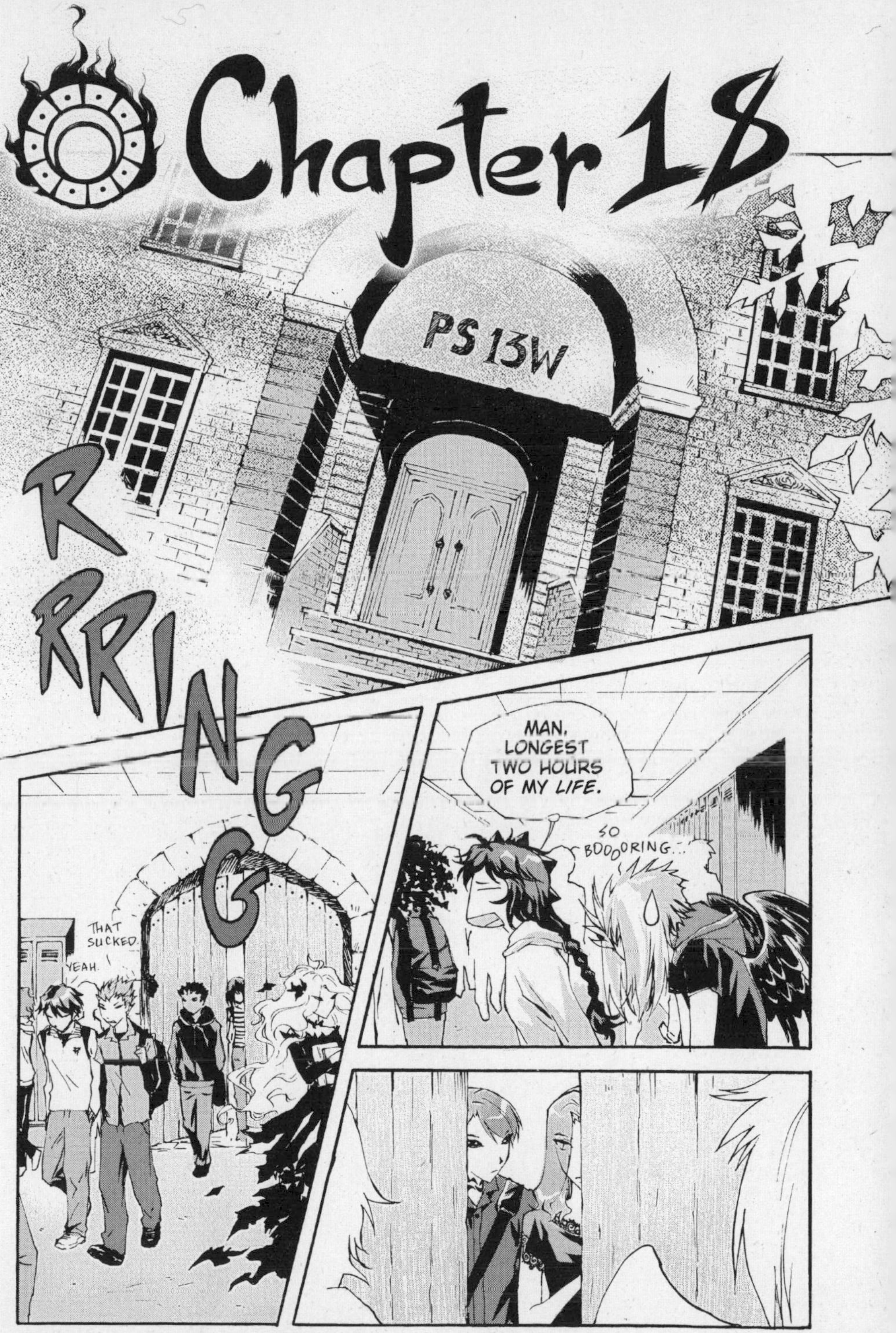
Chapter 18
PS 13W
RRRING
THAT SUCKED.
YEAH.
MAN, LONGEST TWO HOURS OF MY LIFE.
SO BOOOORING...

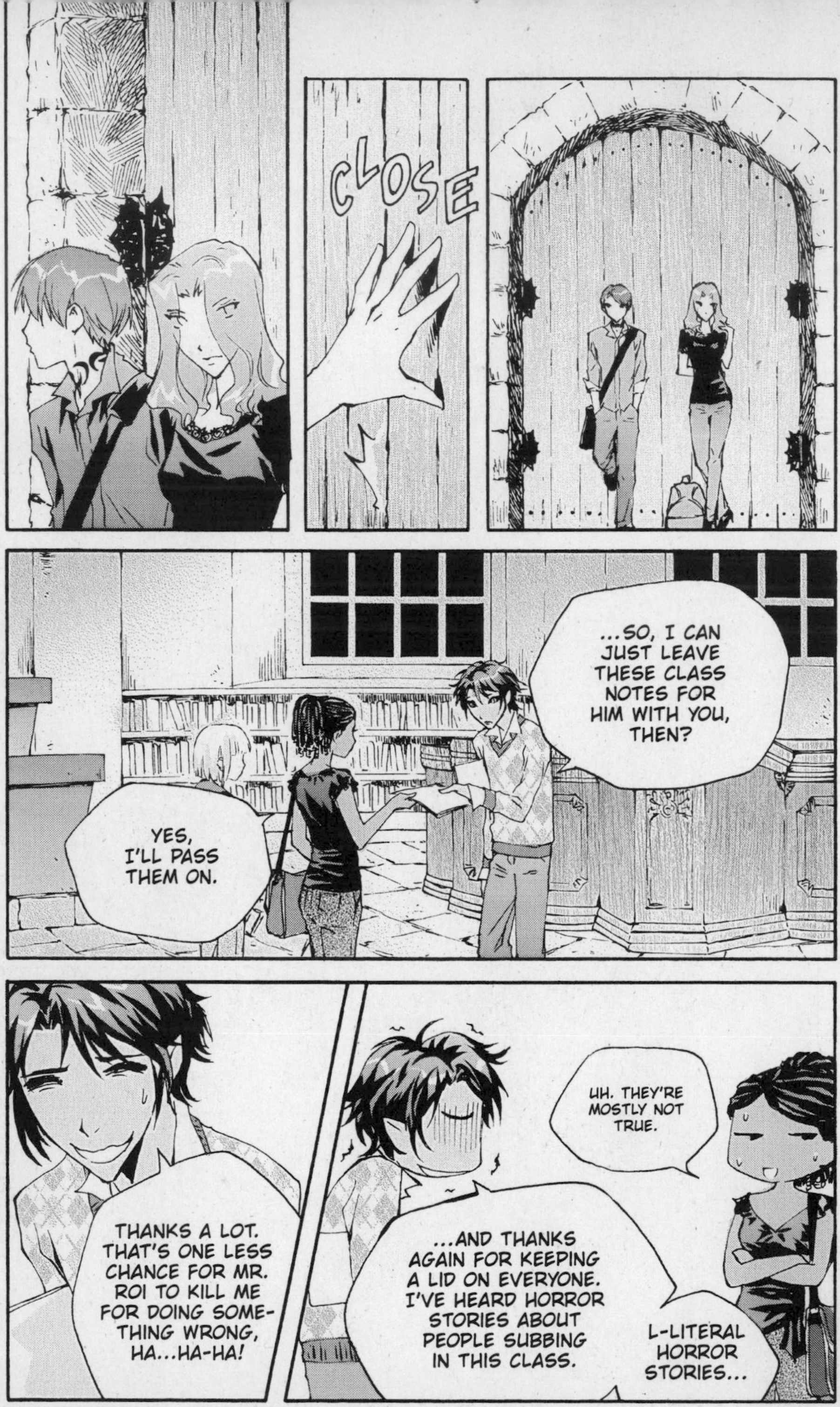
CLOSE
...SO, I CAN JUST LEAVE THESE CLASS NOTES FOR HIM WITH YOU, THEN?
YES, I'LL PASS THEM ON.
THANKS A LOT. THAT'S ONE LESS CHANCE FOR MR. ROI TO KILL ME FOR DOING SOME-THING WRONG, HA...HA-HA!
...AND THANKS AGAIN FOR KEEPING A LID ON EVERYONE. I'VE HEARD HORROR STORIES ABOUT PEOPLE SUBBING IN THIS CLASS.
L-LITERAL HORROR STORIES...
UH. THEY'RE MOSTLY NOT TRUE.

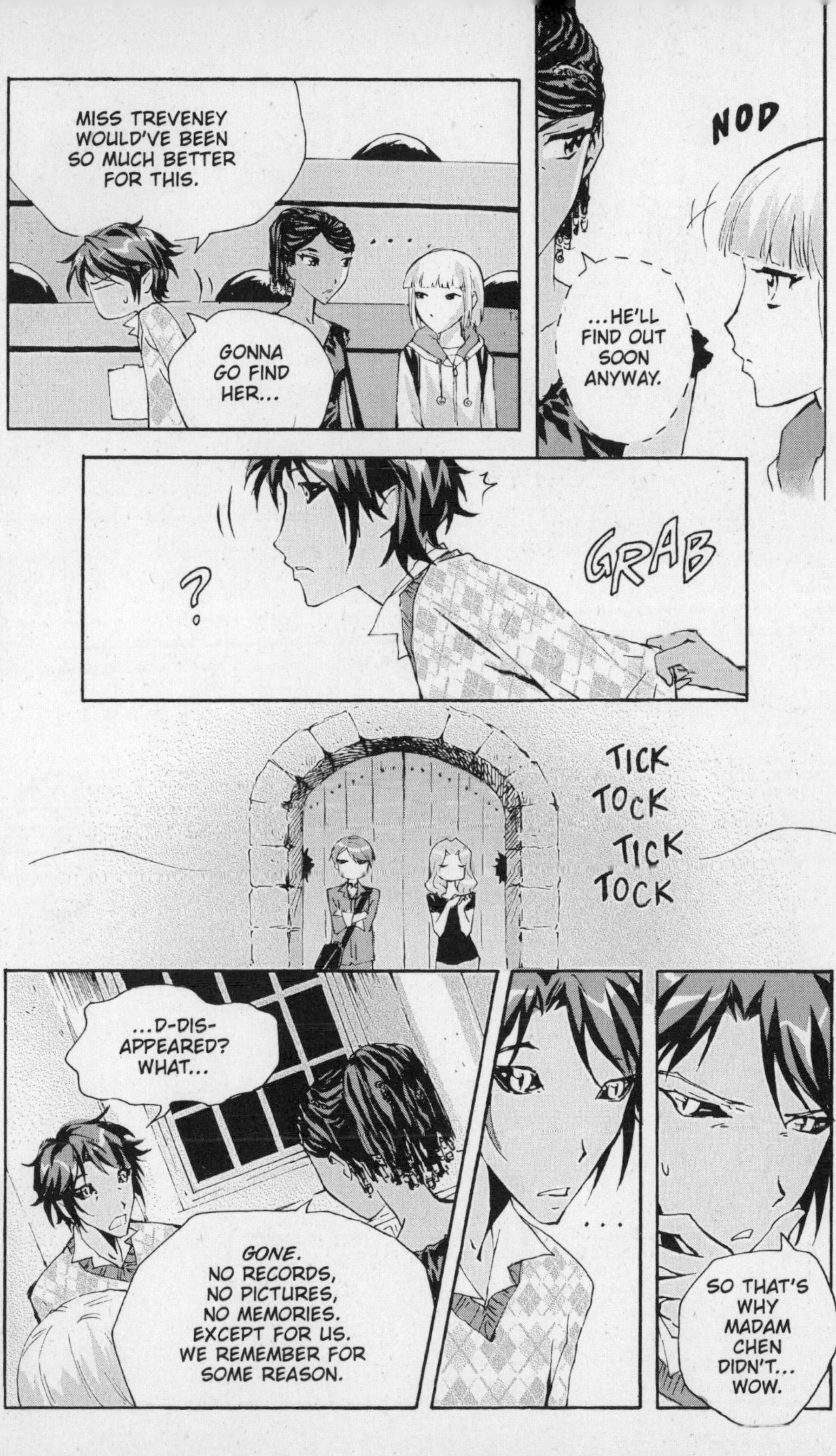
MISS TREVENEY WOULD'VE BEEN SO MUCH BETTER FOR THIS.
...
GONNA GO FIND HER...
NOD
...HE'LL FIND OUT SOON ANYWAY.
?
GRAB
TICK TOCK TICK TOCK
...D-DIS-APPEARED? WHAT...
GONE. NO RECORDS, NO PICTURES, NO MEMORIES. EXCEPT FOR US. WE REMEMBER FOR SOME REASON.
...
SO THAT'S WHY MADAM CHEN DIDN'T... WOW.

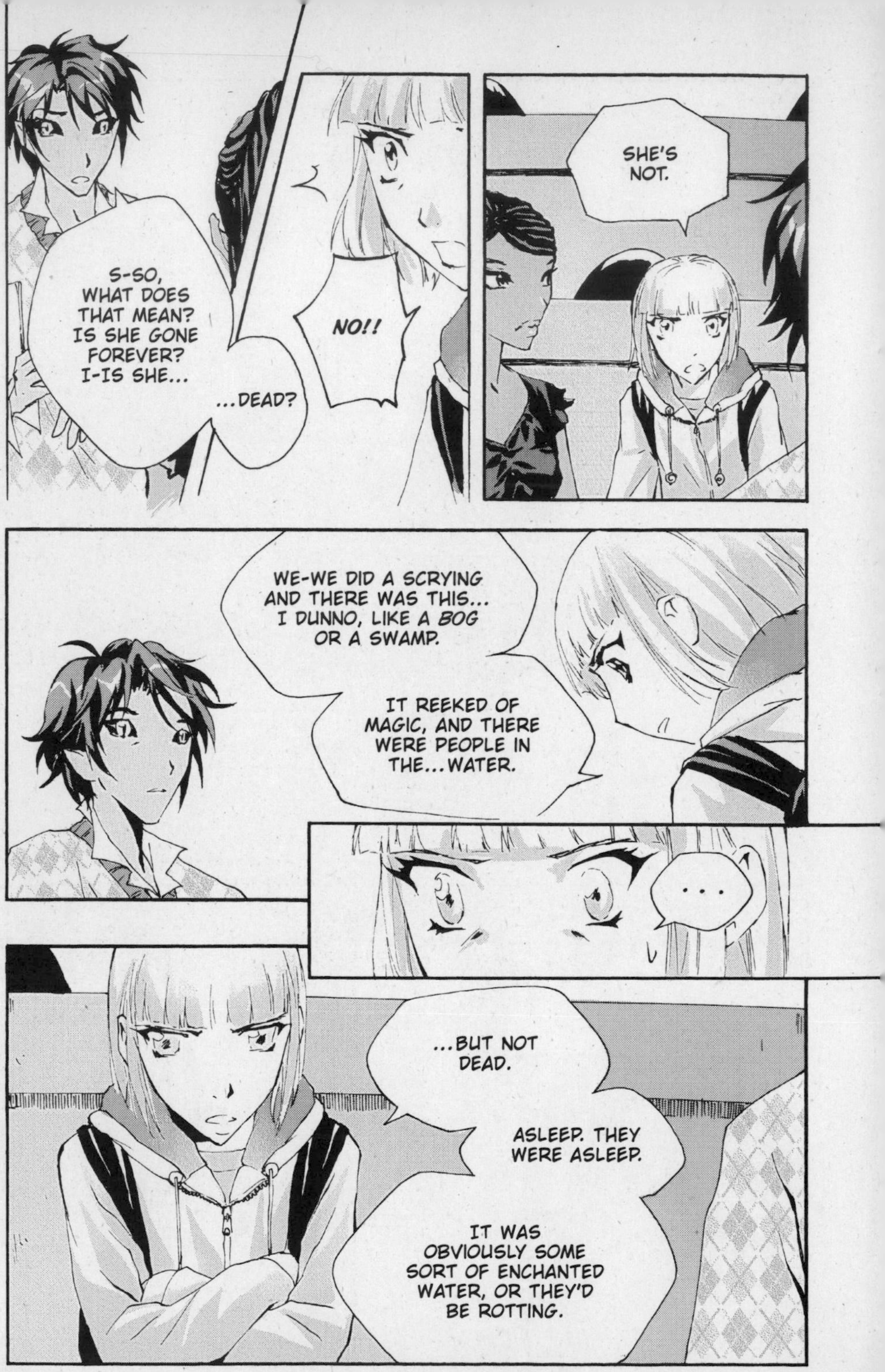
S-SO, WHAT DOES THAT MEAN? IS SHE GONE FOREVER? I-IS SHE...
...DEAD?
NO!!
SHE'S NOT.
WE-WE DID A SCRYING AND THERE WAS THIS... I DUNNO, LIKE A *BOG* OR A SWAMP.
IT REEKED OF MAGIC, AND THERE WERE PEOPLE IN THE...WATER.
...
...BUT NOT DEAD.
ASLEEP. THEY WERE ASLEEP.
IT WAS OBVIOUSLY SOME SORT OF ENCHANTED WATER, OR THEY'D BE ROTTING.

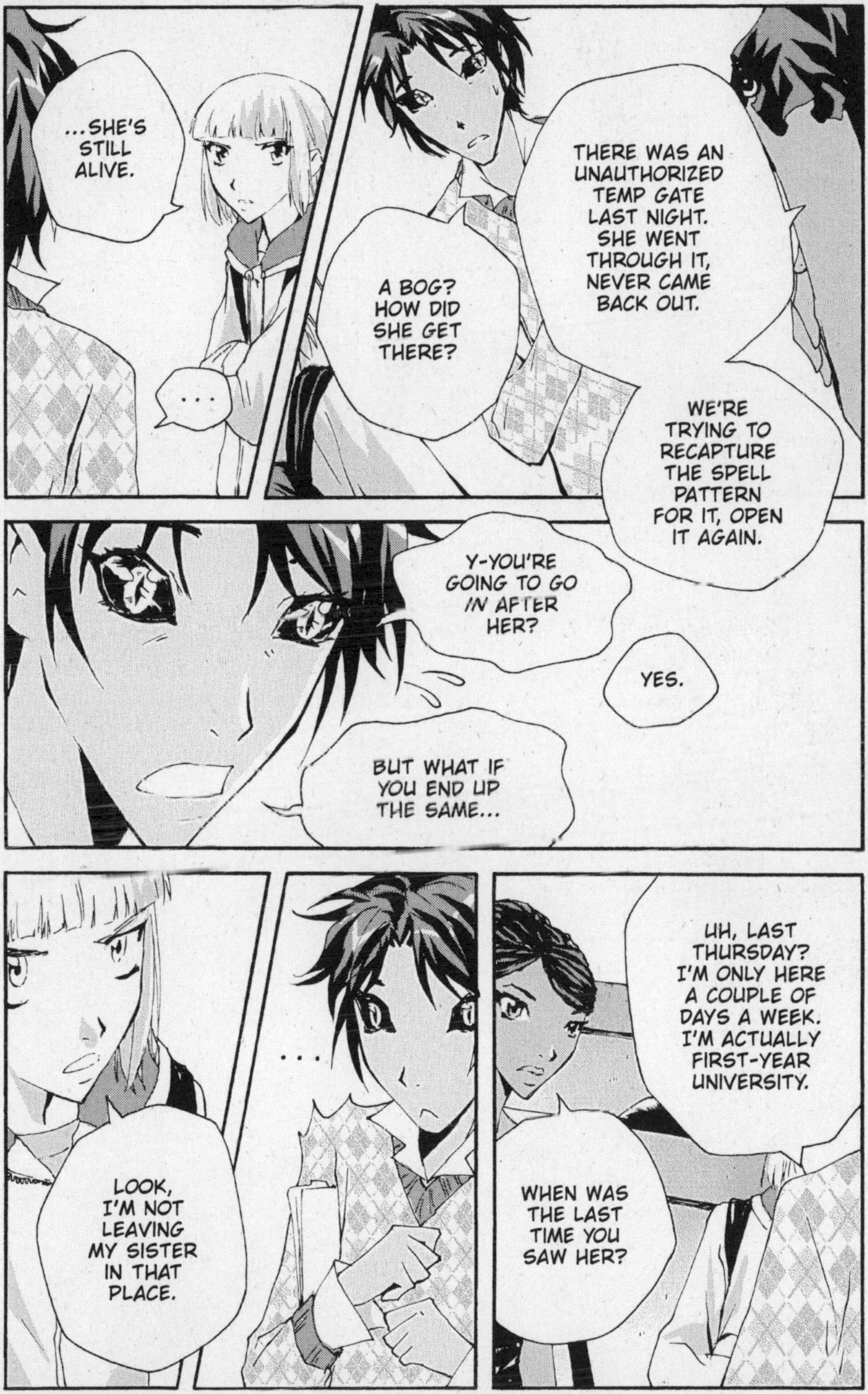
...SHE'S STILL ALIVE.
...
A BOG? HOW DID SHE GET THERE?
THERE WAS AN UNAUTHORIZED TEMP GATE LAST NIGHT. SHE WENT THROUGH IT, NEVER CAME BACK OUT.
WE'RE TRYING TO RECAPTURE THE SPELL PATTERN FOR IT, OPEN IT AGAIN.
Y-YOU'RE GOING TO GO IN AFTER HER?
YES.
BUT WHAT IF YOU END UP THE SAME...
LOOK, I'M NOT LEAVING MY SISTER IN THAT PLACE.
...
WHEN WAS THE LAST TIME YOU SAW HER?
UH, LAST THURSDAY? I'M ONLY HERE A COUPLE OF DAYS A WEEK. I'M ACTUALLY FIRST-YEAR UNIVERSITY.

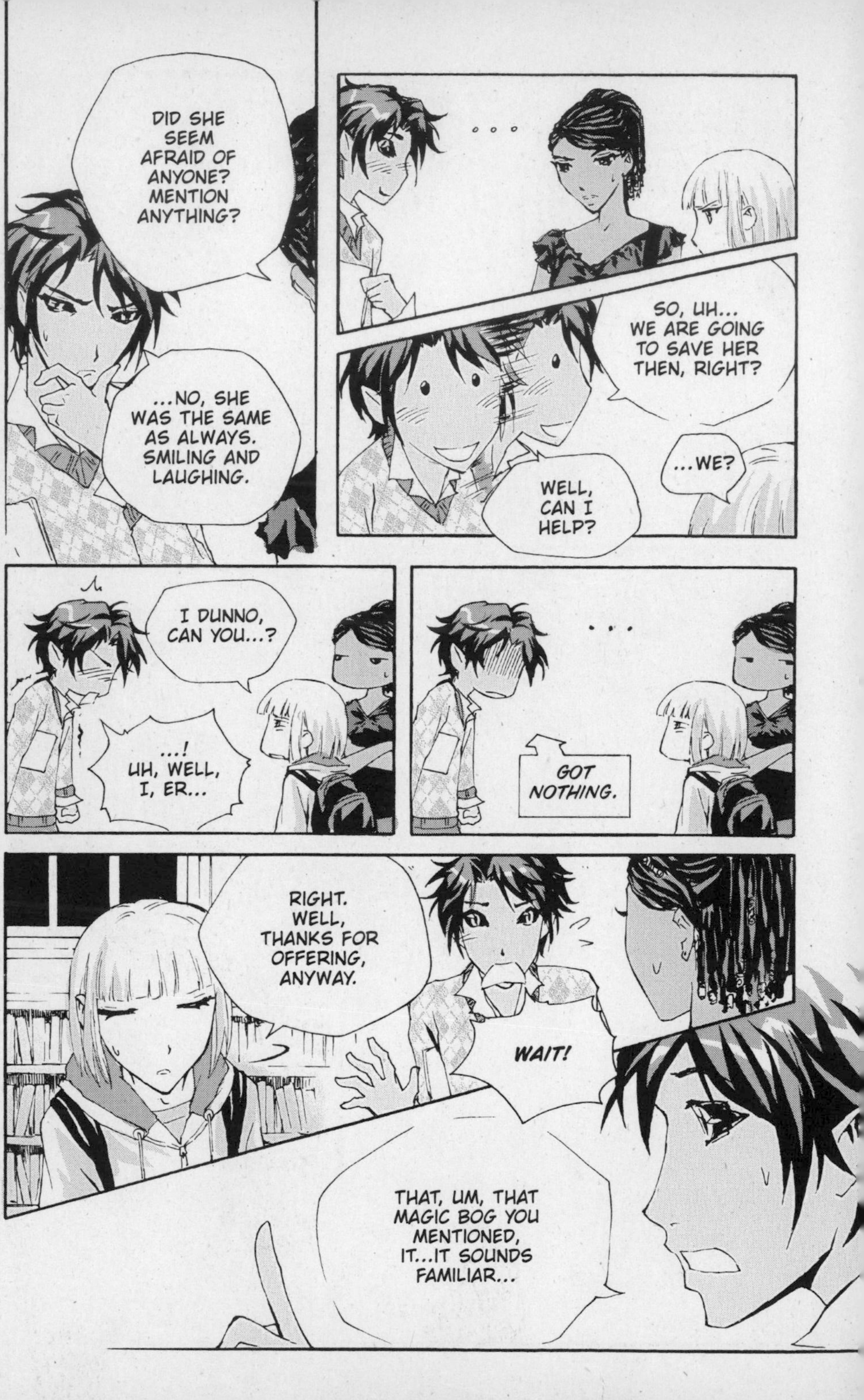
DID SHE SEEM AFRAID OF ANYONE? MENTION ANYTHING?
...NO, SHE WAS THE SAME AS ALWAYS. SMILING AND LAUGHING.
...
SO, UH... WE ARE GOING TO SAVE HER THEN, RIGHT?
...WE?
WELL, CAN I HELP?
I DUNNO, CAN YOU...?
...! UH, WELL, I, ER...
...
GOT NOTHING.
RIGHT. WELL, THANKS FOR OFFERING, ANYWAY.
WAIT!
THAT, UM, THAT MAGIC BOG YOU MENTIONED, IT...IT SOUNDS FAMILIAR...

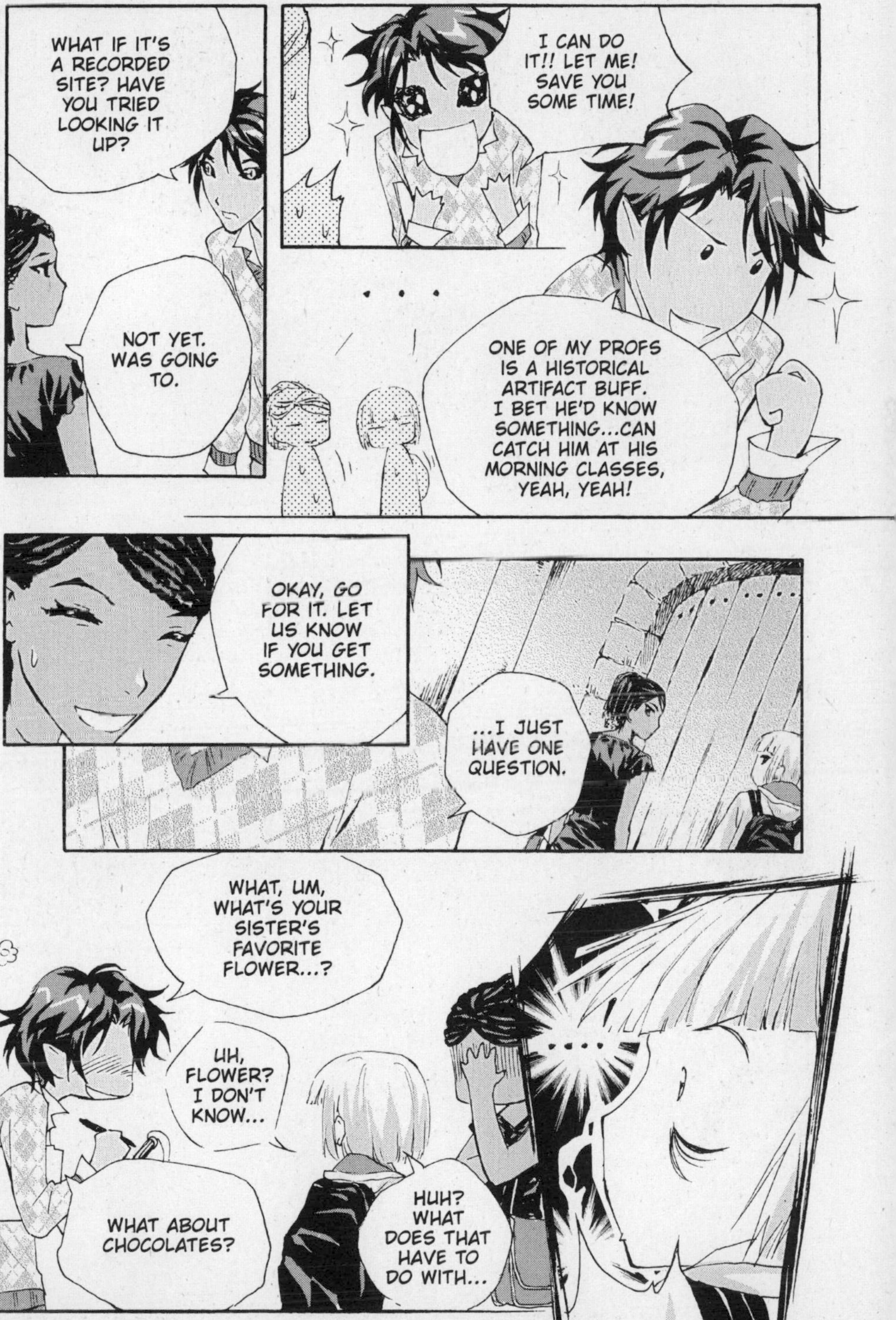
WHAT IF IT'S A RECORDED SITE? HAVE YOU TRIED LOOKING IT UP?
NOT YET. WAS GOING TO.
I CAN DO IT!! LET ME! SAVE YOU SOME TIME!
...
ONE OF MY PROFS IS A HISTORICAL ARTIFACT BUFF. I BET HE'D KNOW SOMETHING...CAN CATCH HIM AT HIS MORNING CLASSES, YEAH, YEAH!
OKAY, GO FOR IT. LET US KNOW IF YOU GET SOMETHING.
...I JUST HAVE ONE QUESTION.
WHAT, UM, WHAT'S YOUR SISTER'S FAVORITE FLOWER...?
UH, FLOWER? I DON'T KNOW...
WHAT ABOUT CHOCOLATES?
HUH? WHAT DOES THAT HAVE TO DO WITH...
.....

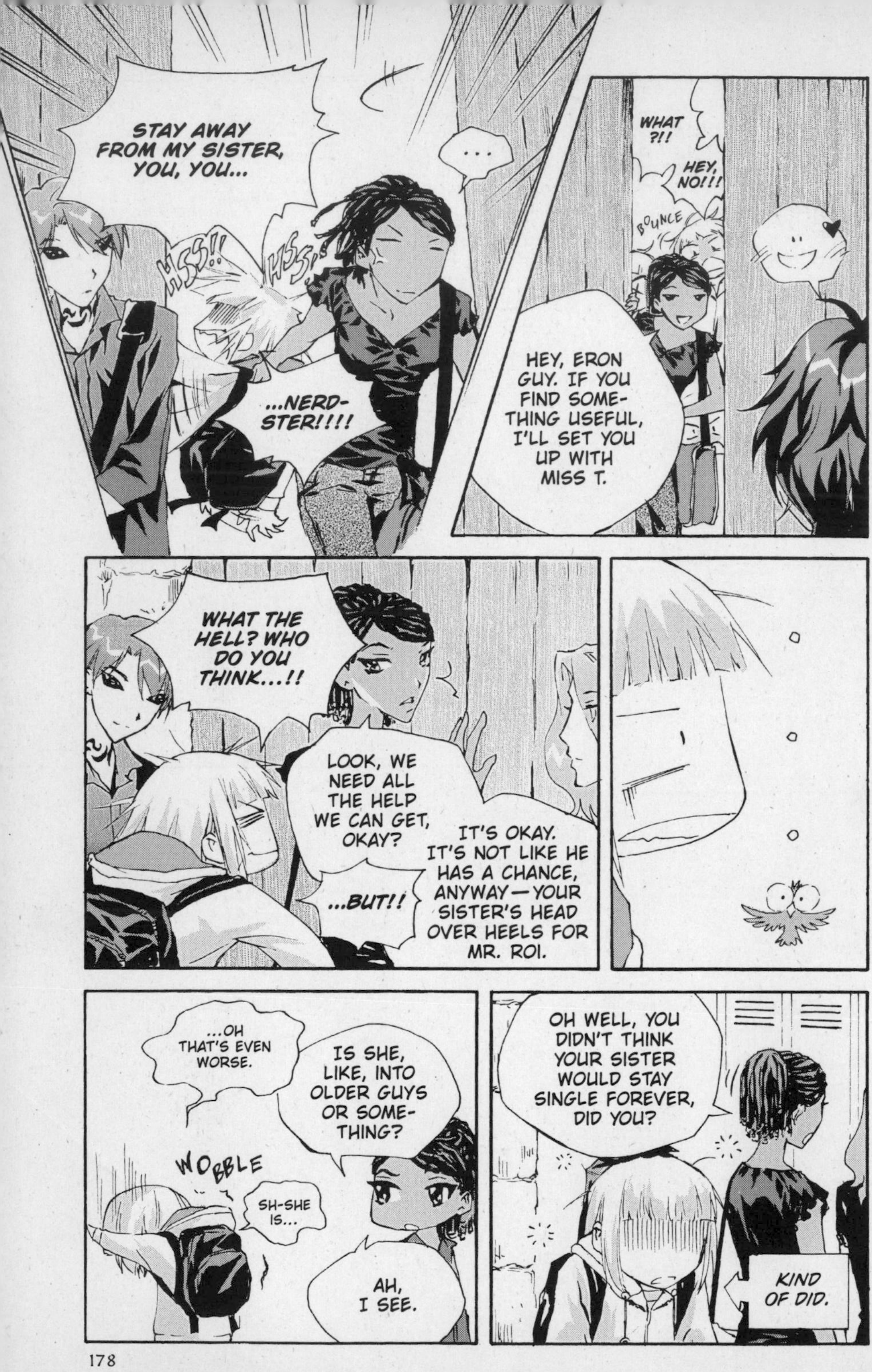
STAY AWAY FROM MY SISTER, YOU, YOU...
...
HSS!!
HSS...
...NERD-STER!!!!
WHAT ?!!
HEY, NO!!!
BOUNCE
HEY, ERON GUY. IF YOU FIND SOME-THING USEFUL, I'LL SET YOU UP WITH MISS T.
WHAT THE HELL? WHO DO YOU THINK...!!
LOOK, WE NEED ALL THE HELP WE CAN GET, OKAY?
...BUT!!
IT'S OKAY. IT'S NOT LIKE HE HAS A CHANCE, ANYWAY—YOUR SISTER'S HEAD OVER HEELS FOR MR. ROI.
...OH THAT'S EVEN WORSE.
IS SHE, LIKE, INTO OLDER GUYS OR SOME-THING?
WOBBLE
SH-SHE IS...
AH, I SEE.
OH WELL, YOU DIDN'T THINK YOUR SISTER WOULD STAY SINGLE FOREVER, DID YOU?
KIND OF DID.

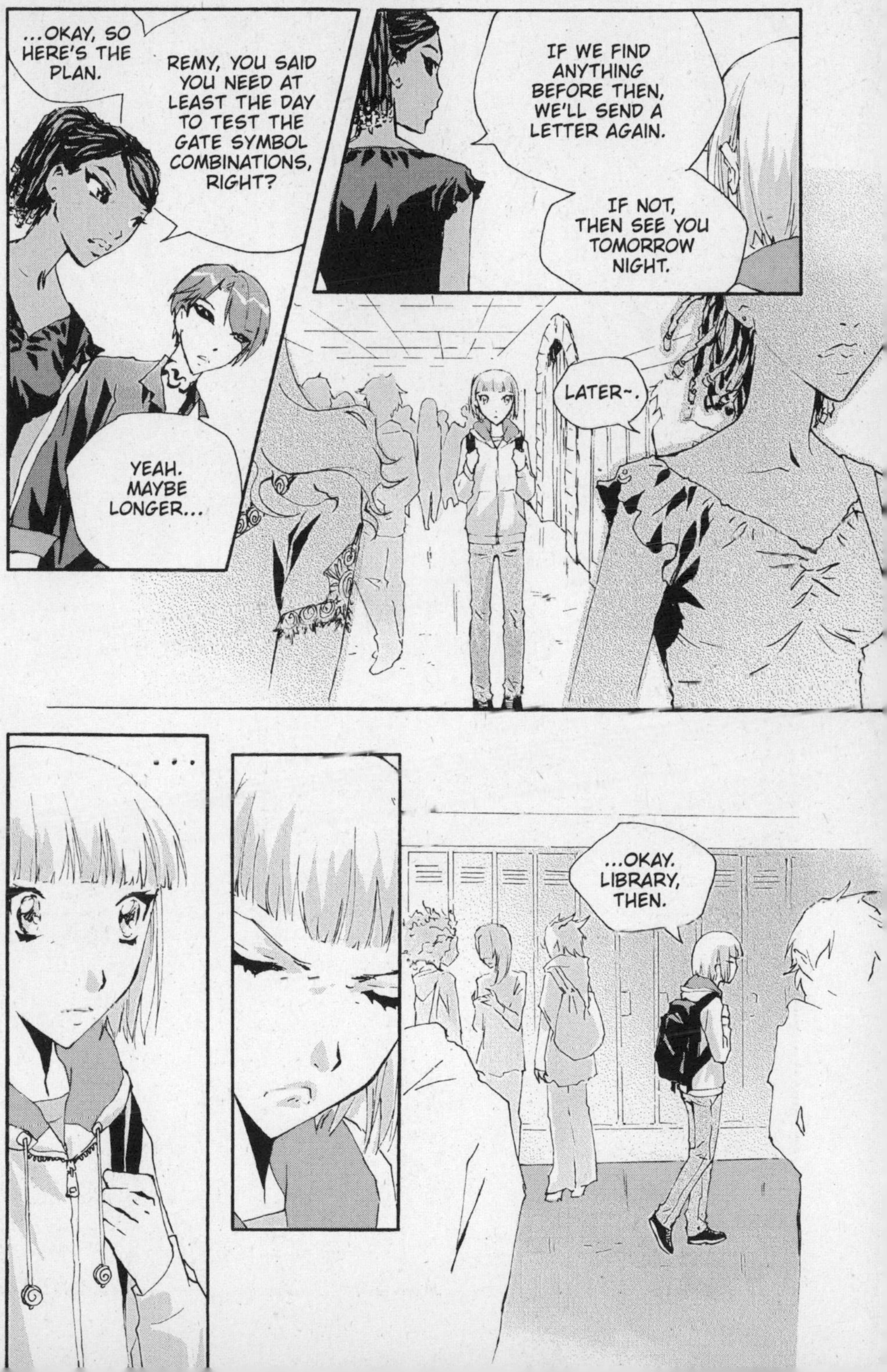
...OKAY, SO HERE'S THE PLAN.
REMY, YOU SAID YOU NEED AT LEAST THE DAY TO TEST THE GATE SYMBOL COMBINATIONS, RIGHT?
YEAH. MAYBE LONGER...
IF WE FIND ANYTHING BEFORE THEN, WE'LL SEND A LETTER AGAIN.
IF NOT, THEN SEE YOU TOMORROW NIGHT.
LATER~.
...
...OKAY. LIBRARY, THEN.

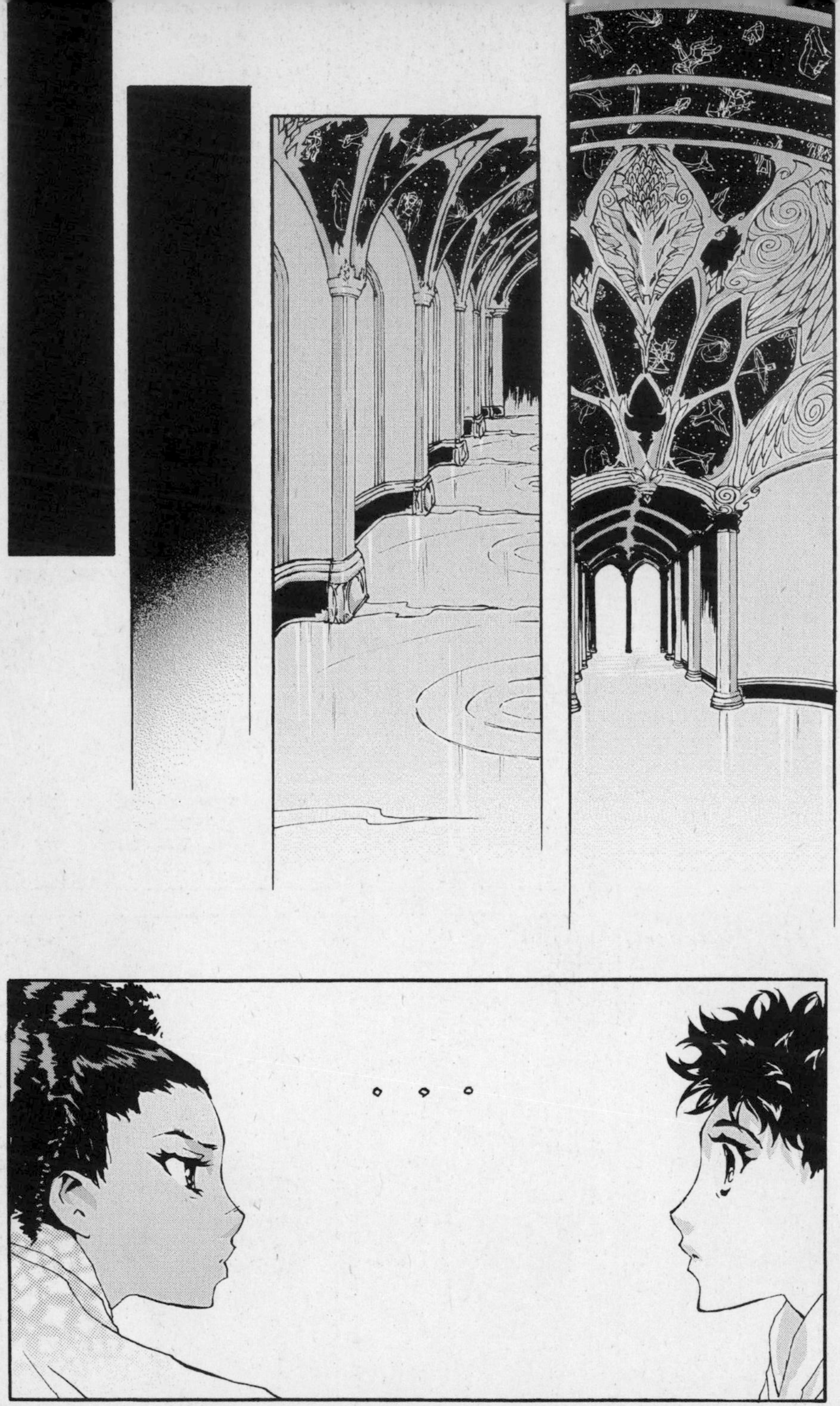
。。。

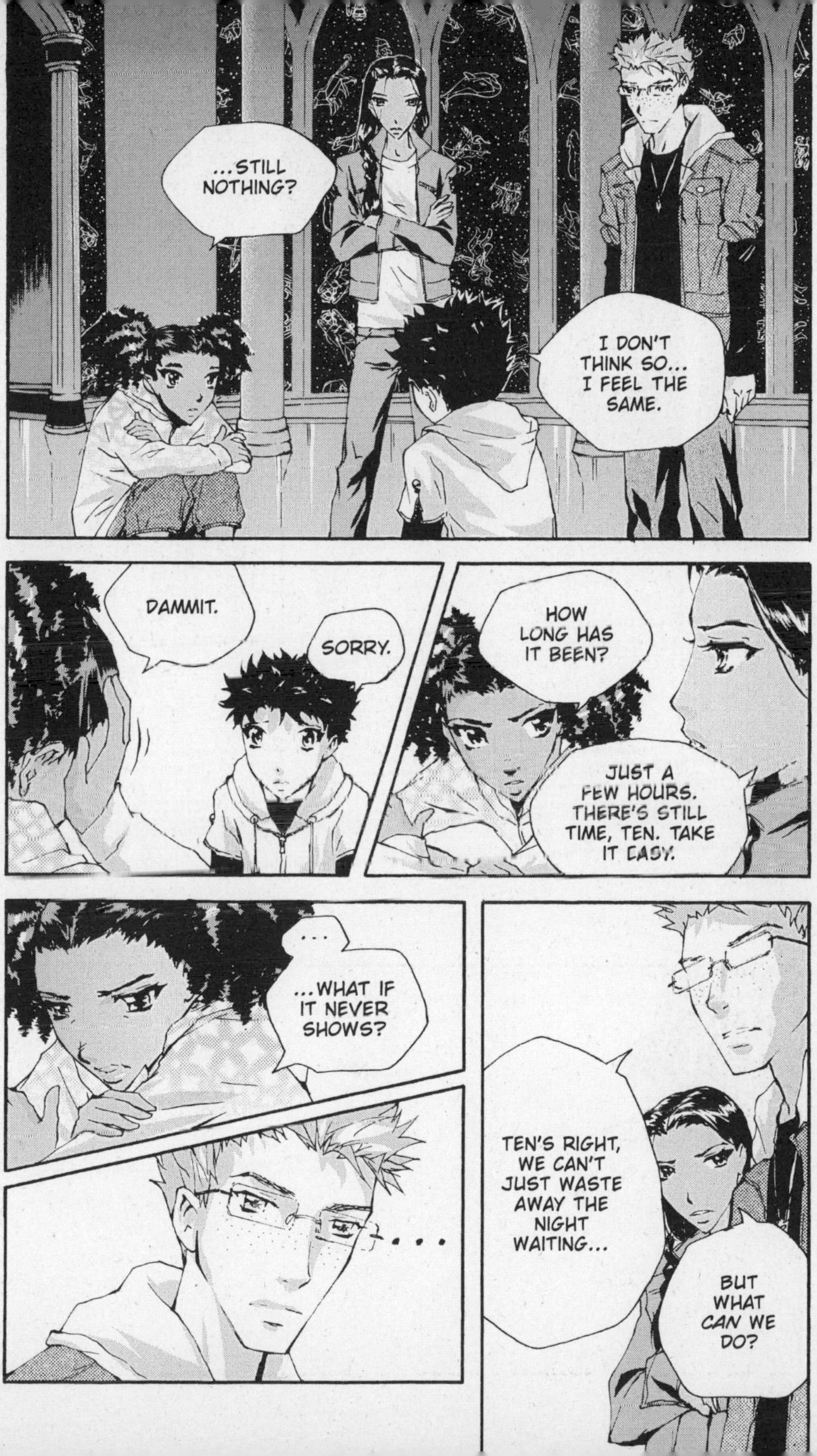
...STILL NOTHING?
I DON'T THINK SO... I FEEL THE SAME.
DAMMIT.
SORRY.
HOW LONG HAS IT BEEN?
JUST A FEW HOURS. THERE'S STILL TIME, TEN. TAKE IT EASY.
...
...WHAT IF IT NEVER SHOWS?
...
TEN'S RIGHT, WE CAN'T JUST WASTE AWAY THE NIGHT WAITING...
BUT WHAT CAN WE DO?

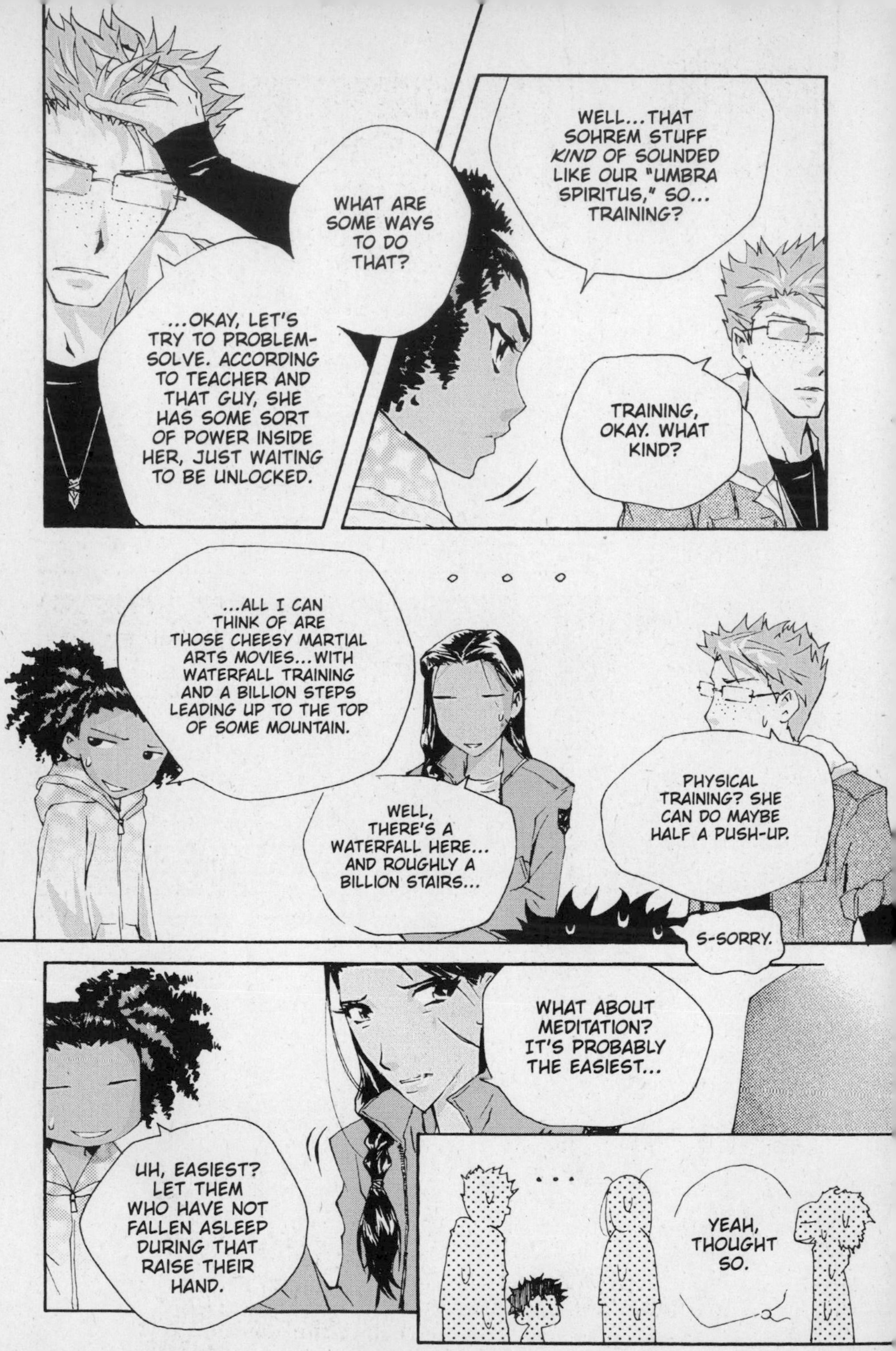
...OKAY, LET'S TRY TO PROBLEM-SOLVE. ACCORDING TO TEACHER AND THAT GUY, SHE HAS SOME SORT OF POWER INSIDE HER, JUST WAITING TO BE UNLOCKED.
WHAT ARE SOME WAYS TO DO THAT?
WELL...THAT SOHREM STUFF *KIND* OF SOUNDED LIKE OUR "UMBRA SPIRITUS," SO... TRAINING?
TRAINING, OKAY. WHAT KIND?
...ALL I CAN THINK OF ARE THOSE CHEESY MARTIAL ARTS MOVIES...WITH WATERFALL TRAINING AND A BILLION STEPS LEADING UP TO THE TOP OF SOME MOUNTAIN.
WELL, THERE'S A WATERFALL HERE... AND ROUGHLY A BILLION STAIRS...
PHYSICAL TRAINING? SHE CAN DO MAYBE HALF A PUSH-UP.
S-SORRY.
WHAT ABOUT MEDITATION? IT'S PROBABLY THE EASIEST...
UH, EASIEST? LET THEM WHO HAVE NOT FALLEN ASLEEP DURING THAT RAISE THEIR HAND.
...
YEAH, THOUGHT SO.

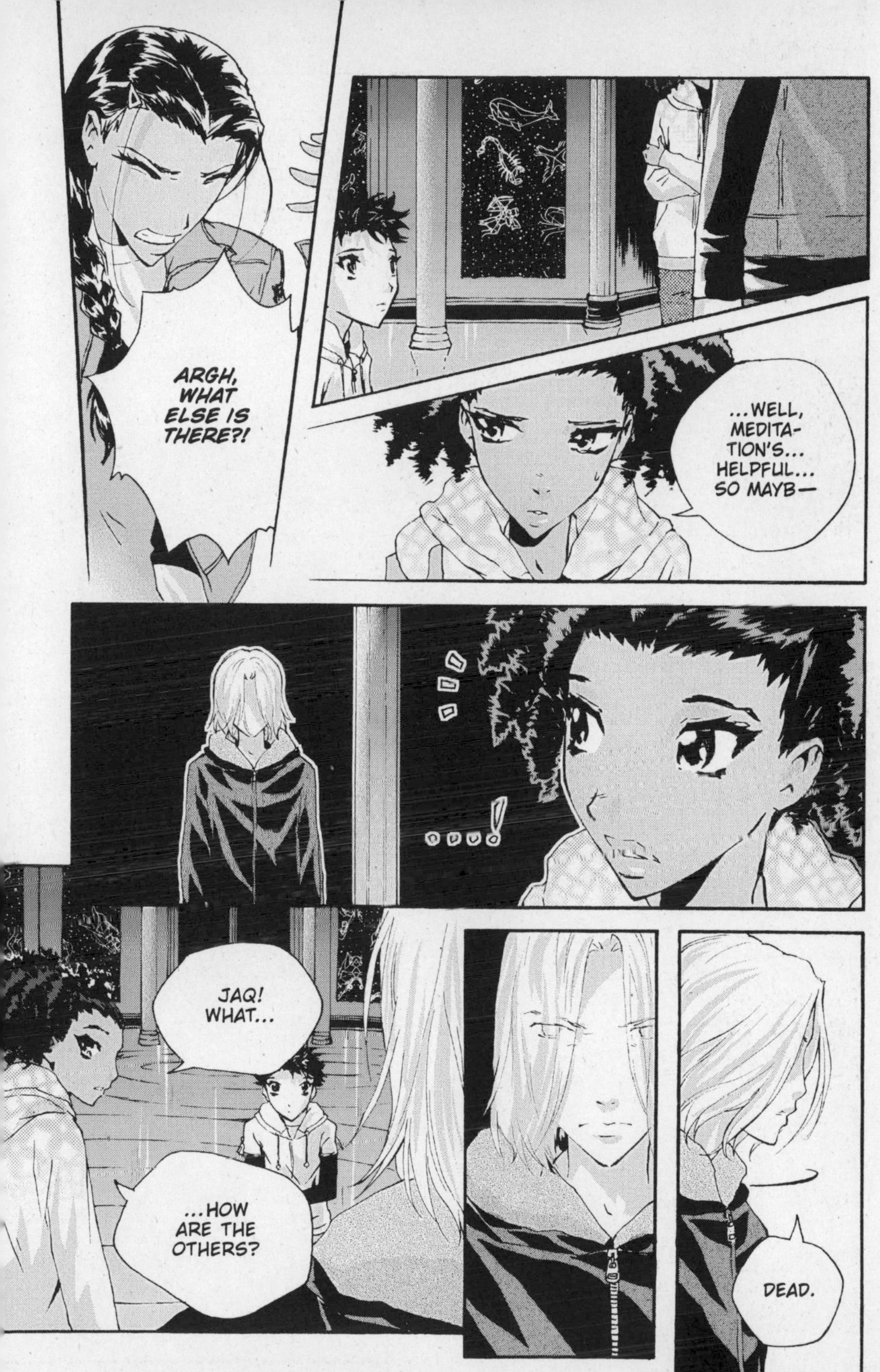
ARGH, WHAT ELSE IS THERE?!
...WELL, MEDITATION'S... HELPFUL... SO MAYB—
JAQ! WHAT...
...HOW ARE THE OTHERS?
DEAD.

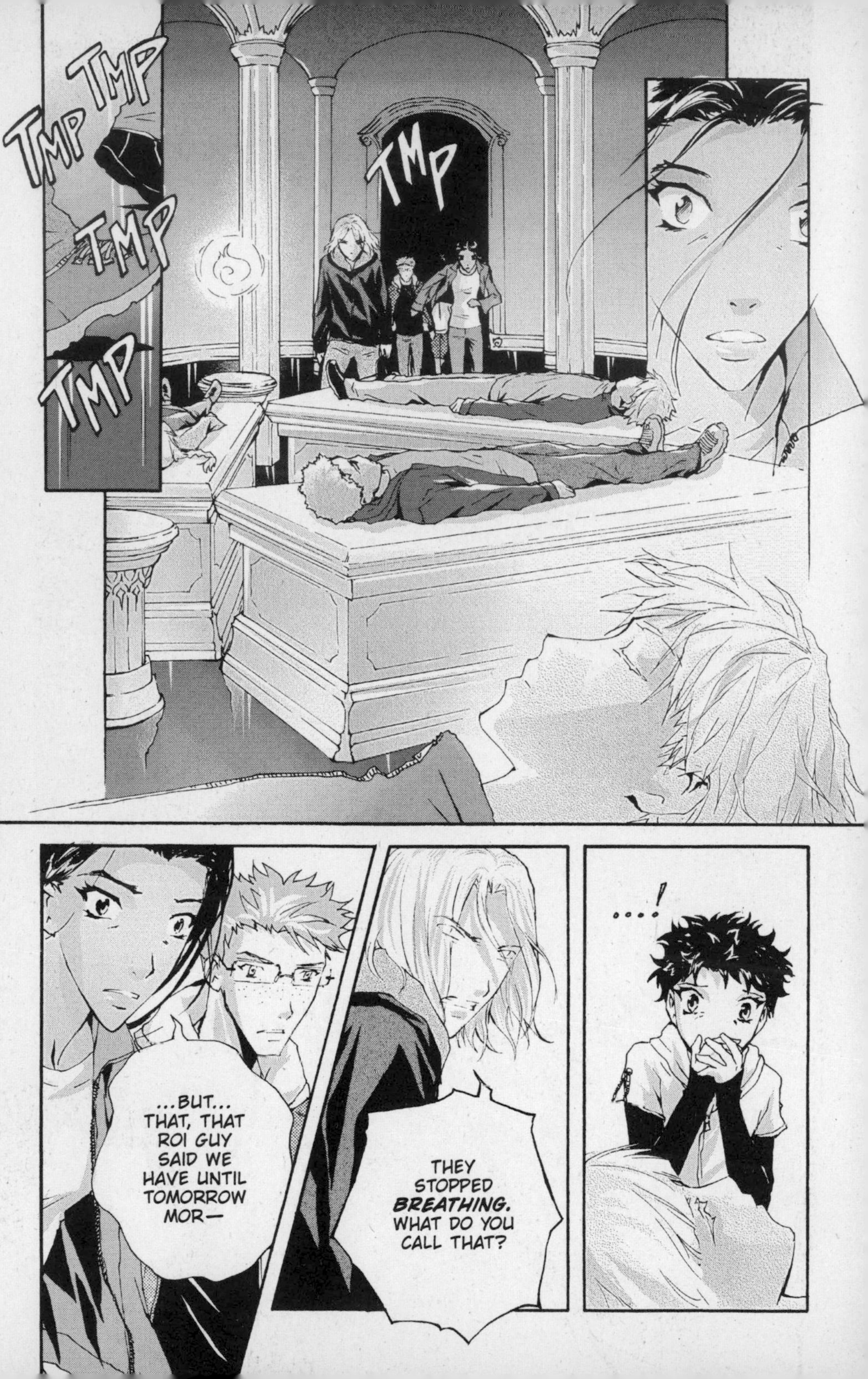
TMP TMP
TMP
TMP
TMP
...BUT... THAT, THAT ROI GUY SAID WE HAVE UNTIL TOMORROW MOR—
THEY STOPPED *BREATHING.* WHAT DO YOU CALL THAT?
...!

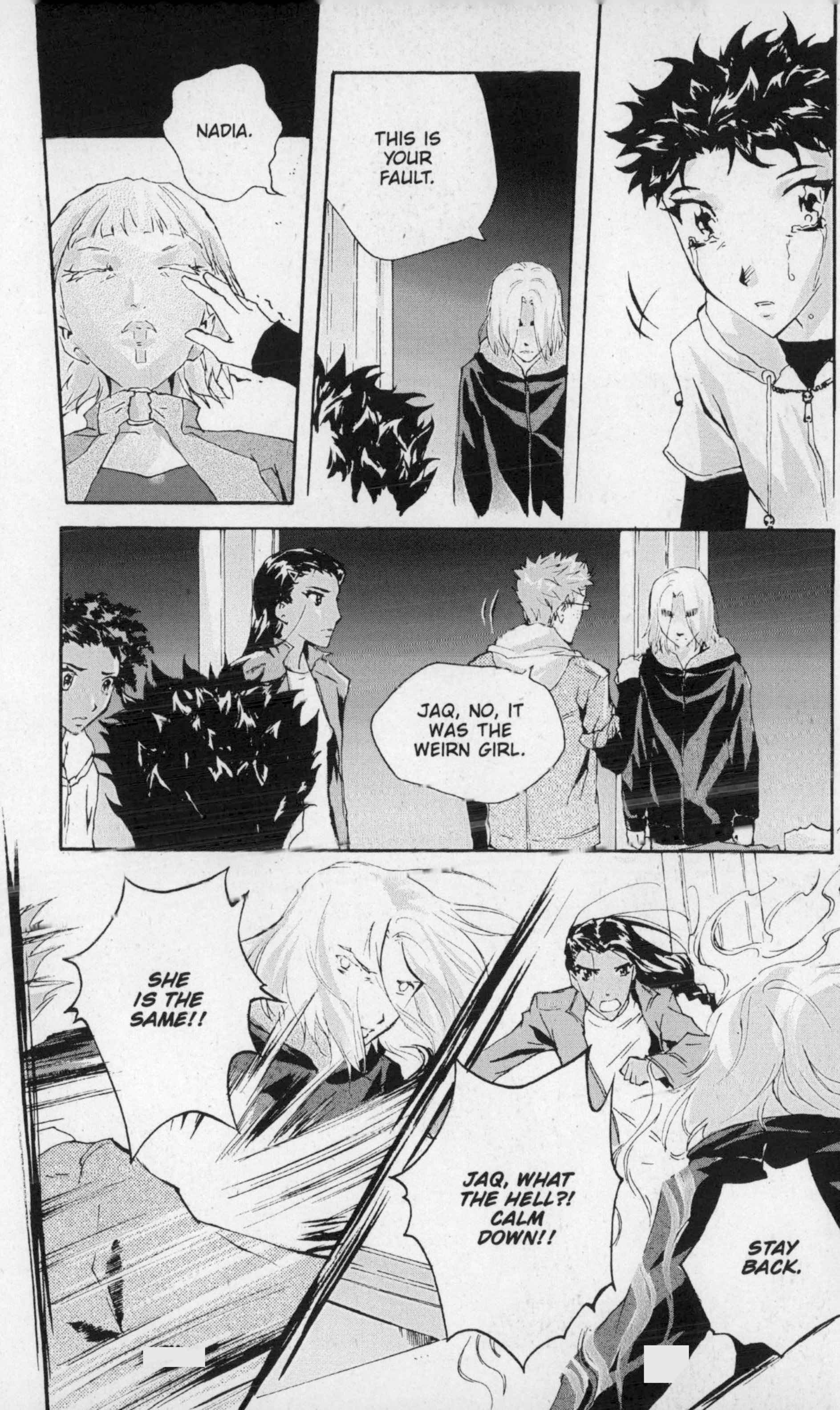
NADIA.
THIS IS YOUR FAULT.
JAQ, NO, IT WAS THE WEIRN GIRL.
SHE IS THE SAME!!
JAQ, WHAT THE HELL?! CALM DOWN!!
STAY BACK.

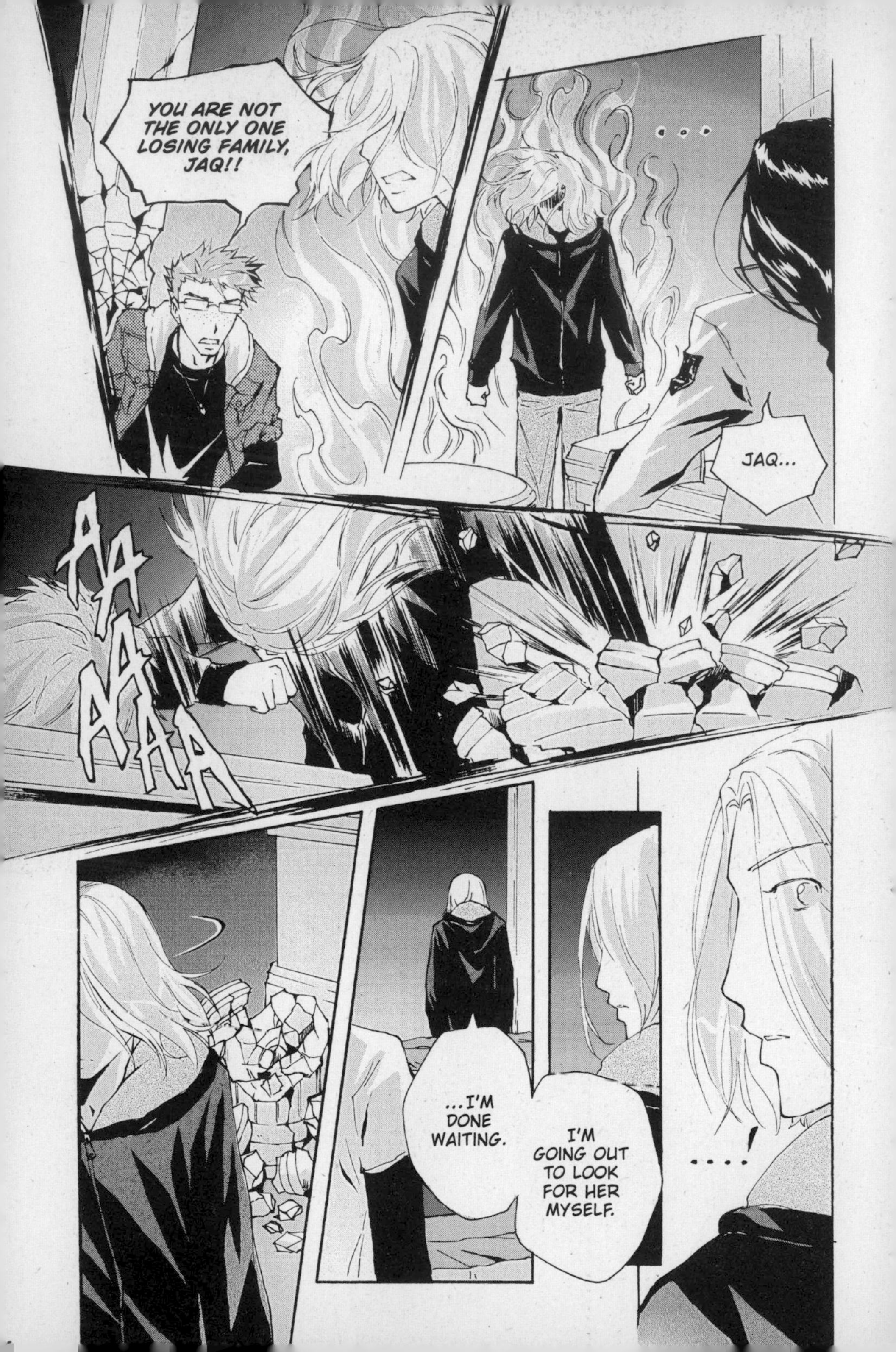

YOU ARE NOT THE ONLY ONE LOSING FAMILY, JAQ!!
...
JAQ...
AAAAAA
...I'M DONE WAITING.
I'M GOING OUT TO LOOK FOR HER MYSELF.
....

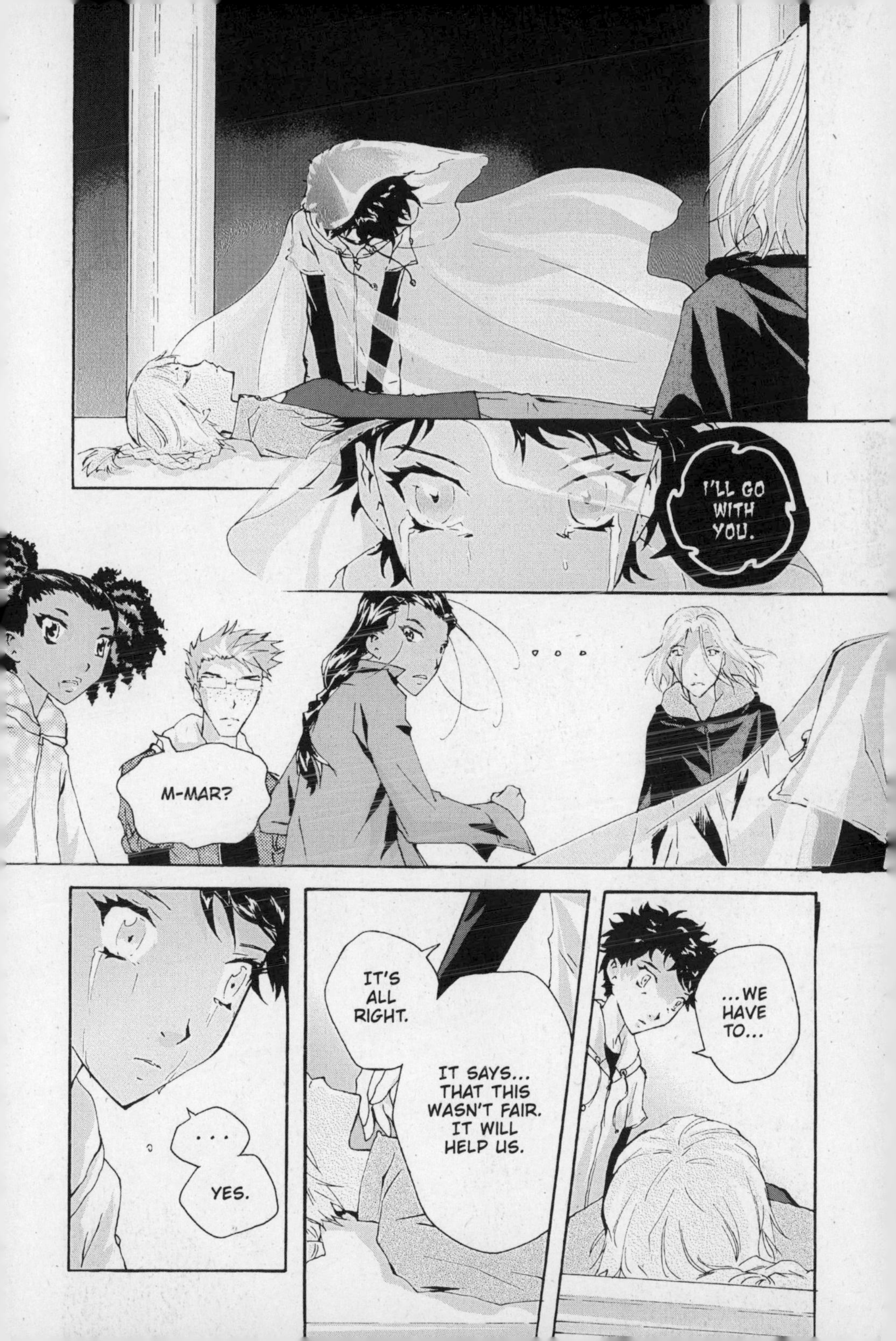
I'LL GO WITH YOU.
. . .
M-MAR?
. . .
YES.
IT'S ALL RIGHT.
IT SAYS... THAT THIS WASN'T FAIR. IT WILL HELP US.
...WE HAVE TO...

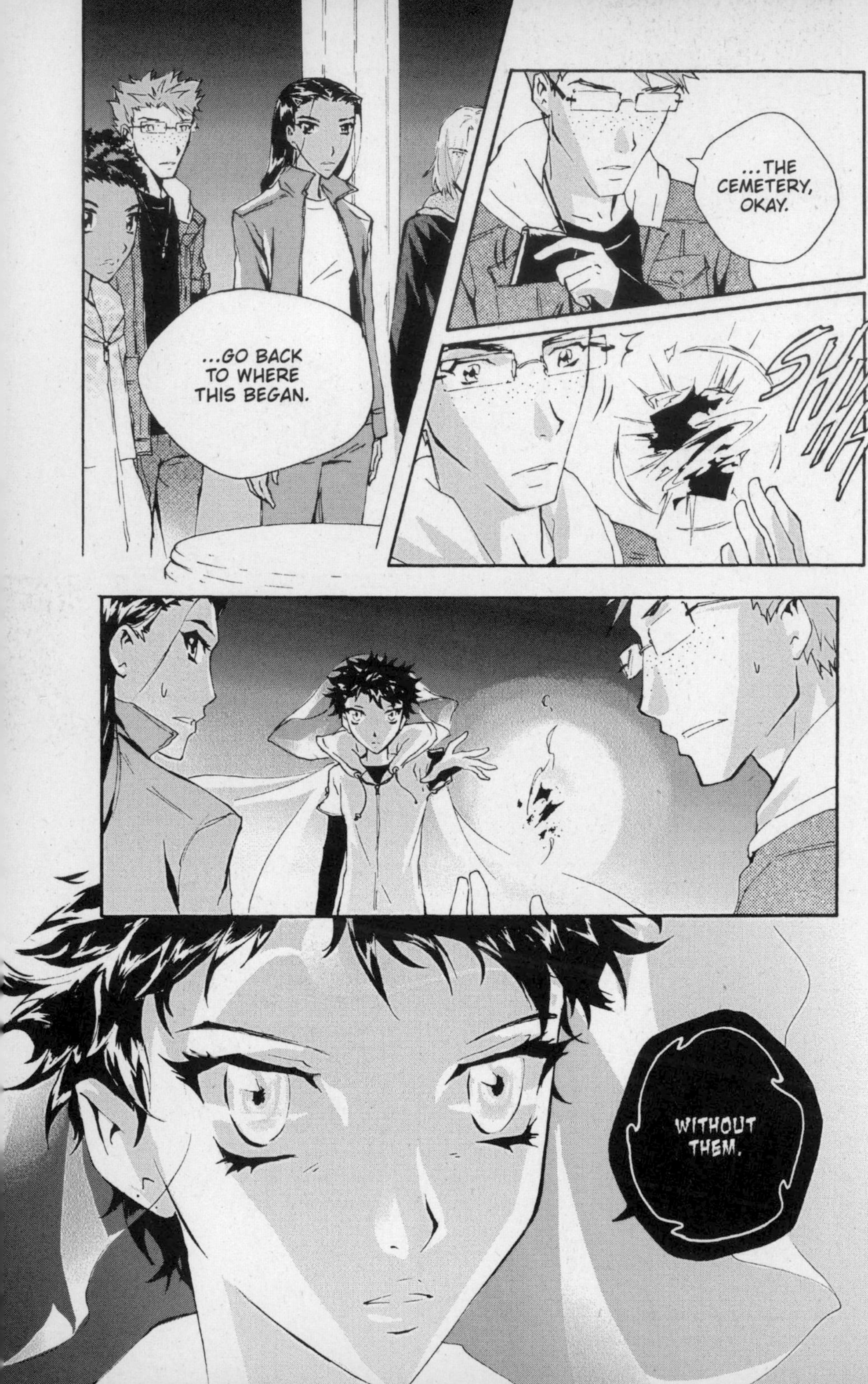
...GO BACK TO WHERE THIS BEGAN.
...THE CEMETERY, OKAY.
SHHH
WITHOUT THEM.

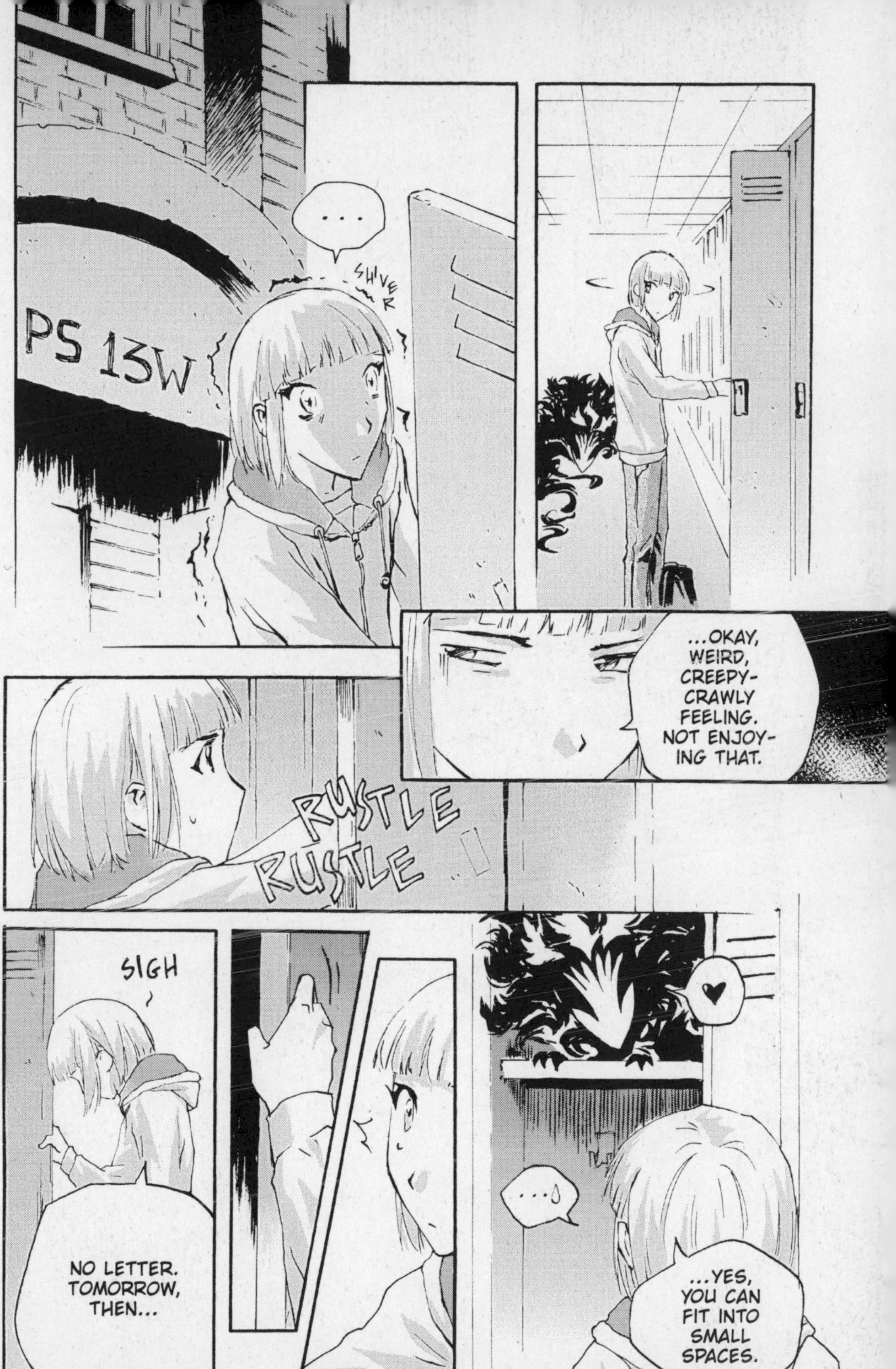

PS 13W
...
SHIVER
...OKAY, WEIRD, CREEPY-CRAWLY FEELING. NOT ENJOYING THAT.
RUSTLE RUSTLE
SIGH
NO LETTER. TOMORROW, THEN...
♥
...
...YES, YOU CAN FIT INTO SMALL SPACES.

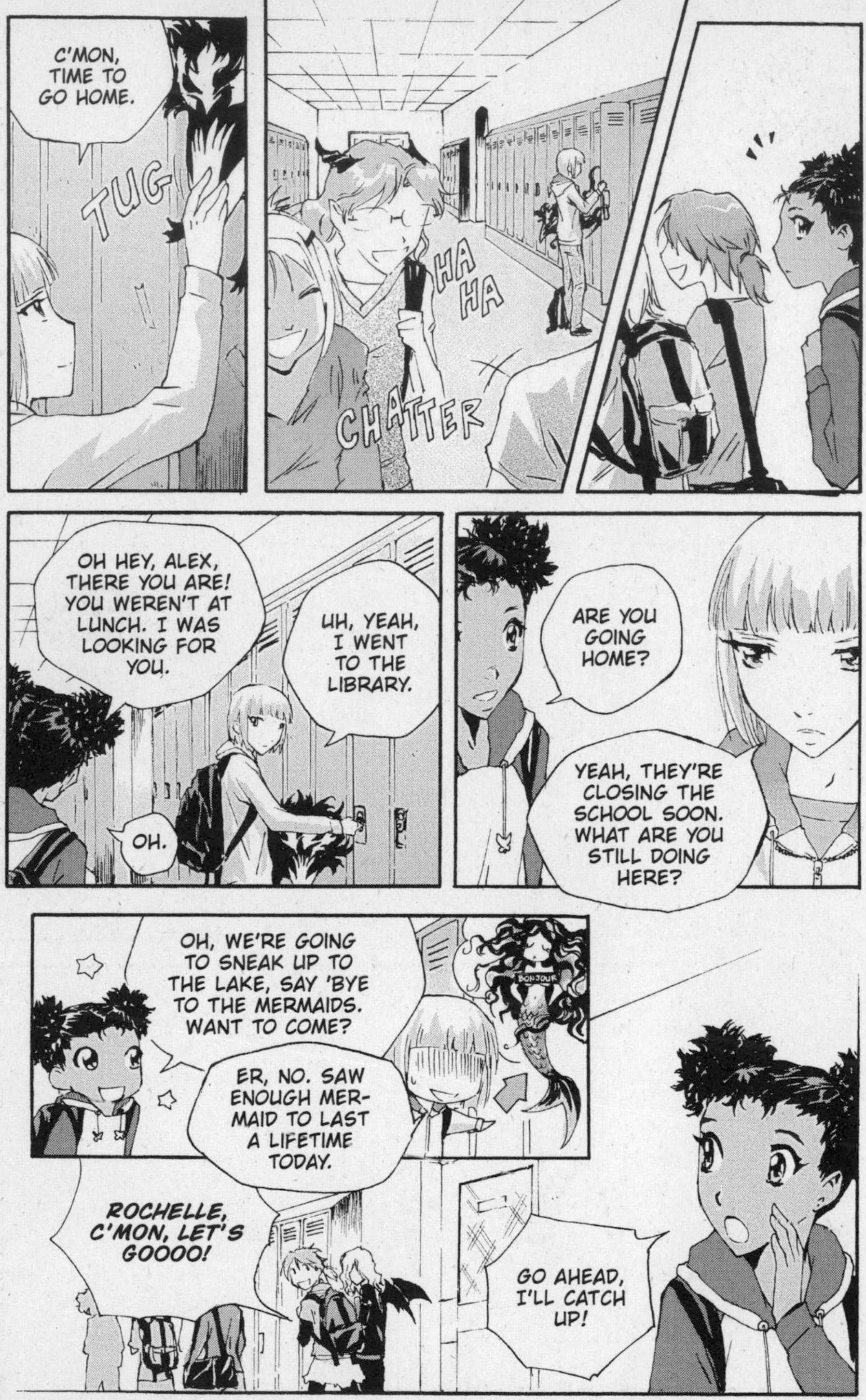
C'MON, TIME TO GO HOME.
TUG
HA HA
CHATTER
OH HEY, ALEX, THERE YOU ARE! YOU WEREN'T AT LUNCH. I WAS LOOKING FOR YOU.
UH, YEAH, I WENT TO THE LIBRARY.
OH.
ARE YOU GOING HOME?
YEAH, THEY'RE CLOSING THE SCHOOL SOON. WHAT ARE YOU STILL DOING HERE?
OH, WE'RE GOING TO SNEAK UP TO THE LAKE, SAY 'BYE TO THE MERMAIDS. WANT TO COME?
BONJOUR
ER, NO. SAW ENOUGH MER-MAID TO LAST A LIFETIME TODAY.
ROCHELLE, C'MON, LET'S GOOOO!
GO AHEAD, I'LL CATCH UP!

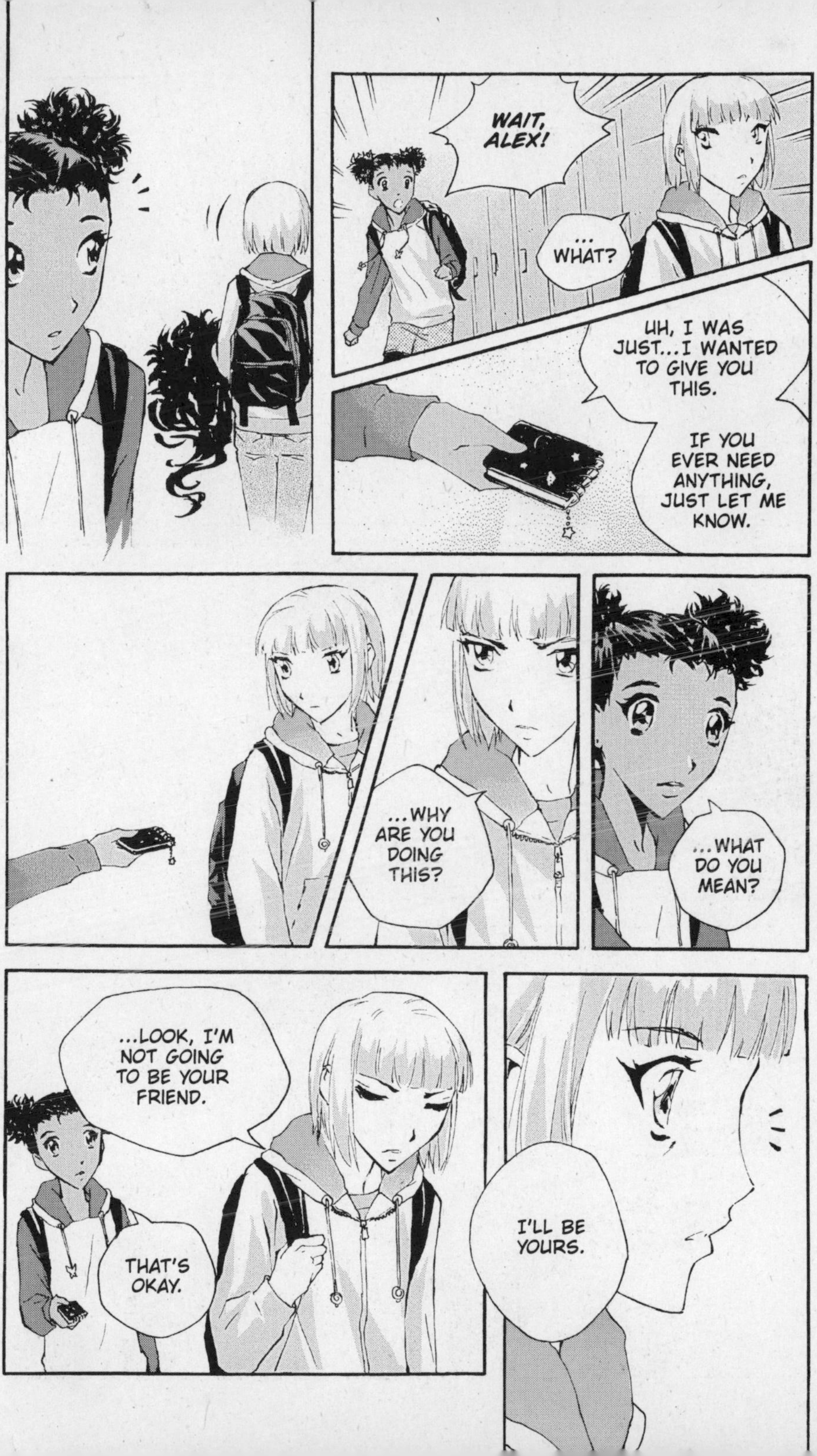
WAIT, ALEX!
... WHAT?
UH, I WAS JUST... I WANTED TO GIVE YOU THIS.
IF YOU EVER NEED ANYTHING, JUST LET ME KNOW.
...WHY ARE YOU DOING THIS?
...WHAT DO YOU MEAN?
...LOOK, I'M NOT GOING TO BE YOUR FRIEND.
THAT'S OKAY.
I'LL BE YOURS.

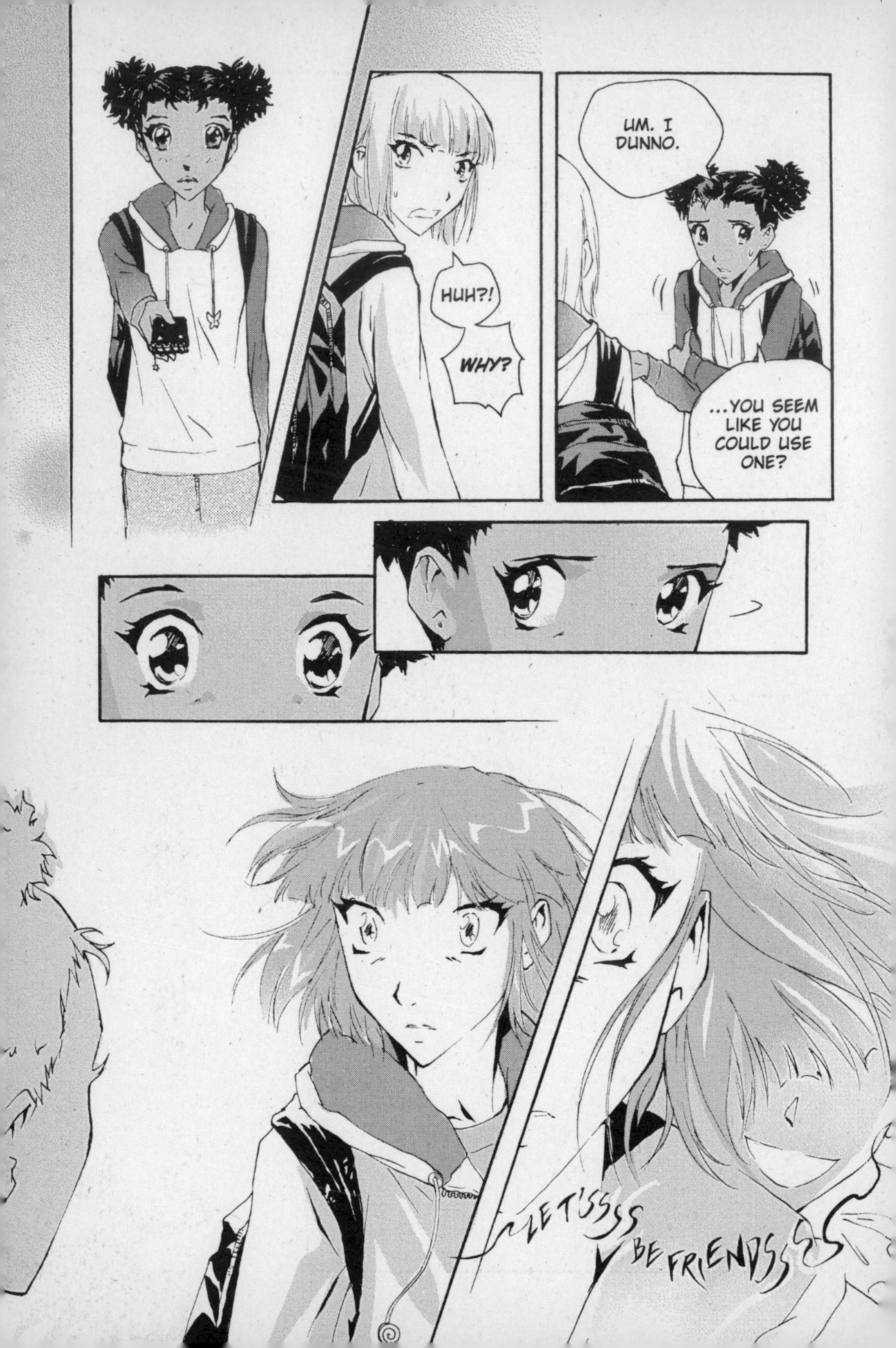
HUH?!
WHY?
UM. I DUNNO.
...YOU SEEM LIKE YOU COULD USE ONE?
LET'SSS BE FRIENDSSS

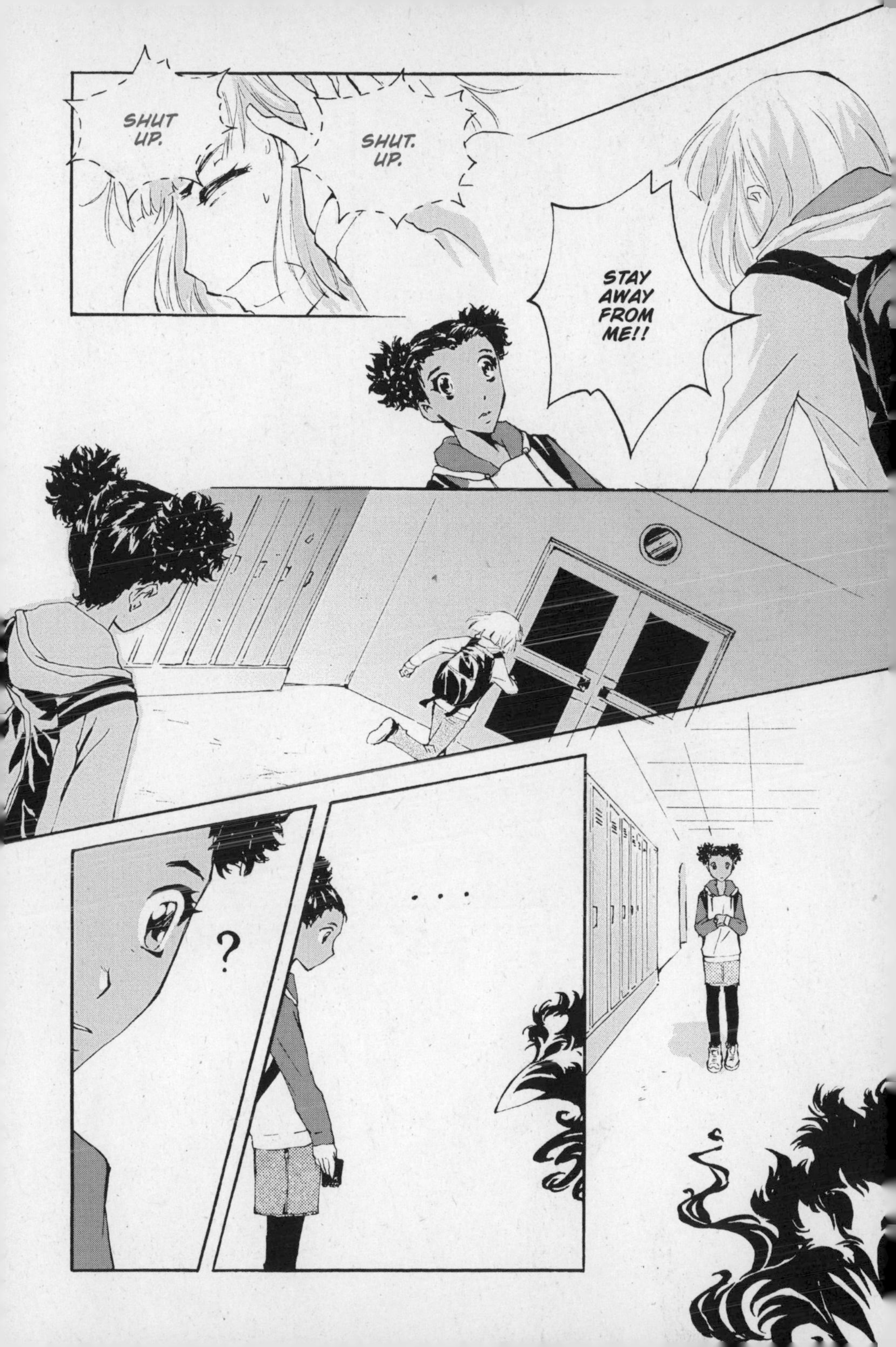
SHUT UP.
SHUT. UP.
STAY AWAY FROM ME!!
...
?

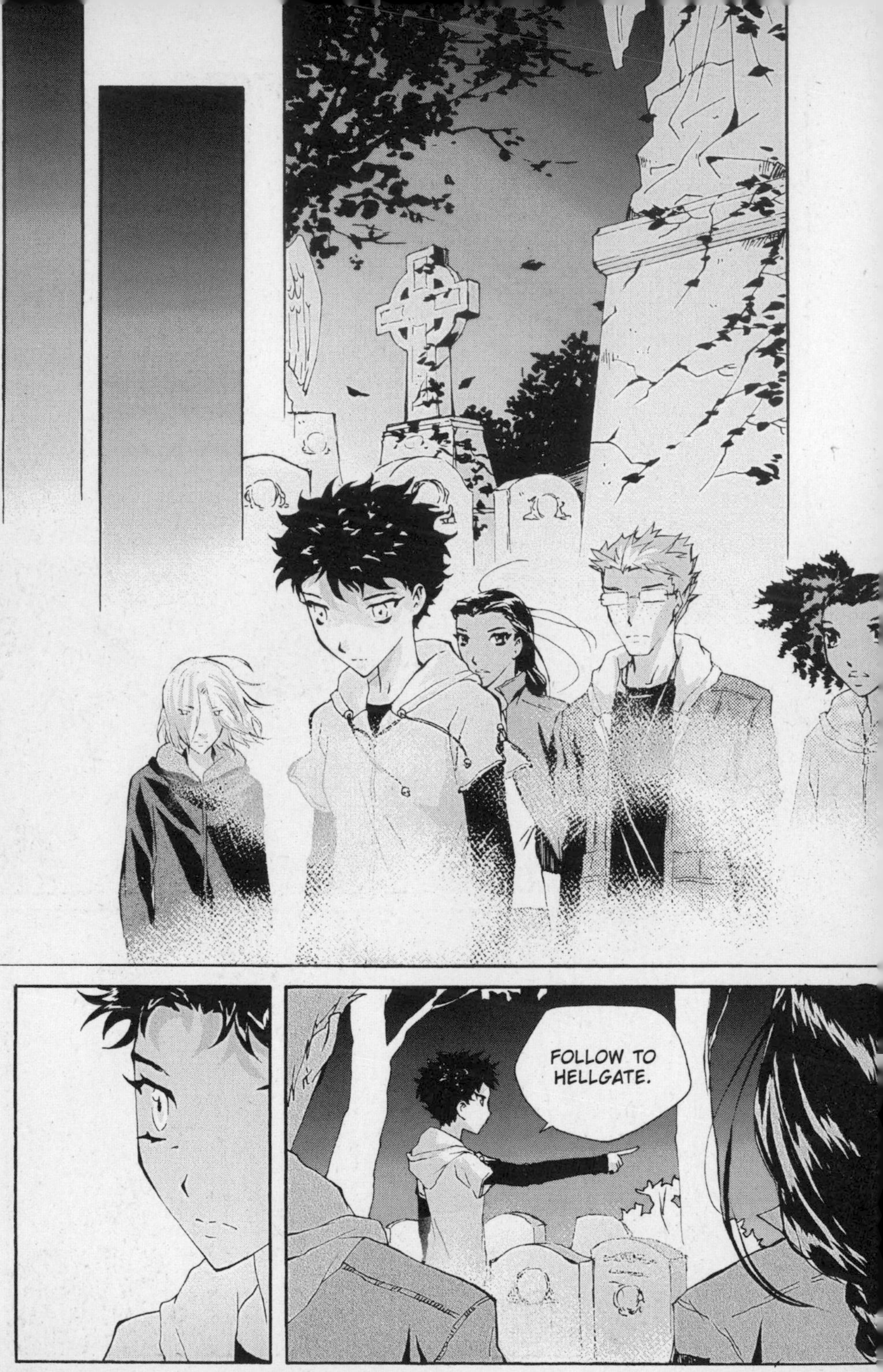
FOLLOW TO
HELLGATE.

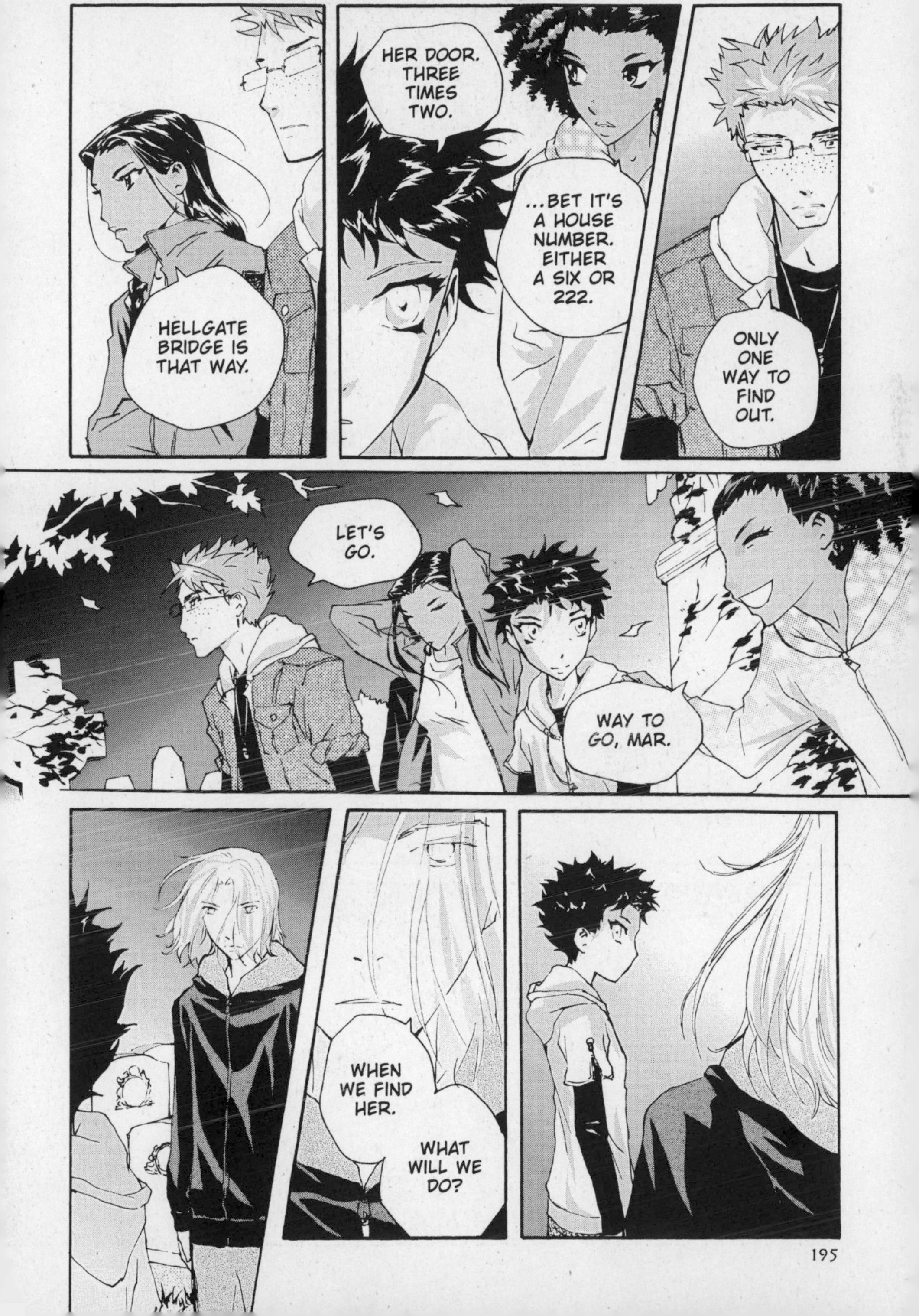
HELLGATE BRIDGE IS THAT WAY.
HER DOOR. THREE TIMES TWO.
...BET IT'S A HOUSE NUMBER. EITHER A SIX OR 222.
ONLY ONE WAY TO FIND OUT.
LET'S GO.
WAY TO GO, MAR.
WHEN WE FIND HER.
WHAT WILL WE DO?

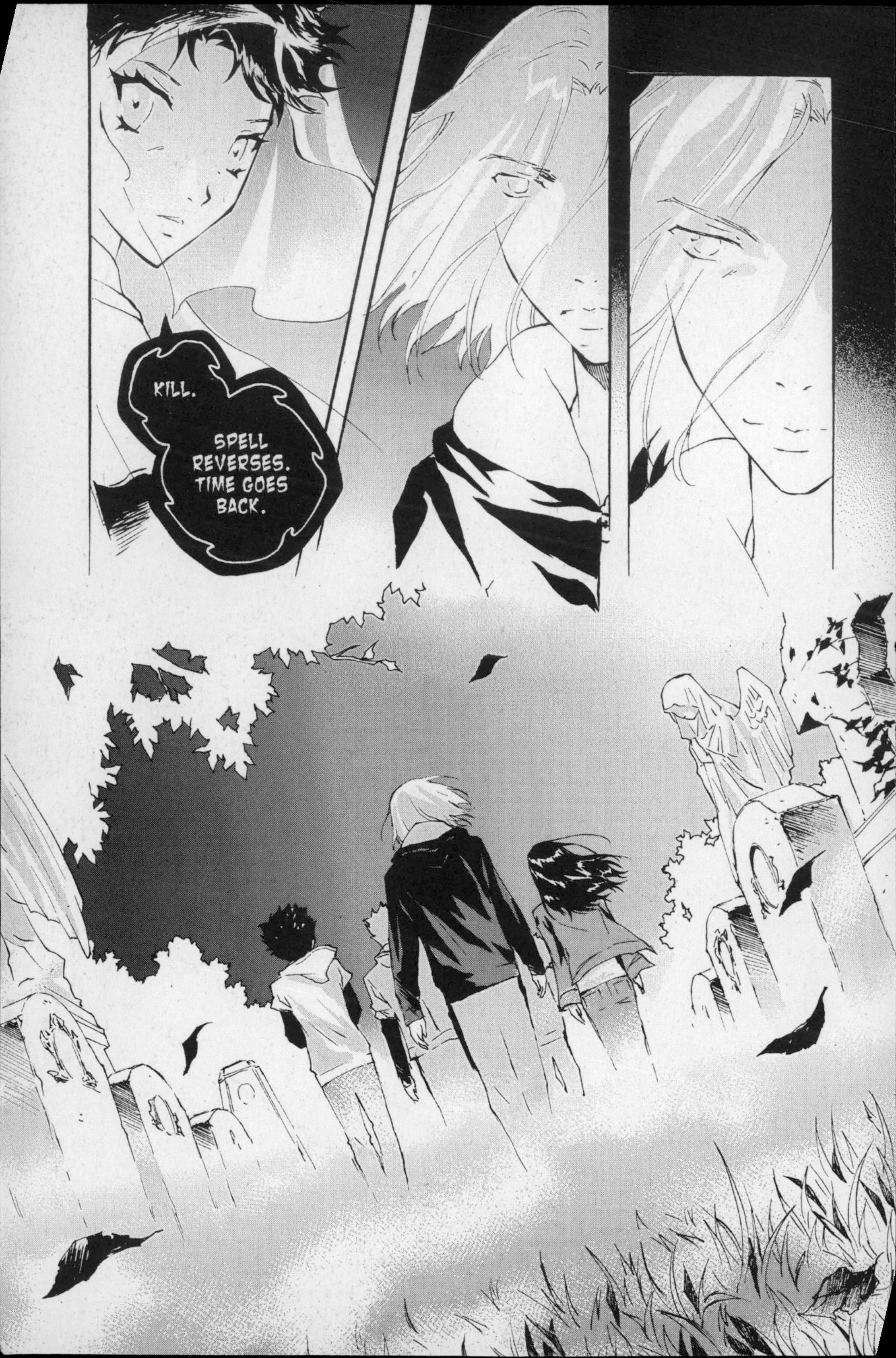
KILL.
SPELL REVERSES. TIME GOES BACK.

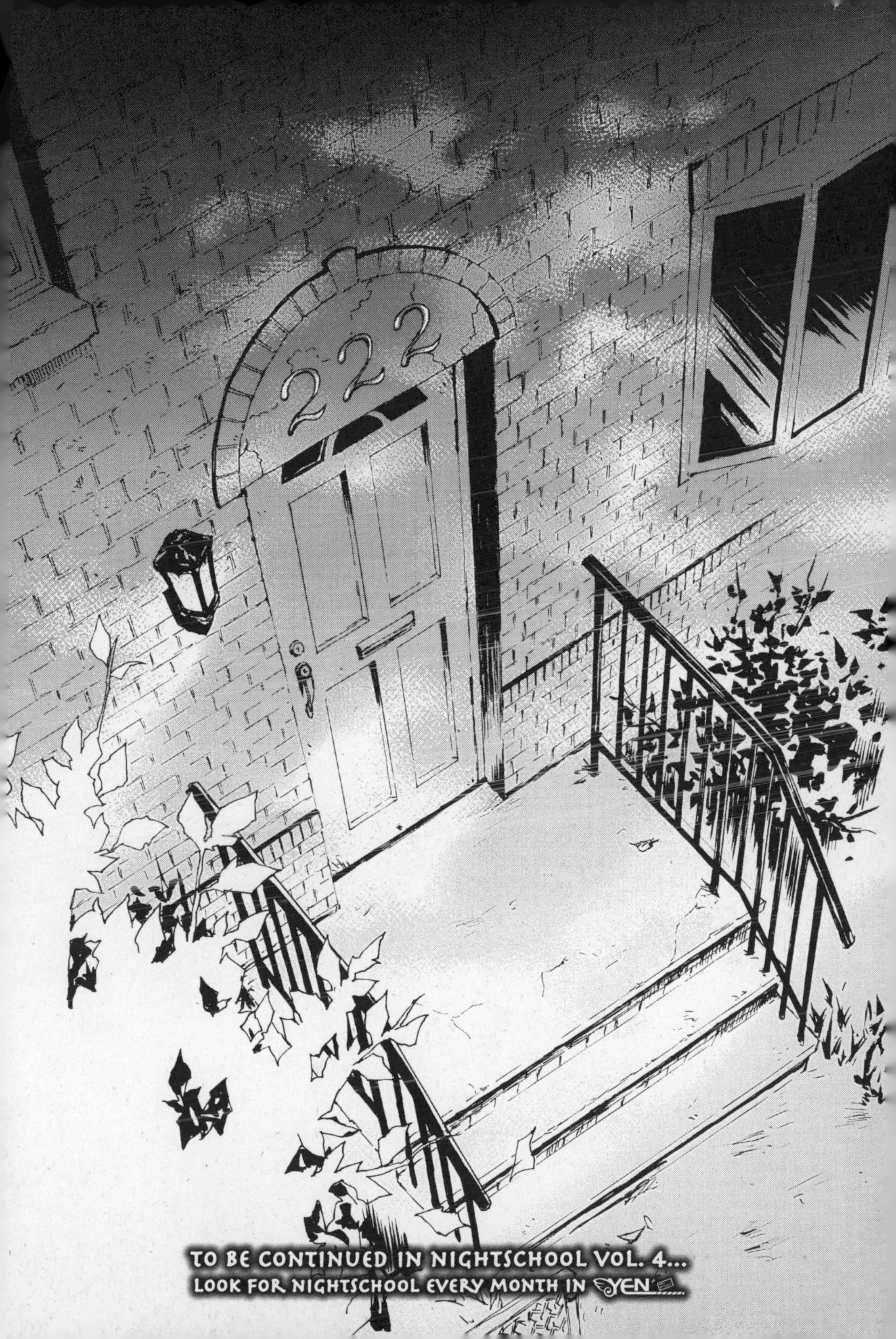
222
TO BE CONTINUED IN NIGHTSCHOOL VOL. 4...
LOOK FOR NIGHTSCHOOL EVERY MONTH IN YEN PLUS

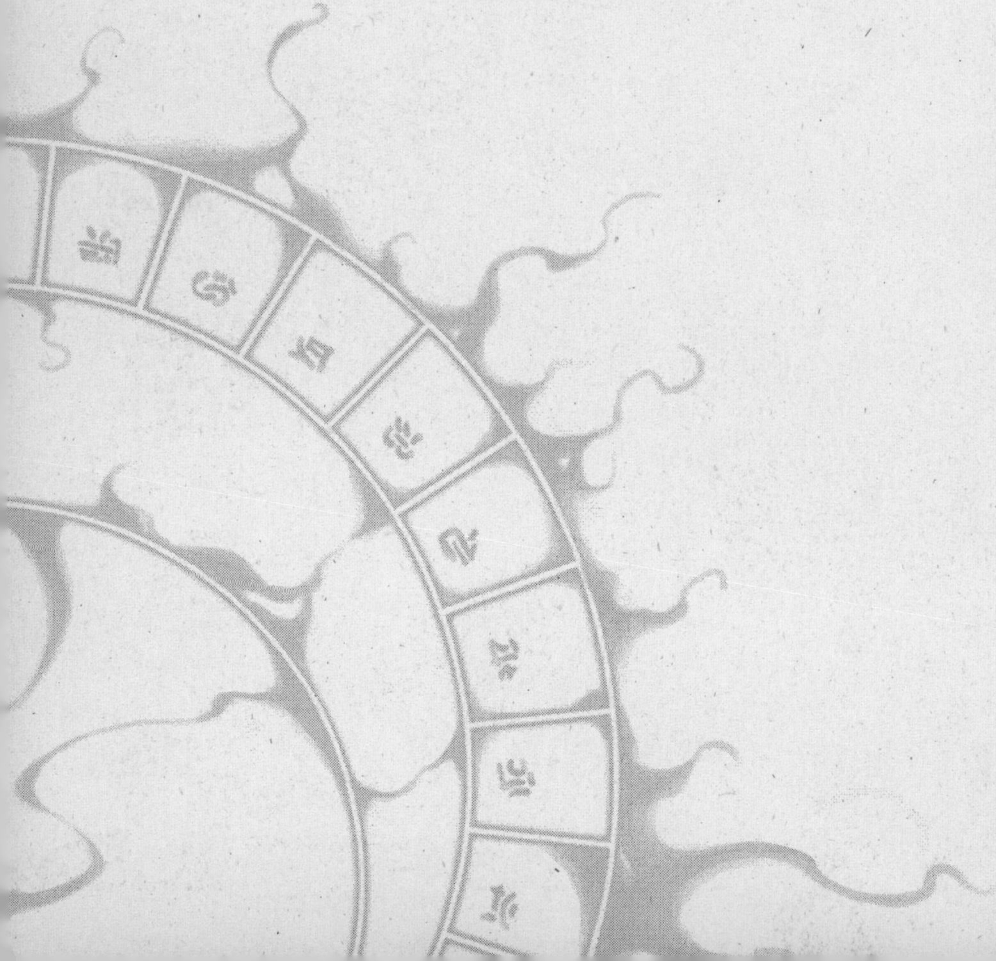

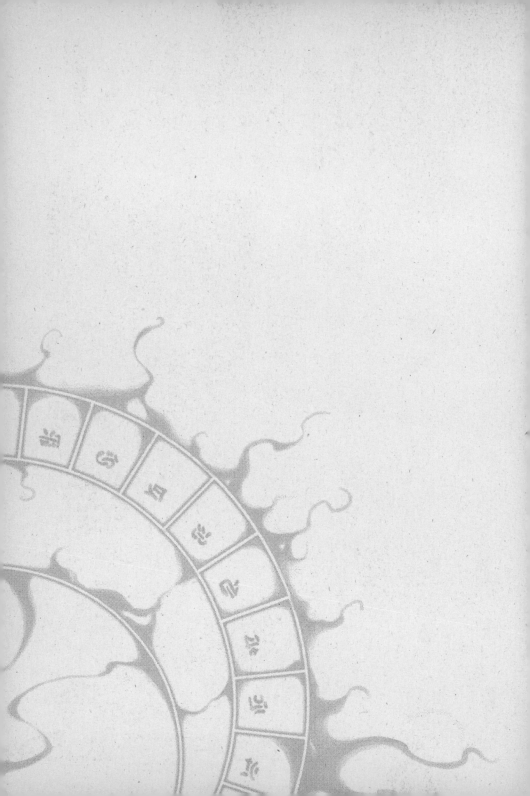

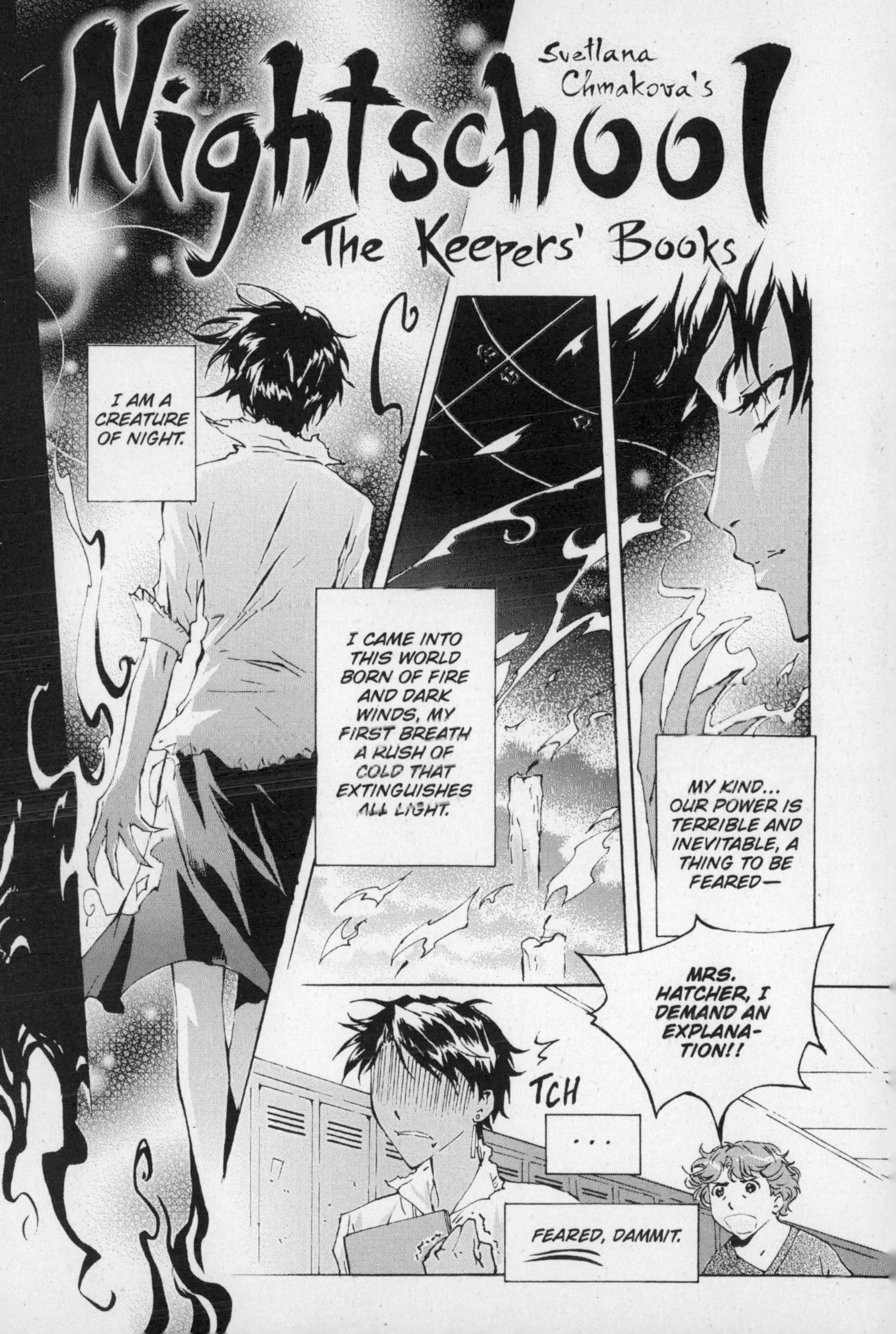
Svetlana Chmakova's
Nightschool
The Keepers' Books
I AM A CREATURE OF NIGHT.
I CAME INTO THIS WORLD BORN OF FIRE AND DARK WINDS, MY FIRST BREATH A RUSH OF COLD THAT EXTINGUISHES ALL LIGHT.
MY KIND... OUR POWER IS TERRIBLE AND INEVITABLE, A THING TO BE FEARED—
MRS. HATCHER, I DEMAND AN EXPLANA-TION!!
TCH
...
FEARED, DAMMIT.

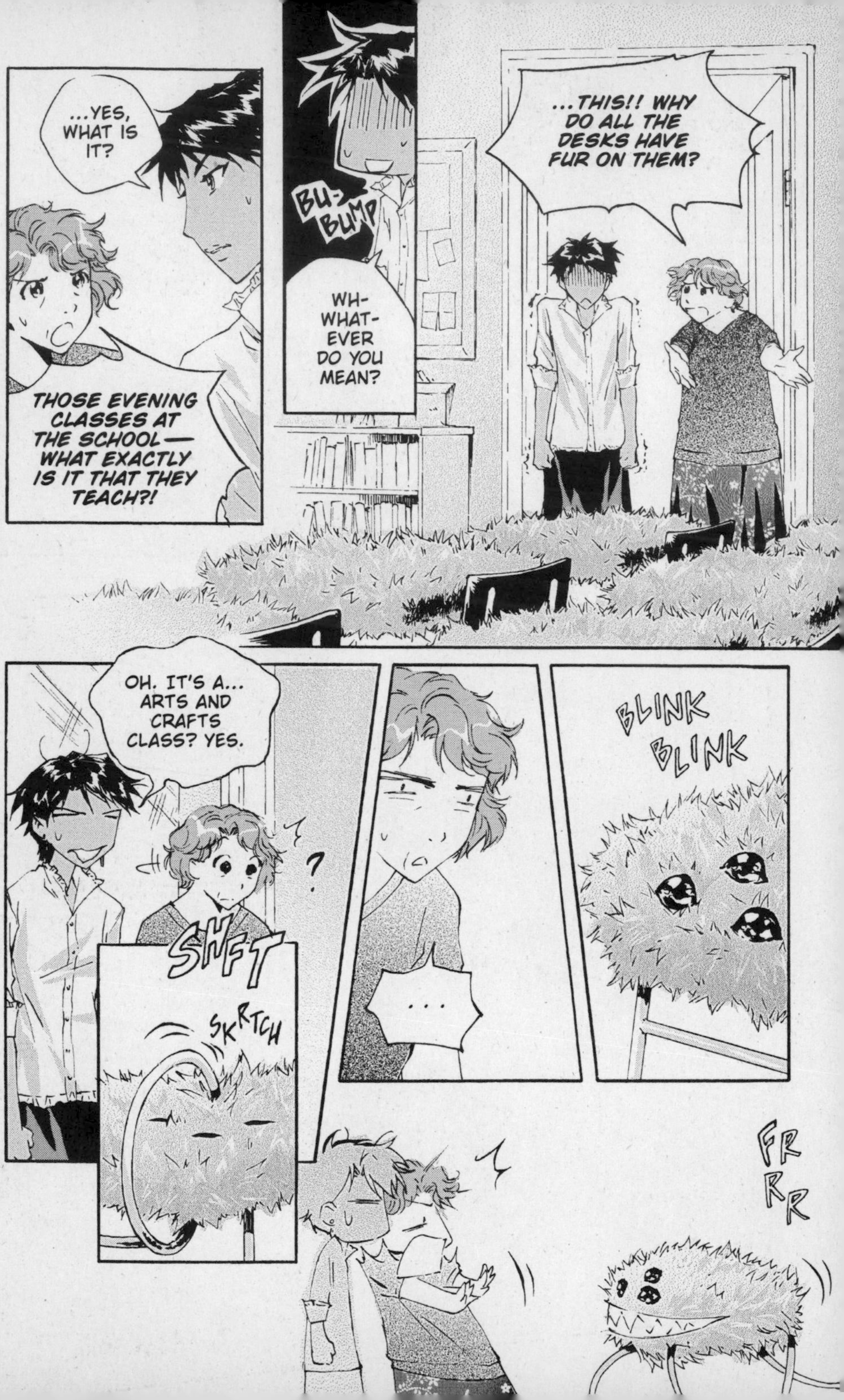
...YES, WHAT IS IT?
THOSE EVENING CLASSES AT THE SCHOOL— WHAT EXACTLY IS IT THAT THEY TEACH?!
BU-BUMP
WH-WHAT-EVER DO YOU MEAN?
...THIS!! WHY DO ALL THE DESKS HAVE FUR ON THEM?
OH. IT'S A... ARTS AND CRAFTS CLASS? YES.
?
SHFT
SKRTCH
...
BLINK BLINK
FRRR

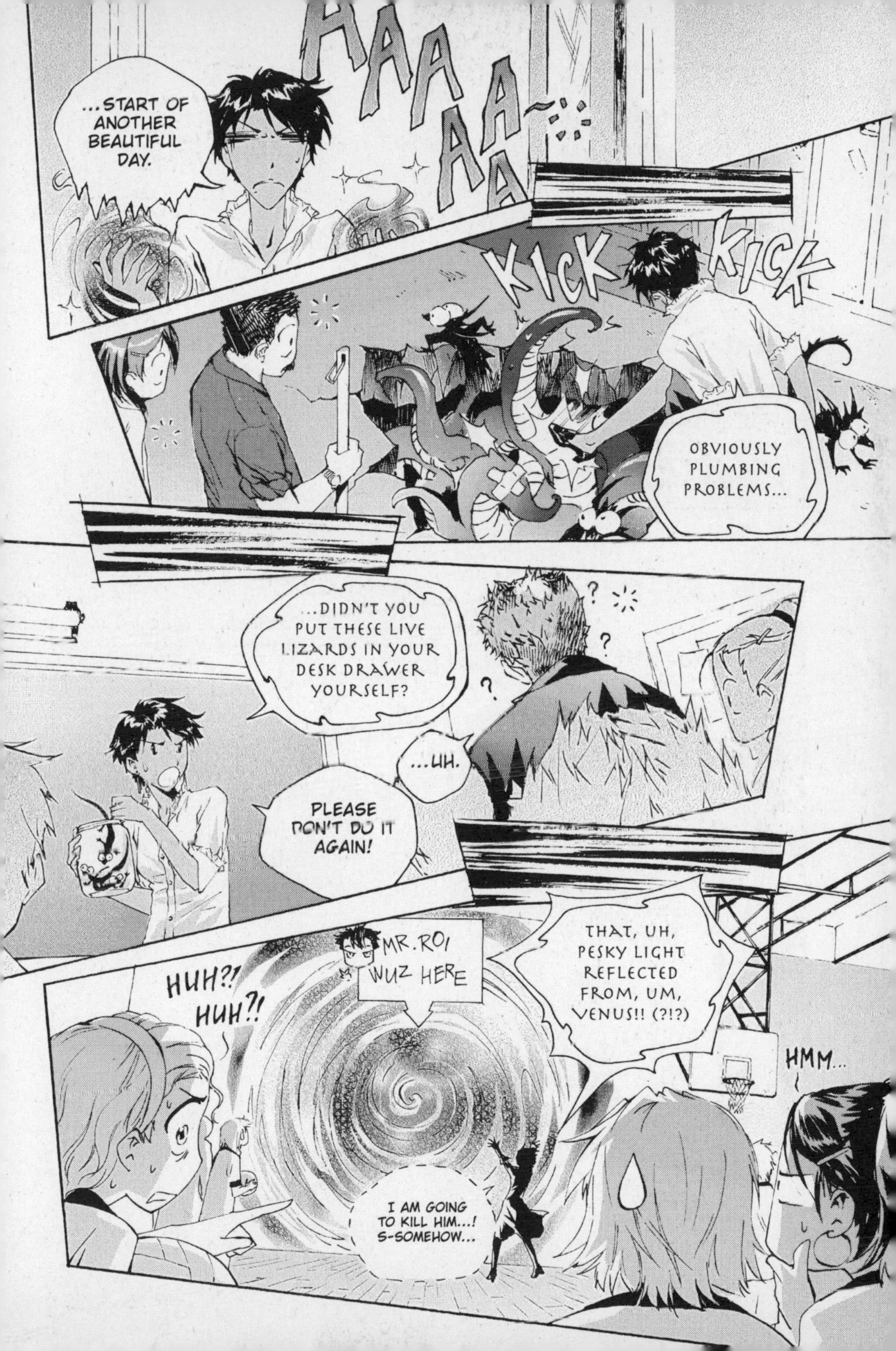
...START OF ANOTHER BEAUTIFUL DAY.
AAAAAAA~
KICK KICK
OBVIOUSLY PLUMBING PROBLEMS...
...DIDN'T YOU PUT THESE LIVE LIZARDS IN YOUR DESK DRAWER YOURSELF?
? ? ?
...UH.
PLEASE DON'T DO IT AGAIN!
HUH?! HUH?!
MR. ROI WUZ HERE
THAT, UH, PESKY LIGHT REFLECTED FROM, UM, VENUS!! (?!?)
I AM GOING TO KILL HIM...! S-SOMEHOW...
HMM...

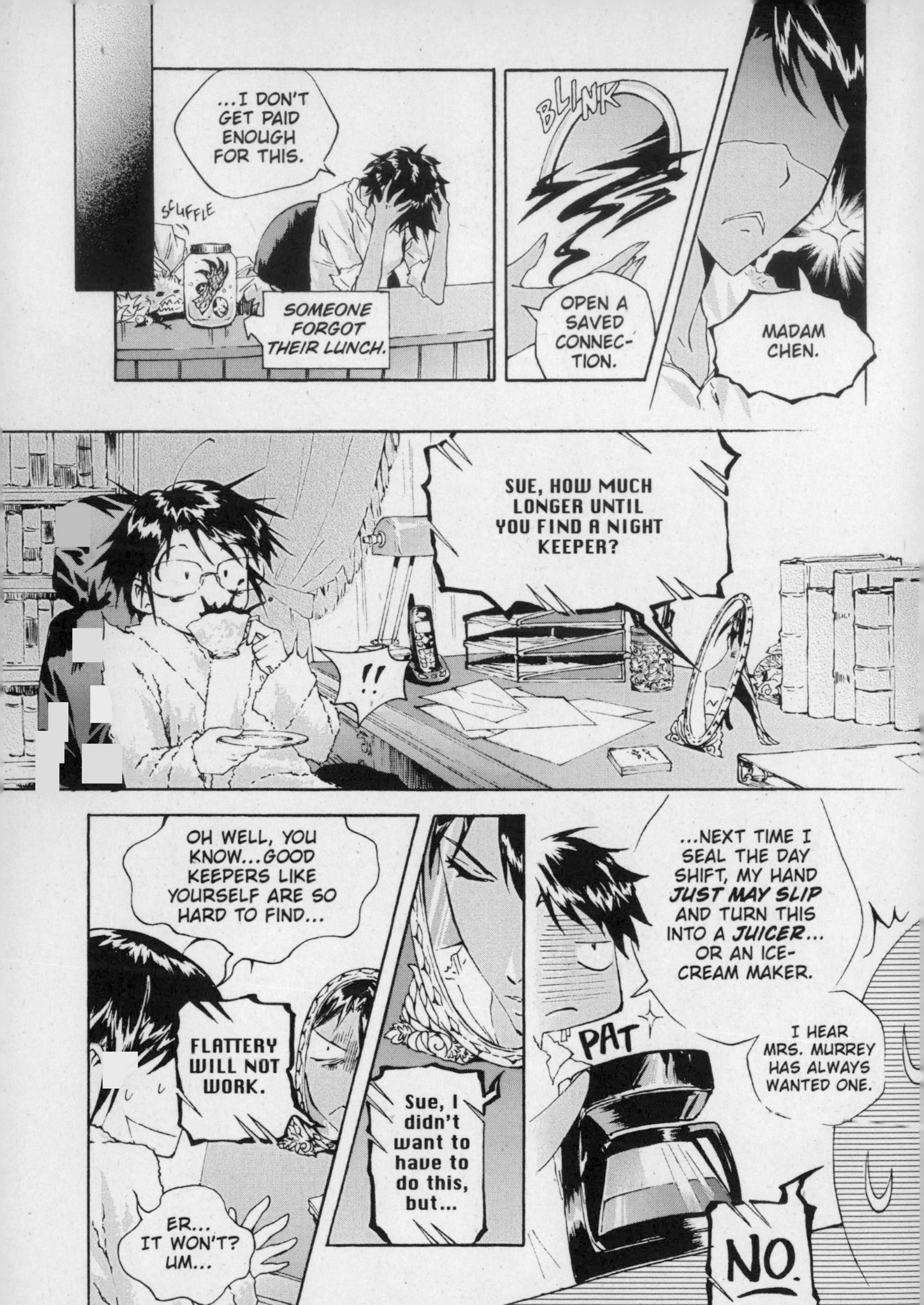
...I DON'T GET PAID ENOUGH FOR THIS.
SCUFFLE
SOMEONE FORGOT THEIR LUNCH.
BLINK
OPEN A SAVED CONNECTION.
MADAM CHEN.
SUE, HOW MUCH LONGER UNTIL YOU FIND A NIGHT KEEPER?
!!
OH WELL, YOU KNOW...GOOD KEEPERS LIKE YOURSELF ARE SO HARD TO FIND...
FLATTERY WILL NOT WORK.
ER... IT WON'T? UM...
Sue, I didn't want to have to do this, but...
...NEXT TIME I SEAL THE DAY SHIFT, MY HAND *JUST MAY SLIP* AND TURN THIS INTO A *JUICER*... OR AN ICE-CREAM MAKER.
PAT
I HEAR MRS. MURREY HAS ALWAYS WANTED ONE.
NO.

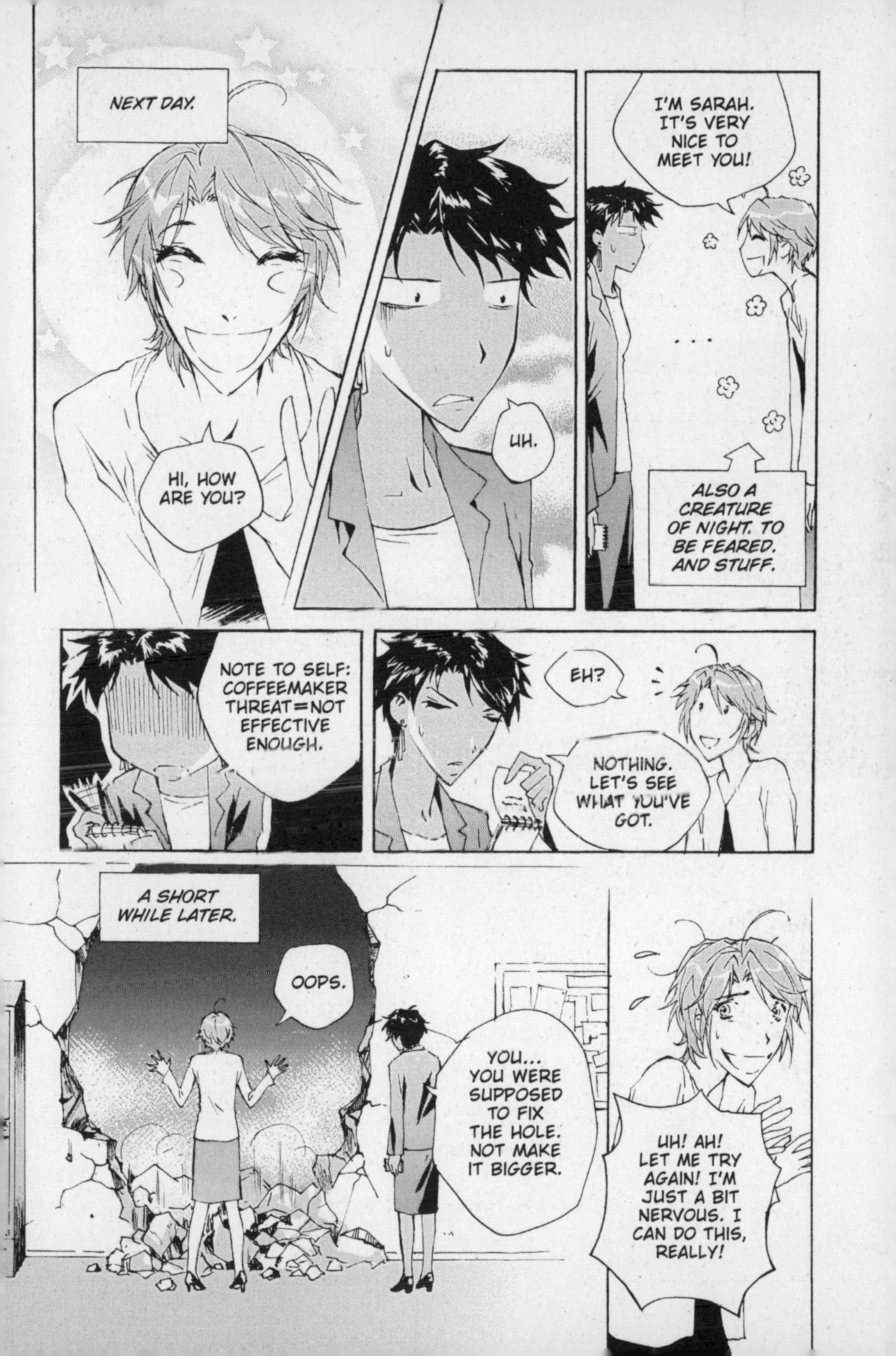
NEXT DAY.
HI, HOW ARE YOU?
UH.
I'M SARAH. IT'S VERY NICE TO MEET YOU!
...
ALSO A CREATURE OF NIGHT. TO BE FEARED. AND STUFF.
NOTE TO SELF: COFFEEMAKER THREAT=NOT EFFECTIVE ENOUGH.
EH?
NOTHING. LET'S SEE WHAT YOU'VE GOT.
A SHORT WHILE LATER.
OOPS.
YOU... YOU WERE SUPPOSED TO FIX THE HOLE. NOT MAKE IT BIGGER.
UH! AH! LET ME TRY AGAIN! I'M JUST A BIT NERVOUS. I CAN DO THIS, REALLY!

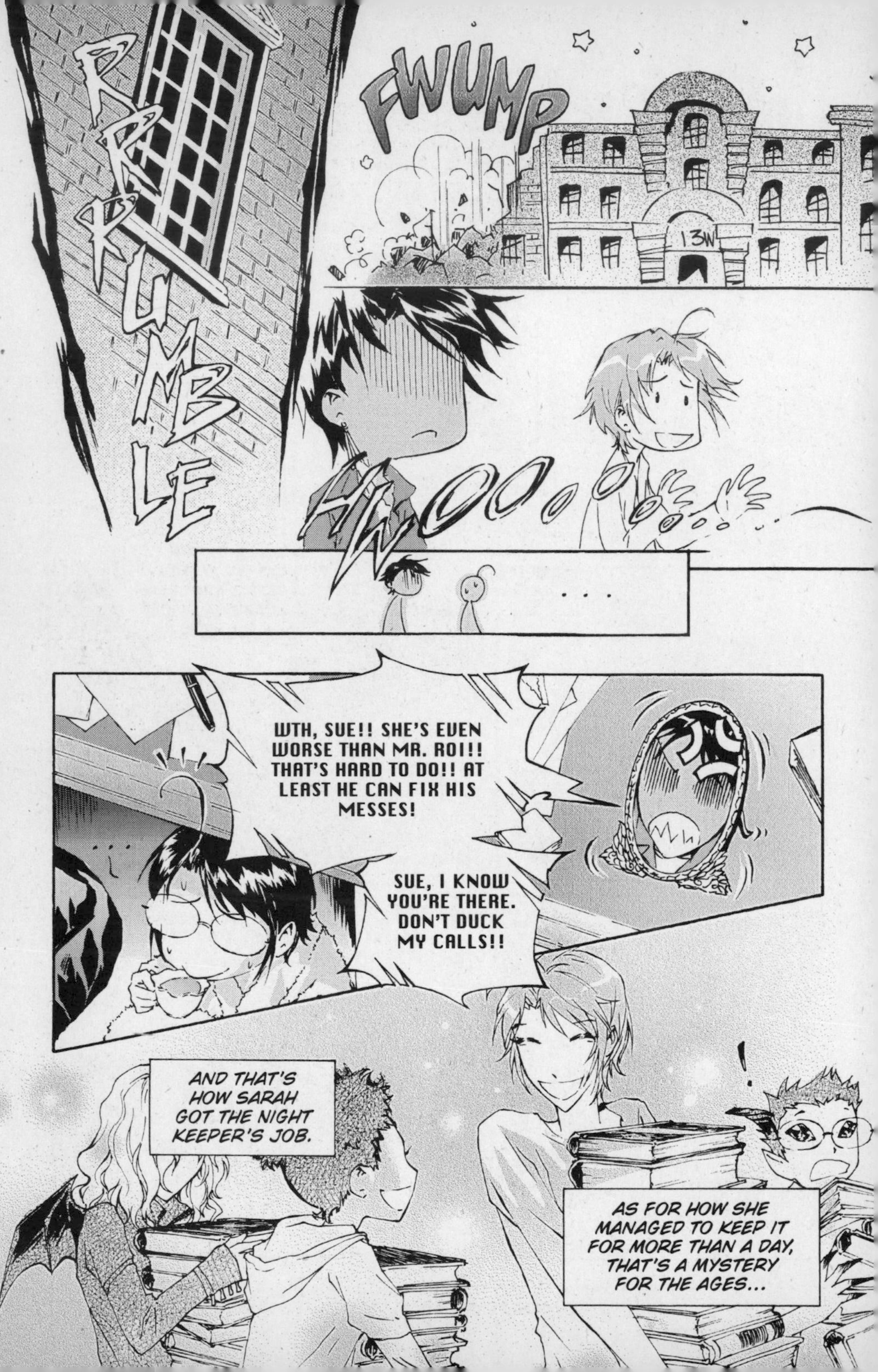
RRRUMBLE
FWUMP
13W
HWOOOoooo...
...
WTH, SUE!! SHE'S EVEN WORSE THAN MR. ROI!! THAT'S HARD TO DO!! AT LEAST HE CAN FIX HIS MESSES!
SUE, I KNOW YOU'RE THERE. DON'T DUCK MY CALLS!!
AND THAT'S HOW SARAH GOT THE NIGHT KEEPER'S JOB.
!
AS FOR HOW SHE MANAGED TO KEEP IT FOR MORE THAN A DAY, THAT'S A MYSTERY FOR THE AGES...

BONUS

NEXT VOLUME! ANSWERS! AND ALL THE BIG SHOWDOWNS AND BATTLES! ***SO EXCITED***. AS FOR LIFE UPDATES, WELL, NOT MUCH HAS HAPPENED SINCE THE LAST VOLUME (HALF A YEAR AGO), BUT HERE ARE A FEW HIGHLIGHTS:

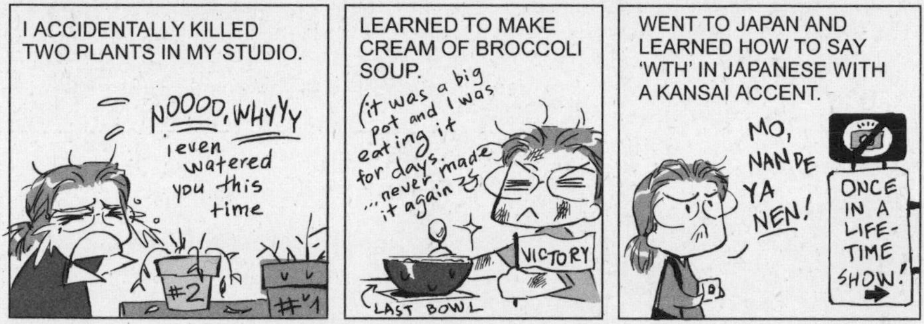
I ACCIDENTALLY KILLED TWO PLANTS IN MY STUDIO.
NOOOO, WHYYY
i even watered you this time
#2
#1
LEARNED TO MAKE CREAM OF BROCCOLI SOUP.
(it was a big pot and I was eating it for days. ...never made it again
VICTORY
LAST BOWL
WENT TO JAPAN AND LEARNED HOW TO SAY 'WTH' IN JAPANESE WITH A KANSAI ACCENT.
MO, NANDE YA NEN!
ONCE IN A LIFE-TIME SHOW!

...BTW, ON THE TOPIC OF SAYING THINGS IN DIFFERENT LANGUAGES!! I COMPLETELY FORGOT TO INCLUDE THE TRANSLATIONS OF THE NON-ENGLISH PHRASES FROM VOLUME 2!! SO IF YOU WONDERED, HERE THEY ARE NOW:

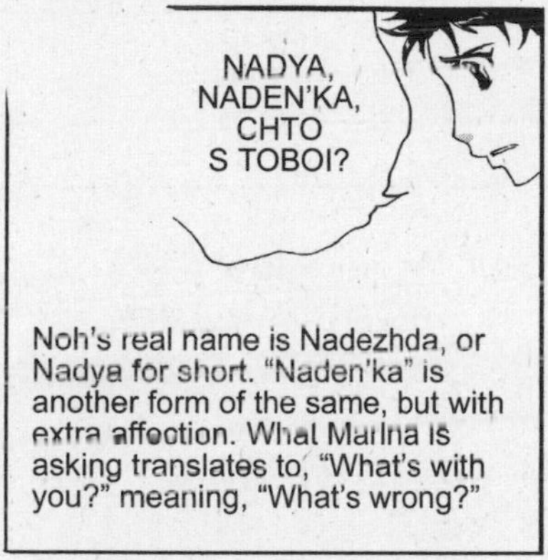
NADYA, NADEN'KA, CHTO S TOBOI?
Noh's real name is Nadezhda, or Nadya for short. "Naden'ka" is another form of the same, but with extra affection. What Marina is asking translates to, "What's with you?" meaning, "What's wrong?"

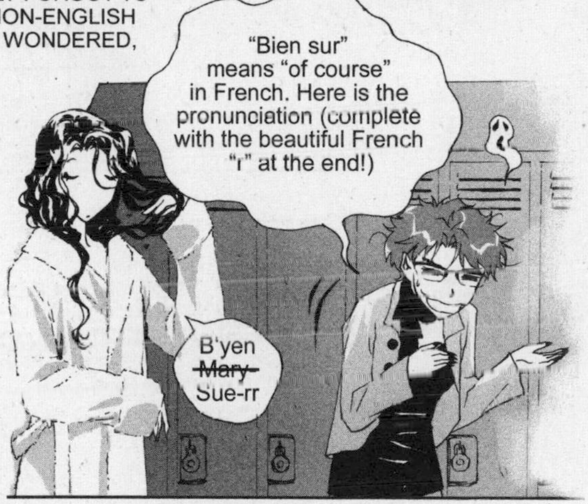
"Bien sur" means "of course" in French. Here is the pronunciation (complete with the beautiful French "r" at the end!)
B'yen ~~Mary~~ Sue-rr

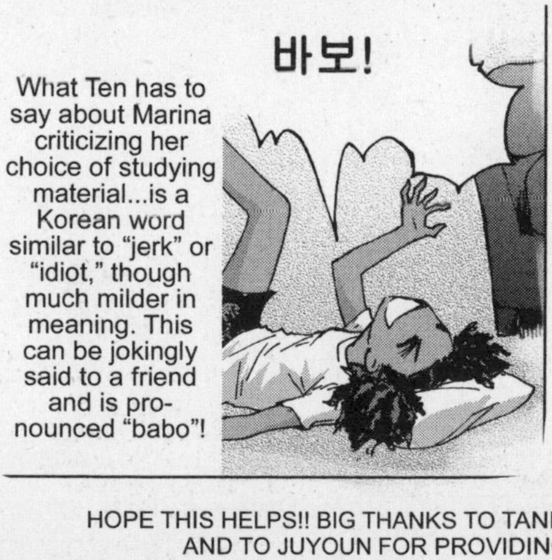
바보!
What Ten has to say about Marina criticizing her choice of studying material...is a Korean word similar to "jerk" or "idiot," though much milder in meaning. This can be jokingly said to a friend and is pronounced "babo"!

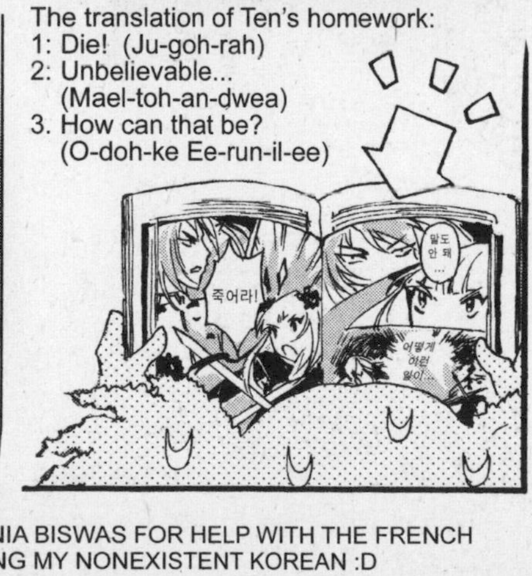
The translation of Ten's homework:
1: Die! (Ju-goh-rah)
2: Unbelievable... (Mael-toh-an-dwea)
3. How can that be? (O-doh-ke Ee-run-il-ee)
말도 안 돼...
죽어라!

HOPE THIS HELPS!! BIG THANKS TO TANIA BISWAS FOR HELP WITH THE FRENCH AND TO JUYOUN FOR PROVIDING MY NONEXISTENT KOREAN :D

FANART!

We've received some truly wonderful fan art for the Fan Art contest again, thanks, you guys!!! I am so glad I'm not the one judging these things – I'd never be able to choose! XD The following pages are the entries that our hardworking judges have picked as winners. Please enjoy!

And what's this, below?! That's...

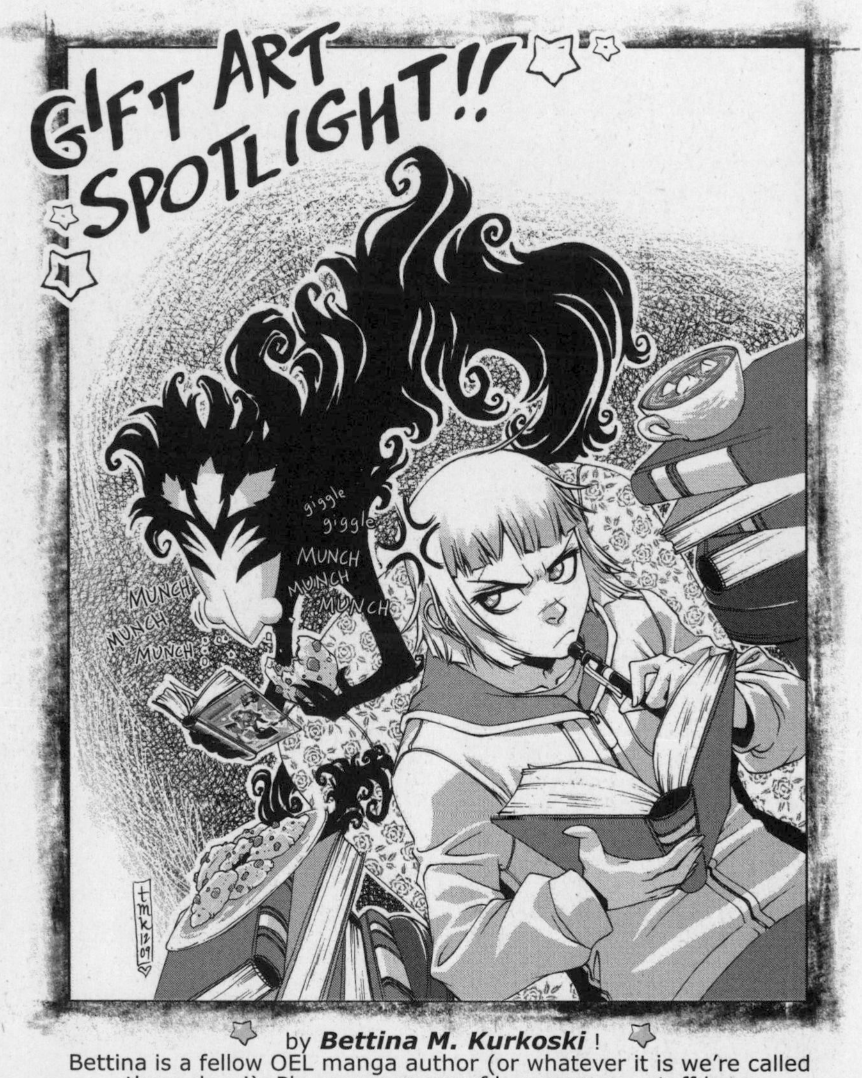
GIFT ART SPOTLIGHT!!
giggle
giggle
MUNCH
MUNCH
MUNCH
MUNCH
MUNCH
MUNCH
tmk 12/09

by ***Bettina M. Kurkoski*** !
Bettina is a fellow OEL manga author (or whatever it is we're called these days!). Please see more of her awesome stuff here:
www.dreamworldstudio.net

♥ CONTEST WINNERS ♥

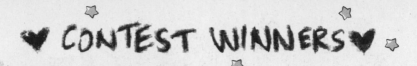

by **Norbert Black**
(Tiny Lego Alex!! Shown almost at
ACTUAL SIZE!!
Incredible with all the painted details.)

by **Amanda S. Kaufman**
Astral cuddle plushie, aw!
Note her cute little paaaws! X3

by **Brittany Lawson**
Wonderful Astral marionette!
(And look, she's waving – hi, Astral!! :D)

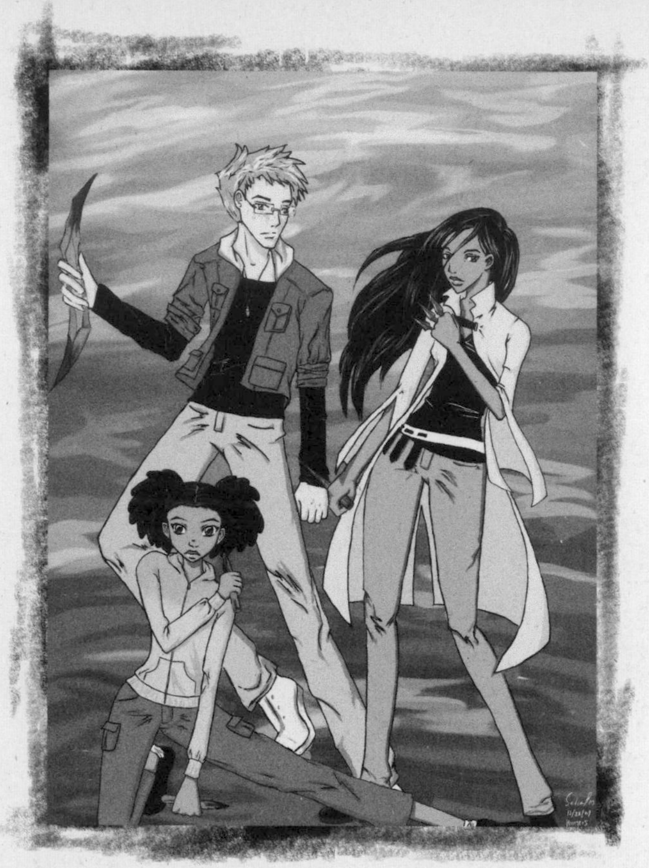

by ***Sadia Bies***
This would make a great cover for *Hunters Monthly*, woo!!
Rippers everywhere beware!!
(...Hey, that kind of rhymed :D /easily amused)

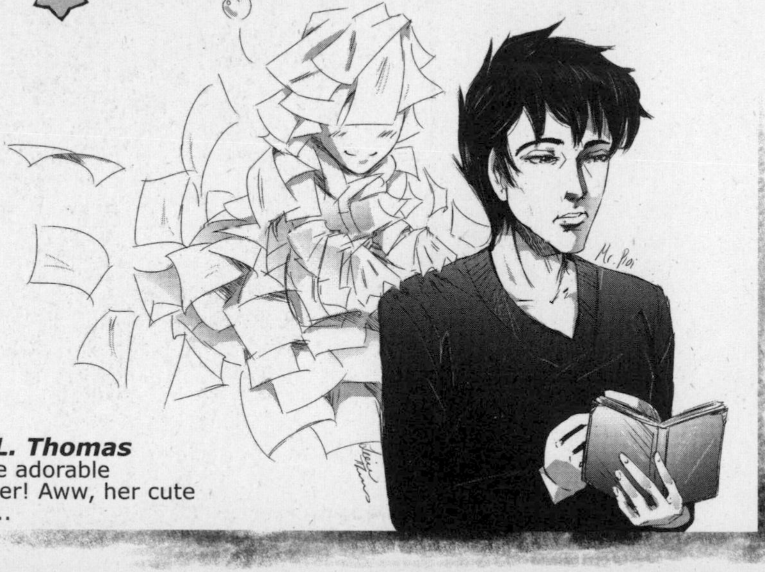

by ***Laurie L. Thomas***
Attack of the adorable
book snatcher! Aww, her cute
little hands...

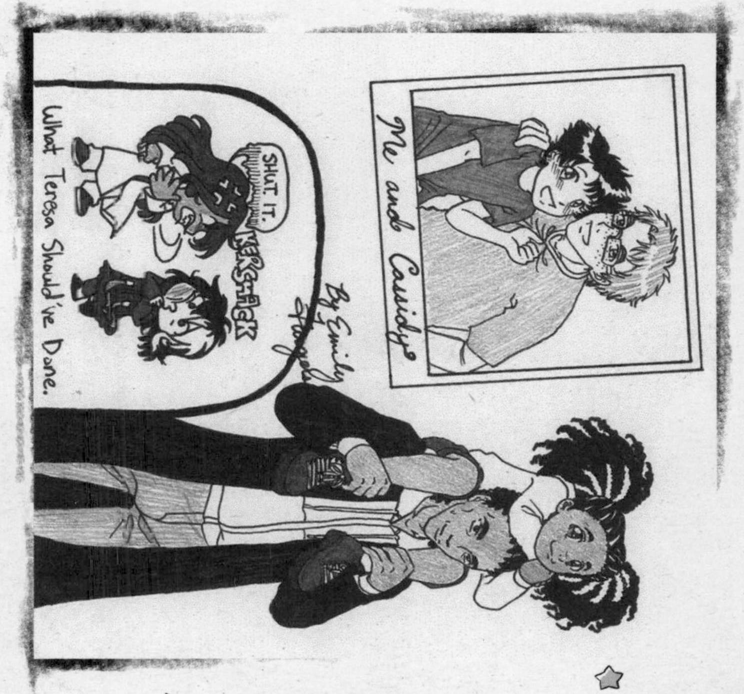
Me and Cassidy
By Emily Furgerson
SHUT. IT.
KERSHACK
What Teresa Should've Done.

by ***Emily J. Furgerson***
(When the camera isn't rolling... Hee-hee!
My favorite is the Ten and Daemon shot, so sweet ^___^)

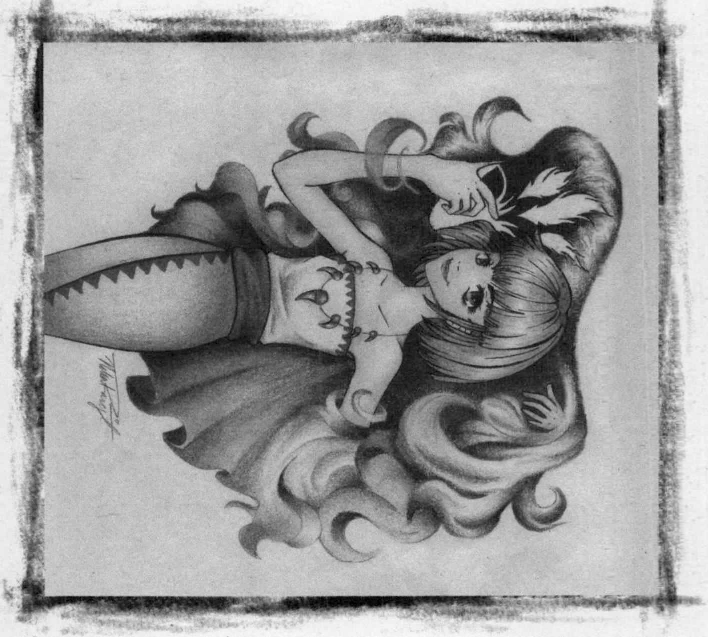

by ***Neha Ranjit***
(The colors of the original submission are very vibrant; it's too bad we couldn't keep them. :(But still, very beautiful!)

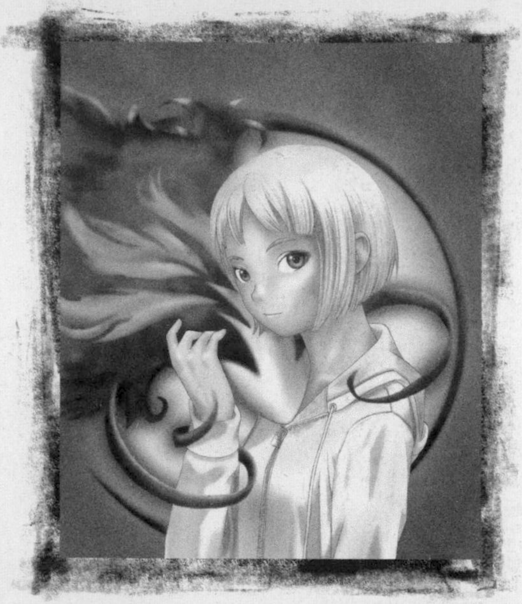

by ***Tim Ferreira***
(Another beautiful color picture! It has a light purple tone in the original.)

by ***Jordan Serra***
(Ha-ha, Astral is sneaking cookies again! <3)

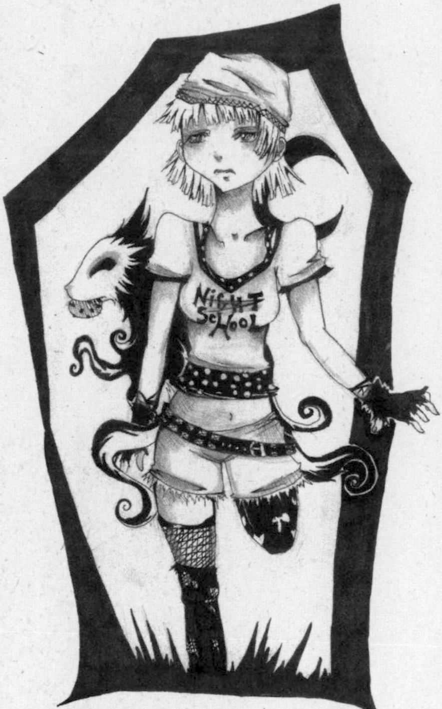
NIGHT SCHOOL

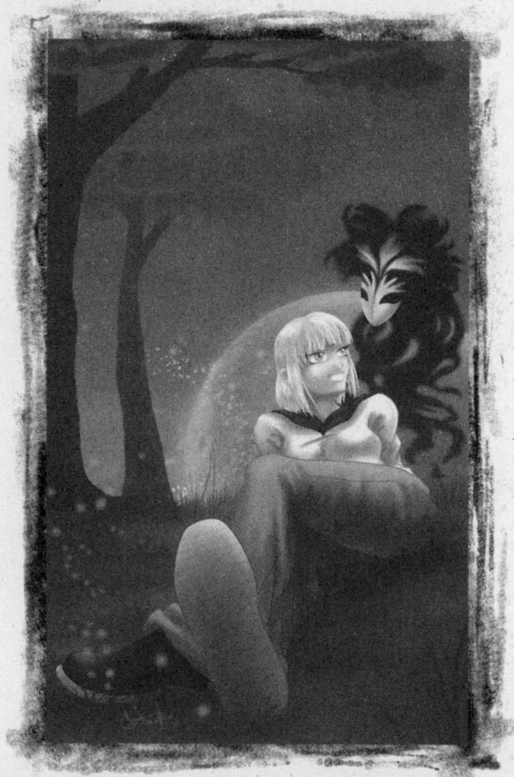

by ***Christine Harcinske***
(Also color! I weep for losing it! A very lovely night magic feel here~)

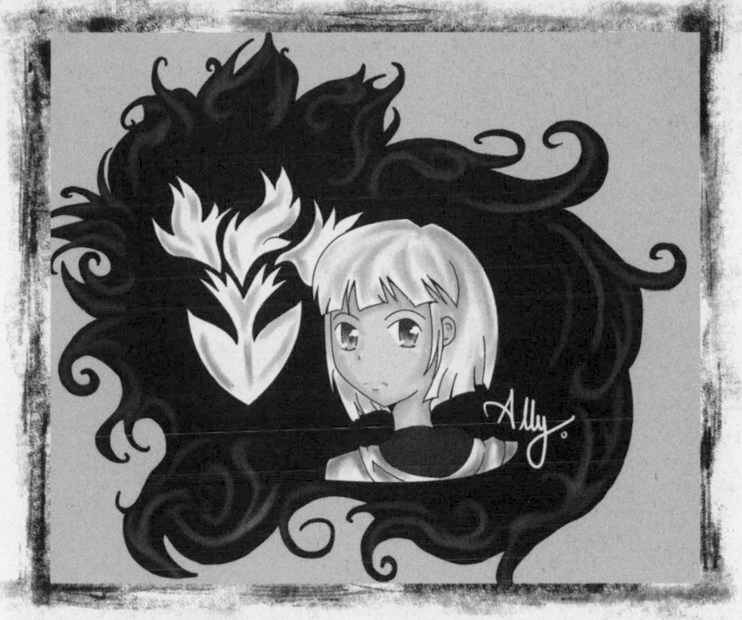
Ally.

by ***Allyson Florez***
(Color lost here, but not forgotten!
...Hey, I think I know who the favorite characters are in this book. XD)

by ***Starlia Prichard***
(...Okay, everyone who wants Mr. Roi's Library,
raise your hands!! ;o;/)

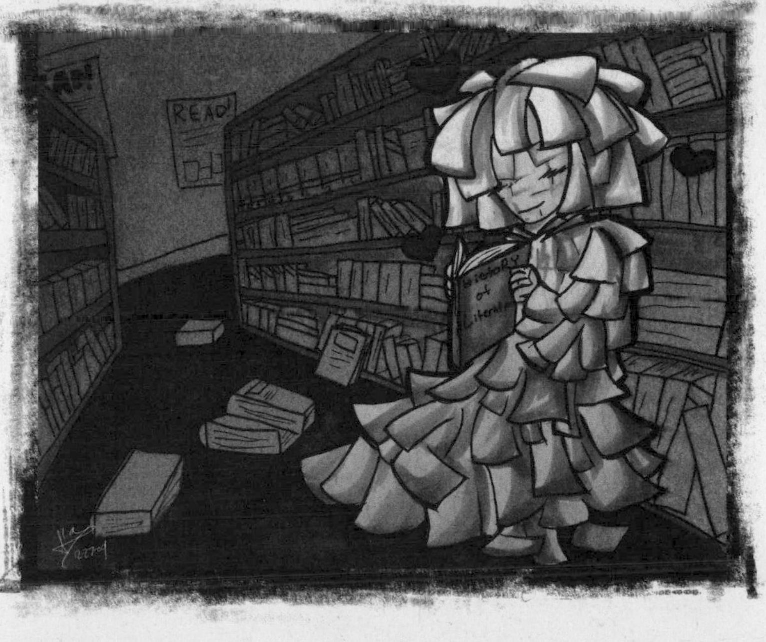
READ!

by ***Sarah Covington***
(And last but not least, a nice large pic of the cast!
I LOVE ERON TOO.)

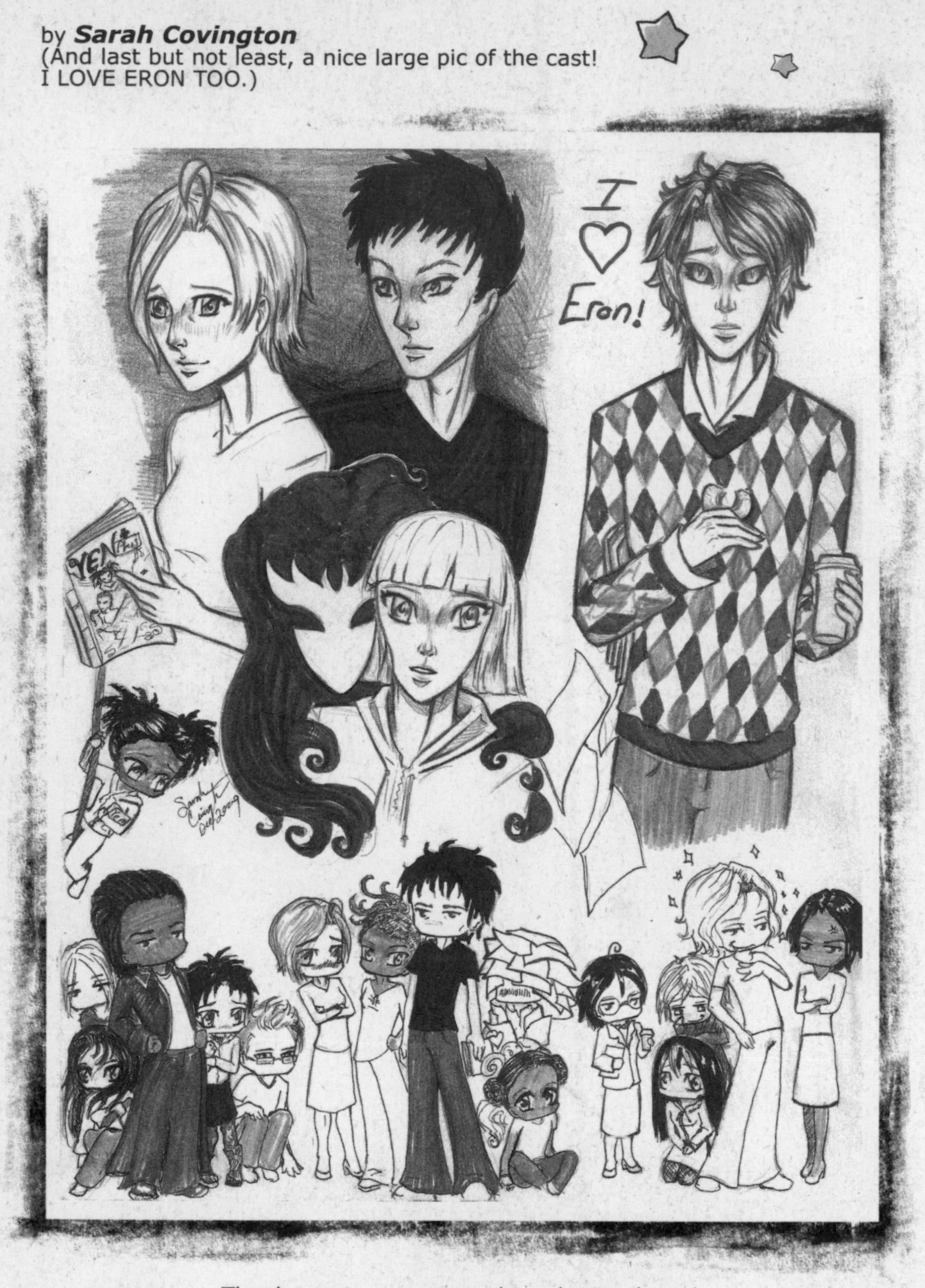
YEN
I ♡ Eron!

Thank you to everyone who submitted, and
congratulations to the winners!! Hope you
enjoy your prizes, and please don't hate me if
I spelled your name wrong; I tried very hard.
;__;

See you all in the next volume!!

NIGHTSCHOOL
THE WEIRN BOOKS ③

SVETLANA CHMAKOVA

Toning Artist: Dee DuPuy

Lettering: JuYoun Lee

NIGHTSCHOOL: The Weirn Books, Vol. 3 © 2010 Svetlana Chmakova.

Yen Press
Hachette Book Group
237 Park Avenue, New York, NY 10017

www.HachetteBookGroup.com
www.YenPress.com

Yen Press is an imprint of Hachette Book Group, Inc. The Yen Press name and logo are trademarks of Hachette Book Group, Inc.

First Yen Press Edition: April 2010

ISBN: 978-0-7595-2861-1

10 9 8 7 6 5 4 3

BVG

Printed in the United States of America